Expert Oracle Application Express Security

Scott Spendolini

Expert Oracle Application Express Security

ISBN 978-1-4302-4731-9

ISBN 978-1-4302-4732-6 (eBook)

President and Publisher: Paul Manning
Lead Editor: Jonathan Gennick
Technical Reviewer: Alex Fatkulin
Editorial Board: Steve Anglin, Ewan Buckingham, Gary Cornell, Louise Corrigan, Morgan Ertel, Jonathan Gennick, Jonathan Hassell, Robert Hutchinson, Michelle Lowman, James Markham, Matthew Moodie, Jeff Olson, Jeffrey Pepper, Douglas Pundick, Ben Renow-Clarke, Dominic Shakeshaft, Gwenan Spearing, Matt Wade, Tom Welsh
Coordinating Editor: Kevin Shea
Copy Editor: Kim Wimpsett
Compositor: SPi Global
Indexer: SPi Global
Artist: SPi Global
Cover Designer: Anna Ishchenko

Distributed to the book trade worldwide by Springer Science+Business Media New York, 233 Spring Street, 6th Floor, New York, NY 10013. Phone 1-800-SPRINGER, fax (201) 348-4505, e-mail orders-ny@springer-sbm.com, or visit www.springeronline.com.

For information on translations, please e-mail rights@apress.com, or visit www.apress.com.

Apress and friends of ED books may be purchased in bulk for academic, corporate, or promotional use. eBook versions and licenses are also available for most titles. For more information, reference our Special Bulk Sales–eBook Licensing web page at www.apress.com/bulk-sales.

Any source code or other supplementary materials referenced by the author in this text is available to readers at www.apress.com. For detailed information about how to locate your book's source code, go to www.apress.com/source-code.

To my wife Shannon, who has always stood by and supported me in my career and in life.

—Scott Spendolini

Contents at a Glance

Contents

Foreword

In May of 1999, Oracle Application Express was begun. I was the only direct report to a great visionary at Oracle Corporation, Michael Hichwa. His passion and creativity led to Oracle Application Express, and I've been proud to be directly involved in the development of this rich framework since day one. I've also had the pleasure to work directly with Scott Spendolini when he was a product manager on the Oracle Application Express team (in the "early years"). I credit Scott and the other product managers for making Oracle Application Express so successful. They were tireless in pitching and demonstrating Oracle Application Express to anyone who would listen. They helped to cultivate the APEX community, engaged them in social media, and ensured that the customer's requirements and concerns were addressed in subsequent releases of Oracle Application Express. They authored countless tutorials, white papers, and presentations to help convince customers of the power and benefits of Oracle APEX.

Scott was so enthused with Oracle Application Express that he formed a company focused solely on Oracle Application Express solutions. He and his colleagues are directly responsible for the successful delivery of solutions for numerous, high profile, large-scale, and security-conscious customers. It is these repeated solutions and repeated security requirements that inspired Scott and his colleagues to author a tool to evaluate and identify possible security issues in Oracle Application Express applications. Scott has years of experience in understanding and assessing the myriad of security vulnerabilities that are possible in Web applications, and in Oracle Application Express environments, in particular.

For many years, it seemed as if security in software development was an afterthought. It was always "build it and assess later," or as my father would always say, "there's always enough time and money to do it right the second time." But this mentality needs to change—security must be a part of the development process and everyone must be conscious of this during design, development, testing and maintenance. There should be a secure coding guidelines document. There must be rules, and equally important, there must be the ability to continually assess whether an application or code violates those rules. The knowledge and experience conveyed in this book will empower the reader to establish this understanding and mindset.

System and database administrators are tasked with setting up and managing Oracle Application Express environments, very often with little to no knowledge of APEX, how it works, how to monitor it, how to diagnose it, or how to secure it. To understand APEX is to understand the architecture, and Scott provides a very lucid and complete overview of the architecture of Oracle Application Express, how it's organized, and why it is so efficient. Additionally, administrators of an APEX environment are provided with a wealth of options and controls to tweak the Oracle Application Express infrastructure. While the typical Oracle documentation will explain what something is, the chapter on instance settings also answers the anticipated questions of why you would want to change something.

How many security vulnerabilities are considered "too many" in an application? One hundred? Ten? Five? I live by the rule that one is too many for the Oracle Application Express framework, because all it takes is a single vulnerability to provide an entrance to a malicious hacker. Once the entrance is established, it can be used to exploit other deficiencies in your application environment. But before you can understand how to assess the security of an application, you first must understand what types of exploits can be perpetrated against an application and environment and how to protect against them. Scott does an excellent job of explaining the type of threats that are possible and conveys very practical solutions to combat these threats.

In 1999 when Oracle Application Express was begun, the <blink> tag was popular, dynamic generation of HTML Web pages was just becoming commonplace, SQL injection, cross-site scripting, and clickjacking were not in the vernacular, and no one really gave much thought to how hackers might gain access to a Web application. While Oracle Application Express has dramatically evolved to help new customers create secure Web applications out-of-the-box, APEX cannot prevent someone from introducing vulnerabilities in their applications. I am confident that the knowledge Scott conveys in this book will make developers and administrators alike quite complete in their understanding of these various types of threats, how to assess their APEX and database applications, and ultimately, instill the confidence in new and seasoned APEX developers that they can develop robust APEX applications both quickly *and* securely.

Joel R. Kallman
Director of Development, Oracle Corporation

About the Author

Scott Spendolini is an executive director at Enkitec, a world-class Oracle® services, education and solutions firm founded in 2004. He has assisted a number of clients from various verticals with their Oracle APEX development and training needs. Spendolini has presented at a number of Oracle-related conferences, including Oracle OpenWorld, ODTUG, and IOUG and is a regular contributor to the Oracle APEX Forums on OTN. He is a recipient of the Oracle Ace Director designation, author of *Expert Oracle Application Express Security* and co-author of *Pro Oracle Application Express* (Apress, 2011). In 2009, Spendolini along with ODTUG was presented with the Oracle Innovation Award for his work on ODTUG's public web site, odtug.com. Spendolini is also an Oracle Certified Oracle Application Express developer.

Prior to joining Enkitec, Spendolini co-founded and ran Sumneva and Sumner Technologies from 2005 through 2012, which focused on Oracle APEX services, education and solutions. Before that, he was employed by Oracle Corporation for almost 10 years, the last three of which he was a Senior Product Manager for Oracle APEX. He holds a dual bachelor's degree in Management Information Systems and Telecommunications Management from Syracuse University. He currently resides in Ashburn, Virginia, with his wife and two children.

About the Technical Reviewer

Alex Fatkulin is a master of the full range of Oracle technologies. His high level of expertise has been essential in addressing some of the greatest challenges his customers meet.

Drawing on years of experience working with some of the world's largest companies, Alex has been involved with virtually every aspect of Oracle databases, from data modeling to architecting high-availability solutions, as well as resolving performance issues of extremely large production sites.

Acknowledgments

First of all, I would like to thank my wife, Shannon, for her support while I wrote this book. Without her help and understanding, it simply would not have happened. I also have to thank my children—specifically my daughter—who would regularly come into my office and ask if I was working on the book and scold me if I answered otherwise.

I would also like to thank the folks at Enkitec—specifically Kerry Osborne and Veronica Stigers—for their support throughout this project. This book would simply not be possible without their understanding of what it takes to write a technical book as a "side project" while starting a new job.

I'd also like to thank my technical reviewer, Alex Fatkulin. Alex is a brilliant individual whose insight on APEX security is shared throughout this book. Individuals like Alex are living proof that you can always stand to learn more on any subject, no matter how well you think you know it.

I would be remiss if I did not mention Doug Gault here, too. Doug and I have been working together in one way, shape or form for the past few years. While we don't always initially agree on things, the "discussions" that we have as a result of this makes us both better developers.

Lastly, I would also like to acknowledge the entire Oracle APEX team, led by Mike Hichwa and Joel Kallman. This group of professionals has produced and continues to enhance one of the most revolutionary and innovative pieces of software that I have ever seen or used. The past 10 years of my career has focused around their innovation, and I am both grateful and privileged to have been a part of their journey. Special thanks also goes out to Christian Neumüeller from the Oracle APEX team for being so willing to help me clarify some of the murkier parts of APEX security.

Introduction

Security is hard. If it's easy, then it's wrong.

Application security is on the forefront of everyone's minds these days. It's almost impossible to go more than a couple of days without reading about another website organization that was hacked or had a data breach. Unfortunately, it seems as if the problem is getting worse with time, not better. This can be attributed directly to the fact that there are simply more people using computers, iPhones and the like today, thus increasing the number of attack vectors for the bad guys.

There is a simple answer for this: severely limit access to information systems. This is, of course, not the best answer, but it clearly would mitigate the problem down to a manageable chunk. Unfortunately, users will always need access to data, and as developers, the responsibility of delivering this task in a secure fashion falls squarely on our shoulders.

Therefore, developers need to build applications that are much more secure today than in the past. But given the workload of the average developer (read: overworked), securing applications is often done hastily right before turning over code to production, if ever at all. As a result of this, more insecure applications are put into production, which leads to more breaches and data leaks.

To compound the problem, developers coming from older client server technologies often don't have the background in web development to even understand what secure is and what it is not. The concept of an end-user being able to manipulate where they go via the URL or view the source code of a page is completely foreign to them. Their lack of knowledge often leads them down the path of building web applications that are simply not secure, as they simply don't know what secure looks like.

As more business turn to the web and mobile technologies to enable their customers and employees to access information, more applications that represent potential security vulnerabilities are created, thus giving hackers and even malicious users more places to attack.

Oracle APEX is not unique, in that like any other web technology, applications can be developed with it in either a secure or not-so-secure manner.

About This Book

The focus of this book is to cover the best practices required to develop secure APEX applications. It is important to understand that the focus is at the APEX level itself, and does not go into great detail about how to secure your database, web server, network and other parts of your infrastructure from other types of attacks. Each one of those components will also need to be secured and monitored as well, but the specifics of doing so are simply out of scope for this book.

This book is based on APEX 4.2, the latest version of APEX as of the publishing date. Many of the concepts discussed also apply to prior versions of APEX in whole or in part, while some are unique to APEX 4.2.

The book is broken out into four sections, as follows:

Security Planning & Assessment

Comprehensive security for any application in any environment will not just happen. It takes a great deal of time, planning and forethought to ensure that the end result is as secure as it needs to be. Thus, a secure APEX application starts with a comprehensive and thorough security plan.

Chapters 1 and 2 will illustrate the potential threats to your applications and how to mitigate each, and how that can be translated into a security plan. It will also highlight what needs to be done to ensure that the security plan is being implemented, and techniques for testing the plan. It provides guidance as to which questions to ask to determine how much security needs to be applied to each application in your infrastructure.

APEX Security

Much of the steps in the other sections won't matter if you don't spend time securing APEX at the APEX level itself. Chapters 3, 4, 5 and 6 will cover APEX security from three levels—the instance of APEX itself, the workspace, and finally, the application. Many security threats can easily by eliminated by changing simple settings. The challenge, of course, is to make sure that all of the settings are properly set, and understand the risk of setting them improperly.

User Access

All of the APEX security best practices in the world will do little good if users can roam anywhere they want once they are authenticated. APEX does provide good controls to implement a solid user access policy, but these control need to be enabled, configured and verified. Chapters 8 and 9 will discuss the different authentication and authentication options that are available to APEX applications.

Data Access & Protection

Often times, data access is one of the last things that a developer considers when building an APEX application. While APEX also provides some options to assist with users accessing records that they are not supposed to see, it's not always the best approach. Chapters 10, 11, 12, 13 and 14 cover some techniques that you can employ in your application to ensure that data can only be seen by those who should see it.

Downloading the Code

The code for the examples shown in this book is available on the Apress web site, `www.apress.com`. A link can be found on the book's information page under the Source Code/Downloads tab. This tab is located underneath the Related Titles section of the page.

Contacting the Author

Should you have any questions or comments—or even spot a mistake you think I should know about—you can contact the author at `scott.spendolini@enkitec.com`.

CHAPTER 1

■ ■ ■

Threat Analysis

No two applications are exactly alike. Thus, the security required to protect one application is likely different—either vastly or slightly—from that required for any other application. Determining to secure your application starts with a proper assessment of the risk posed and corresponding threats. The upcoming section on "Assessment" goes into detail on how to initiate your thinking about security.

As part of this assessment, it may help to classify threats into one of two categories: preventable and unpreventable. The difference between and details of these threats are detailed in the section "Types of Threats."

Assessment

How much security is enough? There is only one correct answer to this question: it depends. Unfortunately, that answer doesn't really *answer* the question.

Choosing how much security to apply to an application largely depends on a number of factors, including

- what you're protecting,

- whom you are protecting it from,

- the likelihood that someone wants to steal your data or compromise your system, and

- the repercussions you would face in the case of a breach.

A helpful, easy-to-understand analogy to application security is home security. Most concepts in home security can easily be translated to application security, especially during the analysis and mitigation phase.

Home Security Assessment

Consider the example of choosing how to provide adequate security for your home. The answer to the first question is simple—you're protecting your home, condominium, or apartment, a physical piece of property or real estate with defined boundaries.

Next question: whom are you protecting your home from? That's where "it depends" comes into play. Before you can answer this question, you must ask yourself a number of others: How safe is the neighborhood? Is there a history of people breaking into homes in the area? If you're in an apartment, do you have a doorman or other security personnel? If so, do you trust them? The answers to these additional questions will help guide you in answering the initial one.

The third question—what is the likelihood that someone will break into your home?—also needs to be thought through and relevant facts and opinions applied in order to arrive at an answer. If you live in a part of town that has a history of break-ins, obviously the likelihood will be greater. If your property is in a rural gated community in a part of town with less crime, then the likelihood will not be as great. When answering this question, it is important to also consider "crimes of opportunity." Even in the best neighborhoods, an iPod or GPS unit sitting in an unlocked car presents an opportunity to otherwise honest people to make the wrong decision.

Lastly—and in many ways, most importantly—the repercussions of an actual breach need to be considered. If you don't have anything expensive in your home, you might not be too bothered by the thought of someone breaking in, as there's little for them to take. If you do have nice things, as well as good homeowners insurance, most stolen items can easily be replaced. However, the loss of family heirlooms and specific items that hold sentimental value could result in great emotional stress. There is also the concern that burglaries these days sometimes take a turn for the worse and end up with the burglar inflicting harm on the residents.

Once all of these questions are answered, it is a lot easier to answer the underlying "how much security is enough?" question. In some cases, simply locking the door when you're not at home will suffice. In others, perhaps locking the door as well as purchasing and activating a home security system would be the best approach. In extreme cases, the best course might be to move into another house in a better neighborhood.

Whatever decision is made, it was greatly influenced by both the answers to the original four questions and the answers to the questions that arose from them. Different people who live in different parts of the world or on different streets within the same community will come to different conclusions.

One of the most easily recognized homes in the United States is located at 1600 Pennsylvania Avenue NW in Washington, DC. The White House is essentially a home with a larger-than-average home office attached to it. While it is perhaps one of the larger homes in its neighborhood, it nonetheless has a physical boundary and surrounding grounds, as evidenced by the tall perimeter fence.

Despite its location in a good neighborhood, the White House has been the scene of several break-in attempts. In fact, only authorized personnel are allowed inside, making the answer to the second question simple: everyone else. Given that there have been many attempts to break into the White House—either in a spectacular fashion via a small airplane or by simply trying to scale the fence and make a run for it—the likelihood that someone will try to break in again is extremely high. The repercussions of such a breach are extremely serious in all cases.

Given that the stakes are a lot higher at the White House, extreme precautions and countermeasures are employed there. The entire property is under constant video surveillance, a highly trained armed security force is present at all times, and many physical barriers are in place to prevent access to the grounds. And these are only the precautions we know about.

Even though, at its core, the White House is not essentially different from anyone else's home, the level of perceived and actual threats to it is obviously much higher than for most homes. Thus, the additional layers of security are more extreme and thorough.

Application Security Assessment

Application security should be assessed and applied in much the same way as in home security. And, also like home security, one size does not necessarily fit all. Given unlimited resources, time, and money, all applications could have all sorts of security layers built into them, making each one as fortified as the next. Unfortunately, unlimited resources have never been nor ever will be available to any organization. Thus, we have to assess and determine what security needs to be applied on an application-by-application basis.

To start, let's consider the same four criteria that were used in assessing the need for home security. What are you protecting? To elaborate on this, what does the application you're protecting do? Is it a simple project management system where tasks are entered and reported on, or does it contain sensitive information, such as Social Security numbers or account numbers? Are there legislative regulations in place that dictate specific precautions to be taken? Is the application based on data that is freely available to anyone in your organization? As in the case of home security, the answers to these questions, as well as to the questions these questions lead to, will determine how much or how little security you should put in place.

The next question—whom are you protecting the application from?—is almost always answered incorrectly. Most organizations hold the view that if the application is within a firewall there is no way anyone from the outside can gain access to the system. While we all know that this has proven to be false in the past, let's ignore that for a moment.

Much less spectacular, yet much more likely, culprits are your authorized users. These users have already gotten past the first hurdle—having a valid username and password—because one has already been given to them. Many applications allow any user to see any record by design. Thus, an authorized user who wanted to steal data would have little difficulty in doing so. In fact, most APEX reports contain a link that allows the user to easily export all of the data to a CSV file, which can easily be carried out of the office on a USB drive or sent as an e-mail attachment.

Consider, for example, how WikiLeaks works. It is not political to point out that WikiLeaks does not actively hack into systems and try to steal data. Rather, they are merely a purveyor of data. Authorized users can anonymously upload sensitive data to the WikiLeaks site, where it is verified and, if deemed legitimate, released to the public en masse. At some point, an authorized user had to have access to all of this data, typically by way of some sort of export function.

Therefore, it is important to consider trusted, authorized users as part of the set of people you want to protect your data from, as not only are they the ones most likely to steal it; they also are the ones who have the least difficulty doing so.

Next, consider the likelihood that someone wants to break into your system and steal data. Depending on what the system does, the likelihood will either increase or decrease accordingly. Obviously systems with more sensitive data or more escalated privileges will be more likely targets. Certain organizations are a target for hackers simply based on their name or business alone. To a hacker, government intelligence agencies and large corporations are much more attractive targets than smaller organizations or government agencies that don't have a focus on national security.

You don't have to be the CIA or Microsoft to take this question seriously, as your data is critical to your business and so requires adequate protection. When evaluating the likelihood that someone wants access to your systems, be sure not to compare your concern directly to that of other organizations. Likelihood does not translate well from one organization to another because it's a relative concept that needs to be evaluated at the level at which it is applied. Regardless of your organization's size and fame, your data is as important to you as the CIA's data is important to them, and any precautions you take should be based on that.

Lastly, consider the repercussions of an actual breach or break-in to one of your systems. If a project management system was compromised, the repercussions would likely be limited, as the data contained therein may be of little interest or value. But if your application has sensitive financial or classified data, the repercussions could include financial loss, physical harm, even death.

Your applications likely fall somewhere in the middle of these two scenarios. For example: If a salesperson leaves to work for a competitor and takes all of his or her contract data, customers may soon start to do business with that competitor. Or if a student is able to break into the grading system at a college, everyone's grades may be made available to the public, thus embarrassing the college and perhaps causing a reduction in enrollment or legal action.

Data and Privileges

In addition to the four factors mentioned earlier, two other key factors need to be considered when assessing the security required for your applications: data and privileges.

The data on which your application is based is a good place to start, as its level of sensitivity tends to dictate how much security is required. If your data is not very sensitive, then implementing data access controls may not be required, as any user can already see any record. But if the data is more sensitive, data access should immediately be brought to the forefront and a solid plan needs to be designed and implemented.

APEX itself does not provide much in the way of tools for securing data. Fortunately, the Oracle Database does. Depending on your needs, you can use something as simple as a secure read-only view to secure your data so that only authorized users can view it. Oracle also provides more robust tools—such as Virtual Private Database—that can assist in providing secure access to your data. Data security is discussed in greater detail in Chapters 11 and 12.

Smaller applications that don't do much—say read-only reporting system or a simple data entry application—may require less attention than an application used to manage user roles or access to other systems, but this is not an excuse to ignore role-based security. APEX applications have a tendency to start very small and then quickly grow to something much larger—either in the sheer size of the application or the number of users. Initially, little access control is needed for many of these applications, but as they grow, access control becomes more and more critical and increasingly difficult to implement. Thus, no matter what the size or scope of an application, attention needs to be paid to basic user management and access control.

APEX does provide a basic user-to-role management utility called Access Control. Developers can easily add this capability to their applications via a wizard, instantly creating a view, edit, and administrator role. While this feature works for basic access control issues, it is somewhat limited in various ways. Chapter 9 addresses additional ways of managing access control in an APEX application.

Types of Threats

As noted before, threats can be grouped into two categories: preventable and unpreventable. The first group, as the name implies, can be prevented as long as secure best practices are adhered to, such as cross-site scripting, URL tampering, and SQL injection. The second group is an unfortunate necessity of doing business. At some point, users will need access to sensitive parts of the system. This requirement cannot be prevented and in fact is required for the system to function. Therefore, the only alternative is to provide solid auditing tools so that in the case of a breach, the perpetrator can easily and unequivocally be identified.

Preventable

Many threats in APEX applications can be prevented with just a little extra effort. Unfortunately, they often go unresolved due to the lack of time and not understanding how to locate and remedy them.

Preventable threats can be broken out into three different types:

- URL tampering,
- SQL injection, and
- cross-site scripting.

When building APEX applications, APEX typically selects the most secure options for page and shared components. However, for a number of reasons, those settings can be and often are changed to less secure settings. Assuming that a page was generated by a wizard and therefore is secure is a bad assumption to make.

URL Tampering

The URL of an APEX application is made up of a colon-delimited string of values that are passed to a parameter "p" of a procedure called "f". This is often referred to as the "f and p" syntax. The string of characters passed in is fixed, and any APEX developer can likely recall the purpose for many, if not all, of the positions. The APEX URL syntax is defined in Listing 1-1 below.

Listing 1-1. The APEX URL Syntax

```
Application ID:Page ID:Session ID:Request:Debug:Clear Cache:Item Names:Item Values:Printer Friendly
```

Given that the definition of the APEX URL syntax is standard across all APEX applications, it doesn't take a lot of skill to learn how to manipulate it. A malicious or simply curious user could easily change the values in the URL bar of a browser and resubmit the page. Listing 1-2 below illustrates a simple APEX URL that references page 1 of application 100:

Listing 1-2. A Simple APEX URL That Refers to Page 1 of Application 100

```
http://localhost/apex/f?p=100:1:12432087235079
```

URL tampering poses one of the most dangerous threats, as it takes zero programming skills to launch an attack. By changing portions of the URL, a malicious user might gain access to pages or to records that the user is not supposed to see. Fortunately, both APEX and the Oracle Database employ a number of techniques that can completely neutralize URL tampering attacks. These are addressed in later chapters of this book.

SQL Injection

SQL injection is much more sophisticated than URL tampering, as these attacks require at least a working knowledge of SQL. An SQL injection attack is designed to pass in actual SQL fragments that then get executed rather than inserted into the database as data. SQL Injection attacks can range in severity from minor to major, depending on a number of factors. Consider the SQL in Listing 1-3 below:

Listing 1-3. An SQL Statement with a Potential SQL Injection Risk

```
SELECT
 customer_name,
 cust_first_name,
 cust_last_name
FROM
 demo_customers
WHERE
 customer_name = '&P1_SEARCH.'
```

By using the APEX &ITEM. substitution syntax, the developer has introduced an SQL injection risk, since APEX will replace the string &P1_SEARCH. with its corresponding value before it parses, binds, and executes the query. If the user entered something like ACME, no danger would be present and the query would execute as expected.

However, if the user was more malicious and entered ACME' OR 'x' ='x for the value of P1_SEARCH in an APEX form, the SQL would actually be modified before it was parsed and executed by the database. The actual SQL that would be passed to the database and run is illustrated in Listing 1-4 below.

Listing 1-4. The SQL That Will Be Executed if a Malicious Value Is Passed In

```
SELECT
 customer_name,
 cust_first_name,
 cust_last_name
FROM
 demo_customers
WHERE
 customer_name = 'ACME' OR 'x' = 'x'
```

Notice that the WHERE clause now has an OR condition that will check for one or the other conditions to be true. If the customer_name is, in fact, ACME, then that record will be returned. If it is not ACME, then the second part of the OR will be evaluated, which will always be true. Thus, all records from the demo_customers table will be returned, which clearly was not the intent of the original SQL.

Fortunately, APEX applications typically don't face a lot of SQL injection risk, largely due to the fact that when referencing APEX items in SQL or PL/SQL regions, most developers use bind variable syntax. When bind variable syntax is used in APEX, the values of items are not passed in until after the query executes, making it impossible for them to influence the SQL itself.

Simply using bind variable syntax everywhere does not make you one hundred percent immune from SQL injection attacks. If bind variable syntax is used in conjunction with dynamic SQL, take care to ensure that the actual SQL is evaluated before the APEX items are. Chapter 7 covers SQL injection in greater detail.

Cross-Site Scripting

Cross-site scripting occurs when a malicious user at a high level passes in a fragment of JavaScript that is later executed by the same or other users in the application. Think of it as a type of SQL injection for JavaScript. Somewhat advanced knowledge of JavaScript is required to execute a successful cross-site scripting attack, so most average end users will simply not be capable of implementing one. But that is not a reason to ignore this type of threat.

Depending on the original version of APEX an application was started with, the number of cross-site scripting vulnerabilities can be quite large. Versions prior to APEX 4.0 did not secure report columns from cross-site scripting attacks by default, resulting in a large number of improperly configured columns. Also, the use of &ITEM. syntax in static APEX components could introduce a potential risk of cross-site scripting.

Cross-site scripting vulnerabilities are far more common than SQL injection in APEX applications and can be just as dangerous. Fortunately, these types of attacks can be mitigated by ensuring that your application settings are properly configured. This also is discussed in more detail in Chapter 7.

Unpreventable

Unfortunately, not all threats are preventable. Some systems, due to the nature of their design, do not employ much security. Take a call center system, for example. Given that calls can be routed to any agent from any customer, that agent will have access to any customer information—orders, personal information, and in some cases, credit card numbers. It would be quite simple for a dishonest agent to capture some of this data and then turn around and exploit, sell, or use it maliciously elsewhere. This type of free-for-all access can become especially troublesome when industry regulations, such as the Health Insurance Portability and Accountability Act (HIPAA), are factored in.

During the 2008 presidential election, Verizon Wireless employees improperly accessed cellular phone records for then-candidate Barack Obama. These employees were not hackers, but authorized users of the system they used to access the records. It was relatively simple to identify the culprits because there was an auditing system in place that recorded who accessed which record. As a result, the employees at fault were either disciplined or terminated.

Consider how difficult it would be to conduct business if there were tighter restrictions on who could access which records in a call center–like environment. If customers were each designated as having their own personal, "trusted" agent, how much more difficult would it be to conduct a simple billing inquiry call? What if your trusted agent was on vacation or not in and you needed access to your information? Companies could never work in such a fashion, and their corresponding systems are designed around this, allowing any agent access to almost any customer's records with no prior clearance.

When system design requires broad access to many users, it is essential that a comprehensive auditing policy be planned and implemented, as in many cases that will be your last and only line of defense against unauthorized data access. Some of the proactive measures that can be taken to reduce risk of unauthorized data access in an APEX application are discussed later in this book.

Auditing can be implemented at almost any level in an APEX application, ensuring that if unauthorized data is accessed, the administrators of the system will be notified immediately. Some controls—such as export to comma-separated values (CSV file)—can also be disabled, preventing users from downloading all records to a portable format. Lastly, and perhaps most importantly, design of these call center–type systems can incorporate controls that limit which records can be viewed. Requiring more than a single field for a query makes it more difficult for the agent to maliciously search the database.

Summary

So how much security is enough? It still depends. And what "it depends" means will change over time as requirements and conditions change. Using the examples outlined in this chapter, you should be able to create a set of guidelines that help determine which security measures to deploy in which circumstances and to clarify "it depends" on a per-application basis.

Your data is one of your organization's most critical assets. Don't get caught in the trap of comparing it to that of other, higher public profile organizations. Rather, look at your data in the context of itself. Use as a guideline what similar organizations do, as you will get a much more accurate picture of the typical security precautions you should be looking at implementing.

CHAPTER 2

Implementing a Security Plan

Security is not something that is bolted on to an application the day before it gets promoted to production. It should be considered as early in the design process as possible. To ensure that this happens, it's a good idea to have a security plan when building applications. The plan should be broad enough to meet your requirements yet brief enough to remain practical.

As part of the security plan, it is essential that some sort of security review process is devised and incorporated into your development process. This review process can be automated, manual, or a bit of both, depending on what you've assessed is necessary.

What Is a Security Plan?

Security plans come in all shapes and sizes. Some are hundreds of pages long and contain countless data points, while others can fit on a single sheet of paper. Regardless of the size, the point of a security plan is to ensure that all security policies are adhered to when designing, deploying, and managing your entire IT infrastructure.

A good security plan will not only identify potential threats to your organization but will also outline how to mitigate those threats and how to deal with them if they ever do come to fruition. It should identify potential risks, and also rank them, so that those with the highest priority get attention first. It should also provide a clear path to follow in the case of any sort of breach. The security plan should address all touch points in your architecture—network, software, hardware, and even physical access to resources.

The APEX security plan should focus on at least the following five categories:

- Assessment
- Design
- Development
- Contingency
- Review and revision

The task of creating a comprehensive security plan is not trivial and therefore should not be taken lightly. For the scope of this book, the security plan will focus exclusively on an APEX.

LESS IS MORE

Like any other type of standards document, if you make your APEX security plan too sophisticated, no one will follow it. But if you make it too broad or ambiguous, then no one will follow it. Thus, the challenge is to come up with a plan that encompasses what it needs to in the least intrusive way possible.

Before the application is designed, you should assess the application's security requirements. This assessment should be used as part of the design phase, not simply determined there. For example, if your application's data is sensitive and it is determined that a virtual private database (VPD) is required, the design of the application will be very different than when not using VPD.

Regardless of the complexity of the plan, one thing should be made clear: security starts before development. APEX is a RAD tool, and in many cases, the first step to building an application is actual development, not design. For the traditional reasons, skipping the design phase is clearly an oversight and a mark of a less experienced developer. From a security point of view, the risks of skipping the design phase are also grave.

Assessment

As discussed in the previous chapter, an assessment of your application's security needs must be the first step in any security plan. It's also one of the most difficult steps, because there are no concrete, one-size-fits-all guidelines that work for any organization.

The following are some areas you'll want to examine as part of your assessment. Some example questions to spark your thinking are included.

Risk Analysis

Risk analysis speaks to the likelihood and impact of something going wrong. We wear seatbelts when riding in cars because of a judgment call that our society has made regarding the likelihood of a wreck. Ride in a subway car in a major city, though, and the judgment call is different. No seatbelts are even available because the risk of a crash or wreck is deemed so very low.

Questions to answer during your risk analysis include the following:

- What is the likelihood that someone wants this data?

- Will this system be inside or outside of the firewall?

- What are the repercussions if someone actually does breach the system?

Keep in mind that the answers are not always objective. You can know for certain whether a system is inside or outside your firewall, but the likelihood of someone wanting your data comes down to a judgment call. You or someone in your organization will need the courage to make that call.

Access Control

Access control is about limiting access to your application and its underlying data. Questions to consider include the following:

- How will users authenticate to this application?

- What roles are required for this application, and what will each one do?

- Who will be assigned each role?

Keep in mind your risk analysis as you answer these questions. Design your answers to mitigate the risks whenever feasible.

Data Access

Aside from the application, how sensitive is your data? What steps beyond access control to the application should you take to protect the data? Here are some questions to think about:

- What level of sensitivity is the data in this application?

- If needed, what technologies are required to help secure the data?

- Should the data be encrypted? If so, how much of it should be encrypted?

Don't just consider the data in the operational data store. Also, consider the data in backups of your database, work files created during extract/transform/load (ETL) processing, temporary tables, and reporting databases. Take a broad view of protecting data throughout the life cycle.

Auditing and Monitoring

In many cases, data simply cannot be protected because authorized users will need to access the data at some point in order to do their jobs. When this occurs, auditing and monitoring are the first and last lines of defense because if a breach were to occur, someone would need to be held accountable.

- What auditing strategy will be used?

- How will this application be monitored?

When determining what to audit, keep in mind that erring on the side of too much is better than erring on the side of not enough. It is much better to discard unused audit data than it is to wish that auditing had been enabled in the first place.

Application Management

Access control is a critical piece of the overall security of your application. Careful thought, planning, and constant reevaluation as to who gets which role needs to occur because business rules and conditions are often fluid and change without notice. The initial design should answer the following questions:

- Who will determine who gets access to the application?

- Who will determine and/or approve which user gets which role?

- Who will be responsible for monitoring the application?

- Where will the application be hosted?

During assessment, focus more on identifying risk rather than the specifics of how to mitigate it. The mitigation steps and associated specifics will come later in the design and development phases. For example, it's OK to determine that Lightweight Directory Access Protocol (LDAP) will be used to authenticate users in this phase, but it makes little sense to start defining the specifics of the connection to the LDAP server, the credentials required, and so on.

Design

Based on the results of the assessment, security should be added as part of the design phase of your application. It should not be an afterthought or something that you attempt to bolt on days or even hours before your application goes live. Sacrifices made at this phase will become painfully obvious should a breach occur.

The design phase is where the findings of the analysis phase will start to be mapped to tangible components. For example, you may have determined to manage your users and groups in LDAP. In the design phase, you'll start to define how many groups you need, what each group will map to by way of APEX components and capabilities, and who will belong to which group.

Let's take the case of building a ten-page application, of which each page contains ten components. If security is ignored until the end, then there will be 100 components that will have to be inspected for any potential threat. Assuming that it will take three to five minutes to check each component, you would have to spend just almost an entire business day inspecting your application for security issues. Additionally, it will be quite cumbersome to keep track of all possible components because, in the real world, the number of pages and components will likely be higher.

Had you taken a different approach and designed your application with security in mind, it will still take about 100 minutes to inspect all 100 components. So, what's the difference? It lies in the order of operations and overall development time.

In the first approach, you built an application that has 100 places that could have a security flaw. Thus, for each flaw that you address and fix, you introduce the potential of breaking the application's functionality. Each piece of functionality that is broken will of course require more time to fix. Thus, the estimate of 100 minutes is on the extreme low side because each flaw fixed will likely break other components in your application and extend the total development time.

The second approach addresses any functionality issues that a more secure application introduces as they occur because the application is being tested with more secure components from the start of development. Thus, the total time it would take to build an application with security in mind is almost always less than applying security at the end. Additionally, it is a lot less likely that components will be skipped because there won't be a long list of components to inspect at the end of development.

Development

After the assessment and design phases are complete, then—and only then—should development start. A builder does not start building the frame of a house before the blueprints are drawn up and signed off on. Developing an application before the design is complete is just as foolish.

Given that adequate time was spent on the assessment and design phases, the development phase should go smoothly and without too many unexpected surprises. This is where the work done in the design phase starts to take form in the application. Implement the controls that were defined by mapping them to either APEX components or database features.

While many of APEX's settings are defaulted to the more secure options, there are still a few that default to less secure options. A simple, concise, best-practices guide for APEX developers will assist in ensuring that all developers are working from the same set of secure properties. Regular security reviews—either by an automated tool such as Enkitec's eSERT or manually by developers or a third party—will ensure that additional risk is not exposed when building the actual applications.

Contingency

Despite all of the careful planning and testing that may have occurred, there is always the chance that a security vulnerability went unnoticed or a new exploit is discovered. Therefore, it is critical to have a plan in place that can be activated in a worst-case scenario.

One mistake many organizations make here is that they focus on the spectacular yet unlikely events, not the unspectacular yet likely events. A large-scale terrorist attack similar to 9/11 is certainly spectacular yet is not very likely at all to occur again, especially at facilities that are not as iconic as the World Trade Center. A rogue user stealing data and selling it to a competitor is much more plausible.

Even if an organization did have a large budget and ample resources, it would not make economic sense to spend that money and effort on something so unlikely when other departments could benefit more. At some point, the laws of diminishing returns would kick in, and each additional hour or dollar spent on trying to secure an application would yield no tangible results and actually become a burden as opposed to a benefit.

Events that get far less media attention are much more likely to occur in your environment. Consider these events as higher priorities because many of them are easy to address, as long as time is spent identifying and mitigating them. Thus, ensure that these much more common events are properly mitigated.

Review and Revision

Your security plan is a fluid document. It will never really be finished. Security is a never-ending process, and your security plan should mirror that fact closely. Hackers and malicious users will stop at nothing to get access to your data. Therefore, your task of ensuring the security of your applications will never end.

Before any APEX application is promoted to production, it should undergo a thorough security review. If all of the best practices previously defined in this chapter are adhered to, then the security review should yield positive results. However, even an automated tool cannot accurately detect all issues with processes, page flows, or sophisticated code. Therefore, it is critical that the entire footprint of the application is reviewed for potential security issues.

On the server side, particular attention needs to be paid to Oracle Database and APEX patches on a regular basis because they will address both published and unpublished security and other issues. In fact, efforts should be made to stay with the current release of APEX for that reason alone. Hackers are aware of exploits that exist in previous versions of APEX and won't hesitate to exploit them. The greater the delta between your release and the the current release, the longer the stride to get back to the current release will be. This also applies to database and operating system patches.

It's rare that any organization will require less security as it moves forward with its development. Additional regulations or situations may arise that require additional security checks or considerations. Don't be afraid to amend the security plan as needed to reflect this. Sure, it will likely cost both time and money, but considering the alternative, you'll be saving a lot of both in the long run.

Security Reviews

The thoroughness and length of the security review process should be established as part of the assessment phase. For practical purposes, it may make sense to create a couple of different levels or types of review and then map each application to one of the levels. For applications that don't contain sensitive data or don't implement any roles, a simple automated test may suffice. But for applications with multiple roles, sensitive data, and complex business rules, an automated test combined with a manual review would make more sense.

Automated Reviews

APEX is a metadata-based tool. This means that when you define components—pages, regions, reports, columns, and so on—you are specifying options, not writing code. Even the SQL in a report region is technically an attribute of that report and stored in a database table.

This architecture is quite powerful for various reasons such as portability, performance, globalization, and security. The developers at Oracle are well aware of this power and hence have exposed this metadata through a set of secured views simply called the *APEX views*. These views can and often are used by developers in their own applications to enhance functionality or provide a window into the application.

In a security context, these views are invaluable. Many components in APEX have a number of different settings that the developer can choose from. When set incorrectly, some of these settings can introduce security risks to an APEX application. Others can be set to any setting without compromising security at all.

Given that the APEX views contain all of these settings and that you can create a list of secure versus insecure options for these settings, the process of inspecting all settings in an application can be greatly automated with a tool that contains mappings of which settings were secure and which weren't.

Enkitec eSERT is one such tool. eSERT is an APEX application that inspects other APEX applications for potential security vulnerabilities based on a configurable set of rules. The result is an interactive dashboard that highlights which components present a security risk and shows advice on how to remedy them. Using such a tool can greatly reduce the time it takes to inspect and remedy all components in an APEX application because eSERT can evaluate thousands of components in just a few seconds.

eSERT was designed to be embedded in your development process and is best utilized when run frequently, not at the end of a development cycle. As mentioned previously in this chapter, it is much more effective and efficient to ensure that components are developed in a secure manner as they are created rather than all at one at the end of the development cycle.

Manual Reviews

Automated reviews are a starting point when it comes to reviewing an application. While the information that they can provide is valuable, they do not inspect all facets of your application. Thus, automated reviews should be augmented with manual reviews when deemed necessary in your security plan.

The manual review should focus on the flow and business rules of your applications, not the individual settings that an automated review can scan. Attention should be paid as to what each computation, process, and branch is for, as well as the corresponding PL/SQL and/or JavaScript code associated with each.

Consider this example: a developer adds a process that applies a 50 percent discount to any order taken, as long as the last name of the customer is Spendolini. If the developer built this process using secure best practices, then an automated tool will simply flag it as secure and move on to the next component. Thus, it is critical to inspect APEX components not only for declarative security flaws but for programmatic exploits that can be discovered only as part of a manual review.

Unfortunately, manual reviews can be time-consuming and expensive, depending on the size and complexity of the application. Thus, the more that developers can stick to using native APEX components versus writing their own code, the less lengthy and costly the manual review will be.

Simulating a Breach

Our society is very much event-driven. We don't take precautions to prevent something from happening until it actually happens. Consider car or home security systems. Oftentimes, the impetus for purchasing either of these is a car or home break-in. Clearly, had we made the investment in the security system earlier, the break-in may have been prevented.

Much of the rationale behind this approach is simple: money. It is a lot cheaper to not buy a car or home security system than it is to buy one. With APEX applications, money definitely plays into the decision-making process. But another factor is at work here, too: time. Most developers—APEX, Java, .NET, or otherwise—work in a high-stress environment. Demands for producing additional applications are high, and oftentimes, developers simply can't spend as much time as they would like on things such as the user interface, documentation, and, unfortunately, security.

Given this scenario, there is really only one way to truly test the security of your infrastructure or application: simulate a breach. This can be done either without your staff's knowledge by a third party or as an internal exercise where all parties are aware of the exercise. The former method tends to be taken more seriously because the breach does seem real, whereas the latter method is almost always written off as just another tedious exercise that distracts from real work that needs to be done.

In either case, it is critical that the breach is taken seriously and the steps to remedy it are implemented. The cost of hiring a third party to test your security may seem high, but compare that to your organization being featured in the media as having a breach and the shattered relationships with your customers that you would have to deal with.

A dose of practicality does need to be applied here because most organizations do not have unlimited time and money to conduct such simulations. The other extreme of simulating any potential breach and accounting for that may also prove counterproductive because the resulting system would be so locked down that it would be nearly impossible for anyone to use.

At the very least, take the time to come up with a few "what if" scenarios, and consider what policy or application design changes would be implemented if one of these scenarios became reality. Then, consider implementing some or all of the application design changes proactively.

Summary

Creating a security plan is relatively simple to do. Ensuring that your organization adheres to such a plan—and revising the plan as conditions warrant—is not as easy. Security plans also don't need to be complex to be effective. A better approach is to keep them lightweight so that developers will more readily adopt them. Instilling secure best practices is also something that should start at the very beginning of the application's life cycle, not at the end.

Automated tools will greatly reduce the time it takes to conduct a security review, but keep in mind that they represent only a portion of the overall plan. Manual reviews should be employed for applications that need more security or scrutiny. Malicious code or rogue processes that circumvent business rules can be detected only by a manual review because there is no other way to discern the purpose of a block of code.

■ ■ ■

CHAPTER 3

APEX Architecture

Flying a modern commercial airliner has never been easier than it is today. Essentially, all a pilot has to do is enter a start point and an end point, get the plane in the air, and let the plane fly itself for the rest of the flight. Should conditions necessitate it, the plane can even land itself. Despite these facts, commercial pilots undergo a massive amount of training before they are allowed to take off with passengers on board. They have to study not only the specifics of the type of plane they want to fly but also the basics of aeronautics. In addition to the education they must receive, they also need to log a large number of hours of actual flying time before they can get a commercial license.

On a good day, little of this knowledge will need to be put to use. But in the case something does go wrong, a pilot needs to be able to draw from this vast array of education and experience in order to solve any potential problem. Without an intimate knowledge of both the principles of aeronautics and the specifics of the aircraft, this is simply not possible.

Similarly, to truly understand how to build secure APEX applications, you have to understand the underlying infrastructure and technologies that make up APEX. That is what this chapter sets out to do: familiarize you with the architecture and building blocks of APEX. It starts out with a high-level overview of the different modules of APEX, from the instance administration console to what a workspace is and how many of them to create. It also briefly covers the application development environment components, namely, the Application Builder, SQL Workshop, Team Development, and Websheets. It then shifts gears a bit and discusses the metadata-based architecture of APEX and how that relates to building applications. Next, it covers the three schemas that make up APEX and how they are managed and secured. The chapter concludes with a detailed overview of how APEX transactions work.

Overview of APEX

What is Oracle Application Express (APEX)? In a sentence, APEX is a web-based development and deployment platform designed in and for the Oracle Database. All that is required to design or use an APEX application is a modern web browser. APEX applications can be as simple as a single page or contain multiple pages and interface with external systems via web services. Figure 3-1 shows the sample database application, which highlights the features of APEX. In fact, the APEX developer tools—Application Builder, SQL Workshop, and Team Development—are actually APEX applications.

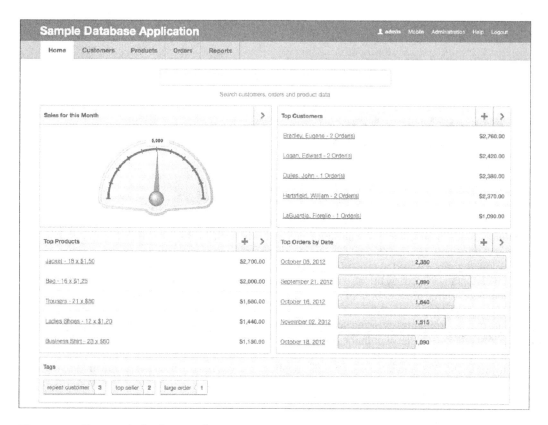

Figure 3-1. *The sample database application*

APEX is built on a declarative architecture. Thus, when pages or reports are created, no additional code is generated. Rather, rows that describe the corresponding components are inserted into APEX's tables. When an application is run, APEX will render the page and its components by combining this metadata with its own internal procedures. This approach is quite scalable, because the same procedures are executed over and over in the database, with the only difference being the data that is used. The Oracle Database can read and write records quite efficiently, which yields extremely fast performance for most APEX application environments.

The APEX environment contains a number of commonly used foundation components integrated directly into the tool. Features such as session state management, user and role management, validations, user interface, and integration via web services are all out-of-the-box features that are ready to use. APEX 4.2 also ships with a number of packaged applications, which are prebuilt applications that solve basic business problems. Examples include a project tracker, incident tracker, art catalog, and bug tracker. Once installed, these packaged applications are ready to use just as they are. Alternatively, they can be easily modified to suit a particular requirement or need.

All components and actions within APEX are accessed via nothing more than a modern web browser. At a high level, APEX is split into two major parts: the instance administration console and the Application Builder. The instance administration console is where all workspaces, developers, and instance settings are managed. Access to the instance administration console should be restricted to either the DBA or system administrator, since users with access to it can perform low-level system administration functions, such as creating new schemas, developers, and workspaces. The instance administration console is discussed in detail in Chapter 4.

The application development environment—which includes the Application Builder, SQL Workshop, Team Development, and Websheets—is where all development takes place. Developers who log in to the application development environment can create applications, pages, reports, charts, and so on. They can also use the SQL Workshop to create and manage database objects and can use Team Development to manage their projects. Chapters 6 and 7 cover using the application development environment, specifically the Application Builder, in much more depth.

Administration Console

The APEX administration console is a web-based interface used by APEX administrators to manage an instance of APEX. From the administration console, an administrator can manage requests, manage the instance settings, create and manage workspaces, and monitor all workspace activity. Upon installation, only a single user—ADMIN—has access to the administration console. The typical APEX developer will never need access to the administration console. If such a case does arise, it is best to have the APEX administrator perform the task on behalf of the developer, rather than grant the developer access.

The APEX administrator is a powerful role; it should be closely guarded and given out only to trusted individuals. While it is often compared to SYS, it does not have the ability to manage and control the Oracle Database; its functionality is limited to only the APEX workspaces and their associated applications and users. However, the APEX administrator can access nearly any schema in the database simply by creating a workspace and associating it to a schema. Thus, the APEX administrator can view any data in the database that does not have any other safeguards.

From a personnel point of view, the APEX administrator is rarely a full-time position. It requires a commitment of only a few hours a month, sometimes even less than that. In most cases, the APEX administrator is also the DBA. This makes sense from a compliance and control point of view in that having access to the APEX administrator is a lesser set of privileges than that of a DBA.

The administration console home page provides a dashboard that summarizes the settings of the instance of APEX, as shown in Figure 3-2.

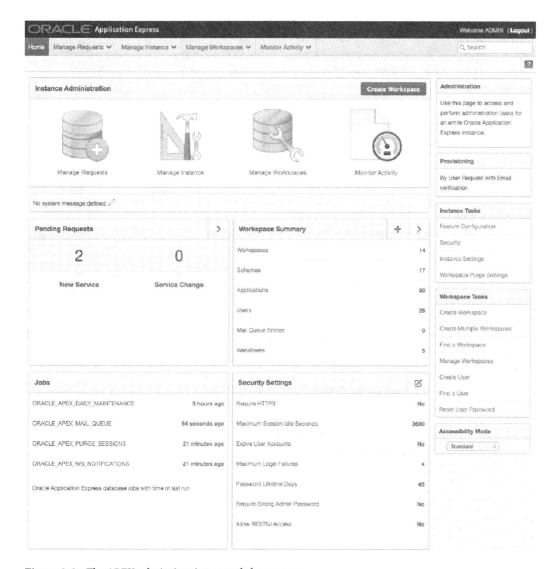

Figure 3-2. *The APEX adminsitration console home page*

On this page, a number of metrics and settings are displayed, broken out into four categories. It is important to note that this is not a conclusive list of attributes, particularly in the Security Settings region. Quite a few additional attributes are critical for the security of an instance of APEX. Recommended secure settings for an instance of APEX are discussed thoroughly in Chapter 4.

Managing Requests

APEX developers can request additional tablespaces, schemas, workspaces, or workspace termination from within APEX. All of these requests need to be approved by an APEX administrator and are done so through the Manage Requests section of the administration console. It is important to point out that schema management can be done outside of APEX as well by the DBA, just as it would for any other database schema. This embedded feature was created namely for APEX in a multitenant, hosted environment where access to SYS is not required. In most on-premises environments, the DBA manages the creation of all schemas for any application, and this feature is simply not utilized.

From a security perspective, there is little risk here by allowing developers to make such requests, because they will all need to be approved by the APEX instance administrator. However, the Provisioning Status setting in the instance settings should be set to Manual. This will prevent anyone from signing up for a workspace without approval and require the APEX instance administrator to create all workspaces.

Managing Instances

The Manage Instance section is where most instance-level settings of APEX are configured. These settings typically impact every workspace and application on the instance. In some cases, a workspace administrator can override some of these settings at the workspace level. Many of these settings have to do directly with the overall security of the instance of APEX, particularly most of those in the Instance Settings region. The bulk of the remainder of the settings have little direct impact on the overall security of an instance and are there purely for instance management purposes.

Aside from initially configuring APEX, little time will need to be spent in this section on an ongoing basis. Most management of an APEX instance is done at the workspace level, either by creating new workspaces or by managing the associated workspace users. Chapter 4 is dedicated to configuring an instance of APEX with secure best practices in mind and highlights any instance setting that pertains to security.

Managing Workspaces

From its earliest days, APEX was intended to be a multitenant, hosted environment. Multiple users from completely different organizations would be able to securely share an instance of APEX that would be hosted on the public Internet. A real-world example of this is Oracle's publicly hosted instance of APEX, at http://apex.oracle.com. Oracle provides this instance free of charge to anyone who wants to try APEX without having to download and install it locally. This instance regularly plays host to more than 10,000 workspaces, or virtual private slices of the APEX environment.

An APEX workspace contains both developers and applications and is typically associated with one or more database schemas. All development activity occurs within a workspace. Each workspace is completely segregated and isolated from all others, thus ensuring that different groups can build and deploy their applications on a single instance of Oracle and APEX. However, most organizations that have adopted APEX have chosen to deploy it on-premise, installing it as close to their production databases as possible. Given APEX's ease of management and installation, this is not a surprise.

The Manage Workspace section provides a set of tools for creating, modifying, and removing workspaces. It also provides a facility for moving a workspace from one instance of APEX to another. Lastly, a few reports summarize the attributes of all workspaces within an instance of APEX.

Details about what makes up a workspace and its associated components can be found in the "Workspaces" section of this chapter. You can find information on how to ensure that workspaces are properly configured and secured in Chapter 5.

Monitoring Activity

The last component of the administration console is Monitor Activity. From here, an APEX instance administrator can keep an eye on all page views that occur within any workspace, including the application development environment. A combination of reports, charts, and even calendars are provided to display the data. Summary data is automatically archived by APEX and displayed here as well.

While APEX does collect a lot of details about itself, the data here has a relatively default short life span of about two weeks. This APEX instance administrator can increase this value up to about a year, which may still not be enough in some cases. Thus, it is recommended that if data retention periods need to be longer, a custom archival procedure be implemented. Archived data is stored only as summary data; discrete details are not archived automatically by APEX.

Workspaces

As previously mentioned, workspaces are virtual private slices of an instance of APEX where developers build and deploy their applications. Each workspace will have a number of users associated with it. Users can be one of three types: workspace administrators, developers, or end users.

Workspaces also have at least one schema associated with them that the different modules can interact with or parse as. Any system privilege granted to that schema will be available to any developer or workspace administrator in the workspace it's associated with. For example, if a schema were created without the CREATE TABLE privilege, then there is no way that any type of APEX user would be able to create a table within that schema from APEX, even though a user would still be able to run the Create Table Wizard. This concept extends to any system privilege.

Depending on how the instance administrator configured it, a workspace will provide access to all or some of the different modules that make up the application development environment. This ability to limit access to modules can even be extended to individual users, if needed.

Users and Roles

APEX users are specific and unique to a workspace. Their credentials are managed internally by APEX and cannot currently be moved elsewhere. If a single person needs access to three workspaces, then three APEX users need to be created—one in each respective workspace. These three accounts are seen as completely separate accounts by APEX and contain no integration or association with one another. Changing the password on one account does not impact the other two at all. Future releases of APEX may support moving these users to an external authentication repository, but as of APEX 4.2, that is not possible.

There are three classifications or types of APEX user: workspace administrator, developer, and end user. The end user is simply a set of credentials that can be used in applications that are developed with APEX. End users can access only the Team Development module. They will not even see the Application Builder or SQL Workshop when they log in to the application development environment, as shown in Figure 3-3. Even though there is a link to the Administration section of the workspace, no functions or actions are available on the corresponding page for APEX end users.

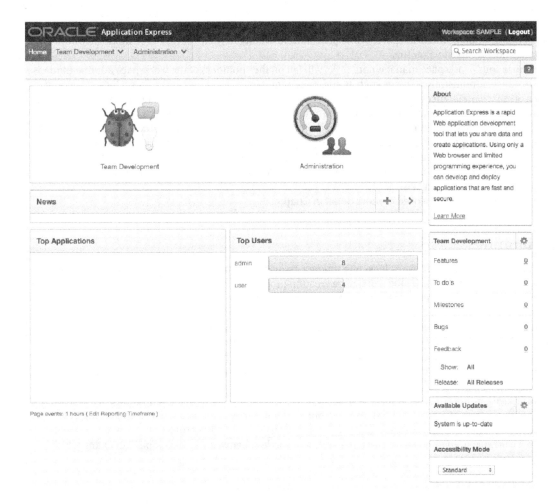

Figure 3-3. *An end user's view of the application development environment*

Using the APEX end-user type of user is acceptable for testing, training, or even applications with a small, static user community. However, because APEX users cannot be used across applications in different workspaces and cannot be easily integrated with external authentication repositories, it is not recommended they be used for most applications.

Most developers within a workspace should be classified as just that—developers. APEX developers can create and build applications, access the associated database objects via the SQL Workshop, use Team Development, and access some of the functionality of the Administration report. Developers can also be limited as to which module or modules they have access to. For instance, a developer could be created who had access only to SQL Workshop but not the Application Builder or Team Development.

It is important to understand that a developer who has access to the Application Builder but not the SQL Workshop can still perform almost any function in the SQL Workshop, including performing any DML or DDL on any schema associated with the workspace. All they would have to do would be to create a simple application that either embeds the desired functionality via PL/SQL processes or allows them to execute any SQL statement passed in via a page item.

The last level of APEX user is the workspace administrator. The workspace administrator can do anything that a developer can as well as manage the workspace. Workspace administrators have full access to all modules within a workspace, and it is not possible to alter this.

In most organizations, workspace management tasks will fall on the shoulders of the workspace administrator as opposed to the instance administrator. Things such as adding or removing a developer, unlocking a locked account, and setting the workspace preferences are all common tasks given to the workspace administrator. The time required to perform these tasks is usually just a few minutes per month.

While the workspace administrator can manage only their specific workspace, it is important to limit who actually gets this role. Developers who spend their time building applications and their associated schema objects do not need to be created as workspace administrators, but rather simply as developers. The workspace administrator role should be reserved for either the development manager or a DBA. This way, there can be more accountability for administrative tasks performed within a workspace.

Workspace users and roles are disused in more detail in Chapter 5.

Schema Mappings

When a workspace is created, it must have at least one schema associated with it. This schema can be an existing one or be created automatically as part of the workspace creation process. This schema will be used to store all database objects and data used in user-developed applications. The metadata that APEX creates as developers build applications is not stored in this schema, but rather in the APEX_040200 schema.

When a schema is associated with a workspace, any developer who has access to that workspace can perform any task that the schema has privileges for. The developer can also see any data stored in the schema, provided it has not been obfuscated by an external mechanism. This is a critical factor when considering which developers have access to which workspace, because any developer will be able to see all objects in any parse-as schema associated with a workspace.

In most workspaces, only a single schema is associated with a workspace. However, if requirements dictate that different applications parse as different schemas, then multiple schemas may be associated to a single workspace. It is also possible for a single schema to be associated with multiple workspaces. Regardless of how many schemas are associated to a workspace, an application can parse only as a single schema, and a developer can change this association only during design time.

Components

The top-level sections of the application development environment consist of four major components: Application Builder, SQL Workshop, Team Development, and Administration. Depending on a user's role and privileges, the user may see one, two, or all of the associated components. Furthermore, some sections will be only partially enabled based on role. For example, a developer will see the Administration tab, but only a subset of the functionality is available to a developer.

An instance or workspace administrator can limit which modules users have access to on a per-workspace or per-user basis, as illustrated in Figure 3-4.

Figure 3-4. *Limiting which modules an individual user has access to*

Under the covers, each module is actually a separate APEX application. Take notice of the URL the next time you log into the application development environment, and you'll see that each module has its own unique application ID. This design was done to facilitate security, as well as make each module more manageable so that a bug or design change in one module will not impact the other modules.

Application Builder

The Application Builder is where developers will spend the bulk of their time when using the tool. Here, applications can be built by creating pages, reports, charts, calendars, and a number of other types of components. Users with either the developer or the workspace manager privilege can access the Application Builder.

As mentioned, each application must be associated with one and only one schema. The developer must make that determination when creating the application and is free to choose any schema that is associated with the workspace. The schema assignment can be changed at any time, but only by a developer at design time. All SQL and PL/SQL within that application will parse as if connected directly to that schema. Applications can also perform any DDL commands that the corresponding schema has access to, if so programmed by the developer.

Application Builder secure development best practices are discussed in detail in Chapters 6 and 7.

SQL Workshop

The SQL Workshop is a web-based interface used to interact with database objects and data. It is by no means a replacement for a desktop-based IDE; rather, it's an alternative that developers can use when a full IDE is not required or not available. The SQL Workshop is further split up into five subsections: Object Browser, SQL Commands, SQL Scripts, Utilities, and RESTful Services, as illustrated in Figure 3-5.

Figure 3-5. *The SQL Workshop home page*

From a security perspective, there is not much that can be configured to limit or restrict access to the SQL Workshop. Either developers have access to it or they don't. And if they don't, they can easily build an application that allows them to perform similar functionality. Thus, when any developer has access to either the Application Builder or the SQL Workshop, they have full access to any schema associated with it. They will be able to run any SQL statement they want, create or drop any type of object the schema has permissions to, view any table or view, and execute any script they can upload. If this level is access is not appropriate for a developer, then the only sure way to limit it is to not make them a developer in that workspace.

Despite there being little control as to what a developer can access within the SQL Workshop, there are a couple of sections that do focus on security, and they are worth mentioning here.

> *Methods on Tables*: Found in the Utilities subsection of the SQL Workshop, the Methods on Tables Wizard automates the creation of a package to manage all DML transactions on a table or group of tables. Using this wizard to create what are called *table APIs* creates a single entry point into inserting, updating, and deleting data for a table. This entry point can be augmented with any number of business rules and additional security checks to ensure that only valid transactions occur.

> Chapter 13 discusses an approach that use a limited privilege schema and table APIs to mitigate a number of threats. The theory behind this approach is that if the parse-as schema that an application is associated with has little to no system privileges, then any successful attack on that schema will also be limited as to what it can impact. The Methods on Tables Wizard is used as part of this approach, and samples are provided as well.

> *Object Reports*: The Object Reports section is broken down into five subsections. Of particular interest here is the Security Reports subsection. There are four security reports: Object Grants, Column Privileges, Role Privileges, and System Privileges. Each of these reports displays information from the corresponding data dictionary views. While this data is not unique to APEX and can be obtained a number of ways, it is convenient that it is included in the SQL Workshop.

Team Development

Team Development was introduced with APEX 4.0. Essentially, it is a project management utility that is integrated with the Application Builder. A development team can use Team Development to plan their milestones, features, and to-dos, as well as manage bugs and feedback reported by end users.

Any type of user—workspace administrator, developer, or end user—can be configured to have access to Team Development. This flexibility works well for nondevelopers such as project managers because they can be created as an end-user account and only be able to use Team Development.

Team Development is, of course, an APEX application, designed by the Oracle APEX team. It functions like any other APEX application and may or may not have potential security vulnerabilities. Unfortunately, if there are any vulnerabilities, there is little that can be done aside from waiting for a patch from Oracle to address them. This fact should not discourage the use of Team Development, though, because it is a supported component of the application development environment and will be patched should a vulnerability be discovered.

Websheets

Introduced in APEX 4.0, Websheets are a feature of APEX aimed at the common business user. More of an online spreadsheet feature than full-blown application development environment, Websheets do not have traditional developers, but rather end-users who can also make changes to the application. The approach works well in some scenarios, as business users can quickly and easily modify both data and its underlying structure without the assistance from a developer, or knowledge of SQL or PL/SQL.

Most Websheets applications are designed with the assumption that any authorized user can see and modify any record. This is often a decision made by necessity, as most of the security controls available in a database application are absent in Websheets. For example, there is no easy way to prevent URL tampering with a Websheet.

Unfortunately, there is no simple upgrade path from a Websheet to a traditional database application. All pages and their associated content will need to be re-created. In fact, Websheets applications will lose some functionality when migrated to a traditional database application, as they allow for updatable interactive reports and database applications do not. Data will also need to be migrated to traditional Oracle tables, since Websheets use a single table to store any and all data.

Thus, when choosing between a Websheet and a traditional database application, these limitations and shortcomings need to be kept in mind. Often times with just a little more work, a database application can be quickly created in place of a Websheet, ensuring the application's longevity as the business and requirements grow.

HOW MANY WORKSPACES?

One of the questions to arise when starting with APEX is this: how many workspaces do I need to create for my organization? Ideally, the answer to this question would be simple: one. A single workspace could be associated with as many schemas as needed, and all developers could be created there as well.

There are a couple of technical benefits of using a single workspace. First, APEX subscriptions work only within a single workspace. Subscriptions allow developers to create master copies of some components and then subscribe to those components across different applications—as long as those applications are in the same workspace. Using this mechanism, a developer could make a change to a component and then publish that change to all subscribers, regardless of which application they are located in. This centralization increases the manageability of an application greatly because changes need to happen in only a single location vs. multiple places.

Second, applications within a single workspace can be configured so that when a user authenticates to one, the user is authenticated to all of them. Configuring an application to behave this way is as simple as setting the cookie name in the authentication scheme to the same value across multiple applications. Details of this approach are discussed in Chapter 8.

While these two benefits may seem compelling, there are also some drawbacks to using a single workspace that may negate the benefits. First, if there is concern that only specific developers should be able to access specific schemas, then a single workspace approach will not work. Since there is no way to restrict which schema a specific developer has access to (aside from the SQL Workshop), multiple workspaces may be required where this requirement is in place.

Also, for organizations with a large number of applications, it may simply be easier to split up the applications into multiple workspaces for organizational sake, at least on the development side. It is possible to develop applications in multiple workspaces and then deploy them to a single workspace on the production instance. While the subscription feature will not work using this approach, the shared authentication will.

While there is no single correct number of workspaces for an organization, a good guideline is that the fewer workspaces that exist, the easier an instance of APEX will be to manage and secure.

Architecture

The architecture of APEX is simple yet extensible at the same time. APEX is a metadata-based environment, meaning that most options specified by developers are stored as data rather than PL/SQL procedures. This approach allows APEX to scale quite well because all of APEX's procedural code is finely tuned and does not change as applications are developed.

As far as languages go, APEX consists of two languages: PL/SQL and JavaScript. While the heavy lifting and all page rendering and processing tasks are done in PL/SQL, all of the client-side interaction and validation code is written in JavaScript using the open source jQuery library. At its core, APEX is a database application and thus makes extensive use of database objects such as tables, views, indexes, triggers, functions, procedures, packages, and so on. Much of APEX's code is written in PL/SQL and called from the interface itself.

jQuery allows for more efficient, cross-browser, client-side interactions and has been integrated with APEX since version 4.0. It provides a set of rich-UI client-side components, such as modal dialog boxes, calendar tools, and tabs, that can easily and quickly be integrated into any web development platform.

■ **Note** There is no Java code anywhere within the tool whatsoever, although it is possible to use Java within any developed APEX application by calling it from PL/SQL.

Metadata-Based Architecture

APEX is a declarative development environment, meaning that every object in an APEX application is actually stored as metadata in a set of database tables. When a page is rendered, APEX will call a set of its own PL/SQL procedures that will, in turn, read the corresponding metadata and use that to generate whatever components live on the page. Thus, when a new APEX page, report, form, chart, calendar, or even process is created, no new objects in the database are created. Rather, the information about that component is stored as metadata by APEX and recalled as an end user renders that page.

Historically, metadata-based tools have been limited as to the level of complexity that they are capable of supporting. If only a finite number of options can be defined, than only a finite number of results are possible. While APEX is also constrained by the number of options that are defined for a given component, it is quite extensible beyond the traditional limitations of a metadata-based architecture. APEX can evaluate and execute PL/SQL at almost any point during the rendering or processing of a page, whether it's a named PL/SQL procedure or an anonymous block. This level of extensibility provides the developer with a limitless palette of options when designing applications.

All of the APEX metadata is exposed through a set of views simply called the *APEX views*. These views provide a view into all of the metadata that makes up everything within an APEX environment—from the workspace itself all the way down to a column in a report. Because a good portion of APEX is metadata-based, it is possible to use an automated process or tool, such as Enkitec eSERT, to inspect the vales of many of the attributes and determine whether they are set to the most secure setting. You can find a list of all APEX views on the application utilities page, as shown in Figure 3-6.

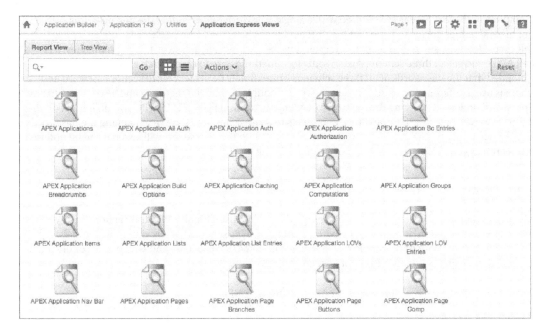

Figure 3-6. *The APEX views report, highlighting some of the APEX views available*

APEX views can be accessed from any schema within the database but will return data only if the views are queried either from a schema that is mapped to a workspace or from SYS and SYSTEM. They can be accessed from any tools that can connect directly to the database, not just APEX itself.

Starting in version 4.1, APEX includes a new database role called APEX_ADMINISTRATOR_ROLE that, when granted to a schema, gives that schema two things: the ability to call the APEX_INSTANCE_ADMIN APIs in order to manage the instance of APEX and the ability to allow that schema to view applications from any workspace when querying any APEX view. This role should be granted with care because any schema it is granted to essentially becomes the equivalent of an instance administrator.

Schemas

Not counting any parse-as schema associated with a workspace, APEX itself consists of three schemas: APEX_040200, FLOWS_FILES, and APEX_PUBLIC_USER. These schemas are created and populated upon the installation of APEX. APEX_040200 is where all of the APEX database objects and metadata are stored. The 040200 portion of the schema name represents the version of APEX. Thus, your installation of APEX may be based on a previous version, depending on the value embedded in the schema name. FLOWS_FILES is a schema dedicated to storing uploaded files, either permanently or temporarily. And lastly, APEX_PUBLIC_USER is the only schema that APEX will directly connect to. All applications—including the application development environment—connect to the database using APEX_PUBLIC_USER and nothing else.

When created, two of these schemas—APEX_040200 and FLOW_FILES—will be locked and should remain that way. There is no reason for any developer to access these schemas directly, especially in a production environment. In fact, if the APEX_040200 schema is accessed and data is manipulated directly there, it could corrupt an application or potentially the entire instance of APEX. The third schema—APEX_PUBLIC_USER—is unlocked because it is the sole schema that APEX uses to connect directly to the database.

By default, all three of these schemas are secured with a single password that is supplied when installing APEX. Given that two of these schemas are locked, the fact that three schemas have the same password is not as critical if they were all unlocked. However, since the installation script does not enforce any password strength policies, it is possible to install APEX and set all three schemas' passwords to something easy to crack, such as *oracle*.

It is recommended that the passwords of all three schemas immediately be set to a more secure password and that all three schemas use a different password. These passwords should be changed regularly and also adhere to any organizational password policies. Changing the password of APEX_040200 and FLOW_FILES will have no impact on the instance of APEX whatsoever, because nothing directly connects to those schemas. However, changing the password of APEX_PUBLIC_USER will impact APEX, because the password stored with the web server will also have to be updated accordingly, if either the Oracle HTTP Server or APEX Listener is being used.

APEX_PUBLIC_USER

The APEX_PUBLIC_USER schema is the single "gateway" schema that will be used for all APEX transactions in any APEX application, including the application development environment itself. This schema itself is extremely limited as to what it has access to. It is created with only a single system privilege—CREATE SESSION—and with no role or object privileges, as illustrated in Listing 3-1. It also does not own any objects.

Listing 3-1. The System, Role, and Object Privileges for APEX_PUBLIC_USER

```
SQL> SELECT * FROM dba_sys_privs
  WHERE grantee = 'APEX_PUBLIC_USER';

GRANTEE                 PRIVILEGE               ADM
--------------------    --------------------    ----
APEX_PUBLIC_USER        CREATE SESSION          NO

SQL> SELECT * FROM dba_role_privs
  WHERE grantee = 'APEX_PUBLIC_USER';

no rows selected

SQL> SELECT * FROM user_tab_privs
  WHERE grantee = 'APEX_PUBLIC_USER';

no rows selected

SQL> SELECT * FROM all_objects
  WHERE owner = 'APEX_PUBLIC_USER';

no rows selected
```

No developer should ever have to connect directly to this schema for any reason, and it should not be modified in any way. It is also not locked by default, because the web server must connect directly to it in order for APEX to run. If the APEX_PUBLIC_USER account is compromised and accessed, there is little damage that can be done, because all of the APIs and views that APEX_PUBLIC_USER makes use of have embedded security controls within them that can't be circumvented without access to a more privileged schema.

For an authenticated APEX session, the APEX engine will allow APEX_PUBLIC_USER to alter the current schema in which it parses based on the schema associated with the current application using DBMS_SYS_SQL.PARSE_AS_USER. Once this switch occurs, all SQL and PL/SQL code executed is actually being executed as if APEX were directly connected to the database as the parse-as schema. This "switch" is built into APEX and cannot be disabled or altered in any way.

> ■ **Note** One gotcha to keep in mind is that any database role associated with the parse-as schema will not work. Many developers coming from an Oracle Forms environment have come to rely on database roles and may be perplexed as to why they will not work anymore in APEX.

Since all APEX applications connect via APEX_PUBLIC_USER, it is impossible to distinguish which APEX session is mapped to which database session by using the USERNAME column alone in V$SESSION. In APEX 4.2, more thorough information about which APEX session maps to which database session has been added to the MODULE, CLIENT_INFO, and CLIENT_IDENTIFIER columns of V$SESSION.

The MODULE column now contains three values delimited by colons: the parsing schema followed by /APEX, APP followed by the APEX application ID, and the APEX page ID. The CLIENT_INFO column contains two values delimited by colons: the APEX-authenticated user name and the workspace ID. Lastly, the CLIENT_IDENTIFIER column contains two values delimited by colons: the APEX-authenticated user name and the session ID. Listing 3-2 shows an example of this.

Listing 3-2. The MODULE, CLIENT_ID, and CLIENT_IDENTIFIER Columns from V$SESSION for APEX_PUBLIC_USER

```
SQL> SELECT module, client_info, client_identifier
  FROM v$session WHERE username = 'APEX_PUBLIC_USER';

MODULE                CLIENT_INFO            CLIENT_IDENTIFIER
--------------------  --------------------   -----------------
SAMPLE/APEX:APP 123:6  DEV:3010820895725282  DEV:931284638673
```

Despite this enhancement, the information stored in these three columns in V$SESSION represents the initial values set when that database session is created by APEX. A single database session may and almost always maps to a number of different APEX applications across different workspaces. Since APEX makes heavy reuse of database sessions, the values in these columns may not represent the current values of the session using them.

One last point to make about APEX_PUBLIC_USER is that if the Embedded PL/SQL Gateway is being used as the web server, the APEX_PUBLIC_USER may not exist in the database. Instead, APEX will use the ANONYMOUS user to connect to the database.

APEX_040200

The APEX_040200 schema is where all APEX database objects and metadata reside. The name of this schema will vary slightly based on the version of APEX. In earlier releases of APEX, the name of this schema substituted the word FLOWS for APEX. This was merely a cosmetic change that reflected the original name for APEX, Oracle Flows.

This schema ships as locked and should remain that way. Developers do not need direct access to this schema, especially in a production environment. However, the APEX_040200 schema contains a number of fascinating and interesting constructs that any curious developer would love to explore. For that type of activity, it is recommended—and even encouraged—for a developer to install APEX on a local virtual machine, unlock the APEX_040200 schema, and do their exploration there. This way, no harm can come to any shared systems. Any damage done will be limited to the virtual machine on the developer's workstation and not impact anyone else.

The password for this schema is also set upon installation and is the same password used for the other two schemas, as well as the APEX instance administrator account. Because of this commonality, the password should be immediately changed to something more secure and different from the other APEX schemas. Unlike the APEX_PUBLIC_USER schema, there is much sensitive information in the APEX_040200 schema, and adequate precautions should be taken to protect it. Changing the password of APEX_040200 will not impact any part of the APEX environment and any associated web server in the least.

When browsing the APEX_040200 schema, it's almost impossible to miss the fact that most objects contain a prefix of WWV_FLOW. The origin of this prefix is twofold. First, the WWV is the three-letter product abbreviation given to APEX when it was first conceived as an idea. Second, FLOW refers to the original name of APEX, Oracle Flows. The prefix has survived numerous product name changes and, from the looks of it, is here to stay.

As APEX's name evolved from Oracle Flows to Oracle HTML DB to Oracle APEX, so did the name of the synonyms APEX used for its own APIs. Fortunately, all of the legacy synonym names have been preserved so that any references to either the FLOW or HTMLDB prefix-based ones will continue to function. For example, the table WWV_FLOW actually has three public synonyms that refer to it, as illustrated in Figure 3-7.

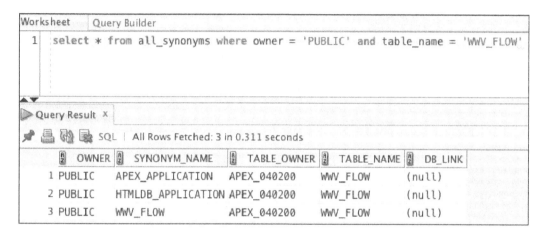

Figure 3-7. *Three synonyms for the same APEX table*

Many of APEX_040200's objects are accessible to PUBLIC, which on the surface seems like a really bad idea. However, all of the objects that can be accessed publicly do have the proper security controls embedded within them, making them useless outside of a properly authenticated APEX context. Listing 3-3 shows the breakdown of what types of privileges are granted to APEX_040200's objects.

Listing 3-3. Privileges by Type Granted to APEX_040200's Objects

```
SQL> SELECT privilege, count(*)
  FROM user_tab_privs
  WHERE grantee = 'PUBLIC'
  GROUP BY privilege
  ORDER BY 2 DESC

PRIVILEGE                              COUNT(*)
-----------------------------------    --------
SELECT                                      164
EXECUTE                                      81
DELETE                                        3
UPDATE                                        1
INSERT                                        1
```

Each of the 81 packages accessible by PUBIC is secured with code that first validates that it is being called from a valid APEX session. If any attempt is made to execute them from outside of a valid session, they simply won't work because the embedded security code will prevent them from doing so.

Of the 164 tables and views that can be accessed from PUBLIC, most of them are APEX views, which are secured in the WHERE clause to restrict who gets to see what data, based on schema-to-workspace mappings or the grant of the APEX_ADMINISTRATOR_ROLE. The remaining tables are either placeholder tables—such as WWV_FLOW_DUAL100, a table with 100 fixed rows—or global temporary tables used internally by APEX.

That leaves the remaining five privileges: an UPDATE, an INSERT, and three DELETEs. Listing 3-4 shows the specific objects these five privileges are granted on.

Listing 3-4. Specific Objects from the APEX_040200 Schema That Are Accessible by PUBLIC

```
SQL> SELECT grantee, owner, table_name, privilege
  FROM user_tab_privs
  WHERE privilege NOT IN ('SELECT','EXECUTE')
  AND grantee = 'PUBLIC';
```

GRANTEE	OWNER	TABLE_NAME	PRIVILEGE
PUBLIC	APEX_040200	WWV_FLOW_FILES	DELETE
PUBLIC	APEX_040200	WWV_FLOW_FILES	INSERT
PUBLIC	APEX_040200	WWV_FLOW_FILES	UPDATE
PUBLIC	APEX_040200	WWV_FLOW_USER_MAIL_ATTACHMENTS	DELETE
PUBLIC	APEX_040200	WWV_FLOW_USER_MAIL_QUEUE	DELETE

All of the objects are actually also secured views, so without a valid APEX context set, no records will be returned, thus ensuring that the data remains protected.

FLOWS_FILES

The third and final schema in the APEX triumvirate is called FLOWS_FILES. This schema exists for the sole purpose of providing an initial repository to upload files. Nothing is ever supposed to connect to this schema, so it is also locked by default. In fact, it goes one step further because FLOWS_FILES even lacks the CREATE SESSION system privilege. The password of FLOWS_FILES can also be changed without impacting any part of the APEX environment.

FLOWS_FILES contains only 11 database objects: a single table, a trigger, and some synonyms and indexes. Listing 3-5 shows a full listing of its objects.

Listing 3-5. FLOWS_FILES Database Objects

```
SQL> SELECT object_name, object_type
  FROM all_objects
  WHERE owner = 'FLOWS_FILES';
```

OBJECT_NAME	OBJECT_TYPE
SYS_C004026	INDEX
WWV_FLOW_FILES_FILE_IDX	INDEX
WWV_FLOW_FILES_USER_IDX	INDEX
WWV_FLOW_FILE_OBJ_PK	INDEX
WWV_FLOW	SYNONYM
WWV_FLOW_FILE_API	SYNONYM

```
WWV_FLOW_FILE_OBJECT_ID        SYNONYM
WWV_FLOW_ID                    SYNONYM
WWV_FLOW_SECURITY              SYNONYM
WWV_FLOW_FILE_OBJECTS$         TABLE
WWV_BIU_FLOW_FILE_OBJECTS      TRIGGER
```

```
11 rows selected.
```

When any file is uploaded via an APEX application, it initially ends up in the WWV_FLOW_FILE_OBJECTS$ table. Whether it stays there permanently is, in some cases, up to the developer. If the file is uploaded from the application development environment, it will remain in the WWV_FLOW_FILE_OBJECTS$ table until it is either purged by a job or deleted manually. The view from which this table is accessed in the application development environment is augmented with security to segregate data based on the underlying workspace.

As a developer, there is the option to move uploaded files to the parse-as schema as part of the File Browse item type. This approach is highly recommended for a number of reasons. First, by moving the file to the parse-as schema, it can be linked via a foreign key to another record. Oracle Text can also easily index it in when it is moved to the parse-as schema. Lastly, by keeping the uploaded files in the parse-as schema, all of the application's data exists in a single schema, making it more portable and manageable.

Transactions

One of the benefits of a metadata-based environment is that all transactions consist of the same components. It doesn't matter how simple or complex, fast or slow, or well-designed or ugly an APEX application is—the fundamental way the APEX engine renders and processes pages is the same. Thus, it doesn't matter who developed the application or how good or bad the SQL is. The underlying infrastructure functions the same, making it a lot easier to both understand how APEX works and take advantage of the architecture.

Like every other web application, APEX uses two HTML methods to facilitate page views and process input: GET and POST, respectively. On a high level, a GET is used to fetch data from the web server, whereas a POST is used to send data to the web server to be processed. In the Application Builder, APEX has its own nomenclature for each of these methods: page rendering and page processing. Any component defined in the page-rendering column can be mapped to the HTML GET method, whereas any component in the page-processing column can be mapped to the HTML POST method. Shared components, which make up the third column, can be called during either phase, depending on their type.

Understanding when APEX uses the GET and POST methods is one of the most critical and fundamental steps to becoming a skilled and security-conscious APEX developer. Almost every facet of the tool itself can be traced back to either a page-rendering or page-processing event, and being able to clearly delineate between the two of them is critical.

Under the covers, each of these two phases can be mapped to different PL/SQL procedures. All page rendering is handled by wwv_flow.show, whereas all page processing is handled by wwv_flow.accept. Experienced APEX users will recognize at least wwv_flow.accept because it is often referenced in error messages when a page or component can't be found.

The f Procedure and WWV_FLOW.SHOW

APEX applications have a unique URL syntax that is easily identifiable. Basically, it starts with an f?p= and contains a string of colon-delimited values, as illustrated in Listing 3-6.

Listing 3-6. An Example of the APEX URL Syntax

```
http://server/apex/f?p=142:1:3514168517778::NO::P1_ITEM:123
```

As with any other web URL standards, the portion to the left of the ? represents the procedure or function to be called, and the portion to the right of the ? represents the value and attribute pairs that are passed to that procedure. When navigating from page to page via the URL, APEX typically uses a procedure called f and passes a colon-delimited string to a parameter called p. The f procedure actually has a number of additional parameters, as shown in Listing 3-7.

Listing 3-7. The f Procedure Used by APEX Pages via the URL

```
SQL> desc f
PROCEDURE f
 Argument Name              Type                 In/Out Default?
 -------------------        -------------------  ------ --------
 P                          VARCHAR2       IN    DEFAULT
 P_SEP                      VARCHAR2       IN    DEFAULT
 P_TRACE                    VARCHAR2       IN    DEFAULT
 C                          VARCHAR2       IN    DEFAULT
 PG_MIN_ROW                 VARCHAR2       IN    DEFAULT
 PG_MAX_ROWS                VARCHAR2       IN    DEFAULT
 PG_ROWS_FETCHED            VARCHAR2       IN    DEFAULT
 FSP_REGION_ID              VARCHAR2       IN    DEFAULT
 SUCCESS_MSG                VARCHAR2       IN    DEFAULT
 NOTIFICATION_MSG           VARCHAR2       IN    DEFAULT
 CS                         VARCHAR2       IN    DEFAULT
 S                          VARCHAR2       IN    DEFAULT
 TZ                         VARCHAR2       IN    DEFAULT
 P_LANG                     VARCHAR2       IN    DEFAULT
 P_TERRITORY                VARCHAR2       IN    DEFAULT
```

In the example URL, when this page is rendered, the value 142:1:3514168517778::NO::P1_ITEM:123 will be passed to the p parameter of the f procedure. The f procedure will then take that string and decompose it into its discrete values. Once decomposed and after performing some basic security and globalization checks, the f procedure will in turn call wwv_flow.show and pass the discrete values to their corresponding parameters where they will be processed, and in turn, the page will be rendered.

Some of the additional parameters that can be passed to the f procedure may be recognizable. For example, passing the value YES to p_trace will cause APEX to generate a SQL trace file. The TZ parameter is used to set the corresponding time zone for a user. Others, however, are not as commonly used and undocumented, and passing values to them may cause erroneous results.

When run, wwv_flow.show will loop through all the components of a particular page and either execute or render them, depending on the component type. It will use a combination of execution/display point and component sequence to determine the order in which the components are rendered. This way, a computation that occurs before the header is rendered will be set so the computed value can be used in a report that is generated as part of the page body. Some components, such as computations and processes, will not have any output, whereas others, particularly almost any region type, will produce output. This process is repeated for each APEX page that is rendered or asynchronous process that is executed.

The WWV_FLOW.ACCEPT Procedure

Once a page is requested by the user and then rendered, the user can interact with it as they see fit—entering, selecting, and changing values, and so on. As soon as the user submits the page by clicking a button or other item that causes the page to be submitted, all the information on the page is sent back to the APEX engine for processing. The procedure that handles all page processing or POSTs in APEX is called wwv_flow.accept. Inspecting any APEX page will reveal an HTML form that looks similar to the example in Listing 3-8 that makes reference to wwv_flow.accept.

Listing 3-8. The HTML Form Definition from Any APEX Page

```
<form action="wwv_flow.accept" method="post" name="wwv_flow" id="wwvFlowForm">
```

Thus, when a page is submitted, all items on the page are passed in as parameters to the wwv_flow.accept procedure, as if it were being called from another PL/SQL procedure. Both items that are visible and hidden are passed back to the APEX engine. Each APEX page will contain a number of hidden items that are generated by APEX. These items store values for the application, page, session, page instance, and any checksums associated with the page.

One way to see all the items on the page is to view the HTML source. All modern browsers support this capability, typically by allowing the user to right-click anywhere on the page and select the corresponding function. The downside to this function is that the HTML document may be quite large and difficult to sift through to locate a specific element, especially in its raw form. A better alternative is to use a free add-on called Web Developer. Web Developer, written by Chris Pederick, will work with both Firefox and Chrome and can be downloaded from http://chrispederick.com/work/web-developer/.

After installing Web Developer, an additional menu bar will be visible in the browser, typically immediately below the bookmark bar, as highlighted in Figure 3-8.

Figure 3-8. The Web Developer toolbar in Firefox

Selecting Display Form Details from the Forms menu will display all item details inline with items on the page. In addition to that, it will also display details for any hidden items, as illustrated in Figure 3-9.

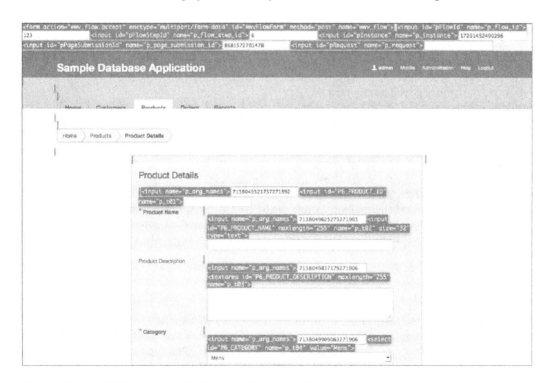

Figure 3-9. An APEX page with Display Form Details enabled

In APEX 4.2, the `wwv_flow.accept` procedure contains 510 parameters! Of these, 470 parameters are designed to accept input from APEX pages and asynchronous processes: 200 for items, 200 for arrays, 50 for tabular form columns, and 20 for items used in AJAX transactions. The remaining 40 parameters are used to specify other options such as application, page, session, and instance.

Since the names of the parameters in `wwv_flow.accept` are fixed and APEX item names can be anything the developer chooses, there has to be some sort of mapping that is done so that the APEX engine knows which item is which. This is what the `p_arg_names` items are used for. For each item on the page, there will always be a corresponding `p_arg_names` item as well. The `p_arg_names` items are always hidden and contain a relatively long numeric value, as shown in Figure 3-10.

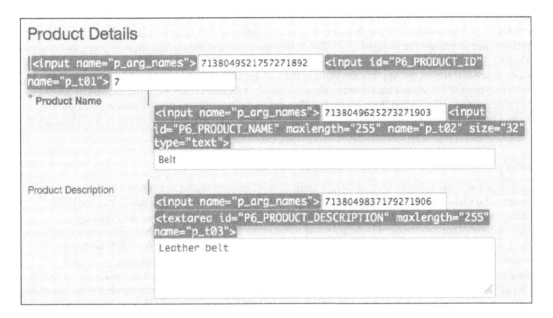

Figure 3-10. *An APEX form, highlighting the p_arg_names hidden items*

The value stored in `p_arg_names` is not arbitrary in the least. It actually refers to the primary key of the item that immediately precedes it in the form. By querying the source table for all APEX items—WWV_FLOW_STEP_ITEMS—the values in the ID column clearly correspond to the values set in `p_arg_names`, as shown in Figure 3-11.

ID	FLOW_ID	FLOW_STEP_ID	NAME	DATA_TYPE	IS_REQUIRED	ITEM_SEQUENCE
7138049521757271892	123	6	P6_PRODUCT_ID	VARCHAR	N	10
7138049625273271903	123	6	P6_PRODUCT_NAME	VARCHAR	Y	20
7138049837179271906	123	6	P6_PRODUCT_DESCRIPTION	VARCHAR	N	30
7138049909063271906	123	6	P6_CATEGORY	VARCHAR	Y	40
7138050128756271906	123	6	P6_PRODUCT_AVAIL	VARCHAR	N	50
7138050207566271907	123	6	P6_LIST_PRICE	VARCHAR	Y	60
6838894211467678574	123	6	P6_PRODUCT_IMAGE	VARCHAR	N	70
6838894532377694063	123	6	P6_IMAGE	VARCHAR	N	80
3607188122931306377	123	6	P6_TAGS	VARCHAR	N	90
3608403328253998914	123	6	P6_BRANCH	VARCHAR	N	100

Figure 3-11. *Item details from the WWV_FLOW_STEP_ITEMS table*

For example, the item P6_PRODUCT_ID has an ID value of 7138049521757271892. In the HTML, the value of p_arg_names that immediately precedes P6_PRODUCT_ID also has a value of 7138049521757271892. Based on the fact that they have the same value, these two elements are clearly related.

When this form is submitted to the APEX engine, the value for P6_PRODUCT_ID will be passed to the parameter p_t01 in the wwv_flow.accept procedure. All of the p_arg_names will be passed as an array to the p_arg_names parameter in wwv_flow.accept. The APEX engine will then begin to map array values with parameters by looping through all of them. The first array value—7138049521757271892—will be used to look up the corresponding page item, which is of course P6_PRODUCT_ID. Once that association is made, APEX will set the session state of P6_PRODUCT_ID to the value that was passed into p_t01. It will repeat this process for each item passed to a parameter in wwv_flow.accept, setting each value in session state.

Tools like Web Developer are invaluable assets that make web development a lot easier and faster. Unfortunately, they can also be used for evil, because when the details of a form are displayed, they can be edited. Thus, it would be simple for a malicious user to change the value of P6_PRODUCT_ID from 7 to 6 and submit the form, causing the wrong record to be updated.

Fortunately, there are features in the Application Builder that will prevent such an alteration from occurring. Session state protection is an APEX feature that detects when the value of a specific item or items have been altered and prevents the resulting page submission from executing. You can find more information on how session state protection works and how to implement it in Chapters 6 and 7.

Session State

A traditional Oracle database session established via SQL*Plus or Oracle Forms is similar to a phone call. In both scenarios, each party—the client and the server—need to invest resources in order to create a connection. For that connection to be maintained, a fixed number of resources need to be reserved, even if little or no data is being transferred. A fixed number of connections can be established and maintained, depending on the server resources. Once that limit is reached or exceeded, all connections will suffer degradation in performance and potentially be dropped.

An APEX session is more similar to a text message than a phone call. Rather than establishing a dedicated connection to the database server, an APEX session is merely a short request for data followed immediately by a short reply. While both parties still need to dedicate resources for this exchange to occur, the amount needed is far less than a dedicated database connection. In fact, multiple APEX sessions can and almost always do share a single database connection because they are logically and physically distinct from a database session.

Since HTTP is a stateless protocol and does not maintain a persistent connection to the server, APEX contains its own robust session state management infrastructure. APEX's session state management is enabled by default and does not require any additional code or configuration. It functions the same, regardless of which authentication scheme an application uses. In fact, it even works for unauthenticated users.

APEX uses a unique session ID to segregate its sessions from one another. That session ID is included in almost every APEX URL, as shown in Figure 3-12. In this example, the session ID is 9546423770164.

Figure 3-12. *The APEX session ID in a typical APEX URL*

The session ID is not the only component that is required to validate a session. When a user accesses an APEX site, a cookie is sent to the user's local computer. That cookie contains a value that, when combined with the session ID, proves that the user is an authenticated APEX user. Therefore, simply copying the URL from one computer to another will not result in successfully hijacking a session, because the corresponding cookie will not be present.

After logging into Application 123, a new cookie is sent to the client. Using the Web Developer toolbar, the cookie that APEX sends to the client can be viewed, as shown in Figure 3-13.

Name	WWV_CUSTOM-F_3010820895725282_123
Value	174B4CB2999CA035609059780172ABBA
Host	vm
Path	/apex/
Expires	At end of session
Secure	No
HttpOnly	Yes

Figure 3-13. *The APEX session cookie, as viewed with Web Developer*

Like most other web technologies, it uses client-side cookies to identify which client has authenticated as which user. The name of the cookie contains both the workspace ID and the application ID. The value of the cookie contains a string that corresponds to a hash of the session ID. In this example, the value is 174B4CB2999CA035609059780172ABBA.

Internally, APEX maps the session ID (ID) to the hashed session ID (SESSION_ID_HASHED) value in the WWV_FLOW_SESSION$ table, as illustrated in Figure 3-14.

	ID	SESSION_ID_HASHED	COOKIE_SESSION_ID	CREATED_BY	CREATED_ON	COOKIE	ON_NEW_INSTANCE_FIRED_FOR
1	15986611255866	6464C25892E17FF444160C5432EDE746	(null)	APEX_PUBLIC_USER	12-DEC-12	nobody	:142
2	15309947387356	92DB89F551B8C87226F07A8776E99F38	(null)	APEX_PUBLIC_USER	12-DEC-12	nobody	:4550
3	5368857203739	04FA377B47296BA8E1414B28435E34AF	(null)	APEX_PUBLIC_USER	12-DEC-12	ADMIN	:142
4	9546423770164	174B4CB2999CA035609059780172ABBA	(null)	APEX_PUBLIC_USER	12-DEC-12	ADMIN	:123

Figure 3-14. *The WWV_FLOW_SESSIONS$ table*

When validating a session, APEX uses this combination of session ID and hashed session ID. If there is a match and the corresponding session ID has not been otherwise invalidated or expired, then the session is deemed valid. Access to this table is obviously restricted to the APEX engine only and cannot be otherwise used by APEX developers.

Once a valid session has been established, APEX will then be able to associate any session state values to that unique session ID. Session state values will always be stored in the database and never in a cookie on the client PC. This is good for a number of reasons. First, it is much more secure to keep those values in the database, where they cannot easily be obtained. Second, since most processing in APEX occurs in the database, it is more efficient to store values there, because the server will not have to fetch them from the client when they are needed. Third, if the database is bounced, users can continue using their applications as if nothing happened. Having database-based sessions is also what makes APEX a RAC-friendly development tool. No code changes or special considerations are required for developing APEX applications deployed on Oracle RAC (real application clusters).

The lifetime of an APEX session will vary and can be terminated by one of a number of events. First, as soon as the user logs out, the session will be terminated, and all associated values in session state will be purged. If a user completely closes all windows of the browser, the session cookie will expire, thus terminating the session. Closing just the browser tab, or even the browser window if multiple windows are open, is not enough because the session cookie may still be valid, meaning that if the session ID were retrievable via the back button, the user may be able to rejoin the existing session. An APEX administrator can proactively terminate APEX sessions based on their duration.

Each application also has a session duration and session idle time attribute. If either of these values is exceeded, the session will also be terminated. If the user attempts to modify the session ID in the URL, APEX will not only allow that user to hijack another session but also immediately expire the current session, should one exist. Lastly, by default, there is a scheduled job that will automatically purge any session—valid or otherwise—that is older than 24 hours old. This job runs every eight hours unless altered to run more or less frequently.

Infrastructure

A key part of the architecture of APEX is the underlying web server. While all the code business rules and security processes are managed in the database via PL/SQL, APEX is, after all, an HTML-based application and needs a delivery mechanism in order to present pages and interact with users.

Since APEX's middle tier resides in PL/SQL, it does not require a traditional middle-tier application server. It does, however, require at least an HTTP server and component that will allow it to communicate with the database. There are currently three supported options that work with APEX: the Embedded PL/SQL Gateway, the Oracle HTTP Server and mod_plsql, and the APEX Listener.

While the details on how to implement and secure the different web servers that work with APEX is out of scope for this book, it is worth at least briefly calling attention to each of them in this section.

Embedded PL/SQL Gateway

Oracle Database 11g contains a built-in web server called the Embedded PL/SQL Gateway (EPG). The EPG runs in the XML DB HTTP server, as shown in Figure 3-15. It provides the same core features as mod_plsql does. All of the supporting files required for APEX—images, Cascading Style Sheets files, and JavaScript libraries—are stored in the database when using the EPG.

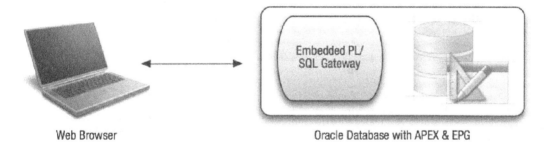

Web Browser   Oracle Database with APEX & EPG

Figure 3-15. *The Oracle Embedded PL/SQL Gateway architecture*

Because of its close proximity to the database, Oracle recommends not using the EPG when deploying applications on the Internet. That recommendation should be extended to any production system for the same reasoning. If not used, the EPG should be disabled immediately so that it cannot be illicitly accessed. To disable it, run the commands in Listing 3-9 as the SYS user.

Listing 3-9. Commands to Run As SYS to Disable the Embedded PL/SQL Gateway

```
EXEC DBMS_XDB.SETHTTPPORT(0);
EXEC DBMS_XDB.SETFTPPORT(0);
```

To verify that it has been disabled, either try to connect to APEX via the port previously configured by the EPG or run the script at @?/rdbms/admin/epgstat to get the status of the EPG.

Oracle HTTP Server and mod_plsql

The oldest and most mature web server in use with APEX is the Oracle HTTP Server and mod_plsql. The Oracle HTTP Server is a for-cost version of Apache that Oracle made some specific changes to. It is a fully supported product that is compatible with most other Apache modules, such as mod_rewrite or mod_security, and offers the most flexibility when it comes to configuration and management.

The Oracle HTTP Server can be installed on the same server as the database, on a separate tier entirely, or in conjunction with a load balancer for additional fault tolerance. Figure 3-16 illustrates the Oracle HTTP Server installed on its own server, providing a layer of additional separation between the web browser and database server. Firewalls can also be added between each and any of the tiers to restrict network traffic.

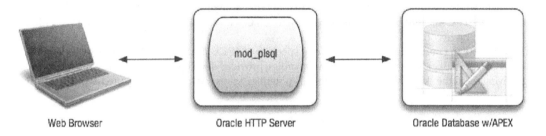

Figure 3-16. *The Oracle HTTP Server with mod_plsql architecture*

For even more security, a second Apache server and reverse proxy architecture can be used to create what's called a *demilitarized zone* (DMZ). If a hacker is successful in breaching the most outward-facing Apache server, they will still be outside of the internal network, or in the DMZ, where the damage they can inflict will be greatly mitigated.

APEX Listener

The third and newest option for serving up APEX pages is the APEX Listener. Introduced around the same time as APEX 4.0, the APEX Listener is a Java application that was designed from the ground up to work with APEX, as illustrated in Figure 3-17. Currently in its second major release, the APEX Listener can run in any J2EE-compliant application server. However, Oracle will provide support only for the following three: OC4J, Oracle Glassfish, and Oracle WebLogic. That is not to say that it won't run in other J2EE application servers such as JBoss and Tomcat, for example; it's just that if an issue arises with the APEX Listener, it will need to be verified with one of the three supported servers before Oracle will take action.

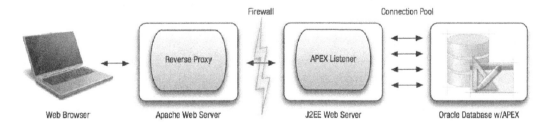

Figure 3-17. *The APEX Listener architecture*

Oracle seems to be moving in the direction of increased support of the APEX Listener, because there have been a number of released and additional functionalities over the past couple of years. The most recent release added the ability for a single listener to service multiple database, added integration with ICAP servers for virus scanning, added the ability to manage the APEX listener via either a command line or the SQL Workshop, and added better support for RESTful web services.

Summary

The underlying architecture of APEX is both simple and sophisticated at the same time, which makes it quite unique. Its simplicity makes it easier to understand, install, and ultimately secure because there are fewer moving parts than most applications. Yet its sophistication allows for a number of different configurations, from the simple and basic to the sophisticated and complex. An APEX implementation can start small with as few as a server or two and expand as the organization requirements do.

Understanding some of the underlying technologies and specifics of APEX ultimately leads to a better and more security-conscious APEX developer. A deeper level of understanding provides developers with a more robust view of the technology, giving them the skills that let them anticipate potential issues and design their systems around them from the start.

CHAPTER 4

∎ ∎ ∎

Instance Settings

Think about when you purchase a new or used car. These days, cars are more complicated than ever, with sophisticated electronic monitoring systems, integrated GPS and iPod docks, and more controls than anyone can ever claim to understand. At first glance, it may seem like a daunting task to understand and master all of these controls and associated settings. But after just a few days or even hours with the car, most of the settings are not only configured but are optimized to your liking. You've positioned the mirrors, you've set the radio presets, and you've integrated your phone to sync contact details, make calls, and even play music.

Occasionally, you may need to tweak a setting or even discover an option that you previously did not know about. But for the most part, things should just work. The only ongoing task that a car owner needs to dedicate constant attention to is monitoring the gauges on the dashboard, such as fuel, oil, engine temperature, check engine, and so on. These gauges will indicate when the car is low on gas or oil or when there are other issues that need to be investigated. If these gauges report no issues, then the car can continue to operate as normal.

Configuring an instance of APEX is very similar to learning the ins and outs of the features of a new car. Up front, there is a level of investment and time that is required to master all of the settings and their impacts. But once everything is configured optimally, there is little additional work that needs to be done, aside from monitoring the APEX logs for potential security breaches and other threats.

This chapter will cover how to configure and manage an instance of APEX with security in mind. It will start by describing some best practices for instance configuration, including a discussion of the benefits and drawbacks of runtime mode. It will then cover all security-related aspects of the instance administration console, from instance configuration and management to the management of the workspaces and their associated users and schemas. It concludes with an overview of monitoring the APEX logs and some pointers for retaining data longer than APEX does, should the need exist.

Overview

Securing an instance of APEX starts with configuring the instance itself. While application security is also a critical component to consider, a misconfigured instance could allow a malicious user to compromise the instance, giving the intruder access to any application within any workspace. The time required to actually secure an instance of APEX is not too significant, making it a step that has no reason to be skipped. It can be done in a matter of hours, not days. But if time is not spent on reviewing all of the settings and ensuring that they are configured properly, the results could be disastrous.

Depending on the instance type—development, test, QA, or production—different settings can be safely selected. Most of the settings covered in this chapter come with recommendations for production instances, as well as information about whether the setting needs to be configured as securely for a nonproduction instance. Keep in mind that individual requirements can and will be different from organization to organization, so the recommendations may have to be adjusted accordingly.

Runtime Mode

One of the first things to consider when configuring a production instance of APEX is whether to convert it to runtime mode. When converted to runtime mode, the APEX development environment is actually removed entirely, leaving only enough database objects to run your applications. The theory here is that if the development and administration environments do not exist, then no one can access it, regardless their intentions.

Converting an instance to runtime mode is relatively simple and should take only a few minutes. However, this is a process that needs to be completed by the DBA, because it requires access to the SYS account. The actual speed at which the script runs is, of course, dependent on the specifications and speed of your server. The script required to convert an instance to runtime mode is called apxdevrm.sql and can be found in the root directory of the APEX .zip file that was downloaded from OTN. If this file is no longer available, a new copy can easily be downloaded from OTN. Be sure to download the same version of APEX that you are running because the scripts are compatible with only a single release of APEX.

Once the script is either downloaded or located, connect to the database as SYS and simply run the script without any parameters, as shown in Figure 4-1. Be warned: there is no confirmation message within the script. As soon as it runs, it will begin to remove the development environment and effectively cannot be stopped.

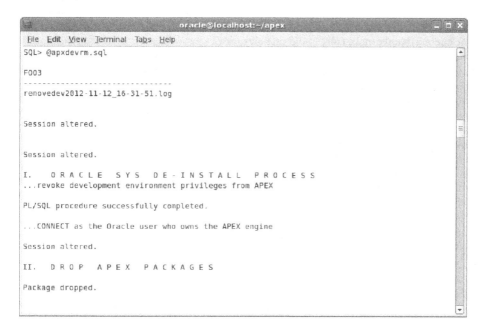

Figure 4-1. *Executing the apxdevrm.sql script, which converts an instance of APEX to runtime mode*

Once the script has completed, the APEX development environment will have been completely removed. To prove this, simply try to access the APEX workspace login page. The results will be a screen similar to that in Figure 4-2. All other developed applications should function as normal from their original URLs.

Figure 4-2. *Attempt to access the workspace login page in a runtime environment*

Should the development environment ever need to be restored, a second script—apxdvins.sql—can be run. This script can be found in the same directory as apxdevrm.sql and should also be run as SYS. It should take just a few minutes to run, and upon its completion, the development environment should be completely restored. The time it takes to complete this script is also dependent on the specifications and speed of the server.

The Instance Administration API

An instance converted to runtime mode is by definition more secure than one not converted, because there is simply no way to log in to the instance administration console or an individual workspace. Even if the proper credentials are known, there is just no place to enter them. But while runtime mode offers an enhanced level of security and assurance, it also presents a few drawbacks.

For example, since the instance administration console is removed, all administration of the instance of APEX will need to be done via the APEX_INSTANCE_ADMIN APIs. Most of the rest of this chapter discusses how to configure an instance of APEX so that it is as secure as it can be. If choosing runtime mode, it may be best to leave that conversion to the very last step because it is much easier to configure the instance via the instance administration console versus calling APIs in SQL*Plus.

The APEX_INSTANCE_ADMIN API is well documented in Chapter 10 of the Oracle Application Express API Reference Guide, which is freely available on OTN. It can be executed from the SYS, SYSTEM, or APEX_040200 schema, or any schema that has the APEX_ADMINISTRATOR_ROLE database role. Should a setting need to be changed to an instance in runtime mode, simply call the APEX_INSTANCE_ADMIN.SET_PARAMETER API and pass in the corresponding setting key and value. The APEX_INSTANCE_ADMIN API can also perform tasks not available in the instance administration console, such as removing applications, saved reports, and subscriptions.

The Instance Administrator Database Role

Introduced in APEX 4.1, the APEX_ADMINISTRATOR_ROLE is a database role that, when granted to a schema, gives that schema the ability to view all applications across all workspaces when querying any APEX view. Additionally, any schema that has been directly granted this role may also execute the APEX_INSTANCE_ADMIN API. The APEX_ADMINISTRATOR_ROLE must be granted directly to a schema and not via another database role; otherwise, it will not work.

Because of its ability to allow access to any schema in the database by creating a workspace, associating that workspace with any schema, and then creating a user in that workspace, this role should be given out sparingly and only when needed. If an instance of APEX is set to runtime mode, then it makes sense to create a schema for the explicit use of managing that instance and grant the APEX_ADMINISTRATOR_ROLE to that schema. This way, a non-DBA schema can manage the instance of APEX, mitigating what that schema can execute.

Other Options

While runtime mode is without question the most secure way to deploy an instance of APEX, it is not always possible or desired. There are a number of reasons why an APEX administrator would not want to set their instance of APEX to runtime mode—some which are valid and others of which are less so. While the validity of these reasons won't be discussed here, it is a reality that many administrators face. Thus, if this is your situation, you can take a number of steps to maintain an almost-runtime mode instance.

First, ensure that all users in every workspace are set to locked. If access is needed, the instance administrator can simply unlock a user, set a temporary password, and then relock the user when the work is done.

Next, consider also disabling the workspace login until it is needed. This will prevent anyone from attempting to log in to any workspace at all by throwing an error message when the user attempts to load the workspace login page. Once a user successfully logs into the workspace, this setting can be once again disabled, because that user's session will remain valid until they either log out or exceed the idle or session duration time.

Lastly, both the workspace login and instance administration console can be disabled and reenabled via the APEX_INSTANCE_ADMIN API by a DBA. While definitely the least convenient approach, this method requires that a DBA—one who is not the same person as the APEX instance administrator—be required to unlock the instance of APEX. This extra step requires that at least two people be involved in making changes to a production environment. While this does not make it any less safe, it does add an additional control that is difficult to overcome. Having said all of this, the best approach is still to convert the production instance of APEX to runtime mode and not have to worry about anyone gaining illicit access to it.

Configuration and Management

The instance administrator can configure a number of instancewide settings. Many of these settings have something to do with security, while others are more focused on the management of the instance. The next section will pay closer attention to those that could impact the security of your instance of APEX. Other non-security-focused settings are in many cases important but are not covered in the scope of this book.

The instance administration console is what the instance administrator will use to manage an instance of APEX. If the instance is converted to runtime mode, then the instance administrator will have to use the APEX_INSTANCE_ADMIN APIs instead. Access to the instance administration console should be given only to trusted users, because they will essentially be able to view any data in any schema simply by creating an APEX workspace associated with that schema. Many organizations give this role to a DBA, since the DBA is already trusted with the management of the instance. It is almost never a full-time role but rather a commitment of just a few hours a month.

To access the instance administration console, simply log in to the APEX INTERNAL workspace with the ADMIN user and password set upon installation. Once authenticated, a screen similar to the one in Figure 4-3 will be displayed.

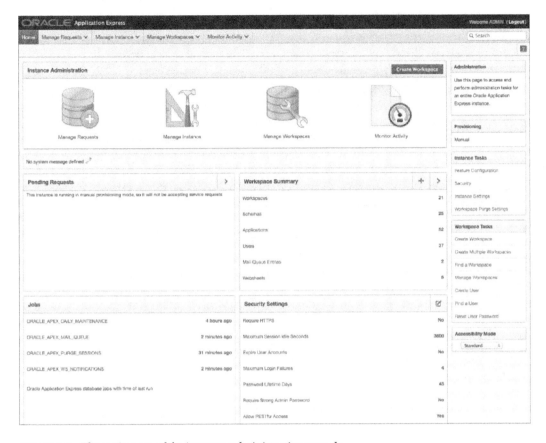

Figure 4-3. *The main page of the instance administration console*

This screen will show some high-level metrics about the settings of the instance, as well as links to the four major parts of the instance administration console: Manage Requests, Manage Instance, Manage Workspaces, and Monitor Activity.

Manage Instance Settings

Most instancewide settings can be found in this section of the instance administration console, as shown in Figure 4-4. While not every subsection of the Manage Instance section has to do with security, many of them do, either directly or indirectly.

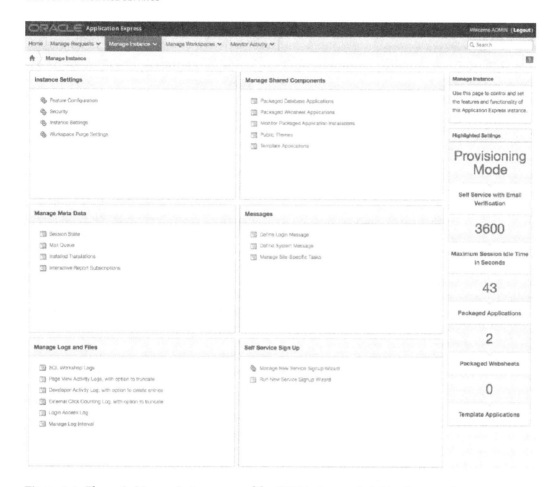

Figure 4-4. *The main Manage Instance page of the APEX instance administration console*

Securing any APEX application starts with the APEX instance settings, all of which can be found on the page shown in Figure 4-4. These settings can be configured only by an APEX instance administrator and, in most cases, will impact all workspaces and applications.

■ **Caution**   Despite the minimum time commitment, the APEX instance administrator is a critical role. If configured incorrectly, an instance of APEX could be open to either attacks or exploits or simply allow access to those who should not have it. The bulk of the remainder of this section covers any setting that has to do with the security of the instance of APEX and how to properly configure it for the most secure environment.

Most settings for an instance of APEX can be found in the Instance Settings section of the Manage Instance section. Instance Settings is further divided into four sections: Feature Configuration, Security, Instance Configuration Settings, and Workspace Purge Settings. All of these sections, with the exception of Workspace Purge Settings, contain settings that are pertinent to application security. Configuring these settings correctly should be done prior to enabling access to any applications in your production instance of APEX.

Feature Configuration

The Feature Configuration section contains a number of features, some of which have to do with security. All of the settings in Feature Configuration apply to all workspaces and, in most cases, cannot be overridden at the workspace level.

Allow PL/SQL Program Unit Editing Setting

This setting will determine whether developers can edit PL/SQL program units—packages, procedures, functions, and triggers—from within the SQL Workshop. By default, it is set to Yes, and it's safe to leave it that way, especially given that no developers should have access to a production instance. Setting this to No on a development or QA instance should not pose a problem.

Create Demonstration Objects in New Workspace Setting

By default, this option is set to No and should remain that way on a production instance. By creating a demonstration application in each workspace, a potential path into a workspace is also created. The default login page for the sample application denotes that it is, in fact, the APEX sample application and even offers advice for which credentials to use. In a properly secured environment—where all APEX developers are either disabled or removed—this presents no risk. However, in workspaces that are not well managed, adding the sample application introduces a potential liability into the overall infrastructure, and for that reason alone, this feature should be disabled.

Create Websheet Objects in New Workspaces Setting

Similar to the previous setting, "Create Websheet objects in new workspaces" should be disabled for similar reasons and is so by default. A malicious user could easily create a script that seeks out active Websheets by manipulating the URL, and if any APEX developers or users are still enabled in a workspace, those websheets could be accessed.

Packaged Application Install Options

This section contains three settings: Allow HTTP Header Variable authentication, Allow LDAP Directory authentication, and Allow Oracle Application Server Single Sign-On authentication. All three of these settings apply only when a developer installs any one of the packaged applications, and these settings have no bearing on anything else in a workspace. The default setting of all three of these settings is No and, for a production instance, should remain that way.

SQL Workshop

Most of the options in the SQL Workshop section have little to do with security and can be safely kept at their defaults. However, there is one that should be considered when securing your instance of APEX: Enable RESTful Services. Enabling this option allows developers to build RESTful services from the SQL Workshop, which could potentially expose data to external systems.

When this feature is enabled at the instance level, a workspace administrator can decide whether to disable the feature for their specific workspace. When disabled at the instance level, the feature will be disabled across all workspaces and cannot be reenabled by a workspace administrator. Thus, if RESTful access from SQL or PL/SQL is required in a specific workspace, the feature will need to be enabled. If it is enabled, close attention should be paid as to which workspace and applications use this feature. If it is not required, then it is best to disable the feature at the workspace level.

Monitoring

Enable Database Monitoring controls whether to enable two additional options to appear in the SQL Workshop portion of all workspaces: About Database and Database Monitoring. There is no harm in enabling this feature, because both functions also require a developer to authenticate as a database user that has been granted the DBA role. If developers need access to this feature on a development environment, then this feature can be enabled there. However, it should be disabled for production environments.

Application Activity Logging

The APEX application activity log automatically captures information about each and every page view in all APEX applications, including APEX itself. Elements captured include the user name, application ID, page, session time, number of rows, error message, and page mode, among others. The activity log data that is stored can be accessed either from within a workspace's activity reports or by querying the APEX view APEX_WORKSPACE_ACTIVITY_LOG.

This setting determines when and how the log is used. By default, it is set to use the corresponding setting as defined in each individual application, leaving it up to developers to determine which applications will be logged and which will not. It can also be set to never log any activity or always log all activity, giving the developer no choice in the matter.

This feature should be set to Always at all times. This will ensure that all APEX application page views are in fact logged, and developers will not be able to override this, even for short periods of time.

Enable Application Tracing

While APEX offers a comprehensive debug mechanism, sometimes even that is not enough to get to the root of a performance issue. When needed, a developer can pass an additional parameter— &p_trace=YES—through the URL, which will cause the result of rendering the page to generate a SQL trace file. This file can then be analyzed using TKPROF or a number of other tools.

For tracing to work, two parameters need to be set. First, the application must have its Debugging option set to Yes. Second, the instance setting Enable Application Tracing must be set to Yes. If either of these setting are set to No, then no trace file will be written.

Thus, from a security perspective, there is little risk in leaving this feature enabled, especially if all applications' debug settings are disabled. The trace file will be securely written to the file system of the database server as per the USER_DUMP_DEST parameter, and as long as that directory is secured, no developer or end user will be able to read that file.

This configuration (Enable Application Tracing enabled and Debug disabled) requires only that an individual application's Debug setting be altered for tracing to be enabled, making it a convenient as well as a secure option.

Enable Service Requests

APEX workspace administrators have the ability to request additional schemas or storage or terminate their workspaces entirely. You can find these functions by navigating to Administration ➤ Manage Service ➤ Make a Service Request.

Since all requests made by a workspace administrator are subject to approval from the APEX instance administrator, there is little risk in leaving this feature enabled. However, if internal policies require that such requests be made externally to APEX, then this feature should be disabled.

Security

As the name implies, many of the core security settings can be found under this section of instance administration. Settings managed here include cookies, HTTPS, passwords, session timeouts, and general login control.

The Security attributes are actually split into two sections: Security Settings and Authorized URLs. The Security Settings section contains the bulk of the parameters that can be configured, whereas the Authorized URLs section pertains specifically to APEX APIs that contain a URL as one of their parameters.

Set Workspace Cookie

Enabling the Set Workspace Cookie option will place a cookie on your local workstation that will remember the last workspace and user name you used to sign into APEX with. Upon returning to that instance of APEX, the workspace and user name will automatically be populated with these values. This cookie will persist on your client workstation for six months.

While this information is not enough for a malicious user to log into your workspace, it does give them two-thirds of the credentials they require. Thus, this feature should be disabled. The added inconvenience of having to enter the workspace, user name, and password is worth the added security of not storing these credentials locally.

If this option was enabled and developers already have workspace cookies stored locally, the cookies can be safely deleted by searching for them with the name ORACLE_PLATFORM_REMEMBER_UN. There may be multiple instances of this cookie, because a separate one will be set for each unique host name and path accessed.

Disable Administrator Login

By setting Disable Administrator Login to Yes, all access to the APEX instance administration console will be revoked for all future sessions. The current session will not be impacted until either exceeding its session time limit terminates it or the user explicitly logs out.

Once this option is disabled, the only way to restore access to the instance administration console is to use the APEX_ INSTANCE_ADMIN.SET_PARAMETER APIs, specifically setting the parameter DISABLE_ADMIN_LOGIN to N. The API will have to be called from a privileged schema, such as SYS or SYSTEM. More details about this API can be found later in this chapter.

If an instance of APEX is not converted to runtime mode, the administrator login should then be disabled. If necessary, a DBA can quickly reenable the administrator login with a simple API call and then redisable it when no longer needed. The URL for any APEX instance administration console is well known, and every effort should be taken to ensure that only legitimate, authorized users can access it.

Many of the instance settings and maintenance activities can be achieved by using either SQL*Plus and/or SQL Developer, so it would be rare that the instance administration console would need to be accessed in a production environment for any significant length of time.

Disable Workspace Login

Setting the Disable Workspace Login setting to Yes will effectively prevent developers and workspace administrators from logging in to any workspace in an instance of APEX. Applications that were developed in workspaces are not impacted at all.

If an instance of APEX is not converted to runtime mode, then the workspace login should be disabled. Basic management and deployment of applications can be done via the APEX_INSTANCE_ADMIN as either the SYS or SYSTEM API and/or via SQL Developer as the corresponding workspace's parse-as schema. Additionally, APEX developer management can be done via the instance administration console or the APEX_UTIL APIs.

Allow Public File Upload

The File Browse APEX item type allows users to upload files into either a table in their own schema or a table in a shared schema. If the Allow Public File Upload setting is set to Yes, then users who are both authenticated and unauthenticated can use this item type without any issues. However, if this setting is set to No, then only users who have successfully authenticated to an APEX application will be allowed to upload files. Thus, this option should be set to No so that only authenticated users can upload files to the database, unless there is a specific business rule that requires otherwise.

For additional security and to ensure that viruses are not present in uploaded files, consider installing the Oracle APEX Listener 2.0. One if its features is built-in integration with an Internet Content Access Protocol (ICAP) virus-scanning site to ensure that uploaded files are virus-free.

Restrict Access by IP Address

Using a list of valid IP addresses can also restrict access to the APEX development and instance administration environments. Individual IP addresses can be entered separated by commas. It is also possible to restrict a block of IP addresses using the * character, provided that it is the last character in the IP address. For example, 192.*.100.1 is not valid, but 192.168.* is.

While this feature may seem like a reliable way to protect an instance of APEX, it is possible for a malicious user to spoof their IP address, effectively changing it to one of those allowed to access the APEX environment. Additionally, many organizations use DHCP, thus assigning a potentially different IP address to the same client each time they connect to the network. Therefore, this feature should not be used as the only line of defense against unauthorized users.

Instance Proxy

While not an essential setting for security, the Instance Proxy setting will route all outgoing HTTP and HTTPS traffic to the proxy server specified. If no proxy server is used, then this setting can safely be left blank. If specified at the instance level, this setting will supersede settings made at either the application or web service reference level.

Require HTTPS

When set to Yes, the Require HTTPS setting will allow access only to the APEX development environment and administration console over HTTPS. Attempts to access either over HTTP will result in a redirection error, because the APEX cookie will not be set.

This setting should always be enabled for any instance of APEX, because at any point in time, sensitive information may be transmitted as part of any APEX page, especially the workspace login page. However, it should be activated only after it is verified that HTTPS has been properly configured and tested, because once it is enabled, access to the administration console will be permitted only over HTTPS. Should this setting be accidentally enabled, it can be disabled by calling the APEX_INSTANCE_ADMIN.SET_PARAMETER API.

Require Outbound HTTPS

Similar to Require HTTPS, the Require Outbound HTTPS setting will require all outbound calls to use HTTPS when it is enabled. This includes calls made to web services from APEX applications. This setting should also be enabled because sensitive data is just as likely to be outbound as inbound.

Allow RESTful Access

Starting with APEX 4.1, any APEX report can be exposed as a RESTful web service, as long as three conditions are met: the page on which the report resides is public, the report itself has RESTful access enabled, and the instance setting Allow RESTful Access is enabled. Once these three conditions are met, the RESTful version of the report can be accessed via the URL.

While this is a quick and easy way to expose a dataset via web service, it is also not a very secure way to do so. First, it requires the page to be public, so anyone who can access the APEX instance can access the web service. Second, since there is no authentication required, the same data set is served for any user and cannot be altered based on which user is accessing it. Third, by calling the apex_rest.getServiceDescription API via the URL, it is possible to get a list of all RESTful reports exposed as web services for any application, as illustrated in Figure 4-5.

Figure 4-5. *The results of calling the apex_rest.getServiceDescription API*

Thus, Allow RESTful Access should always be set to Disabled. If there is a need for a report or reports to be exposed as RESTful web services, great care should be taken to ensure that no sensitive data is contained in such reports.

Maximum Session Length and Idle Time in Seconds

The Maximum Session Length in Seconds and Maximum Session Idle Time in Seconds settings determine the maximum duration and idle time of an APEX session, respectively. By default, the maximum length is set to 28800, or 8 hours, and the maximum idle time is set to 3600, or 1 hour. Setting either to null will also revert to their default settings. Any setting at the application level will override this setting.

To prevent any session from expiring, these values can be set to 0. However, by default sessions older than 12 hours will still be expired as they are cleaned up hourly via the ORACLE_APEX_PURGE_SESSIONS job.

In addition to being used as the default for applications that do not specify this setting, what is entered in the APEX instance administration console is the value that is used for instance administration console and Application Builder sessions.

For best results, these values should be set to an appropriate value for the instance administration console and Application Builder. Individual applications can be set depending on their individual security needs. For example, an application that is typically used for an entire business day, eight hours for a maximum session duration and one hour of idle time may be adequate. However, for any mobile application, the session length and idle time are best reduced so that if the mobile device is lost, the session duration may expire by the time it is recovered.

Domain Must Not Contain

Any domain name entered in this setting will be restricted in two places: the region of type URL and web service calls. Domain names should be colon delimited and should not include any ports.

Since this setting uses a blacklist approach, it is of limited utility. The number of valid domains that could offer a nefarious web service are too numerous to even attempt to collect a list, let alone supply and keep that list updated here. It would be more valuable if this setting were a whitelist of valid URLs that could be accessed versus ones that should be restricted.

Known domains that are flagged as dangerous could certainly be entered here, but little trust and confidence should be placed in this setting to protect against any potential threat, since it is trivial for a malicious user to create a new domain not on this list.

General Login Controls

New in APEX 4.2, the General Login Controls section consists of three settings designed to make user logins more secure. The gist of this feature is that if an end user enters an invalid password, they will have to wait the specified amount of time before they can try again, reducing the possibility of a brute-force password attack.

Delay After Failed Login Attempts in Seconds

When an invalid password is entered, this setting determines how long the user will have to wait before trying again. By default, it is set to 5, but it can be increased if security concerns dictate that it be higher. Setting it to 0 will disable this feature, allowing a user to be able to reenter their password immediately.

Method for Computing the Delay

If a delay of one second or more is set in the previous setting, the "Method for computing the Delay" setting will determine how the delay is computed. There are four options for this setting, in order of least restrictive to most restrictive:

- Username and Client IP Address

- Username

- Client IP Address

- Username or Client IP Address

The last setting—Username or Client IP Address—should be used because it is the most restrictive of the group and provides the most security.

Inbound Proxy Servers

If there are any proxy servers that typically are used to access your instance of APEX, they can be entered here in a comma-separated list. This list will be used to assist APEX in recording the proper IP address a user came from when a proxy server is used.

Require User Account Expiration and Locking

When enabled, this setting will require all APEX developers to adhere to the password reset and locking policy as specified in the next two settings. By default, this setting is disabled. However, it should always be enabled, and the next two settings—Maximum Login Failures Allowed and Account Password Lifetime (days)—also should be configured appropriately.

Maximum Login Failures Allowed

This setting will determine how many invalid passwords are allowed when APEX developers are logging into their respective workspaces. It has no impact on external repositories used for applications created with APEX. If this value is exceeded, the account will be locked and will need to be unlocked by either a workspace or instance administrator. A workspace administrator can override this setting at the workspace level for that specific workspace.

By default, this value is set to 4, which is adequate for most scenarios. Attention should be paid to the workspace-level setting of this attribute, because that will override anything set at the instance level.

Account Password Lifetime (Days)

The Account Password Lifetime (days) setting determines the length that a particular password is valid. This applies only to users in the instance administration console and Application Builder and not any external authentication scheme used in deployed APEX applications. Additionally, this setting can be overridden at the workspace level by a workspace administrator.

By default, this setting is set to 45 days. In many cases, this should be sufficient. However, if local password expiration policies are more or less restrictive, it can easily be adjusted accordingly. Attention should be paid to the workspace-level setting of this attribute because that will override anything set at the instance level.

Workspace Password Policy

There are two options for determining the Workspace Password Policy setting. One option is to use the default strong policy, whereas the other is to define your own. The default strong password policy is defined as the following:

- At least six characters

- At least one lowercase alphabetic character, one uppercase alphabetic character, one numeric digit, and one punctuation character

- Cannot include the username

- Cannot include the word *internal*

- Cannot contain any words shown in the Must Not Contain field specified in Workspace Password Policy

A custom policy should be implemented because the six-character password associated with the default strong policy, even with the associated special characters, is simply too easy to compromise.

■ **Note**   The specific passwords and padding patterns outlined in this chapter should *not* be used verbatim by anyone for any purpose. Rather, it is recommended you apply this concept to your own secure passwords with your own unique padding strings or phrases.

Let's take a look at a couple of examples to prove this: *oracle* and *0raC!3*. To determine how long it would take to crack each one, we'll use GRC's Password Haystacks site, which can be found at https://www.grc.com/haystack.htm. First, the relatively simple password *oracle* was entered in the tool. Figure 4-6 shows the complete results.

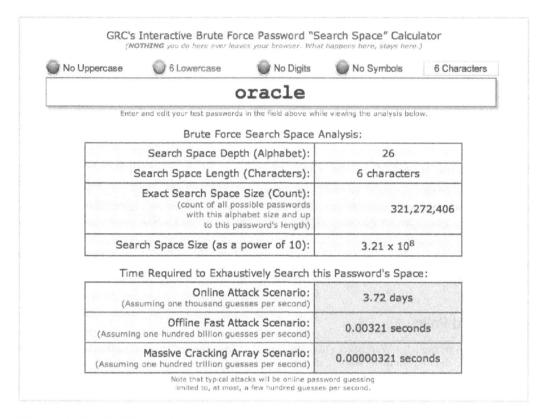

Figure 4-6. *Results of the simple password oracle*

Notice that the time it would take for an offline attack is insignificant, because the password would be instantly available to the malicious user. Even the online scenario does not offer much solace, because it would take less than a business week to crack the password.

Next, let's add some entropy and use at least one special character, an uppercase letter, a lowercase letter, and a number, as per the default APEX-recommended password policy. The password that will be tested next, *0raC!3*, meets and exceeds those criteria. Figure 4-7 shows the results of this test.

Figure 4-7. *Results of the short yet high-entropy password 0raC!3*

This time, all four criteria—one lowercase, one uppercase, one special character, and one number—were met. Thus, the time to crack the password in an online scenario increased dramatically to a comforting 23.5 years. However, despite the addition of mixed-case, special, and numeric characters, the offline scenarios are still almost instant, with the worst case being just seven seconds to crack the password.

The core problem here is simply password length, or lack thereof. With a relatively short password, it does not take that long for a competent malicious user to write and execute a program that cycles through all potential password combinations. Even adding more entropy essentially made no difference in the time it would take to crack the passwords.

The recommendation made by this site is that a combination of some entropy and a longer password are the best approach. And as long as at least one mixed-case, special, and numeric character are present in your password, the rest of it need not be complex at all. In line with these recommendations, what if a string of six periods were added to the end of the high-entropy password? Figure 4-8 details those results.

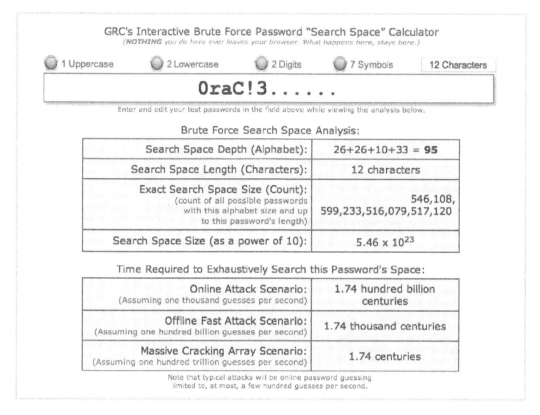

Figure 4-8. *The results of a "padded" high-entropy password*

By simply adding six periods, the time it would take to crack this password in an offline scenario went from 7 seconds to 1.74 thousand centuries, or roughly 174,116 years! Even in the massive offline scenario, it would take close to 200 years to reveal the password. And to increase this duration even more, additional periods can be added anywhere in the password.

Thus, for the most secure password policy, a minimum password length of 12 characters combined with a high level of entropy (at least one uppercase, one lowercase, one special, and one numeric character) is best.

Instance Configuration Settings

The Instance Settings section contains a variety of settings having to do with provisioning workspaces, configuring Oracle Wallet, and configuring e-mail settings. Most of the settings here have something to do with the overall security of an instance of APEX.

Provisioning Status

The Provisioning Status setting, or method in which APEX workspaces can be created, determines how workspaces are created. There are three possible settings:

- *Manual*: An administrator manually creates each workspace.

- *Request*: A link is displayed on the login page enabling users to request workspaces.

- *Request with Email Verification*: A link is displayed on the login page enabling users to request workspaces and validate via e-mail before creating a workspace.

This setting should always be set to Manual so that only an APEX instance administrator can create new workspaces. Setting it to Request could be considered for a nonproduction or sandbox environment that is on an internal network. In this case, each request must still be approved or rejected by an instance administrator. The third setting—Request with Email Verification—should never be selected because it allows anyone with network access to the instance to automatically create workspaces in an instance of APEX.

Require Verification Code

If the Provisioning Status value is set to Request with Email Verification, this setting will determine whether to include a CAPTCHA-like verification code. Users will need to correctly enter the string in the CAPTCHA in order to complete the workspace request. Failure to do so will prevent the request from going through. The purpose of this feature is to eliminate sign-ups by automated services.

If for some reason the Provisioning Status value is set to Request with Email Verification, then this setting should also be enabled as an extra layer of security. Otherwise, it does not matter what this setting is.

Notification E-mail Address

If the Provisioning Status value is set to either Request or Request with Email Verification, the e-mail address entered here will receive a notification when new requests are made. If no e-mail address is entered, then no notification will be sent as new requests are made.

If your provisioning status is set to either Request or Request with Email Verification, then the Notification E-Mail Address value should contain the e-mail address of the APEX instance administrator. This is important so that in the case of any questions, end users have a point of contact to reference.

E-mail Provisioning

When the Provisioning Status value is set to Request with Email Verification, an e-mail asking the requestor to verify the workspace by clicking the link will be sent. Upon clicking the link, the requestor is taken to an APEX page to confirm the request and, in turn, activate the workspace. If this setting is set to Disabled, then clicking the link will not provision the workspace but rather display the message as defined in the Message setting.

It is unlikely that this setting will ever need to be changed, and it is safe to leave it enabled. A better name for this setting would be Email Response Processing, because essentially that is what it controls, not whether e-mail provisioning itself is enabled or disabled.

Message

The Message setting works in conjunction with the previous setting, Email Provisioning. When Email Provisioning is set to Disabled, the text in the Message setting will be displayed to the user when they attempt to provision a workspace by clicking the link provided in the e-mail.

Require New Schema

If the Provisioning Mode value is set to either Request or Request with Email Verification, this setting determines whether a workspace can be created and associated with an existing schema or whether a new schema is required. It does not apply if Provisioning Status is set to Manual.

Encrypted Tablespaces

If this setting is enabled, then APEX will use Transparent Data Encryption (TDE) to encrypt the associated data files. This setting will apply regardless of which provisioning mode APEX is set to. TDE will encrypt all database files that are written to disk, making them unreadable to anyone who tries to access them.

Before this feature will work, a couple of conditions must be met. First, TDE is part of the Oracle Advanced Security Option (ASO), which is a for-cost feature of the Enterprise Edition of the Database. Thus, a proper license for ASO is required in order to use this feature. Second, since the encryption key used in creating the encrypted tablespaces is stored outside of the database, an Oracle Wallet must be configured and opened.

Schemas that are not created as part of the workspace creation process will not be impacted by this feature. However, a DBA can still manually create a schema and associate that schema with an encrypted tablespace.

This feature should be set to Yes, as long as the appropriate licenses and database versions are procured, so that any data written to the disk is protected with encryption.

Delete Uploaded Files After (Days)

Anytime a file is uploaded via the Application Builder, that file is stored securely in a common table, regardless of the workspace. Oftentimes, these files are nothing more than scripts that are executed immediately to create a variety of APEX components or even data in tables. Files that fit these criteria include the following:

- Application export
- CSS export
- Images export
- Page export
- Plug-in
- Script export
- Spreadsheet/text data import
- Static files export
- Themes
- User interface defaults
- Websheet export
- Workspace export
- XML data import

If the Delete Uploaded Files After (days) feature contains a number greater than 0, then files in this shared table will be purged that many days after they are initially uploaded. To retain all files and never purge anything, set this feature to null. The value of this setting will impact all workspaces and cannot be overridden at the workspace level. In most cases, it is not necessary to retain these files because their purpose has been served and they are simply taking up space.

There is no hard and fast recommendation for this setting because it largely depends on whether data stored in the shared upload table needs to be retained for any period of time or is being used in any applications. If your applications use this table—as may be the case with older APEX applications that made more use of the shared table—it should be retrofitted so that any uploaded data is stored in the parse-as schema. This way, it is not accidentally deleted by this process. Applications that use the shared upload table should at some point be retrofitted to store uploaded files in their respective data schemas.

On a development server, it would be acceptable to disable this feature and thus preserve all uploaded files. However, on a production server, it would be ideal to set the value of this setting to 1 so that uploaded files are retained for as short a time as possible.

E-mail

A number of settings have to do with e-mail in the Email section, as the name implies. Most of these settings have little to do with security and therefore will not be discussed in any detail here.

One setting that should have a value is Default Email From Address. When APEX sends messages regarding to workspace provisioning or service requests, this is the address that those messages will come from. Thus, it should be set to an address that is monitored by the APEX instance administrator or DBA, in case replies are sent.

The Email options also provide settings for credentials to the SMTP server, should they be required.

Wallet Path

If any application requires communicating via outbound HTTPS, then an Oracle Wallet must be created and configured. This includes, but is not limited to, web service calls that require HTTPS. Oracle Wallet is a secure certificate store that is used to share credentials with external sites so that secure communications can occur. It is relatively straightforward to set up, but it does require the assistance of a DBA. Refer to the Oracle Wallet documentation for more information on how to install and configure it.

Once a wallet is configured, the Wallet Path and Wallet Password must be entered here for APEX to be able to reference it. The Wallet Path must point to the physical directory in the file system where the wallet is stored. It does not need to refer to the name of the wallet, just the directory. Lastly, the Wallet Path needs to have a prefix of `file:`, regardless of the operating system. For example:

- On a Windows system: `file:c:\WINNT\Profiles\oracle\WALLETS`
- On a UNIX or Linux system: `file:/home/oracle/wallets`

Wallet Password

Enter the password for the wallet specified in Wallet Path. APEX will store an encrypted version of that password and use it when accessing the wallet. If the password of the wallet is changed via the Oracle Wallet tool, the value here must also be changed to match the new password. Be sure to select Check to confirm that you want to change the wallet password when entering a new Wallet Password value.

Report Printing

Most of the Report Printing options have little to do with security and should be configured as per the requirements and specifications of the report server selected. However, it is worth noting that the protocol used to access the reporting server should be set to HTTPS, when possible.

Workspace Purge Settings

When enabled, the settings in the Workspace Purge Settings section will determine the interval at which inactive workspaces are purged. This feature should be disabled on any instance—production, development, or otherwise—because it introduces the risk of a valid yet inactive workspace being purged.

The genesis of this feature lies with the management task associated with running `http://apex.oracle.com`, Oracle's publicly hosted instance of APEX. `http://apex.oracle.com` gets hundreds of workspace requests each week, many of which are used for a short period of time and then abandoned. Like any other server, there are limited resources available, and cleaning up stale workspaces ensures that those resources are best allocated. Thus, this feature was added to APEX largely to assist Oracle with this task. While anyone can take advantage of this feature, it has little practical use outside of a truly hosted, shared instance of APEX.

Manage Other Instance Settings

As discussed, most of the options under Instance Settings clearly have an impact on the overall security of an instance of APEX. There are also a few additional settings scattered throughout the rest of the Instance Settings section that can also impact security, which are discussed next.

Session State

The Manage Meta Data section of the Manage Instance portion of the APEX administration console is a collection of four completely unlike components of APEX: session state, e-mail, translations, and interactive report subscriptions. These components don't have much in common, but there is a security angle to the first: Session State.

APEX administrators can both monitor and purge session state information associated with any application from any workspace. This essentially allows the instance administrator to view any value set in session state from any application. Thus, if sensitive information is stored in APEX session state and not properly encrypted, it will be visible in clear text to an APEX instance administrator from the reports located here. See Chapter 14 for information on how to properly protect items that will contain sensitive data.

Recent Sessions Report

The Recent Sessions report is perhaps one of the most powerful reports in all of APEX. It details all recent sessions and provides a link that drills down to associated session state values. You can see the report and the link in the Session Number column, as shown in Figure 4-9.

Session Number	Database User	Created ▼	User	Workspace Name
16431264674855	APEX_PUBLIC_USER	11/01/2012 13:34:20 Thursday	ADMIN	SERT
9583683736439	APEX_PUBLIC_USER	11/01/2012 13:34:16 Thursday	nobody	SERT
13326503725725	APEX_PUBLIC_USER	11/01/2012 13:32:34 Thursday	ADMIN	SERT
1336526081815	APEX_PUBLIC_USER	11/01/2012 13:32:26 Thursday	ADMIN	SERT
4116226965021	APEX_PUBLIC_USER	11/01/2012 13:06:48 Thursday	nobody	INTERNAL
14979792656408	APEX_PUBLIC_USER	11/01/2012 13:06:12 Thursday	nobody	SERT
5436850548467	APEX_PUBLIC_USER	11/01/2012 13:04:08 Thursday	nobody	INTERNAL
367263472828	APEX_PUBLIC_USER	11/01/2012 13:02:25 Thursday	nobody	INTERNAL
10667153445286	APEX_PUBLIC_USER	11/01/2012 13:01:56 Thursday	nobody	INTERNAL
5245351467337	APEX_PUBLIC_USER	11/01/2012 13:01:18 Thursday	ADMIN	INTERNAL
20697656833609	APEX_PUBLIC_USER	11/01/2012 13:01:13 Thursday	nobody	INTERNAL
3610915076855	APEX_PUBLIC_USER	11/01/2012 12:57:51 Thursday	ADMIN	INTERNAL
18496947312093	APEX_PUBLIC_USER	11/01/2012 12:55:07 Thursday	nobody	SERT
1207673984944	APEX_PUBLIC_USER	11/01/2012 12:55:04 Thursday	nobody	INTERNAL

Figure 4-9. *The Recent Sessions report, with links to session details*

Clicking any of the session numbers will display another report that not only provides details about the session ID itself but also details the current values set within that session, as shown in Figure 4-10.

Session Number	16431264674855
Created By	APEX_PUBLIC_USER
Created	29 seconds ago
Cookie (User)	ADMIN
On New Instance Fired For	:200
Security Checks Passed	: 12061358972338764: 28673616059325285:
Workspace	1044509116395059

Item Name	Session State Value	Session State Status	Flow Id
G_APEX_ADMIN_ROLE	NO	Inserted	200
G_APEX_SCHEMA	APEX_040200	Inserted	200
G_APEX_SESSION_ID	13326503725725	Updated	200
G_APEX_VERSION	4.2.0.00.27	Inserted	200
G_APPROVE_REJECT_ALL_LINK	f?p=200:18:16431264674855:::18:P18_EXCEPTION_PK:BAT%7C&cs=3C36C8C8&A39DF21E80A9F320C83F670D	Inserted	200
G_COMPONENT_ID	-	Inserted	200
G_COPYRIGHT	Enkitec eSERT - Copyright © 2012 <a target="_blank" href="http://www.enkitec.com">Enkitec</a> - Version 2.1.0	Inserted	200
G_HELP_CLASS	formRegionIRHelp2	Updated	200
G_ITEM	01-NOV-12	Inserted	200
G_LOGO	<img src="#WORKSPACE_IMAGES#enkitecLogo.png"> <span class="sumnevaLogo">eSERT</span> 	Inserted	200
G_PAGE_ID	-	Inserted	200
G_PREF_SET	YES	Inserted	200
G_SUBMIT_ALL_LINK	f?p=200:10:16431264674855:::10:P10_EXCEPTION_PK:BAT%7C&cs=3538F9B6DADCCC0C6F449481B011FC836	Inserted	200
G_VERSION	020100	Inserted	200
G_VERSION_DISP	2.1.0	Inserted	200

Figure 4-10. *The Session Details report*

Values that are encrypted in APEX session state will be displayed as *****, whereas values that are not are displayed normally.

Purge Sessions by Age Function

An APEX instance administrator can purge a range of sessions based on the duration of the session combined with a maximum number of sessions to purge. Thus, if there are 20 sessions that are older than 1 hour and the maximum number of sessions to purge is set to 10, only the oldest 10 of those sessions will be purged. These options are illustrated in Figure 4-11.

Purge Sessions

Maximum Sessions to Purge: 1000

Only Purge Sessions Older Than: 1 day

Cancel | Count Sessions | Purge Sessions

Figure 4-11. *The Purge Sessions region*

Unfortunately, there is no way to purge a specific session outside of the boundary of session duration. For instance, if a user were determined to be a threat to the system, it would be impossible to purge just that specific user's session. A block of sessions that would include that user's session would have to be purged instead.

Session State Statistics Report

The term *session state statistics* may not be the best term to use in describing this section because the report simply counts the number of recent sessions and their associated item values. Figure 4-12 shows an example of this report.

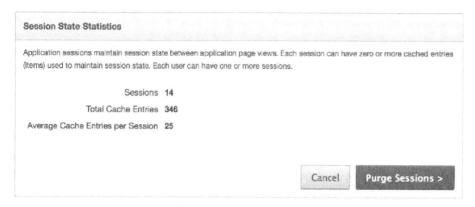

Figure 4-12. *The Session State Statistics report*

Clicking Purge Sessions will simply redirect to the "Purge Sessions, by age" report that is also available from the main Session State page.

Logs and Files

The Manage Logs and Files section, as depicted in Figure 4-13, allows an APEX instance administrator to truncate most of the APEX logs: SQL Workshop, page views, developer activity, external clicks, and login attempts. Details of these logs are not available here but rather can be found on the Monitor Activity tab in their respective sections.

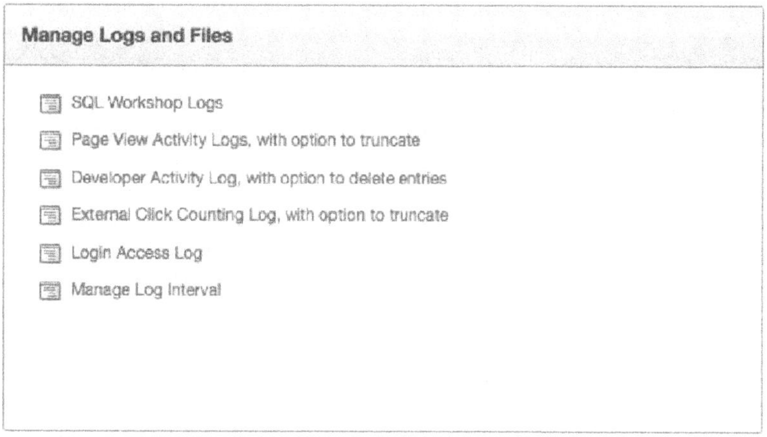

> **Manage Logs and Files**
>
> 📄 SQL Workshop Logs
>
> 📄 Page View Activity Logs, with option to truncate
>
> 📄 Developer Activity Log, with option to delete entries
>
> 📄 External Click Counting Log, with option to truncate
>
> 📄 Login Access Log
>
> 📄 Manage Log Interval

Figure 4-13. *The Manage Logs and Files section*

Table 4-1 maps which APEX views and tables are used to store which log. Note that not all logs are associated with an APEX view. In that case, the corresponding APEX table is listed.

Table 4-1. *Mapping Logs to Their Corresponding APEX Views*

Log Name	APEX View/Table
Page Activity Logs	APEX_WORKSPACE_ACTIVITY_LOG
External Click Logs	APEX_WORKSPACE_CLICKS
Login Access Log	APEX_WORKSPACE_ACCESS_LOG
Developer Activity Logs	WWV_FLOW_BUILDER_AUDIT_TRAIL
SQL Workshop Logs	WWV_FLOW_SW_SQL_CMDS

The Manage Log Interval section allows the instance administrator to determine the intervals before a log switch occurs for each log, as shown in Figure 4-14.

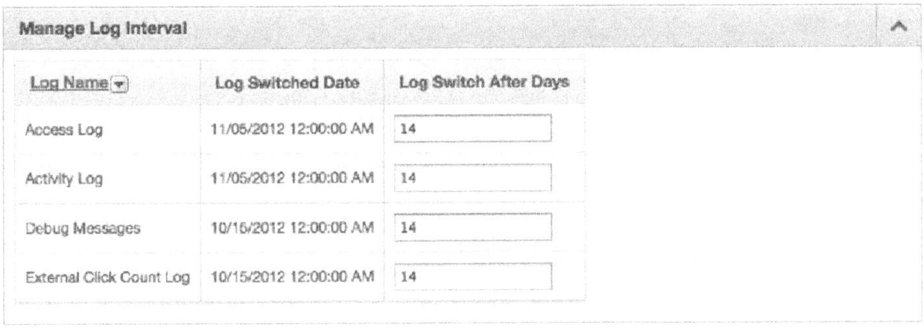

Figure 4-14. *The Manage Log Interval page*

Log switch intervals can be set as short as 1 day or as long as 180 days, thus allowing storage of logs anywhere from a couple of days up to about a year. Unfortunately, the larger the value specified, the more likely a performance issue will arise.

Given that an APEX administrator or log switch can easily truncate data from almost any of these logs, an automated process that archives all details from these logs to a more permanent place should be implemented. A simple scheduled job can be configured to copy all records from the previous tables or views to another table outside of the APEX schema so that in if the logs need to be reviewed, they will be available.

APEX does have built-in automatic archiving for the page activity log only. However, the data stored is rolled up and summarized by date and application. Thus, the details of individual page views are not preserved in the archived data.

Messages

The Messages section is used to set the Login and System message, as well as provide site-specific tasks or links that are displayed on the home page. Unfortunately, any HTML entered into both the Login and System message will not be properly escaped before it is rendered. Thus, it is possible for an APEX instance administrator to implement a cross-site scripting attack using either of these messages.

Granted, an APEX instance administrator is a trusted individual because this administrator has near SYS-level access to an instance of Oracle. Unfortunately, it would not be the first or last time if someone with such lofty credentials turned out to be dishonest. Thus, extra precautions may need to be taken when verifying how these two settings are set.

To illustrate just how a simple cross-site scripting attack could take place, enter the snippet in Listing 4-1 into the Message field. Ensure that Login Message is set to Custom Message and click Apply Changes.

Listing 4-1. Malicious HTML That Illustrates How a Cross-Site Scripting Attack Could Be Implemented from the Login Message by the Administrator

```
Seemingly Innocent Login Message<script>alert('This could be an XSS attack');</script>
```

When the APEX login page is run by any user—unauthenticated or otherwise—an alert will be displayed, as illustrated in Figure 4-15. In a real-world scenario, this alert could instead be malicious code that sent the workspace and user name to the malicious user so that they would have two-thirds of what is required to access an APEX workspace.

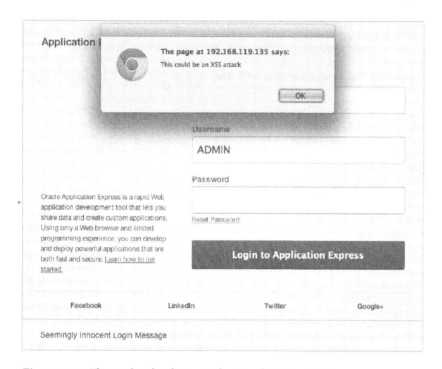

Figure 4-15. *The results of malicious code entered into Login Message*

Self Service Sign Up

While the Self Service Sign Up section does not have anything directly to do with security, it is mentioned because it suffers from the same weakness as the Message section. Any HTML entered into the Agreement Text, Questions, Answers, Pre Text, or Post Text fields will not be properly escaped when rendered. Thus, any illicit JavaScript entered there will be executed versus simply displayed harmlessly. Care should be taken to have these values inspected by someone other than the main APEX instance administrator to ensure that no cross-site scripting attack is subversively implemented there.

Manage Workspaces

Most of the management tasks associated with managing an individual APEX workspace can be handled by the individual workspace administrators because they have the ability to change workspace settings, manage users, and deploy and manage applications. However, because workspace administrators are limited to their own individual workspaces, they cannot manage the instance of APEX. The Manage Workspaces section offers instance administrators the capability to do almost anything that a workspace administrator can, as well as manage the instance of APEX itself, such as creating, removing, and locking workspaces and their corresponding schema assignments.

■ **Note**   In the case of settings that can be managed by both the instance and workspace administrators, the instance administrator's choices will always take precedence over the workspace administrator. For example, if a workspace administrator disables Team Development, the instance administrator could easily reenable it.

The Workspace Actions section is the core of the Manage Workspaces section. Here, an instance administrator can create, remove, lock, or modify any workspace within the instance of APEX. All user management of any user from any workspace is also done at this level.

Create Workspace

The Create Workspace option will initiate the Create Workspace Wizard, which will step through the process of creating a new workspace. This three-step wizard will prompt for the workspace name, schema details, and workspace administrator credentials before creating the workspace. When the provisioning status of an instance of APEX is set to Manual, this is the only way to create new workspaces.

When the wizard is started, it will initially ask for the workspace name and, optionally, the workspace ID, as depicted in Figure 4-16.

Figure 4-16. *The first step of the Create Workspace Wizard*

Workspace ID is an optional value, and it is rare that any value would have to be specified here, because it is a surrogate or synthetic key for the workspace. However, there are times when entering a specific workspace ID is required. If there are subscriptions between any number of applications within a single workspace on one instance of APEX, the only way to preserve those subscriptions across other instances of APEX is to ensure that the workspace ID remains constant.

One way to ensure this is to simply export the workspace from one instance and import it into the other one. When exporting and reimporting a workspace, APEX will automatically attempt to preserve the workspace ID. Another way to achieve the same thing is to create the workspace manually, using the specific workspace ID of the original workspace.

To determine the workspace ID of a specific workspace, simply execute the query in Listing 4-2 from the SQL Workshop while logged into that specific workspace. Executing the SQL from SQL*Plus or any other tool will not work.

Listing 4-2. SQL Used to Determine the Current Workspace ID

```
select v('WORKSPACE_ID') from dual
```

After the workspace name and, optionally, workspace ID, are specified, the next step is to determine what the initial parse-as schema for the workspace will be. There are essentially two ways to associate a schema with a workspace: select a schema that already exists or allow APEX to create one for you. If electing to reuse an existing schema, the Schema Name value will have to match an existing schema in the database. Almost any schema can be associated with a workspace, save for a few that are restricted or reserved by APEX.

When specifying a new schema, the schema name, password, and tablespace size will need to be specified, as illustrated in Figure 4-17.

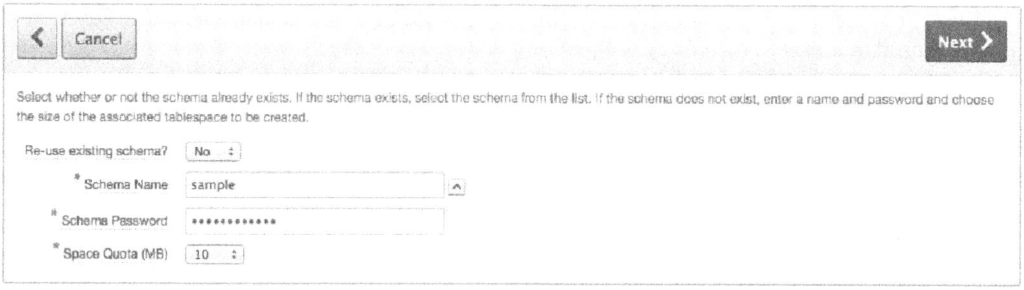

Figure 4-17. *Creating a new schema for a new workspace*

APEX will also associate the following system privileges with any new schema that it creates:

- CREATE CLUSTER
- CREATE DIMENSION
- CREATE INDEXTYPE
- CREATE JOB
- CREATE MATERIALIZED VIEW
- CREATE OPERATOR
- CREATE PROCEDURE
- CREATE SEQUENCE
- CREATE SESSION
- CREATE SYNONYM
- CREATE TABLE
- CREATE TRIGGER
- CREATE TYPE
- CREATE VIEW

Should any of these privileges not be required, they must be manually revoked by the DBA. Additionally, any privileges that are required but not listed must be manually granted by the DBA.

It is important to note that no roles are granted to a new schema by APEX. This is done intentionally for two main reasons. First, it is more secure to grant discrete privileges; they can be revoked individually and allow a schema to perform only one or two operations. Second, role-based security does not work directly in an APEX environment. Since all APEX applications connect to the database as the same common schema—APEX_PUBLC_USER—but parse as a different schema, all code executed by an APEX application is being done so with definer's rights. Since roles are not applied when using definer's rights, roles are not applied or evaluated from within any APEX application. Thus, explicit grants should be made by way of system privileges to ensure that they are secured properly.

It is also important to note that the workspace password policy is not applied here, because this password is for the database schema, not the workspace user. Because of this, it is possible for a weak password to be created here, because there are simply no verification rules applied.

Each schema created as part of this wizard will be associated with its own, unique tablespace. If this is not desirable, which in many cases it is not, then the DBA should precreate schemas and assign them to their proper tablespaces prior to creating an APEX workspace. Then, the schema can simply be referred to, and APEX won't make any changes to the underlying tablespace.

After the schema has been defined, the last step in the wizard is to define the initial workspace administrator account. There is no way to circumvent this step, because the wizard requires a workspace administrator to be created. The instance administrator can always lock or remove this user upon completion of the wizard, should they deem that necessary.

When entering a password, the workspace password policy will be applied here. Also, an e-mail address is required for the administrator. The first name and last name are optional, as pictured in Figure 4-18.

* Administrator Username	ADMIN
* Administrator Password	••••••••••••••••••••
First Name	APEX
Last Name	Administrator
* Email	admin@enkitec.com

Figure 4-18. Creating the workspace administrator account for a new workspace

Even though a valid e-mail address is required, no credentials will be e-mailed to the new workspace administrator. However, a notification will be e-mailed to the address specified in the Notification Email Address area under Instance Settings. Also, the workspace administrator will be prompted to change their password upon their initial login. The workspace password policy will, of course, be applied.

Once the workspace is created, APEX will display a success message, detailing the tablespace name and data file used, as per Figure 4-19.

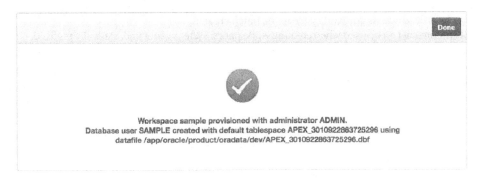

Workspace sample provisioned with administrator ADMIN.
Database user SAMPLE created with default tablespace APEX_3010922863725296 using
datafile /app/oracle/product/oradata/dev/APEX_3010922863725296.dbf

Figure 4-19. Successful creation of a workspace

At this point, the workspace is active, and the workspace administrator can log into it and start creating users and/or applications.

Create Multiple Workspaces

If multiple workspaces need to be created, the Create Multiple Workspaces Wizard can be used in place of having to use the Create Workspace Wizard multiple times. New in APEX 4.2, the Create Multiple Workspaces Wizard asks for a common set of information and then applies that to each of the workspaces created, as shown in Figure 4-20.

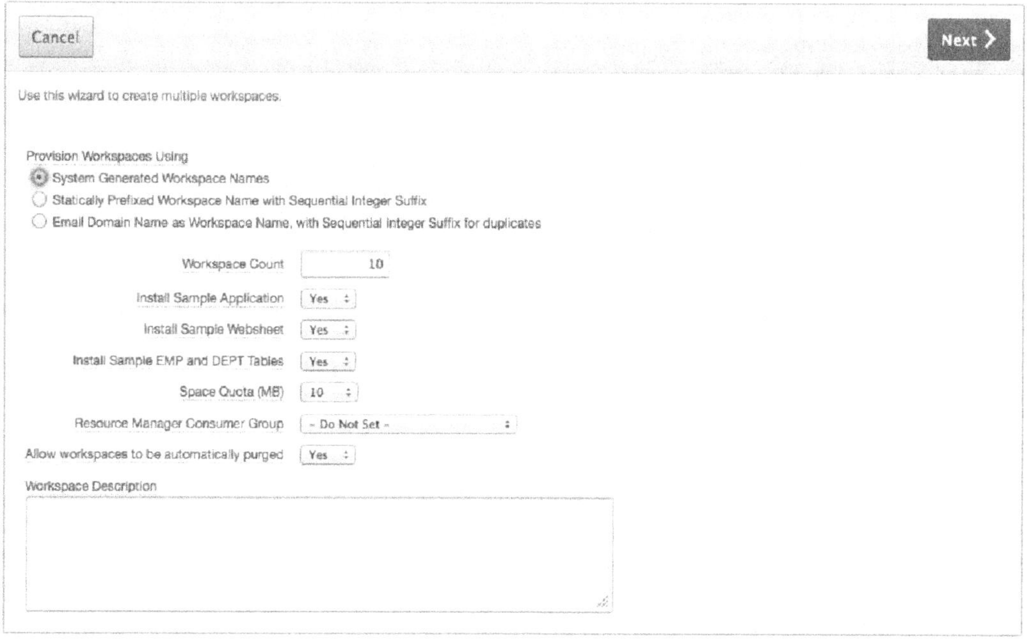

Figure 4-20. *The Create Multiple Workspaces Wizard*

This wizard is ideal for creating multiple workspaces for use in training environments or other nonproduction systems, because it is rare that a large number of workspaces would need to be created on a production system. Because a single password will be applied to all workspaces created with this wizard, it should be used with the assumption that any user may be able to access any workspace in the batch created.

There are three different criteria that can be used when creating workspaces: system generated, statically prefixed, or a list of e-mail addresses. Figure 4-21 illustrates a statically prefixed set of five workspaces using the prefix *TRAINING*.

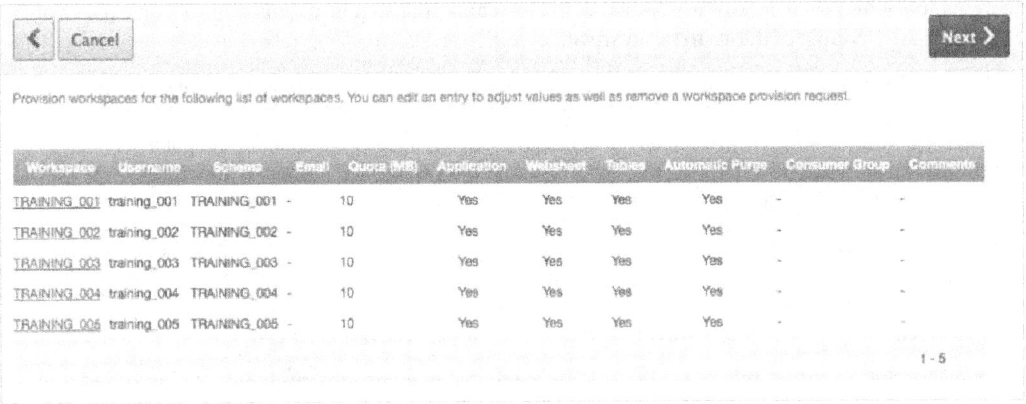

Figure 4-21. *A statically prefixed set of five workspaces from the Create Multiple Workspaces Wizard*

Regardless of which creation method is selected, each workspace can have a different set of sample objects installed or have some of its options altered, as illustrated in Figure 4-22. For example, if 10 generic workspaces were created, 5 of them could include the sample database application, while 5 of them would not.

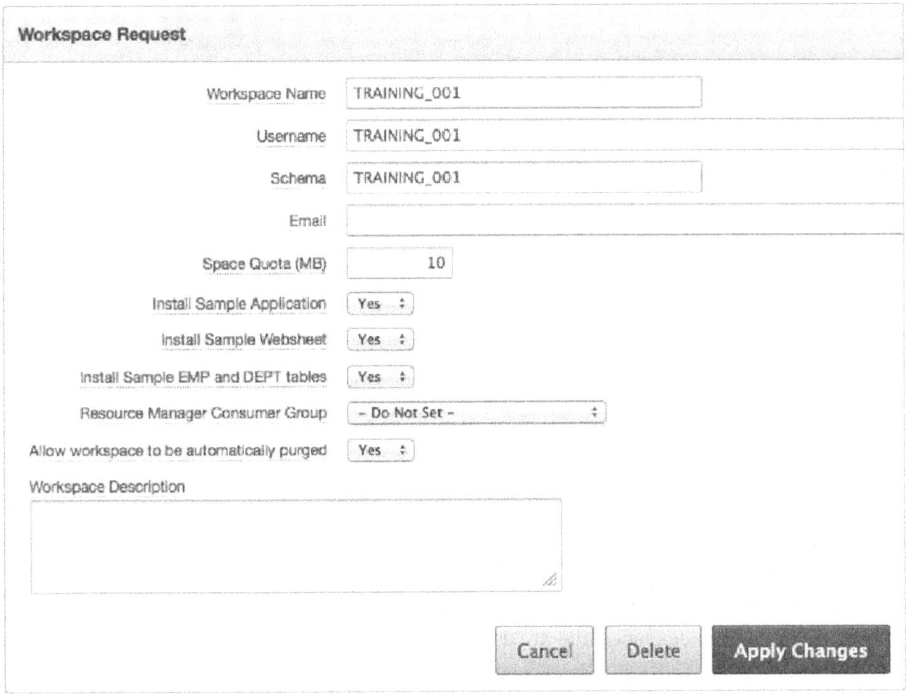

Figure 4-22. *Editing an individual workspace in the Create Multiple Workspaces Wizard*

Once all the individual workspace options are tweaked, the next and final step is to determine a single password for all workspaces. There are a couple of things to be aware of.

- First, the same password is used for all workspaces. Thus, it would be trivial to access any other workspace if a static prefix were used. If e-mail addresses were used when creating the workspaces, it would still be relatively easy to access the others, as long as a user could get a list of the e-mail addresses used. Using the system-generated workspace names would make this much more difficult to do, if not impossible.

- Second, the workspace password policy is not enforced with the Create Multiple Workspaces Wizard. Because of this, it would be easy for an instance administrator to either purposely or accidently create ten workspaces that all shared the same short, easy-to-guess, insecure password. According to Oracle, this will be addressed in a future release of APEX.

Until these conditions are remedied, this wizard should be used only in environments where it is assumed that any user can access any workspace in the group created with this wizard.

Remove Workspace

Removing a workspace is a simple, two-step procedure. First, use the pop-up window to locate the workspace to be removed, as shown in Figure 4-23.

Figure 4-23. *Selecting a workspace to remove via Remove Workspace Wizard*

Next, ensure that the confirmation check box is checked and click Next, as shown in Figure 4-24.

Figure 4-24. *Confirming the removal of a workspace*

There is one more confirmation step to complete before the workspace is actually removed. The final page will display any schemas and their associated tablespaces that are associated with the workspace, as illustrated in Figure 4-25.

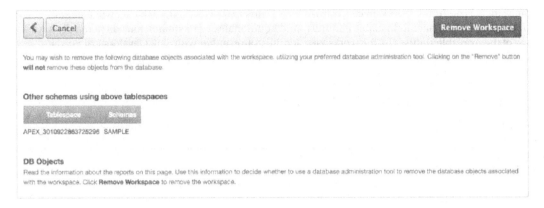

Figure 4-25. *The final step in the Remove Workspace Wizard*

Removing a workspace will simply remove the workspace and its associated users and applications. As noted in the confirmation page, it will not remove the schemas and tablespaces associated with the workspace. That task will have to be later completed manually by a DBA, should those components need removal.

Lock Workspace

Locking a workspace is a bit misleading because a workspace itself cannot technically be locked. When run, this wizard will actually lock all workspace users and then set the status of all applications to Unavailable. Before the wizard actually completes, a list of user and applications that will be impacted will be displayed, as shown in Figure 4-26.

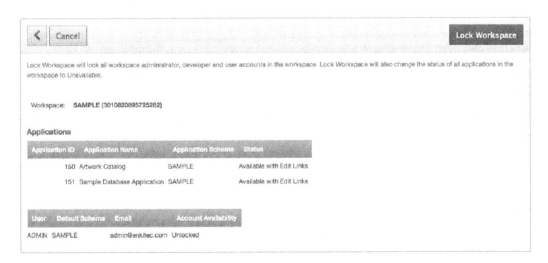

Figure 4-26. *Confirmation before the Lock Workspace Wizard completes*

When an application's status is set to Unavailable, the application will be inaccessible to all users. Users will instead see a message that states that the application is currently unavailable. Nothing else about the application is changed or altered in any way.

Unfortunately, there is no "unlock workspace wizard." Once a workspace is locked, each user will manually have to be unlocked by the workspace or instance administrator. Additionally, each application will manually have to be reset to one of the Available statuses by the workspace administrator, either with SQL Developer or via the APEX_ADMIN API.

Manage Workspace to Schema Assignments

When a workspace is created, an associated parse-as schema has to be associated with that schema. Workspaces must have at least one parse-as schema associated with them at all times. In some cases, a workspace can have multiple parse-as schema associated with it. Only an instance administrator can create those mappings using the Manage to Workspace to Schema Assignments page.

An interactive report will list all existing schema-to-workspace mappings. If a new mapping is desired, simply click the Add Schema button. Similar to when creating a new workspace, the first question from the wizard will ask whether the schema is new or existing, as shown in Figure 4-27.

Figure 4-27. *The first step when adding a new schema to an existing workspace*

Next, identify the workspace that the schema will be associated with. Use the pop-up region to locate and select the workspace and then click Next. Depending on whether the schema is existing or new, the next step will be to either select the schema or create a new schema, respectively. When creating a new schema, both the default and temporary tablespaces will also have to be specified, as shown in Figure 4-28. Workspace password policies do not apply in the latter case because the password is for the database user, not the workspace user.

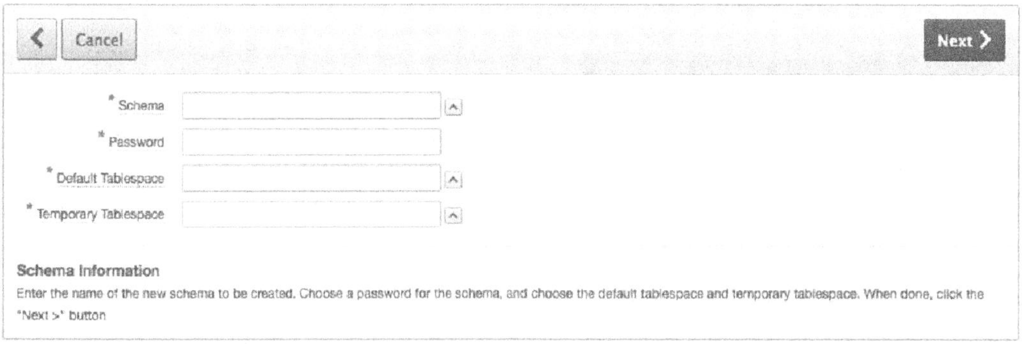

Figure 4-28. *Associating a new schema with an existing workspace*

Upon completion of this wizard, the selected workspace will now have access to its original parse-as schema as well as the schema specified in this wizard. This means that any workspace administrator or developers will also have access to that schema from both the Application Builder and the SQL Workshop. Whatever system and object privileges that schema has will also be available to any workspace administrator or user.

Oftentimes, developers may need access to a specific table or view from a schema other than the one that their application parses as. While associating the desired schema to the developer's workspace may seem like the intuitive thing to do, it is not. Applications can parse only as a single schema, a setting that can be changed only by a developer at design time. Thus, if a developer needs access to objects in schema B and has an application that parses as schema A, associating schema B to the workspace will not allow schema A to see any of schema B's objects.

The correct way to grant access across schemas is no different as when using SQL*Plus or any other database tool: create a database grant. A simple SELECT grant on a table in schema B to schema A would allow the developers to refer to that object in their application that parses as schema A. Associating the schema with the workspace won't work, and it also introduces the risk of the developer being able to access any object in that schema whatsoever.

A workspace or instance administrator can limit which schemas each developer has access to, but this limitation is applied only to the SQL Workshop. Thus, if both schema A and schema B were associated with a workspace, a user could be set up to be able to access schema A only. That user would not be able to view any of schema B's objects from any part of the SQL Workshop. However, it would be trivial for that user to create an application that parses as schema B, which would enable that user to see any of schema B's objects by creating simple reports based on data dictionary views. Thus, this limitation should be considered ineffective for all intents and purposes.

Manage Developers and Users

The Manage Developers and Users section gives the instance administrator the ability to manage all users across all workspaces in an instance of APEX. Instance administrators can modify any properties of a user, create additional users, and either lock or remove users from this section. Access to modules on a per-user basis can be managed from this section. This is also where instance administrators can reset passwords for users who have forgotten them.

An important concept to keep in mind here is that APEX users are unique within each workspace. It is possible and likely that there will be multiple users with the same name across multiple workspaces. For example, if there are multiple users named ADMIN, as depicted in Figure 4-29, each user is a separate, distinct object with its own unique credentials and settings. Future versions of APEX should alleviate this deficiency by allowing APEX accounts to use an external authentication repository such as LDAP or Oracle Access Manager.

	User	Full Name	Workspace ▲	Default Schema	Created	Updated	Password	Workspace ID
✎	ADMIN		ADMIN	SV_ADMIN_010000	1.2 years ago	1.2 years ago	-	1634407994788480
✎	ADMIN		APEXLEAKS	APEXLEAKS	1.3 years ago	6 months ago	-	12145420870660223
✎	DEV		APEXLEAKS	APEXLEAKS	7 months ago	6 months ago	Reset	12145420870660223
✎	ADMIN		BEHIND THE SCENES	BTS	9 months ago	7 weeks ago	-	3409418001853220
✎	ADMIN		DATA	DATA	2 weeks ago	2 weeks ago	-	2765609666880404
✎	ADMIN		ENKITEC	ENKITEC	6 weeks ago	6 weeks ago	-	8842630810673089
✎	KING		ENKITEC	ENKITEC	6 weeks ago	6 weeks ago	Reset	8842630810673089
✎	ADMIN		FWK	FRAMEWORK	2 weeks ago	2 weeks ago	-	2770619209311700
✎	ADMIN		INTERNAL	-	1.7 years ago	25 minutes ago	-	10
✎	ADMIN		NEW FEATURES	NEW_FEATURES	1 years ago	1 years ago	-	1904829752065586

***Figure 4-29.** The main report for Manage Developers and Users*

APEX Account Types

It is important to clarify the types of APEX accounts. In order of least to most privileged, they are user, developer, and workspace administrator.

An APEX user (sometimes referred to *end user*) is the least privileged of the three. APEX users will have access only to the Team Development module when they log into the workspace. Because of this, APEX users are most often used as end users for applications or Team Development participants because they will not be able to modify applications or any schema objects. Using APEX users as end users is possible and easy but is not a recommended approach for production applications. Refer to Chapter 8 for more details.

APEX developers are what almost every user account in every workspace should be set to. Developers can create, modify, and remove applications; use any part of the SQL Workshop and Team Development; and view all workspace activity reports and logs. It is rare than an APEX developer will need any more access than this level.

APEX workspace administrators can do everything that an APEX developer can do with the added abilities of managing the workspace settings, users, and even some application settings. It is strongly recommended that the APEX workspace administrator accounts be given out sparingly, perhaps even to development managers or other nondevelopers. If all users in a workspace are APEX administrators, then essentially no one is an APEX administrator because any user can change any setting without any additional controls. Since it is rare that workspace settings need to be changed or users need to be added or removed, these tasks can easily be centralized and given to the instance administrator instead of workspace administrators, if so desired.

The Internal Workspace

The Internal workspace is a special workspace. If a user is created in this workspace, the user will essentially become an APEX instance administrator, regardless of the type of user added. By default, APEX ships with a single user in this workspace named ADMIN. The password for the ADMIN user is set during the installation of APEX. Additional users can be added here, should they be needed. Nothing else special needs to be done to these users; their membership in the Internal workspace is enough to make them instance administrators.

Not only are the user type settings ignored in the Internal workspace but so are the module access settings because the instance administration console does not have an Application Builder, SQL Workshop, or Team Development module. Thus, a user in the internal workspace who is set up as an administrator with access to all modules has the same privileges as a user in the Internal workspace set up as an end user with no access to any modules.

Forgotten Internal ADMIN User Passwords

Even instance administrators will forget their passwords, especially if they are not accessing APEX frequently. If the instance password settings are set to lock an account after a number of invalid attempts, it is quite possible and even likely that the ADMIN user in the internal workspace can essentially lock them out of the entire instance of APEX.

Should this happen, there is a script that ships with APEX called `apxchpwd.sql`. This script can be found in the top-level directory where the APEX download was extracted. When run as SYS, it will reset the user ADMIN's password in the internal workspace.

An important thing to note: the script will work only for a user specifically named ADMIN in the internal workspace. If additional users were created in the internal workspace and the ADMIN user was subsequently removed, the script will not work. Editing the script and changing the line that sets the value of `wwv_flow_security.g_user` to the user that you need to reset the password for will work.

It is also important to note that this script is APEX-version specific. Thus, be sure to run the script that coincides with the version of APEX you are running. Inspecting the script and looking for the line that resembles Listing 4-3 will determine which version the script is set to work with.

Listing 4-3. This Line of the apxchpwd.sql Script Will Determine What Version of APEX It Is Designed to Work With

```
alter session set current_schema = APEX_040200;
```

If the version listed in the script does not coincide with your version of APEX, be sure to download the corresponding version of APEX from the Oracle Technology Network.

Users

The APEX instance administrator can create and manage users from any workspace within an instance of APEX from this section of the instance administration console. The first page presents all users in all workspaces in an interactive report. Administrators can quickly and easily filter the report to locate the user or users they need to update. Refer to Figure 4-29 for an illustration of the manage developers and users report.

From a security perspective, a few attributes are worth mentioning when creating new users. First, each user is created and associated with a specific workspace. There is no way to change this mapping after the user is created. If more than one schema is associated with a workspace, it is possible to change the default schema.

The default schema is what will be selected when using the SQL Workshop and creating new applications. The Accessible Schemas (null for all) attribute allows an administrator to limit which schemas a user can access in the SQL Workshop, should more than one schema be associated with the workspace. As the label implies, leaving this attribute set to null will allow the user to access any schema that is associated with the workspace now and in the future. Use a colon-delimited string when referring to multiple schemas.

It is important to note that the Accessible Schemas (null for all) attribute does not apply to the Application Builder, only to the SQL Workshop. Thus, limiting which parse-as schema a user has access to does not restrict that user from being able to see anything in that schema, because they can simply create an application that queries any object from any schema associated with the workspace.

The type of user is determined by a pair of radio groups: User is an Administrator and User is a Developer. If the user is a workspace administrator, then the User is a Developer radio group is disabled because an administrator can do anything that a developer can do. If the user is set to a developer, it is possible to control which modules that user has access to: Application Builder, SQL Workshop, and Team Development. Lastly, if the user is neither an administrator nor a developer, then the user is considered an end user and access to all modules is disabled because end users cannot access any modules.

If the user has locked their account by exceeding the maximum number of invalid passwords, the Account Availability setting will be set to Locked. When this is the case, either an instance administrator or the corresponding workspace administrator will have to log in and set this attribute to Unlocked before the user can log in again. Oftentimes when this occurs, the administrator will reset the user's password and also force them to change it upon their next login.

All users – no matter what the type – should be created with the Require Change of Password on First Use value set to Yes. This will force the user to change their password upon their first login, thus rendering any password contained in an e-mail invalid. It will also force the user to adhere to the workspace password policy.

An administrator can also force expire a user's password, which will require them to change it the next time they log in. This can be achieved by selecting the Expire Password check box and saving the user. A user's password can also be reset by an administrator entering and verifying a new password and saving the user. If no password is entered in either field, the user's password will remain unchanged.

Manage Component Availability

The Manage Component Availability report simply displays which components are enabled in which workspace, as illustrated in Figure 4-30.

Workspace ▲	Allow Application Building	Allow SQL Workshop	Allow PLSQL Editing	Allow Team Development
✎ ADMIN	Yes	Yes	Yes	Yes
✎ APEXLEAKS	Yes	Yes	Yes	Yes
✎ BEHIND THE SCENES	Yes	Yes	Yes	Yes
✎ DATA	Yes	Yes	Yes	Yes
✎ ENKITEC	Yes	Yes	Yes	Yes
✎ FWK	Yes	Yes	Yes	Yes
✎ NEW FEATURES	Yes	Yes	Yes	Yes
✎ PLPDF_DEMO	Yes	Yes	Yes	Yes
✎ SAMPLE	Yes	Yes	Yes	Yes
✎ SEOUC	Yes	Yes	Yes	Yes

Figure 4-30. *The Manage Component Availability report*

Clicking the corresponding edit link will allow the instance administrator to select which components will be available within that workspace. A workspace administrator can override anything that an instance administrator sets in this case. The only way to ensure that this setting be maintained is to not have workspace administrators for those workspaces. In that case, workspace management would be delegated to the instance administrator.

Export and Import

Workspaces can be exported and imported from the same instance or across different instances via the Export Import section of the instance administration console. Workspace exports will not include any applications or associated database objects. Rather, they will simply contain the workspace definition and all associated users and their corresponding credentials. The workspace export will be in the form of a SQL script that can be reimported via the Import feature in the instance administration console.

The benefits of exporting and importing workspaces are that the internal workspace ID will be preserved when possible. This will ensure that shared component subscriptions will not break across different instances of APEX. Also, all users accounts, such as administrators, developers, and users alike, will be preserved. This makes it easy to clone workspaces from development to QA or training, for instance, because all credentials will not have to be re-created.

View Workspace Reports

Workspace Reports is perhaps not the best name for this section because this is where the actual workspace management, as well as a number of other reports, occurs. Only a couple of the reports in this section have to do with security, so only those will be discussed in any detail here.

Existing Workspaces Report

The Existing Workspaces report displays all workspaces within an instance of APEX, as shown in Figure 4-31. To edit any workspace, simply click any workspace name.

Workspace Name	Display Name	Users	Developers	Applications	Provision Status	Workspace Status	Provisioned	Auto Purge	Source Identifier	Action	Consumer Group
ADMIN	ADMIN	1	1	1	Approved	Assigned	1.2 years ago	Yes	ADMIN	Delete	-
APEXLEAKS	APEXLEAKS	2	2	5	Approved	-	1.3 years ago	Yes	APEXLEAK	Delete	-
BEHIND THE SCENES	BEHIND THE SCENES	1	1	3	Approved	Assigned	9 months ago	Yes	BEHIND T	Delete	-
DATA	DATA	1	1	0	Approved	Assigned	3 weeks ago	Yes	DATA	Delete	-
ENKITEC	ENKITEC	2	2	2	Approved	Assigned	6 weeks ago	Yes	ENKITEC	Delete	-
FWK	FWK	1	1	4	Approved	Assigned	3 weeks ago	Yes	FWK	Delete	-
INTERNAL	INTERNAL	2	1	14	-	-	-	Yes	-		-
NEW FEATURES	NEW FEATURES	1	1	1	Approved	Assigned	1.1 years ago	Yes	NEW FEAT	Delete	-
PLPDF_DEMO	PLPDF_DEMO	1	1	2	Approved	Assigned	5 months ago	Yes	PLPDF_DE	Delete	-
SAMPLE	SAMPLE	3	2	0	-	Assigned	-	Yes	SAMPLE	Delete	-

Figure 4-31. *The Existing Workspace report*

Editing a workspace will include attributes that were not available when creating the workspace. These attributes include Feedback Synchronization Source Identifier, Resource Consumer Group, Builder Notification Message, and Display Name. While none of these attributes is specifically security related, they can be seen only when editing a workspace.

The Login Control section allows the instance administrator to specify whether password expiration and locking for APEX users is enabled and, if so, what criteria to use. A workspace administrator can easily override these settings. The Component Availability section allows an instance administrator to specify which components are available in a specific workspace. Similar to Login Control, the selections here can be overridden by a workspace administrator.

Deleting a workspace can be done only from the main Existing Workspaces report. Simply click the corresponding Delete link to remove that workspace. When deleting a workspace, all applications within that workspace will also be deleted, and a list of those applications will be presented as part of the wizard. Any associated schemas and tablespaces will not be deleted as a result of this wizard. Workspaces can also be deleted by clicking the Remove Workspace link in the Workspace Actions section of Manage Workspaces.

Workspace Database Privileges

The Workspace Database Privileges report, as shown in Figure 4-32, displays all system privileges associated with any schema that is associated with any workspace within the instance of APEX. While there is no way to manage these privileges from the instance administration console, this report provides useful insight as to which schema and workspace combination has which system privileges.

Workspace ▲	Schema	Privilege	Administration Option
SAMPLE	SAMPLE	CREATE SEQUENCE	NO
SAMPLE	SAMPLE	CREATE SYNONYM	NO
SAMPLE	DATA	CREATE DIMENSION	NO
SAMPLE	DATA	CREATE SEQUENCE	NO
SAMPLE	SAMPLE	CREATE TABLE	NO
SAMPLE	DATA	CREATE MATERIALIZED VIEW	NO
SAMPLE	DATA	CREATE TRIGGER	NO
SAMPLE	SAMPLE	CREATE SESSION	NO
SAMPLE	SAMPLE	CREATE TRIGGER	NO
SAMPLE	SAMPLE	CREATE TYPE	NO

Figure 4-32. *The Workspace Database Privileges reports*

Since this is an interactive report, it is simple to apply filters, search for specific workspaces, and so on, to locate a specific workspace or privilege.

Manage Applications

Only one attribute of an application can be managed from the instance administration console: the application build status. All other application attributes are managed from within their corresponding workspaces. Thus, the Manage Applications section contains mostly read-only reports that provide high-level summaries of applications across all workspaces.

View Application Attributes

The Application Attributes report displays a high-level overview of all applications across all workspaces within an instance of APEX, as shown in Figure 4-33.

Workspace ▲	Application	Parsing Schema	Application Name	Updated By	Updated	Pages	Language	Logging	Build Status	Application Status	Created	Workspace ID
FWK	1000	FRAMEWORK	Launchpad	ADMIN	2 weeks ago	4	en-us	YES	RUN_AND_BUILD	AVAILABLE_W_EDIT_LINK	10/17/2012	277081920401700
FWK	999	FRAMEWORK	Shared Components Master	ADMIN	2 weeks ago	8	en-us	YES	RUN_AND_BUILD	AVAILABLE_W_EDIT_LINK	10/17/2012	277081920401700
FWK	998	FRAMEWORK	Starter Application	ADMIN	2 weeks ago	2	en-us	YES	RUN_AND_BUILD	AVAILABLE_W_EDIT_LINK	10/17/2012	277081920401700
NEW_FEATURES	122	NEW_FEATURES	Sample Database Application	ADMIN	2 weeks ago	29	en	YES	RUN_AND_BUILD	AVAILABLE_W_EDIT_LINK	10/19/2011	1904829752085088
PLPDF_DEMO	139	PLPDF_DEMO	PLPDF	ADMIN	2 weeks ago	10	en	YES	RUN_AND_BUILD	AVAILABLE_W_EDIT_LINK	08/19/2012	611371819473663
PLPDF_DEMO	138	PLPDF_DEMO	Sample Database Application	ADMIN	2 weeks ago	25	en	YES	RUN_AND_BUILD	AVAILABLE_W_EDIT_LINK	08/19/2012	611371819473663
SEOUC	131	SEOUC	Help Desk	ADMIN	2 weeks ago	15	en	YES	RUN_AND_BUILD	AVAILABLE_W_EDIT_LINK	11/02/2011	2480109929115716
SEOUC	125	SEOUC	Sample Database Application	ADMIN	2 weeks ago	26	en	YES	RUN_AND_BUILD	AVAILABLE_W_EDIT_LINK	11/02/2011	2480109929115716
SERT	133	SERT	4.0 New Features	ADMIN	2 weeks ago	34	en-us	YES	RUN_AND_BUILD	AVAILABLE_W_EDIT_LINK	04/22/2011	1044508116385059
SERT	111	SERT	ADMIN 01	ADMIN	2 weeks ago	3	en	YES	RUN_AND_BUILD	AVAILABLE_W_EDIT_LINK	03/03/2011	1044508116385059

Figure 4-33. *The Application Attributes report*

While no changes to any of the application attributes can be made here, a couple of columns are of interest securitywise. The Build Status and Application Status columns show those corresponding attributes for an application. Discussed in Chapter 5, these attributes control whether an application can be edited by a developer and whether an application is available to end users.

Build Status Report

The Build Status report displays the corresponding build status for all applications across all workspaces, as shown in Figure 4-34.

Edit	Workspace ▲	Application	Application Name	Parsing Schema	Build Status	Updated	Pages
✏	FWK	998	Starter Application	FRAMEWORK	Run and Build Application	2 weeks ago	2
✏	FWK	999	Shared Components Master	FRAMEWORK	Run and Build Application	2 weeks ago	0
✏	FWK	1000	Launchpad	FRAMEWORK	Run and Build Application	2 weeks ago	4
✏	NEW FEATURES	122	Sample Database Application	NEW_FEATURES	Run and Build Application	2 weeks ago	29
✏	PLPDF_DEMO	139	PLPDF	PLPDF_DEMO	Run and Build Application	2 weeks ago	10
✏	PLPDF_DEMO	138	Sample Database Application	PLPDF_DEMO	Run and Build Application	2 weeks ago	25
✏	SEOUC	126	Sample Database Application	SEOUC	Run and Build Application	2 weeks ago	26
✏	SEOUC	131	Help Desk	SEOUC	Run and Build Application	2 weeks ago	15
✏	SERT	200	Enkitec eSERT 2.1	SV_SERT_APEX	Run Application Only	2 weeks ago	211
✏	SERT	100	XSS	SV_SERT_APEX	Run Application Only	44 hours ago	7

Figure 4-34. *The Build Status report*

Editing an application allows the administrator to change the build option of that application, as shown in Figure 4-35.

Figure 4-35. *Editing the build option of an application*

There are two possible options for this setting: Run Application Only and Run and Build Application. Run Application Only will prevent any APEX user—developer or workspace administrator—from editing the application itself. Run and Build Application is the default and will allow the application to run and be edited by an APEX developer or administrator. A developer can change this setting to Run Application Only but cannot change it back to Run and Build Application. Only a workspace administrator or instance administrator can do that.

For nonruntime production instances of APEX, all applications should be set to Run Application Only. This will ensure that no developers will be able to modify any part of the application at all.

Monitor Activity

The Monitor Activity section provides a range of reports that display monitoring and logging information across all workspaces and applications. In the workspace administration console, there is a similar section that looks almost completely identical to this one. The only difference is that the reports in the workspace administration console only report on data associated with the application(s) of that workspace.

Many of these reports are security related because reports for all of the APEX logs can be found here. The information in these reports does not do much good if they are not regularly monitored for anomalies. For instance, if someone is attempting to break into an account or accounts, those attempts will be recorded and available in the Login Attempts report. If no one is monitoring this report, then the break-in attempt will go undetected, and the malicious user may have enough time to eventually compromise an account with a weak password.

If the instance of APEX is set to run in runtime mode or access to the instance administration console is disabled, these reports will not be available. Thus, it will be the responsibility of the APEX instance administrator to monitor the logs via either a custom-built APEX application, SQL Developer, or any other reporting tool that can connect to the APEX database.

All of the data presented in the logs in the Monitor Activity section is available via the APEX views. APEX views are secured based on the embedded workspace to parse-as schema mappings. Thus, if the APEX views are queried from outside of APEX from a schema associated with a workspace, only data from that workspace is returned. If that schema has the APEX_ADMINISTRATOR_ROLE granted to it or if the user connects as either SYS or SYSTEM, then all workspace data will be included in the results.

To view the APEX views as they would appear in the instance administration console while the instance is in runtime mode, an administrator could grant the APEX_ADMINISTRATOR_ROLE to a schema and then query the APEX views while connected directly to the database as that schema. This method is preferable over connecting as SYS or SYSTEM, because the recipient of the APEX_ADMINISTRATOR_ROLE cannot perform DBA-type tasks like SYS or SYSTEM would be able to. Additionally, that schema could be associated with a workspace, and then custom APEX monitoring applications that are built on top of the APEX views could be deployed as regular applications, the only difference being that only the instance administrator would be able to access them.

One thing to keep in mind about the APEX views used for logging is that, by default, the data is retained for only about a month or so. Thus, all of the reports in the Realtime Monitor Reports section will go back only as far as the least recent log entry. APEX will archive summary data and make that available in the Archived Activity section. However, the data that is archived is summary data and does not contain the individual rows. In almost every case, this level of data is not sufficient for auditing purposes.

This limitation is important to keep in mind, because several of the select lists throughout the Monitor Activity section make reference to longer time periods. Those select lists—some of which claim to display data for periods up to a year—are not dynamically adjusted based on the amount of data that is being retained.

Realtime Monitor Reports

The Realtime Monitor Reports are all based on the most up-to-date logs that APEX has available. Reports here mostly focus on two APEX views: APEX_WORKSPACE_ACTIVITY_LOG and APEX_WORKSPACE_ACCESS_LOG. While different reports will present data in different formats or with different predicates, most of the data on this page can be traced to just a couple of logs.

Several of these reports are a bit redundant and present similar views of the same thing. This is largely because prior to the introduction of interactive reports, it was not possible for an end user to manipulate a report outside of sorting the columns. For legacy purposes, most of those original reports remain in this section.

Page Views

Any time an APEX page is viewed, including while in the development environment, it is logged in APEX_WORKSPACE_ACTIVITY_LOG. The Page Views report breaks down that data in a number of different ways, as shown in Figure 4-36.

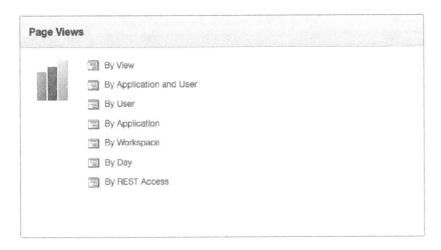

Figure 4-36. *The available Page Views reports*

The By View report, shown in Figure 4-37, will show each discrete page view, no matter what the application. It can be sorted or filtered almost any way, because it is an APEX interactive report.

Time	User	Workspace	Application	Page	Page Name	Elapsed	Page Mode	Information	Content	Component
3 seconds ago	admin	internal	4050	30	Activity by Page View	0.06	Partial Page	-	0	ACTIVITY BY PAGE VIEW
4 seconds ago	admin	internal	4050	30	Activity by Page View	0.02	Dynamic	-	0	ACTIVITY BY PAGE VIEW
12 seconds ago	admin	internal	4050	30	Activity by Page View	0.08	Partial Page	-	0	ACTIVITY BY PAGE VIEW
17 seconds ago	admin	internal	4050	30	Activity by Page View	0.02	Dynamic	-	0	ACTIVITY BY PAGE VIEW
24 seconds ago	admin	internal	4050	30	Activity by Page View	0.11	Partial Page	-	0	ACTIVITY BY PAGE VIEW
26 seconds ago	admin	sample	157	2	Page 2	0.03	Dynamic	-	0	PAGE 2
27 seconds ago	admin	sample	157	1	Home	0.03	Dynamic	-	0	HOME
28 seconds ago	admin	sample	157	4	Page 4	0.03	Dynamic	-	0	PAGE 4
29 seconds ago	admin	sample	157	1	Home	0.03	Dynamic	-	0	HOME
30 seconds ago	admin	sample	157	5	Page 5	0.08	Dynamic	-	0	PAGE 5

Figure 4-37. *The By View report*

The By Application and User report will list which user has logged into which application and display some performance and page view metrics, as shown in Figure 4-38. This report would be useful in determining which users were more active than others. For example, a user with an unusually high number of page views could be deemed suspicious because they may be trying to manually export large volumes of data or trying to access components that they are not allowed to see.

Workspace	Application	User	Median Elapsed	Maximum Elapsed	Minimum Elapsed	Page Views ▾	Content
INTERNAL	4550	nobody	0.008	11.655	0.007	4,362	0
INTERNAL	4050	ADMIN	0.089	33.160	0.010	1,011	0
SERT	4000	ADMIN	0.185	21.318	0.011	311	0
SERT	4600	ADMIN	0.109	9.421	0.008	121	0
PLPDF_DEMO	4500	ADMIN	0.049	1.314	0.011	103	0
SAMPLE	4000	ADMIN	0.150	23.109	0.014	100	0
FWK	4000	ADMIN	0.149	2.648	0.022	90	0
INTERNAL	4500	nobody	0.018	13.028	0.009	71	0
PLPDF_DEMO	4000	ADMIN	0.170	1.752	0.071	71	0
SHADOW	4600	ADMIN	0.079	0.958	0.008	67	0

Figure 4-38. The By Application and User report

Next, the By Users report, as illustrated in Figure 4-39, focuses more on the individual users and their associated metrics. Users with unusually high values for Page Views, Report Rows, or IP Addresses could be deemed suspicious for the same reasons described in the previous section.

Workspace	User Name	Page Views ▾	Percentage	Report Rows	IP Addresses	Total Elapsed	Average Elapsed	Distinct Hours	Distinct Days	Content
internal	Unauthenticated User	4,555	61.44	0	2	137.83	0.03	46	17	0
internal	admin	1,074	14.49	10,676	2	217.42	0.20	39	14	0
sert	admin	619	8.35	2,435	2	275.37	0.44	22	10	0
plpdf_demo	admin	251	3.39	692	1	44.09	0.18	3	2	0
sample	admin	208	2.81	215	1	92.99	0.45	6	4	0
-	admin	192	2.59	259	1	34.10	0.18	2	2	0
shadow	admin	171	2.31	231	1	34.61	0.20	1	1	0
fwk	admin	108	1.46	179	1	23.33	0.22	1	1	0
sert	Unauthenticated User	79	1.07	0	2	10.70	0.14	13	7	0
data	admin	48	0.65	46	1	8.10	0.19	2	2	0

Figure 4-39. The By Users report

The By Applications report provides a hybrid report and histogram that illustrates the number of page views for the corresponding application, as shown in Figure 4-40. Applications with an abnormally large numbers of page views in relation to the other applications could be the subject of some sort of attack and should be investigated further. Unfortunately, there is no way to link directly to the application in question. Instead, navigate to the By View report and create a filter on the application ID of the suspicious application.

Workspace	Application	Application Name	Page Views ▼	Percentage	Graph
INTERNAL	4050	Oracle APEX Internal Administration	98	41.35	
SERT	105	Sample Database Application MASTER	63	26.58	
INTERNAL	4000	Oracle APEX AppBuilder	25	10.55	
INTERNAL	4550	Oracle APEX Login	14	5.91	
SAMPLE	157	ADMIN 01	13	5.49	
SERT	103	4.0 New Features	10	4.22	
INTERNAL	4500	Oracle APEX SQL Workshop	5	2.11	
SERT	104	Ask the Expert 0.9	3	1.27	
SERT	100	XSS	2	0.84	
SERT	101	Sample Database Application	2	0.84	

Figure 4-40. *The By Applications report*

The By Workspace report looks almost identical to the By Applications report but rather summarizes the data by workspace. While it may be cause for alarm if any one workspace has a significantly higher number of page views than the rest, it may also be completely normal, because without looking at the corresponding number of applications, the data presented here is a bit vague. Instead of using the By Workspace report, it would be more interesting and revealing to use the By Applications report with a break on the Workspace column, as shown in Figure 4-41.

Workspace ☑

Workspace : INTERNAL

Application	Application Name	Page Views ▼	Percentage	Graph
4600	Oracle Application Express Learn More	9	0.12	
4800	Oracle APEX Team Development	8	0.11	

Workspace : PLPDF_DEMO

Application	Application Name	Page Views	Percentage	Graph
139	PLPDF	64	0.85	

Workspace : SAMPLE

Application	Application Name	Page Views	Percentage	Graph
157	ADMIN 01	13	0.17	

Workspace : SERT

Application	Application Name	Page Views	Percentage	Graph
105	Sample Database Application MASTER	63	0.83	

Figure 4-41. *The By Application report, with a break on Workspace*

The By Day report simply summarizes the number of page views for each day. Should a suspicious number of page views be discovered, the details would have to be investigated via the By View report.

Lastly, the By REST Access report displays any access to a region that was exposed as a RESTful web service. If this feature is not enabled, there should be no data here. Otherwise, any time a RESTful report is accessed, it will be logged and displayed in this report.

Calendar Reports

Despite their name, only one of the three calendar reports is actually a calendar. The other two have to do with dates but are standard APEX reports. The Workspace Last Used report displays the last time a workspace was accessed by a developer or administrator. It does not take into consideration the applications within the workspace.

The By Day by Application and User is the sole calendar report of the group. It displays the total number of page views, users, and applications for each day of the week in a calendar report, as shown in Figure 4-42. Presenting the data on a calendar may make it easier to spot trends that may otherwise go undetected in a traditional report.

Figure 4-42. *The By Day by Application User calendar report*

Last is the By Hour report. This report displays a wide variety of page view metrics broken out by hour of the day, as shown in Figure 4-43.

Hour	Page Events	Page Views	Page Processing	Maximum Elapsed	Minimum Elapsed	Average Elapsed	Cached Regions	Distinct Users	Distinct Minutes	Distinct Applications	Distinct Pages
2012.11.11 22	13	13	0	.189505	.021677	0.07	0	1	4	1	1
2012.11.11 21	222	222	0	1.018358	.00571	0.07	2	2	23	10	37
2012.11.11 20	85	85	0	6.092626	.010857	0.35	0	2	7	5	28
2012.11.11 19	24	24	0	1.035899	.061677	0.28	0	2	2	2	21
2012.11.11 12	9	9	0	.878471	.071824	0.32	0	2	2	2	5
2012.11.10 08	21	21	0	.808079	.021522	0.17	0	2	3	2	7
2012.11.09 11	17	17	0	1.540449	.031836	0.38	0	2	4	3	6
2012.11.08 20	113	113	0	.379038	.014513	0.05	0	1	13	2	7
2012.11.08 19	133	133	0	4.642539	.00877	0.18	4	3	24	5	40
2012.11.08 18	18	18	0	.516649	.06964	0.15	0	2	6	3	8

Figure 4-43. *The By Hour report*

While the raw data itself is interesting, it is a lot more revealing to display this data in a chart, such as shown in Figure 4-44. This way, outlier data points become much more obvious, potentially revealing suspicious activity.

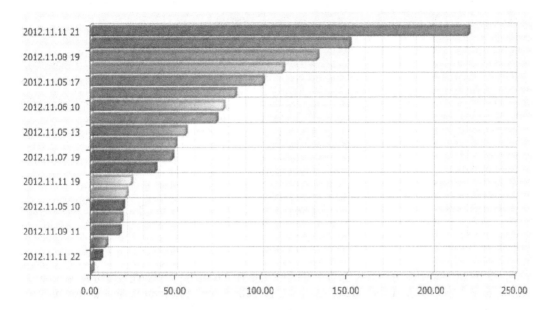

Figure 4-44. *The By Hour report, shown as a chart*

Should more sophisticated or precise charting be required, a custom APEX application could be built on top of the APEX views and configured to meet any specific requirement.

Login Attempts Reports

The Login Attempts reports are critical to the overall security of an instance of APEX because they are the sole source of detecting a potential hacking attempt. The first report—also called Login Attempts—shows all attempts at logging into any APEX application, including the development environment. Figure 4-45 shows a sample of this report.

Login Name	Workspace	Application	Owner	Authentication Result	Authentication Method	Access Date ▲	Accessed	Custom Status
ADMIN	SERT	4500	APEX_040200	Normal, successful authentication	Internal Authentication	10/15/2012 10:17:12 PM	3 weeks ago	-
ADMIN	SERT	4500	APEX_040200	Normal, successful authentication	Internal Authentication	10/16/2012 06:24:08 AM	3 weeks ago	-
ADMIN	SERT	200	SV_SERT_APEX	Normal, successful authentication	APEX Authentication	10/16/2012 06:24:27 AM	3 weeks ago	-
ADMIN	INTERNAL	4500	APEX_040200	Account Expired	Internal Authentication	10/16/2012 07:13:10 PM	3 weeks ago	Password Expired
ADMIN	INTERNAL	4500	APEX_040200	Incorrect Password	Internal Authentication	10/16/2012 07:13:42 PM	3 weeks ago	Invalid Login Credentials
ADMIN	INTERNAL	4500	APEX_040200	Normal, successful authentication	Internal Authentication	10/16/2012 07:13:52 PM	3 weeks ago	-
ADMIN	PLPDF_DEMO	4500	APEX_040200	Normal, successful authentication	Internal Authentication	10/16/2012 07:15:17 PM	3 weeks ago	-
ADMIN	PLPDF_DEMO	139	PLPDF_DEMO	Normal, successful authentication	Application Express Authentication	10/16/2012 07:15:29 PM	3 weeks ago	-
ADMIN	INTERNAL	4500	APEX_040200	Normal, successful authentication	Internal Authentication	10/17/2012 06:59:03 AM	3 weeks ago	-
ADMIN	-	4500	APEX_040200	Password First Use	Internal Authentication	10/17/2012 07:10:28 AM	3 weeks ago	Invalid Login Credentials

Figure 4-45. *The Login Attempts report*

The Authentication Result column will display the actual result of the login attempt. When a user provides a valid user name and password, the result here will be normal, successful authentication. If for some reason the user did not successfully authenticate, the reason why the result failed will be displayed here. The Custom Status column can also provide additional details as to why a failed attempt occurred.

The Developer Last Login report displays the last login time, IP address, and agent of the most recent successful authentication for each developer, as shown in Figure 4-46. Unsuccessful login attempts are not reported here.

Workspace	User	Login ▼	IP Address	Agent
INTERNAL	ADMIN	81 minutes ago	192.168.191.1	Mozilla/5.0 (Macintosh; Intel Mac OS X 10.8; rv:16.0) Gecko/20100101 Firefox/16.0
SERT	ADMIN	14 hours ago	192.168.191.1	Mozilla/5.0 (Macintosh; Intel Mac OS X 10.8; rv:16.0) Gecko/20100101 Firefox/16.0
SAMPLE	ADMIN	14 hours ago	192.168.191.1	Mozilla/5.0 (Macintosh; Intel Mac OS X 10.8; rv:16.0) Gecko/20100101 Firefox/16.0
INTERNAL	USER	6 days ago	192.168.191.1	Mozilla/5.0 (Macintosh; Intel Mac OS X 10.8; rv:16.0) Gecko/20100101 Firefox/16.0
SERT	SV_DEV	2 weeks ago	192.168.191.1	Mozilla/5.0 (Macintosh; Intel Mac OS X 10_8_2) AppleWebKit/536.26.14 (KHTML, like Gecko) Version/6.0.1 Safari/536.26.14
PLPDF_DEMO	ADMIN	3 weeks ago	192.168.191.1	Mozilla/5.0 (Macintosh; Intel Mac OS X 10_8_2) AppleWebKit/536.26.14 (KHTML, like Gecko) Version/6.0.1 Safari/536.26.14
SHADOW	ADMIN	3 weeks ago	192.168.191.1	Mozilla/5.0 (Macintosh; Intel Mac OS X 10.8; rv:15.0) Gecko/20100101 Firefox/15.0.1
DATA	ADMIN	3 weeks ago	192.168.191.1	Mozilla/5.0 (Macintosh; Intel Mac OS X 10.8; rv:15.0) Gecko/20100101 Firefox/15.0.1
FWK	ADMIN	3 weeks ago	127.0.0.1	Mozilla/5.0 (X11; Linux i686; rv:12.0) Gecko/20100101 Firefox/12.0
ENKITEC	ADMIN	6 weeks ago	192.168.191.1	Mozilla/5.0 (Macintosh; Intel Mac OS X 10_8_2) AppleWebKit/536.26.14 (KHTML, like Gecko) Version/6.0.1 Safari/536.26.14

Figure 4-46. *The Developer Last Login report*

When using a custom authentication scheme, it is critical to properly instrument that scheme to call the APEX_UTIL.SET_AUTHENTICATION_RESULT API as part of the function. Failure to do this will result in the Authentication Result column being set to Unknown User Name regardless of what actually happened. Therefore, it will seem as if every attempt to log in to your application was done from a user who doesn't exist.

The APEX_UTIL.SET_AUTHENTICATION_RESULT API takes in one numeric parameter. According to the APEX documentation, it claims that any numeric value is acceptable and even cites using values of 24567 and -666. The reality is that there is a finite set of values that should be called here, each of which returns a meaningful message into the Authentication Result column based on the actual result of the authentication. Table 4-2 outlines the valid codes and corresponding messages for the APEX_UTIL.SET_AUTHENTICATION_RESULT API.

Table 4-2. *Valid Codes and Their Corresponding Results for the*
APEX_UTIL.SET_AUTHENTICATION_RESULT API

Code	Authentication Result
0	Normal, successful authentication
1	Unknown User Name
2	Account Locked
3	Account Expired
4	Incorrect Password
5	Password First Use
6	Maximum Login Attempts Exceeded
7	Unknown Internal Error

In addition to setting the Authentication Result column, it is also possible to provide a value for the Custom Status column when a login attempt occurs. To do this, simply pass any message to the APEX_UTIL.SET_CUSTOM_AUTH_STATUS API as part of the custom authentication scheme. The message passed to this API will then be recorded in the Custom Status column of the Login Attempts report.

Please see Chapter 8 for more details on how to instrument a custom authentication scheme with calls to both APEX_UTIL.SET_AUTHENTICATION_RESULT and APEX_UTIL.SET_CUSTOM_AUTH_STATUS.

Developer Activity Reports

The Developer Activity reports provide a high-level summary of all changes that developers or workspace administrators make to their corresponding applications. Unfortunately, there is little actionable information available in either of the reports here. For specific developer activity reports, log into a workspace as a workspace administrator and view the Developer Activity reports. Please see Chapter 5 for more details of the Developer Activity reports.

Archived Activity Reports

The Archived Activity reports provide high-level summary data of all page views. There are no detail records archived, so any anomaly that warrants further investigation cannot be done from the built-in APEX logs alone. This is yet another reason for creating a better, custom log archival solution that retains all APEX log data indefinitely, in the case that it is needed.

Dashboard Report

The Dashboard provides summary data for top users, workspaces, and applications for a specific period. The data is displayed in chart format and can be clicked to view the summary records, as shown in Figure 4-47.

Figure 4-47. *The Dashboard report*

Like all other APEX logs, the data here is subject to deletion based on the retention settings.

Summary

While the APEX instance administrator is a critical role within an organization, it by no means is a time-consuming one. Once the initial settings of an instance are set and locked down, most of the day-to-day administration can be easily and safely delegated to the individual workspace administrators.

However, constant attention must be paid to the APEX logs in order to identify any illicit attempt to access the system or, even more likely, suspicious activity by authorized users. Since APEX purges logs every couple of weeks, it may be necessary to build and deploy a more robust archiving system as well so that all events will be audited and retained forever.

CHAPTER 5

Workspace Settings

In an APEX environment, a *workspace* is what matches developers with applications. It's where all of the hard work to design, develop, and deploy an application takes place. Fortunately, APEX makes it quite simple to configure and manage any number of workspaces within an instance of APEX.

Since APEX is designed to be a multitenant environment, there are many settings that can be managed at the individual workspace level. By distributing the management of the day-to-day tasks in this fashion, an instance of APEX becomes easier to manage because each workspace administrator needs to worry only about their specific workspace.

This chapter will provide an overview of the tasks of a workspace administrator. It will start by covering the different settings of a workspace and how to control access to different modules. It will then discuss some of the lesser-known yet powerful utilities available to workspace administrators. Lastly, it will conclude with an overview of the different user types and advice on how to manage users and groups.

You can find all administration utilities for a workspace on the Administration tab in the application development environment. While this tab is visible to all types of APEX users, a workspace administrator will see far more options than others. From a security point of view, it is important to understand how to configure the settings within a workspace to ensure that users cannot see data that they are not supposed to see. It is also important to understand the difference between the user roles available and what each role gives a user.

Manage Service

You can find most options for workspaces in the Manage Service section, as shown in Figure 5-1. Here, a workspace administrator can make requests for additional schemas or storage, configure which modules are available across the entire workspace, and configure module-specific options.

Figure 5-1. *The Manage Service page of the Administration section of a workspace*

While some of the options here are not directly related to security, they are worth noting.

Service Requests

Workspace administrators can make three service requests: request an additional schema to be associated with the workspace, request additional storage, or request termination of the workspace itself, as illustrated in Figure 5-2.

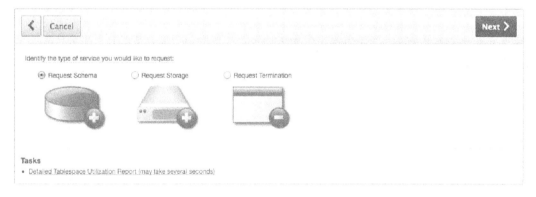

Figure 5-2. *The Make a Service Request options*

When any of these requests are made, the instance administrator is notified and can either approve or deny them via the APEX instance administration console. Only then is the result of the actual request applied or not.

A workspace can have any number of schemas associated with it. This mapping can be made directly by the instance administrator at any time or via a request from the workspace administrator. In either case, the instance administrator has to be involved in this process, so a workspace administrator cannot self-grant access to a schema.

As soon as a schema is associated with a workspace, any developer within that workspace will be able to view and manage any database objects that the schema owns or has access to. Therefore, before any additional schemas are associated with a workspace, ensure that all developers in that workspace are authorized to view the new schema's database objects and associated data.

When editing a workspace user in the Manage Users & Groups section, there is an attribute called Accessible Schemas that would seem to allow more granular developer-to-schema mappings, as shown in Figure 5-3.

Figure 5-3. *The Accessible Schema option for an APEX developer*

Unfortunately, this attribute applies only to the SQL Workshop. It has no impact on which schema a developer can access in the Application Builder. And since a developer can easily build an application to provide access to all of the parse-as schema's objects and data, this feature does not protect against a developer accessing a seemingly restricted schema. The online help for this attribute accurately states that it impacts only the SQL Workshop, but if you don't read the help documentation, it is easy to misinterpret the purpose of this attribute.

Thus, it is important to confirm that all workspace users are allowed to access a schema before it is associated with a workspace. If you cannot confirm this, then you might have to create an additional workspace that contains the mapping of the new schema and only those developers authorized to see it.

Workspace Preferences

Workspace administrators can also manage several workspace preferences. These preferences come in two categories: Account Login Control and Module Access. Account Login Control preferences are used to manage APEX account password expiration and locking conditions, as shown in Figure 5-4.

Figure 5-4. *The Account Login Control preferences*

The Account Expiration and Locking setting should be immediately enabled in each and every workspace. When enabled, accounts will be subject to a specific number of invalid passwords used to access them and a password lifetime duration. The values for these two attributes can also be altered to adhere to any specific security policies within an organization.

The remainder of the preferences are used mainly to control whether a specific module is available within the workspace, as illustrated in Figure 5-5.

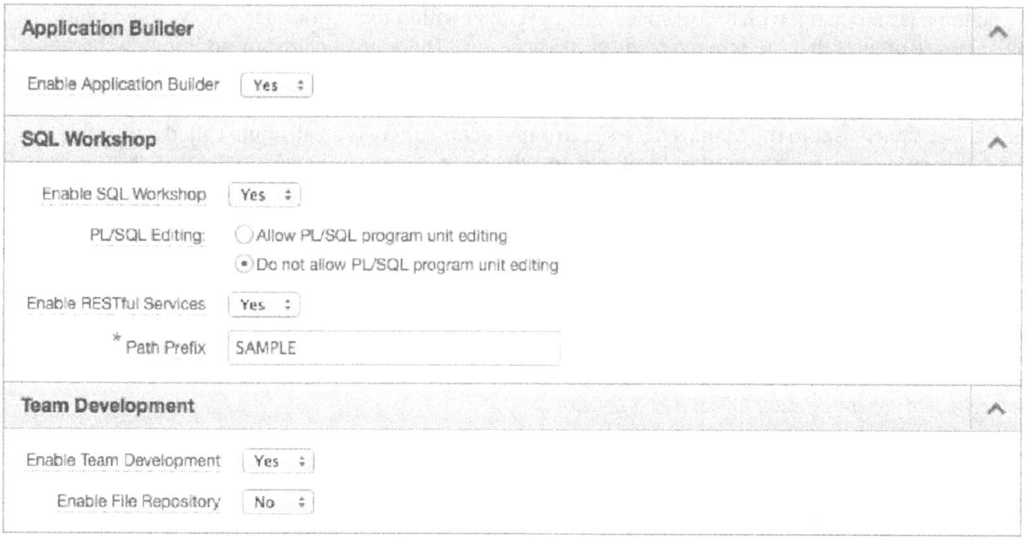

Figure 5-5. *Controlling access to each of the workspace modules*

By disabling a specific module, all access to that module is removed from all users. The workspace-level attribute will supersede what is set at the account level. For more granular control, access to each module can be controlled on a user-by-user basis.

In the SQL Workshop section, there is an attribute used to control whether RESTful services are enabled. This applies to whether a user can create RESTful services via the SQL Workshop. It has nothing to do with whether a report from an application can be published as a RESTful service. When enabled, a developer who has access to the SQL Workshop can create and publish RESTful services that expose data from the underlying schemas associated with the workspace. Thus, if there is no need to use RESTful services, then this option should be disabled.

The Workspace Announcement setting provides the workspace administrator with a tool that will display an announcement on the home page of the application development environment. As previously mentioned, the output of this attribute is not properly escaped. Therefore, a malicious workspace administrator could potentially implement a cross-site scripting attack by using this attribute. However, this possibility is quite remote, and a workspace administrator would have little to gain by this since that person already has complete control of the workspace.

Manage Meta Data

Tucked away on the right side of the page are another set of administration reports and utilities labeled Manage Meta Data. These reports and utilities allow for the more discrete management of a workspace and its associated components. Some of them provide a simple interface used to purge one type of data, while others display only data. Some of these reports are worth noting in the context of security.

The Session State link leads to a page with a number of additional reports and utilities, as shown in Figure 5-6.

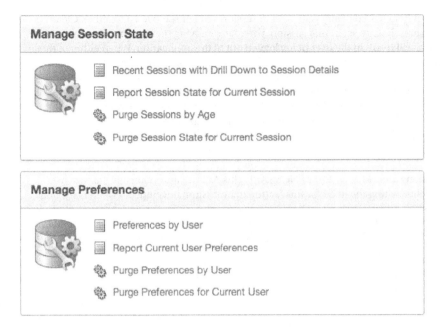

Figure 5-6. *The Manage Session State and Preferences reports*

The first report in the Session State section allows a workspace administrator to view details of any active session state from applications within the current workspace, including those in the application development environment. After selecting a session to inspect, both the session details and any items and their values are displayed on the next page, as illustrated in Figure 5-7.

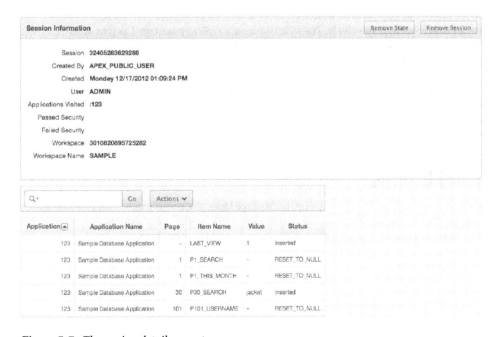

Figure 5-7. *The session details report*

Additionally, the session can be either cleared of any values set in session state or removed altogether. Clearing the session will simply remove any values that are set in that session, whereas removing the session will terminate the session and any associated values and will result in the user being logged out of the application. When either of those options is selected, there is no confirmation page or alert. The action selected will be performed immediately and cannot be undone.

Workspace administrators can use these reports to assist in troubleshooting issues from users. Here, they can view any item set in a user's session state and compare that against the expected results. This greatly assists in the troubleshooting process because users do not always communicate the most accurate results when encountering an issue.

Sessions can also be purged based on how old they are via the Purge Sessions report. Unfortunately, there is no other metric than can be used when purging a batch of sessions.

On a similar note, the workspace administrator can also view and purge user preferences. Preferences are defined in an APEX application by calling the APEX_PREFERENCES API. This API will automatically manage user preferences in internal APEX tables, eliminating the need for this feature to be custom developed. Preference values can be purged only on a per-user basis.

The next utility in the Manage Meta Data list that has to do with application security is the application build status report. This report lists all applications within a workspace in a tabular form that allows their status and build status attributes to be updated, as illustrated in Figure 5-8.

Application ▲	Name	Status	Build Status	Group	Updated
123	Sample Database Application	Available with Edit Links	Run and Build Application	-	8 days ago
142	ADMIN 02	Available with Edit Links	Run and Build Application	-	13 days ago
143	DEV 01	Available with Edit Links	Run and Build Application	-	2 hours ago
157	ADMIN 01	Available with Edit Links	Run and Build Application	-	4 weeks ago

Figure 5-8. *The application build status report*

Applications have two attributes that control their availability and whether a developer can edit them. Those attributes are called Status and Build Status, respectively. These attributes are typically managed as part of an application's shared components on a per-application basis. This report provides a place to modify these two attributes for more than one application at a time. You can find more details about the different settings for these attributes in Chapter 7.

An important thing to note when considering the build status of an application is that if a developer updates the build status to Run Application Only, that application can no longer be edited in the workspace by anyone—developer or workspace administrator alike. The only recourse at this point would be for a workspace administrator to reset that attribute to Run and Build Application using this report.

Manage Users and Groups

Most of the workspace administrator's tasks will be spent using the Manage Users & Groups pages. This is where all APEX users and groups for a specific workspace are created and managed. The instance administrator can also create and manage users from any workspace but does not have the ability to create and manage groups.

User Types

As mentioned in previous chapters, there are three types of APEX users: end users, developers, and workspace administrators. In all cases, a workspace user is specific and unique to a single workspace. For example, a user named SCOTT in workspace A would be a completely different user than one named SCOTT in workspace B. The two accounts are in no way related and could have different levels of access in their respective workspaces. A future release of APEX has pledged to allow all APEX users be managed from an external repository.

End Users

End users in APEX have little access to any part of the application development environment, save for Team Development. End users can be used in conjunction with any application developed with APEX. While this approach is simple and straightforward to implement, it is not recommended for most applications because of a number of reasons.

First, APEX end users are associated only with applications from the same workspace in which they were created. End users from workspace A would not work with applications created in workspace B, for example. This severely limits the utility of APEX end users across applications from multiple workspaces.

Second, there is no way to discretely create a user who can only manage APEX users. Since access to the workspace administrator role is an "all or nothing" approach, any user who would be able to manage users could also potentially modify applications in production or create additional developers within the workspace. Also, in order to access these controls for production applications, the instance of APEX cannot be placed in runtime mode, thus reducing the overall security footprint.

Finally, any additional user repository, regardless of whether it is APEX end users or something else, detracts from a solid identity management strategy. Duplicating credentials in multiple places make things that much harder to manage and introduces the possibility of abandoned, valid accounts when employees leave the organization without all of their credentials being revoked.

In some cases in development or training environments, using APEX end users is acceptable. First, when developing an APEX application, APEX users can be used in place of a more robust, enterprise-grade identity management system when one is not available. For testing purposes, a portion of the users and roles of a system can be mimicked with APEX users, and the application can be tested against that. APEX cannot differentiate where and how a user was authenticated, and thus all associated authorization schemes will treat a user called SCOTT the same. APEX end users can also be used in classroom or training environments where the data is artificial and security concerns about user access are low.

Developers

Most APEX users should be configured as developers. An APEX developer has full access to build any application and interact with any schema mapped to a workspace. While much of their time will be spent in the Application Builder, they typically also have access to the SQL Workshop and Team Development. Developers will also be able to see the Administration tab but have access only to a subset of its functionality.

Any individual who will be developing applications should always be assigned the developer role in APEX. The developer role has ample privileges within a workspace to be able to build both applications and the associated database objects. Only a handful of functions within a workspace cannot be executed by a user with the developer role.

Workspace Administrators

The last and most powerful user role is the workspace administrator. This role encompasses all features of the developer role but also includes the functions associated with managing the workspace. Workspace administrators are limited to managing only the workspace in which they are created. They do not have the ability to do anything outside of their specific workspace. Most of the functionality described in this chapter requires the workspace administrator role.

In most organizations, the workspace administrator role is given to one or two people for a given workspace. These people are sometimes not even developers but rather act as administrators for the workspace and are called upon only when needed. This allows a level of separation to be added between the developers and the workspace administrator that many organizational policies require.

Another way to manage workspace administration is to delegate the task to the instance administrators. Many of the day-to-day administration tasks can be done via the instance administration console. For those tasks that cannot be performed through the console, the instance administrator can easily create a workspace administrator within any workspace.

Regardless of which strategy is adopted, it is important to keep the workspace administrator account separate and out of the hands of all developers. This way, only trusted personnel will be able to manage and create users and perform other administrative tasks within the workspace.

Managing Users

One of the primary tasks that the workspace administrator will be faced with is managing workspace users and their associated options. While this task is simple and not time-consuming, it is nevertheless a critical one because it establishes access to the workspace and its associated applications and schemas.

Creating a user is simple and can be done in a single step. Simply click the Create User button on the main Manage Users & Groups page and fill out the resulting form. Editing a user results in the same form, only this time populated with information about the user being edited.

In the User Identification section, only the user name and e-mail address fields are required, as shown in Figure 5-9. All of the rest of the fields are optional but, in many cases, should be completed with at least the user's first and last names.

Figure 5-9. *The User Identification region when creating or editing a user*

Next, the Account Privileges section, as shown in Figure 5-10, needs to be completed. This is where the user's role and access to modules are defined. Additionally, the default and any additional schemas that the user will have access to in the SQL Workshop are defined here.

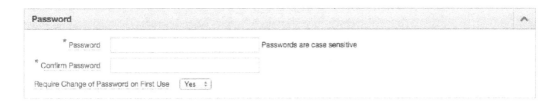

Account Privileges

Default Schema | SAMPLE ⬦
Accessible Schemas (null for all) |
User is a workspace administrator: | ○ Yes ◉ No
User is a developer: | ○ Yes ◉ No
Application Builder Access | No ⬦
SQL Workshop Access | No ⬦
Team Development Access | Yes ⬦
Set Account Availability | Unlocked ⬦

Figure 5-10. *The Account Privileges region when creating or editing user*

If an account were to be locked because of it exceeding the maximum allowed logins with an invalid password, the Set Account Availability attribute would be set to Locked. Unlocking a locked account is as simple as setting the Set Account Availability option to Unlocked and saving the user.

The next section is where the password of the user is set, as pictured in Figure 5-11. Any password entered not only must be confirmed by reentering it but also must adhere to whatever password policy was created by the instance administrator.

Password

* Password | | Passwords are case sensitive
* Confirm Password |
Require Change of Password on First Use | Yes ⬦

Figure 5-11. *The Password region when creating a user*

When editing a user, the Password region will contain two additional attributes, as shown in Figure 5-12.

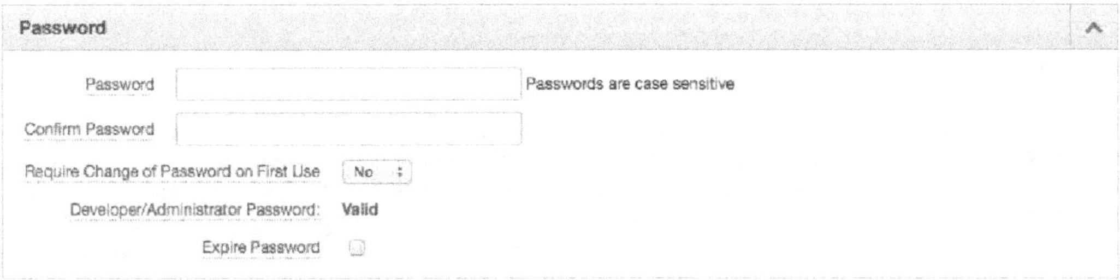

Password

Password | | Passwords are case sensitive
Confirm Password |
Require Change of Password on First Use | No ⬦
Developer/Administrator Password: | Valid
Expire Password | ☐

Figure 5-12. *The Password region when editing a user*

The first new attribute—Developer/Administrator Password—will determine whether the password is valid for the APEX development environment. The second new option—Expire Password—allows a workspace administrator to expire the user's password, automatically forcing that user to create a new password upon the next login.

Any time the password of a user is changed and the credentials are sent out in e-mail, the Require Change of Password on First Use attribute should be set to Yes. This way, the user is forced to reset their password as soon as the account is created. The new password will also have to adhere to the instance password policy as determined by the APEX instance administrator.

Lastly, the user can optionally be assigned to a group or groups, as illustrated in Figure 5-13.

Figure 5-13. *The User Groups region when creating a user*

For some reason, the User Groups region uses a different item type when creating a user versus when editing a user. The one used when creating a user is a simple multiselect list. When assigning a user to a group when creating them, simply select the corresponding group. If assigning more than one group, use either Ctrl+click on a Windows or Linux machine or Cmd+click on a Mac when selecting multiple groups.

When editing a user, the User Groups region contains a shuttle item, as shown in Figure 5-14.

Figure 5-14. *The User Groups region when editing a user*

In this case, simply either double-click a group to move it from one side to another or use the built-in controls. Upon completion of creating or editing a user, simply click either Create or Apply Changes to complete the task.

Managing Groups

Groups in APEX are simply collections of users that are can be mapped to some form of security role. Each workspace can contain any number of groups. Groups themselves are not hierarchical, meaning that all groups are peers of one another and membership in a single group will not automatically include membership in another group.

Mapping users to groups is done at the user level, where any number of groups can be assigned to a single user. Because of this design, groups work best when used in conjunction with APEX users. If an authorization scheme other than APEX users is used, then APEX groups are relatively useless. In this case, it is recommended to create and manage groups and user-to-group associations outside of APEX in a table or via LDAP.

Creating a group is fairly straightforward. From the Administration home page, click the Manage Users and Groups icon. At the top of the page, there is a Groups tab, immediately next to the Users tab, as highlighted in Figure 5-15.

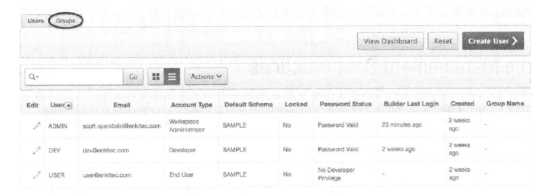

Figure 5-15. *The Manage Users & Groups page, with the Groups tab circled*

Click that tab to switch to the Manage Groups page. To create a group, click the Create User Group button. Next, simply fill out the form with a group name and optionally a description, as shown in Figure 5-16.

Figure 5-16. *Creating a new user group*

Clicking Create Group will do just that. To assign the group to a specific user or users, edit the user, and in the User Groups region, select the group or groups that user is to be assigned. This process will have to be repeated for each user.

To determine whether a user is a member of a specific group, the API APEX_UTIL.CURRENT_USER_IN_GROUP can be called. When passed the name of a group, the API will return a TRUE if the currently logged in user is a member of that group or a FALSE if they are not. A call to this API can be associated with an authorization scheme, and then APEX components associated with that scheme would be accessible only by members of that group. You can find more details on authorization schemes in Chapter 9.

Monitor Activity

The Monitor Activity section in a workspace contains a similar set of the reports available from the instance administration console. While there are a few subtle differences in reports, the major difference between the workspace reports and their counterparts at the instance level is that the workspace reports contain data only from that specific workspace.

While it is possible that the responsibility for monitoring an instance of APEX be delegated to the respective workspace administrators, that is rarely the case. Typically, this falls on the shoulders of the instance administrator. Thus, the workspace administrator is typically not concerned with monitoring the workspace for usage and potential hackers, especially in a development environment.

Refer to Chapter 4 to see more details about the specific reports that have to do with security. Keep in mind that when similar reports are run within a workspace, only activity and applications from that workspace will appear in the data.

Workspace Management Best Practices

Perhaps one of the most common oversights that are made about workspaces in a development environment is that little or even no real security needs to be applied to them. Organizations simply make all developers administrators and allow weak passwords to be used. This approach of lax security is anything but a best practice. All workspaces—whether on the development, test, or production server—need to be secured and treated as if they were production. The same or at least similar security principles and criteria should be applied everywhere.

The following list highlights some of the best practices that should be applied when managing APEX workspaces:

Use HTTPS to access the APEX development environment: An instance administrator can restrict access to the APEX development environment to only HTTPS. This is recommended so that all data that is displayed on a development instance is also encrypted. It is not only likely but also probable that your developers have changed their passwords to match those on either production or even other applications, internal or external. Thus, ensuring that these passwords are encrypted as they travel from their local PCs to the web server is of utmost importance.

Use HTTPS to secure any and all applications: Using HTTPS for the APEX development environment is not enough. All applications should also be configured to use only HTTPS so that any actual data that is displayed is also encrypted. In many organizations, the development instance is a clone of the production instance and little, if any, effort is put forth to obfuscate the actual data. To ensure that this data is secured, HTTPS should also be enforced at the application level. You can find details on how to configure an application to use only HTTPS in Chapter 6.

Ensure that developers are given the developer role: It cannot be stressed enough that developers should be given the developer role, not the workspace administrator role. The developer role provides adequate functionality for developers to do their job. A designated individual and perhaps a backup can act as workspace administrators, or the task can be delegated to the instance administrator.

Maintain a strong password policy: The password policy in a development workspace should be as strict and robust as that on production. Longer, more complex passwords are better, and keeping the interval at which they need to be changed shorter is best. Also, ensure that after four or five invalid password attempts the account will be locked and require the assistance of a workspace or instance administrator to unlock.

Remove stale or terminated users: Since APEX users cannot easily be synchronized with a central identity management system, it is up to the workspace administrator to be proactive and ensure that as developers leave the organization for whatever reason, their APEX accounts are summarily expired and/or deleted. This is especially important in an environment where contractors are present because they tend to come and go much more often than full-time employees. Stale accounts present a simple way for malicious ex-employees or contractors to access the database and cause all kinds of trouble.

Summary

Securely managing a workspace is neither a difficult nor involved task. But it is something that does need to be taken seriously because APEX users have the same access to the database as schemas do. After configuring some of the workspace options and ensuring that both the workspace and applications are running over HTTPS, only occasional service and user-related tasks will need to be addressed, all of which take only minutes to complete.

CHAPTER 6

Application Settings

Securing an instance of APEX starts at the instance level and continues down to the workspace level. However, merely securing a few attributes or even putting the entire instance in runtime mode is nowhere near enough protection to completely secure your applications. Some of the most important security settings can be controlled only at the application level. Fortunately, many of these settings are declarative in nature, making it relatively simple to secure.

This chapter is dedicated to outlining these attributes and the best values for the most secure applications possible. It starts with the highest level of settings—those at the application level—and drills down from there to attributes on pages and even regions that need to be configured properly. It also discusses one of APEX most powerful constructs—conditions—and why using them for security is not always the best idea. It concludes with a brief discussion of securing mobile applications.

This chapter also discusses how to use an automated security tool, such as Enkitec's eSERT. Such tools save a tremendous amount of time and also detect potential vulnerabilities that developers may have missed.

Application Settings

Each application contains a fixed set of attributes that control the high-level properties of the application. Found in an application's shared components, these settings can be broken up into four categories in APEX 4.2: Definition, Security, Globalization, and User Interface. APEX 4.1 and some previous releases did not have the User Interface section but did contain the other three. Each of these sections contains a group of attributes that controls how the application runs, applies security, works in an international environment, and renders, respectively.

While it is obvious that the Security section has a lot to do with security, there are several key attributes that can be found in the Definition and User Interface sections that are covered here as well.

Definition

The Definition section of an application contains a number of attributes that impact everything from the name and alias of the application to whether it can be edited. Most of the attributes here have a direct correlation to the overall security of an application. In some cases, the values specified in a development instance will be different from those in a production instance.

Logging

Logging determines whether page views are logged automatically by APEX to the table APEX_WORKSPACE_ACTIVITY_LOG. Starting in APEX 4.2, there is an instancewide feature that, when enabled, will automatically set this attribute to Yes for all applications. This setting cannot be overridden by anyone at the workspace level, even a workspace administrator. If this setting is disabled, then the Logging attribute can be set on a per-application basis by either a developer or workspace administrator.

All applications should have their Logging attribute to Yes, either by forcing it from the instance level on down or by doing it for each application. This way, all page views from within an application get recorded to the internal APEX logs, where they can be inspected in the case of suspicious or malicious activity.

As mentioned in Chapter 4, APEX will store at most up to a year or so worth of log data. If a longer period of data is required, then a custom routine will need to be set up to archive older data to a more permanent place.

Debugging

The Debugging attribute of an application determines whether an application can be run in debug mode. While in debug mode, APEX will write detailed information about all the steps that occur as pages are rendered and processed to the central debug tables.

For development instances, this attribute is quite often enabled because the information gained from running a page in debug mode often assists developers in troubleshooting and resolving issues. However, debug mode should be disabled in production because passing the value YES through the fifth parameter of the URL for any APEX page can easily activate it. Disabling debug mode will prevent such alteration of the URL from triggering debug mode. Starting with APEX 4.2, and when logged into APEX as both a developer and user of an application in the same workspace, debug mode will always be enabled, regardless of the setting. Thus, debug mode can safely be disabled for all environments.

Also new in APEX 4.2, it is now possible to programmatically call debug mode, regardless of what the status of the Debugging attribute is set to. By using the new API APEX_DEBUG, a developer can instrument PL/SQL code to either enable or disable debug mode. Please consult the Oracle Application Express API Reference guide for more details about the capabilities of APEX_DEBUG.

Allow Feedback

While enabling this setting is not a direct security risk, it could become one if a developer modified the process that inserts the feedback into the database and introduced a SQL injection or cross-site scripting risk. In its default state, the process that is called to record feedback resembles Listing 6-1.

Listing 6-1. Default Code Used to Submit Feedback

```
apex_util.submit_feedback (
    p_comment          => :P102_FEEDBACK,
    p_type             => :P102_FEEDBACK_TYPE,
    p_application_id   => :P102_APPLICATION_ID,
    p_page_id          => :P102_PAGE_ID,
    p_email            => null);
```

Since this code is using the bind variable syntax, an attempt at passing SQL into the p_comment parameter would not result in that SQL being executed, but rather it would simply be passed into the APEX feedback table. If a developer altered the call to this API so that instead of referencing the item P102_FEEDBACK using the bind variable notation, they referenced it using the item notation, there would be the potential for a SQL injection attack.

However, if a cross-site scripting attack was implemented and malicious JavaScript was passed into the p_comment parameter, there is a chance that it could be executed when querying the APEX_TEAM_FEEDBACK view, if all columns are not properly escaped. In the Team Development module, all feedback is properly escaped, so if a cross-site scripting attack were implemented via the feedback page, it would prove to be unsuccessful when that feedback is viewed in Team Development. Custom reports on the feedback tables would need to be properly secured from such an attack.

From a security point of view, it is acceptable to use feedback in an application so as long as the default constructs or properly secured methods are used to call the feedback APIs and precautions are taken if data from `APEX_TEAM_FEEDBACK` is ever queried directly.

Compatibility Mode

New in APEX 4.2, this attribute will change some of the core behavior of the APEX engine based on the value that is selected. The intention of adding this attribute is to allow the developer to provide some legacy support for applications that do not work as well with some of the new features in APEX 4.2.

There are three options for this attribute: 4.2, 4.1, and pre-4.1. The differences are outlined here:

- *Pre 4.1*: When set to Pre 4.1, the APEX engine will allow items mapped to column names to render and process, even if the corresponding column does not exist in the underlying table. Obviously, no value is set in session state if the column mapping is incorrect. Additionally, in Pre 4.1 mode, there are two attributes that are automatically defaulted to less secure values: Browser Cache and Embed in Frames. APEX will default these two attributes to Enabled and Allowed, respectively. These settings are the least secure of those available and could cause numerous security issues. The specifics of each of these attributes are discussed later in this chapter.

- *4.1*: Setting Compatibility Mode to 4.1 requires all items mapped to a database columns to have a corresponding column in the underlying table. Failure to do so will result in an error message. Additionally, the attributes Browser Cache and Embed in Frames will respect the value that is set at the application or page level.

- *4.2*: Lastly, if Compatibility Mode is set to 4.2 (which is the default for all new applications), there are a few changes with regard to how regions are rendered and processes and computations are executed. First, all regions that are mapped to a specific display point are first evaluated to determine whether they will render. Only after all regions are evaluated will the rendering begin. In 4.1 and previous releases, regions were evaluated to determine whether they were to render and, if so, were immediately rendered. This is done to support the new grid layout feature in APEX 4.2. Additionally, computations and processes that are set to fire Before Regions and After Regions will now fire before or after any region at all is rendered, respectively. Despite the name, in APEX 4.1 and earlier releases, Before Regions and After Regions actually fired just before and just after Page Template Body (1-3), respectively.

The Compatibility Mode attribute should always be set to 4.2 or, if necessary, 4.1. Some testing and perhaps modifications may need to be made in order for the application to function properly when changing this attribute to 4.2 or even 4.1. However, as APEX as a product progresses, it will be important to ensure that all applications function properly at the latest release possible.

Application E-mail from Address

This attribute will be used when e-mails are sent from an application via an interactive report download via e-mail or subscription. While this attribute supports both a static e-mail address and an APEX item that can store an e-mail address, it is best to use a static e-mail because the APEX item will not be evaluated when an interactive report is sent out via a subscription.

Set this value to a well-monitored e-mail address so that if any issues with the reports arise, the user will have a place to easily reply to and report them.

Availability

The Availability attribute determines whether the application can be used by end users and, if not, what is displayed instead. Depending on the setting, it is used in conjunction with the "Message for unavailable application" and "Restrict to comma separated user list (status must equal Restricted Access)" attributes. The following list outlines the options for the Availability attribute:

- *Available*: This is the only setting that should be considered for a functioning application in a production environment. When Availability is set to Available, the application functions as normal but will not display the developer's toolbar when the end user is also logged into the corresponding workspace.

- *Available with Edit Links*: When Availability is set to Available with Edit Links, the application will be available for end users like it is when set to Available. However, if an end user is also signed on as an APEX developer, the developer's toolbar will be available. Since the build status of an application in production should be set to Run Application Only, the developer will not be able to make any changes anyway. Thus, using this attribute in production may be acceptable, but for consistency's sake, Available is a better option.

- *Available to Developers Only*: This option will allow only end users who are also logged in as an APEX developer to access the application. Designed to be a temporary status used during troubleshooting an issue, this option is viable only for short periods of time where access to an application needs to be restricted.

- *Restricted Access*: Setting an application's Availability option to Restricted Access will allow only those users specified in the "Restrict to comma separated user list (status must equal Restricted Access)" attribute. The users specified can be from any repository and do not have to be APEX developers. As long as the user name is in the list, they will be able to access the application. Again, this is a temporary value that should be used when actively troubleshooting an issue and other users need to be kept out.

- *Unavailable*: When Availability is set to Unavailable, the application is unavailable to all users, regardless of whether they are logged in as an APEX developer or otherwise. A simple generic message will be displayed to any user who attempts to access any portion of the application. This status is useful if access to a single application needs to be immediately halted because of a security breach or other issue.

- *Unavailable (Status shown with PL/SQL)*: Similar to Unavailable, this option will prevent any access to the application. However, rather than displaying a generic message, a PL/SQL block entered in the "Message for unavailable application" field can be called to either render a custom message or even dynamically redirect the end user to a different application or URL. For instance, a more specific message can be displayed by using a little bit of PL/SQL like this:

  ```
  htp.prn('Site will be back at 12:00 PM EST');
  ```

  Instead of a message, a line of PL/SQL can be used to redirect the user to a different application or URL entirely:

  ```
  owa_util.redirect_url('http://somewhere-else.com');
  ```

- *Unavailable (Redirect to URL)*: A slightly more limited version of Unavailable (Status shown with PL/SQL), this option will simply redirect the user to a static URL entered in the "Message for unavailable application" field.

The Availability status of an application can also be controlled via Oracle SQL Developer or with the WWV_FLOW_API API. If your instance of APEX is set to Runtime mode, this is the only way to modify the application's availability status.

From SQL Developer, connect to the database as either SYS, SYSTEM, or the parse-as schema that is associated to the application that will be modified. Expand the schema's tree to reveal all of the different objects and components. Locate the Application Express node and expand it, revealing any application associated with that schema. Next, right-click the application name, select Modify Application, and then select Status from the second menu, as illustrated in Figure 6-1.

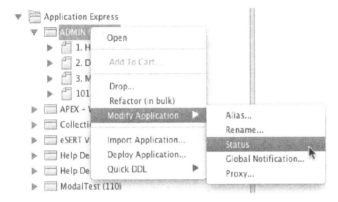

Figure 6-1. *Editing an application's availability status via SQL Developer*

Next, set Status to the level desired, and click Apply. Notice that not all values that are available within the application are presented in this list. Inspecting the SQL used to alter the application's status reveals that there are two API calls made, as shown in Listing 6-2.

Listing 6-2. The SQL Used to Change an Application's Status via SQL Developer

```
declare
  PRAGMA AUTONOMOUS_TRANSACTION;
begin
  wwv_flow_api.set_security_group_id
  (
  p_security_group_id => 1044509116395059
  );
    wwv_flow_api.set_flow_status
    (
    p_flow_id          => 117,
    p_flow_status      => 'AVAILABLE'
    );
  commit;
end;
```

The first call sets the workspace ID, while the second one sets the actual availability status of the application. By inspecting the signature of the SET_FLOW_STATUS procedure, it is evident that a couple of different parameters are not available via SQL Developer, as shown in Listing 6-3.

Listing 6-3. The Description of the WWV_FLOW_API.SET_FLOW_STATUS Procedure

```
PROCEDURE SET_FLOW_STATUS
Argument Name            Type          In/Out  Default?
----------------------   ------------  ------  -------
P_FLOW_ID                NUMBER        IN
P_FLOW_STATUS            VARCHAR2      IN
P_FLOW_STATUS_MESSAGE    VARCHAR2      IN      DEFAULT
P_RESTRICT_TO_USER_LIST  VARCHAR2      IN      DEFAULT
```

These additional parameters—p_flow_status_message and p_restrict_to_user_list—can be mapped to the "Message for unavailable application" and "Restrict to comma separated user list (status must equal Restricted Access)" attributes, respectively.

The last piece of the puzzle can be found in the HTML source of the Definition page. By inspecting the HTML for the Availability page item, you can see the valid values that can be passed to the SET_FLOW_STATUS procedure, as shown in Figure 6-2.

```
<select id="F4000_P4001_FLOW_STATUS" class="selectlist" size="1" name="p_t13">
    <option value="AVAILABLE">Available</option>
    <option selected="selected" value="AVAILABLE_W_EDIT_LINK">Available with Edit Links</option>
    <option value="DEVELOPERS_ONLY">Available to Developers Only</option>
    <option value="RESTRICTED_ACCESS">Restricted Access</option>
    <option value="UNAVAILABLE">Unavailable</option>
    <option value="UNAVAILABLE_PLSQL">Unavailable (Status Shown with PL/SQL)</option>
    <option value="UNAVAILABLE_URL">Unavailable (Redirect to URL)</option>
</select>
```

Figure 6-2. *The HTML source of the Availability item, including values*

Armed with all the parameters and valid values, it is possible to programmatically change the Availability status of an application from SQL*Plus or other SQL utility that can connect to the database. This makes the decision to move to a runtime-only environment easier because the same management tools are available outside of APEX, even if it's not as obvious as it could be.

Build Status

The Build Status setting of an application determines whether developers will be able to edit the application. If it's set to Run and Build Application, then developers will be able to modify the application in any way they see fit. If it's set to Run Application Only, then developers will not be able to even view the pages or components of an application. It will function the same when run by end users, however.

For development, the Build Status setting obviously has to be set to Run and Build Application; otherwise, it would be impossible to actually build the application. For a production environment, set the Build Status setting to Run Application Only. This will prevent any developer who needs access to the workspace from being able to edit the application on a production server.

A note of caution: once the Build Status setting is set to Run Application Only, only a workspace administrator can change it back.

Global Notification

The Global Notification attribute is designed to display its contents on every page of an application, replacing the #GLOBAL_NOTIFCATION# substitution string in templates. By default, all APEX templates contain the #GLOBAL_NOTIFCATION# substitution string. This attribute can be useful to broadcast a message to all active users of an application. For example, if an application needed to be taken offline, a message could be added to the Global Notification attribute that stated so and offered guidance as to when it would return.

Similar to the Availability attribute, the Global Notification attribute can be managed via the SQL Developer or the WWV_FLOW_API API, making the management of a runtime-only installation easier. There is, however, one security concern about the Global Notification attribute: its output is not properly escaped when rendered on a page. Thus, it is possible that a cross-site scripting attack could be implemented via the Global Notification attribute. This type of attack would have to be implemented either by a workspace administrator or by someone with access to the parse-as schema, however, making it an unlikely put possible scenario.

Substitutions

APEX provides up to 20 generic substitution strings for use in any application. These value-attribute pairs can be defined only by the developer at design time and can be named and reference any value at all. They are similar to application items in that they do not have a UI component. In fact, they act as a combination of an application item and a static computation all in one.

The benefit to using substitution strings is that it is a lot faster and easier to create a value-attribute pair because it can be done with just two fields. Despite this, they should be avoided for a couple of reasons. First, if the value of a substitution string needed to change, the entire application would need to be redeployed. Aside from editing an application in production, there is no other way to make a discrete change to the value of a substitution string.

Second, when rendered on the page using either the &ITEM. or bind variable syntax, the values of substitution string are not escaped anywhere by design—including places such as region titles, items, tabs, lists, and breadcrumb entries. Therefore, if a developer were to implement a cross-site scripting attack by using a substitution string, it would likely succeed. Although this is an unlikely scenario, it is possible.

ENKITEC'S VULNERABILITY SCANNER

Enkitec eSERT is an APEX application that quickly evaluates other APEX applications for potential security vulnerabilities. When run, eSERT produces an intuitive, easy-to-use report that highlights any vulnerability it discovers.

Figure 6-3 shows the results of a scan. Most results are green, indicating no trouble. Two of the results are red, indicating that a possible problem has been found by the scanner.

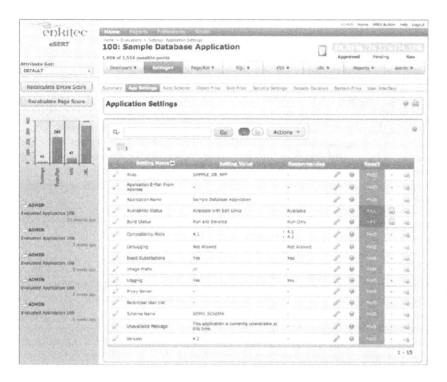

Figure 6-3. *Example of output from an eSERT scan*

eSERT also outlines the details of each vulnerability as well as the steps used to remedy it. Completely integrated with the APEX development environment, fixing any identified issue takes only seconds. For more details, please visit www.enkitec.com/esert.

Security Attributes

The security attributes of an application determine the high-level security settings for the application, including the parse-as schema, how it authenticates, session timeout, and session state protection, among other things. Unlike the Definition section, the values here are typically unchanged when moving an application from development to production.

Public User and Authentication Scheme

This attribute is a bit of an enigma. By default, it is typically set to APEX_PUBLIC_USER, and it should be left that way in almost every case. According to the APEX documentation, the value of this can be derived from APEX_APPLICATION.G_PUBLIC_USER, but as of APEX 4.2.1, this global variable does not exist.

The authentication scheme selected is the current scheme or the one that the application will use when users log in to validate their credentials. While there can be more than one authentication scheme associated with a single application, only one of them can be the current scheme at any given time. A developer can set this attribute only at design time. While there is no "correct" value for this attribute, it is important to ensure that the authentication scheme selected as the current scheme is the intended one. In many cases, an application in development may be pointed to a development LDAP server, for instance. Before promoting the application to production, ensure that the authentication scheme is pointing to the production set of credentials.

■ **Note** You can find more details on authentication schemes in Chapter 8.

Deep Linking

The Deep Linking attribute of an application determines whether users will be able to bookmark a specific page and be able to return to that page. This extra overhead is required because the bookmarked URL will likely contain a stale session ID. When enabled, the APEX engine will be able to "remember" the original page, authenticate the session, and then redirect the user to the bookmarked page.

However, there are a number of potential issues with enabling deep linking. First, if the page that is being bookmarked has session state protection enabled, the user will likely get an error when trying to view the page because the checksum bookmarked may not be what APEX expects. More details about session state protection are provided later in this chapter.

Second, a bookmarked page may cause functional issues, especially if it is the third page in a four-page wizard. Session state values may be set on the first two that determine what is displayed on the third or even fourth page. If the user skips the first two pages, then the third page may erroneously display content or items that should otherwise be hidden. To combat this, a check can be made on each page to ensure that the values on previous pages are set. If they are found to be null, then a redirect to the first page of the wizard can be initiated.

If necessary, Deep Linking can be set to Enabled and then disabled on pages where it is not appropriate. The drawback to this approach is that users will likely assume that it will work on any page and thus encounter errors on pages where it is not enabled. Thus, it may be best to simply set Deep Linking to Disabled at the application level and publish that this feature is simply not supported.

Authorization Scheme

Each application can have an authorization scheme associated it. This scheme will evaluate before every page, and if the result of the scheme is false, the user will be denied access to that application. Each and every application should have an authorization scheme associated with it to limit which users can use it.

Consider this example: a 25,000-person organization starts to use APEX. They integrate APEX with their LDAP server so that users can use their own credentials to log in and not have to remember another user name and password. They deploy their first APEX application, with the intended audience of a small group of 10 people. By not associating an authorization scheme with the application to limit who can use the application, what they have essentially done is allow any one of the 25,000 valid users to be able to log in to this application. This was clearly not the original intent. Therefore, some sort of "gatekeeper" authorization scheme should always be associated with every application in order to allow only authorized users for that application.

Run on Public Pages

Associating an authorization scheme with your application means that the authorization scheme will fire on every page—public or otherwise. This presents quite a predicament for end users. On one hand, you want to protect your application from unauthorized end users. But on the other, you at least want to give your end users a change to authenticate so that you can check to see who they are and determine whether they can run this application.

Thus, the Run on Public Pages option, when set to No, will forgo checking the authorization scheme for pages that are set to public. The idea here is that if the page was purposely set to public by the developer, it should not be restricted by the application-level authorization scheme.

Run on Public Pages should normally be set to No so that public pages can properly run. Be sure to verify that all pages that are set to public are intended to be set to public and were not accidentally left that way.

Parsing Schema

The Parsing Schema setting will be the schema in which all SQL and PL/SQL will be executed from. It can be set to any schema that is associated with the workspace, even if the developer doing the modification does not have direct access to that schema in the SQL Workshop. Parsing Schema is a required value, and while there is no correct answer, ensure that the schema selected has the appropriate privileges that the application requires and nothing more. Chapter 13 discusses techniques to limit the privileges the parse-as schema contains for better security.

Session Timeout

APEX has a built-in mechanism that allows the developer to set the maximum length of a session and the maximum session idle time permitted before a session times out. For each of these two events, the user can be directed to a different URL, as illustrated in Figure 6-4.

Figure 6-4. *The Session Timeout attributes of an application*

If either of the URLs is left blank, APEX will redirect the user to the Session Not Valid location as per the authentication scheme definition. The values specified for the Maximum Session Length and Maximum Session Idle Time settings really depend on the level of sensitivity of the application. A general rule of thumb is that the more sensitive the data, the shorter the time span. Leaving either of the duration fields will cause APEX to default to the instance-level settings.

Keep in mind that there is an APEX job—ORACLE_APEX_PURGE_SESSIONS—that is by default configured to run every hour and kill any session that is older than 24 hours. This means setting the Maximum Session Length option to a value larger than 86,400 seconds (60 seconds per minute x 60 minutes per hour x 24 hours) will have little impact because that session will be purged by the job automatically.

Session State Protection

The Session State Protection option is a feature of APEX that prevents a hacker or malicious user from changing values that are passed through the URL when calling an APEX page. It works by adding an additional checksum as part of the URL itself. Before the page is rendered, the APEX engine will compare the checksum in the URL to a precomputed value. If there is any difference at all, APEX will cease all operations and display an error message because some portion of the URL was tampered with.

The first step in getting the Session State Protection option to work is to ensure that it is enabled at the application level. This is done by simply setting it to Enabled, as shown in Figure 6-5, and saving the changes. Once it is enabled here, each page and item that needs to be protected also needs to be configured.

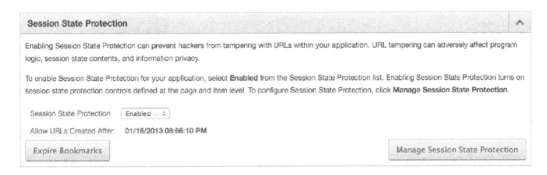

Figure 6-5. *Enabling the Session State Protection option*

Items that are protected with session state protection can be expired by clicking the Expire Bookmarks button. This will invalidate any bookmark that also includes a reference to an item that is protected. Clicking Manage Session State Protection will display a page with four additional options, as shown in Figure 6-6.

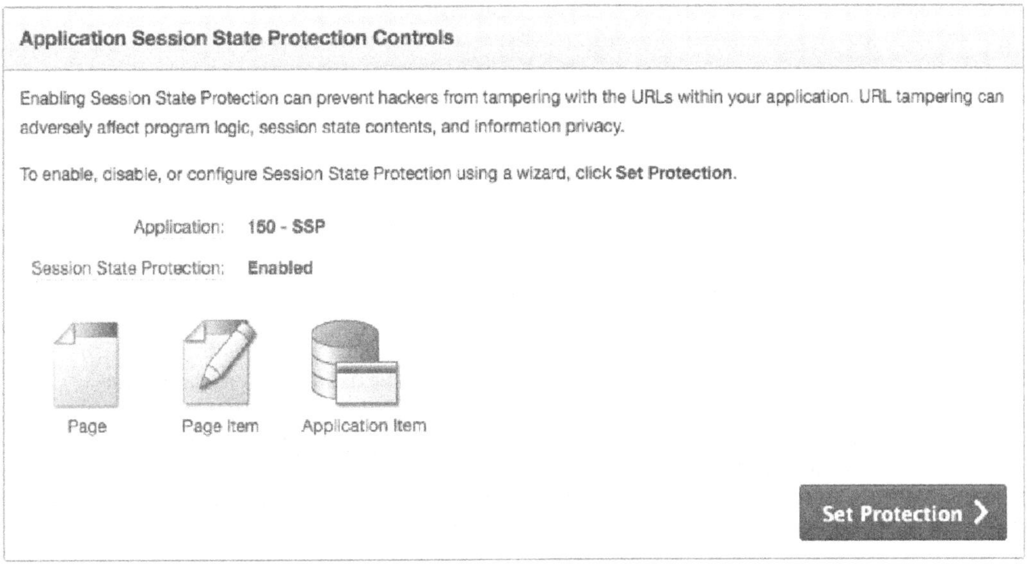

Application Session State Protection Controls

Enabling Session State Protection can prevent hackers from tampering with the URLs within your application. URL tampering can adversely affect program logic, session state contents, and information privacy.

To enable, disable, or configure Session State Protection using a wizard, click **Set Protection**.

Application: 150 - SSP

Session State Protection: **Enabled**

Page   Page Item   Application Item

Set Protection >

Figure 6-6. *The Application Session State Protection controls page*

Clicking either Page, Page Item, or Application Item will produce a report that displays the current session state protection for the respective component. That report will allow the developer to click the corresponding page number for Pages and Page Items, which will lead to the same updatable report for both components. The updatable report will allow a developer to set both the page- and item-level session state protection attributes all at once, as illustrated in Figure 6-7.

111

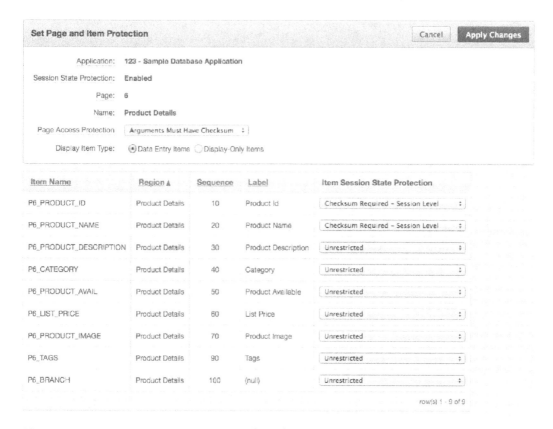

Figure 6-7. *Setting session state protection attributes for a page and its associated items*

Alternatively, the value of session state protection can be set at the page or item level, depending on which component is being secured. Session state protection for application items can be defined only as part of the application item definition.

The fourth option—Set Protection—allows the developer to enable, disable, or configure session state protection. By default, the Session State Protection option is set to Enabled, and it should be left that way. There is a third option available on this page: Configure. Configure allows the developer to pick a setting for the four categories and have that setting applied to all components within an application, as shown in Figure 6-8.

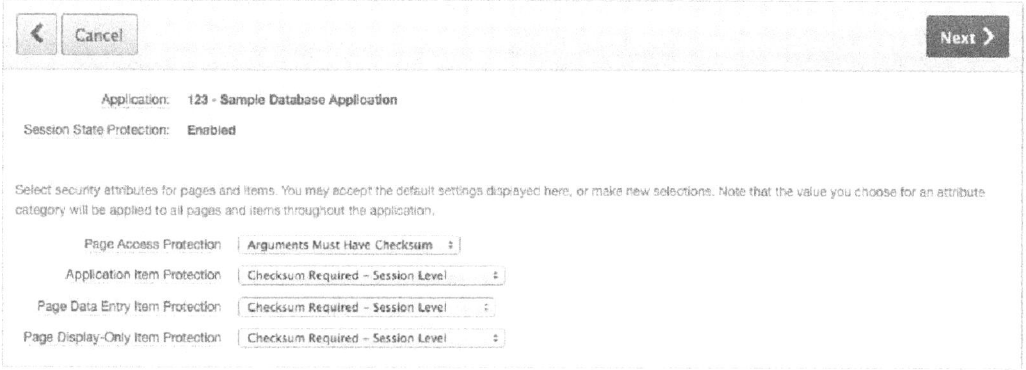

Figure 6-8. *The Configure option in session state protection*

It is best to exercise some level of caution when using the Configure option because certain parts of your application—specifically JavaScript that sets item values—may no longer function properly when session state protection is applied. Also, if the settings chosen are too strong, things such as the ability to pass parameters via the URL may stop working altogether. To be safe, it is a good idea to make a backup of your application before using the Configure feature so that it can be restored to its previous state if need be.

Again, enabling session state protection is only the first step. Additional configuration needs to be done at both the page and item levels for the feature to take effect. You can find details about how to configure pages and items with session state protection later in this chapter in the "Page & Region Settings" section and in Chapter 7.

Cache

If the Cache attribute is enabled, then the browser will store previously viewed pages in both memory and on disk. This offers a convenience to the user because they can use the back button to quickly navigate through previously viewed pages because the browser can use the copy of the page from disk rather than have to retrieve a new copy from the server. However, this convenience comes with a high price because sensitive data may be stored locally on a user's workstation, where it can be accessed by anyone who gains access to the workstation.

Thus, the Cache attribute should always be set to Disabled so that no sensitive data is left on the client. When that is done, an additional directive—Cache-Control—is sent to the browser via the HTTP header, as illustrated in Figure 6-9.

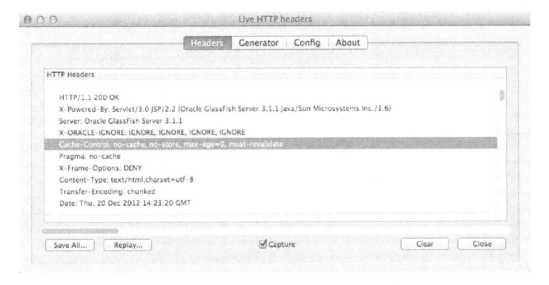

Figure 6-9. *The Cache-Control directive when the Cache attribute is set to Disabled*

A common misconception is that if a web page is served over HTTPS, it won't be cached. While this may be true from some browsers, it is not true for all. Thus, even when running over HTTPS, it is critical that the Cache attribute be set to Disabled.

Embed in Frames

One type of attack that hackers use is called *clickjacking*. The attack is relatively simple to implement. Basically, a hacker sets up a web site that displays some sort of link—say a banner ad that offers a free iPad. On that same site, the hacker also renders an iFrame with content from another site. The properties of the iFrame are set so that it is not visible, but it is actually rendered in front of the original content. When the user clicks the link for the free iPad, the click is actually registered within the iFrame. Oftentimes, the iFrame will contain content from popular sites that users don't need to authenticate to each day, like Facebook or Twitter. So, what happens is that the user thinks he is clicking an ad for an iPad when essentially the click is passed to Facebook as a "like" for a specific page. Thus, the term *clickjacking* was coined to describe this type of attack.

One of the methods used to combat this type of attack is adding the X-Frame-Options response header to all pages. When set to DENY, this directive will prevent a web page from being rendered as an iFrame if the source page's site or origin is different from its own. When set to SAMEORGIN, a page can be rendered within an iFrame only if the origin sites of both the iFrame and containing page are the same. A third option—ALLOW_FROM *uri*—allows the developer to specify a specific site that the content is allowed to render within an iFrame from.

The Embed in Frames attribute is designed to help combat these clickjacking attacks by allowing the developer to specify the value of the X-Frames-Options directive. Setting this value to Deny will prevent any page within that application from rendering within an iFrame. "Allow from same origin" will restrict the application to render only in iFrames from the same origin, and Allow will not restrict the application from rendering within iFrames at all, regardless of the origin. APEX currently does not support an option that would let a developer specify a valid site where the content could be rendered as an iFrame from.

When Embed in Frames is set to Deny and the HTTP page headers from any page in the application are inspected, the directive is clearly visible, as shown in Figure 6-10.

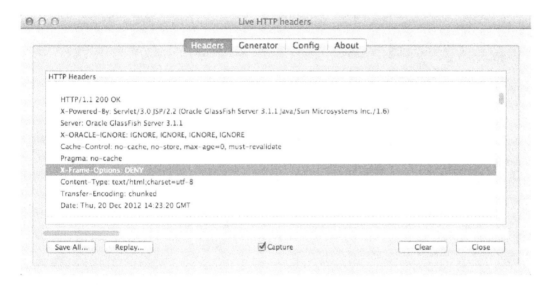

Figure 6-10. *The X-Frame-Options directive in the HTTP header*

This option should be set to at least "Allow from same origin" or Deny, depending on whether there is a legitimate need for an APEX application to be used within an iFrame. While the chance that an APEX application would be used in a clickjacking attack is small, a simple setting change can reduce that chance to zero.

HTML Escaping Mode

The core of a cross-site scripting attack has to do with being able to inject and execute an external, illicit JavaScript function on a valid web page. One of the best defenses against cross-site scripting attacks is to ensure that all data generated on the page is properly escaped. Escaping data will yield special characters, such as < and >, completely harmless. Rather than be interpreted as HTML, they will be rendered on the page just like all of the other text, and the scripts they attempted to inject will fail to execute.

The APEX engine itself goes great lengths to ensure that any output it produces is also escaped. Prior to APEX 4.2, content was escaped with the htf.escape_sc function, which is installed in conjunction with APEX. Starting with APEX 4.2, all instances of the older htf.escape_sc have been replaced with the new apex_escape.html function.

The HTML Escaping Mode attribute actually controls how apex_escape.html will escape content. When set to Basic, apex_escape.html will escape content just like htf.escape_sc did. For this reason, applications that have been upgraded from a prior release of APEX will have this attribute set to Basic. When set to Extended, apex_escape.html will escape everything that htf.escape_sc did and then some. New applications created in APEX 4.2 will have this attribute set to Extended by default.

Figure 6-11 shows the subtle differences between how the two functions escape special characters.

ASCII Character	htf.escape_sc	apex_escape.html
&	&amp;	&amp;
"	&quot;	&quot;
<	&lt;	&lt;
>	&gt;	&gt;
'	n/a	&#x27;
/	n/a	&#x2F;

Figure 6-11. *The differences between htf.escape_sc and apex_escape.html*

What is not illustrated is that the newer apex_escape.html function will also escape Unicode characters if the database or web server's character set is not set to UTF-8. This is done to protect against an attack that attempted to hide its malicious payload in Unicode characters. Because of this, the results for the same string may be longer when rendered in Extended mode versus Basic mode.

Thus, the Extended mode should be used where possible. Before switching from Basic to Extended mode on older applications, they should each be thoroughly tested to ensure that no new issues arise as a result of the change.

Initialization PL/SQL Code

Previously called and slightly misnamed "Virtual Private Database PL/SQL call to set security context" in APEX 4.0 and previous releases, the Initialization PL/SQL Code attribute is designed to give the developer a place to execute PL/SQL code before any other APEX component executes. Unlike the previous name implied, there are no limitations as to what the code executed here can do. However, this attribute is quite frequently used to set a security context that is later used in conjunction with VPD or secure views in other APEX components.

By adding a call to apex_debug.info to the Initialization PL/SQL Code attribute and running any page in debug mode, it can be seen that this code is executed just before the Before Header position, as illustrated in Figure 6-12.

20121221105054.962576	0.00724	0.00010	...Session ID 757449123832 can be used
20121221105054.962678	0.00734	0.00006	...Application session: 757449123832, user=nobody
20121221105054.962740	0.00740	0.00004	...fetch session state from database
20121221105054.962783	0.00745	0.00033	fetch items (exact)
20121221105054.963113	0.00778	0.00010	...Setting session time_zone to -05:00
20121221105054.963215	0.00788	0.00089	Session: Fetch session header information
20121221105054.964107	0.00877	0.00156	...Execute Statement: begin apex_debug.info(p_message => 'DEBUG: Init PL/SQL'); end;
20121221105054.965666	0.01033	0.00028	DEBUG: Init PL/SQL
20121221105054.965950	0.01062	0.00032	Branch point: Before Header
20121221105054.966265	0.01093	0.00127	Fetch application meta data
20121221105054.967535	0.01220	0.00016	...metadata, fetch computations
20121221105054.967694	0.01236	0.00016	...metadata, fetch buttons
20121221105054.967858	0.01252	0.00003	...http header processing
20121221105054.967886	0.01255	0.00019	...set mime type: text/html
20121221105054.968073	0.01274	0.00008	...set additional http headers
20121221105054.968150	0.01281	0.00006	Process point: BEFORE_HEADER
20121221105054.968205	0.01287	0.00005	Processes - point: BEFORE_HEADER

Figure 6-12. *Debug output from a page, highlighting where code in the Initialization PL/SQL Code attribute executed*

It is worth noting that there are several additional calls that APEX makes before the Initialization PL/SQL Code contents that are not shown in Figure 6-12. Most of these additional calls are used to set the NLS settings for this specific APEX session. Since there is no way that APEX can guarantee that each of its page views will be done by the same database session, the NLS settings must be set for every page. They are also set before anything else so that any calculation in any subsequent process is performed after the proper data and numeric format masks have been applied.

Several practical examples of how to use the Initialization PL/SQL Code setting to add data security controls to an APEX application can be found throughout this book in later chapters.

Cleanup PL/SQL Code

Introduced in APEX 4.1, the Cleanup PL/SQL Code setting is similar to the Initialization PL/SQL Code setting except it gets executed at the end of an APEX page view versus close to the beginning. There is nothing else that gets executed after the Cleanup PL/SQL Code contents, as highlighted in Figure 6-13.

20121221105054.976516	0.02118	0.00003	Evaluate which regions should be rendered for display point REGION_POSITION_03
20121221105054.976541	0.02120	0.00004	...No regions to render
20121221105054.976583	0.02125	0.00003	Process point: AFTER_BOX_BODY
20121221105054.976613	0.02128	0.00004	Processes - point: AFTER_BOX_BODY
20121221105054.976653	0.02132	0.00003	Process point: BEFORE_FOOTER
20121221105054.976681	0.02134	0.00005	Processes - point: BEFORE_FOOTER
20121221105054.976726	0.02139	0.00002	Evaluate which regions should be rendered for display point BEFORE_FOOTER
20121221105054.976749	0.02141	0.00003	...No regions to render
20121221105054.976777	0.02144	0.00004	Show page footer
20121221105054.976814	0.02148	0.00004	Show page tempate footer
20121221105054.976851	0.02151	0.00044	Rendering form close tag and page checksum
20121221105054.977288	0.02195	0.00003	Process point: AFTER_FOOTER
20121221105054.977321	0.02198	0.00027	Processes - point: AFTER_FOOTER
20121221105054.977594	0.02226	0.00003	gv$sesstat.statistic# = 436: execute count=2
20121221105054.977627	0.02229	0.00020	Final commit
20121221105054.977823	0.02249	0.00128	...Execute Statement: begin apex_debug.info(p_message => 'DEBUG: Cleanup PL/SQL'); end;
20121221105054.979099	0.02377	-	DEBUG: Cleanup PL/SQL

***Figure 6-13.** Debug output from a page, highlighting where code in the Cleanup PL/SQL Code attribute executed*

A common use of the Cleanup PL/SQL Code attribute is to unset any security context values that may have been set in the Initialization PL/SQL Code attribute. This best practice is employed so that another APEX session that happens to be sharing the same database session does not inherit any security context values that may have been previously set by it. When a security context is set in the Initialization PL/SQL Code attribute, it should also be unset in the Cleanup PL/SQL Code attribute.

User Interface

The User Interface attributes of an application are new in APEX 4.2. As the name implies, these attributes deal with user interface attributes of an application. However, there is one that is worth highlighting in the name of security: Include Legacy JavaScript.

When enabled, this attribute will include an additional JavaScript library called `legacy.js` when rendering any APEX page. Located at `/i/libraries/apex/` on the web server, `legacy.js` contains a number of older, deprecated JavaScript functions that APEX has made use of throughout the years. By disabling this attribute, the `legacy.js` file will no longer be included when APEX pages are rendered.

There are a couple of things to consider with this attribute. First, simply disabling the legacy functions may negatively impact existing, older applications that make use of them. Some advice for switching to more modern, supported versions of these functions exist within the file itself for a portion of the legacy functions.

Second, and just as important, it may be the case that Oracle will no longer be supporting these functions, given that they are referred to as *legacy*. If that is in fact true, then any security or even functionality issues with them may potentially never be addressed by Oracle. For many organizations, this is a deal-breaker because their internal policies dictate that any software used must be supported in full by the vendor.

Therefore, you should replace any instance of legacy JavaScript functions in your application with either a supported version or a corresponding dynamic action. While simply disabling this attribute may not be possible, effort should be made to break any relationship with these legacy functions.

Page and Region Settings

Like application settings, page settings need to be properly configured in order to have a secure application. However, depending on the page, including its purpose and sensitivity, page settings may vary greatly from one page to another. Some pages may be available to any user, whether they are authenticated or not, while others will require a user have a specific authorization scheme in order to be accessed.

The same holds true for region settings. Some regions may be available to any user who can view the page, whereas others may have multiple rules that are evaluated to determine whether a specific user can view it. Additionally, APEX reports also contain a few attributes that security-conscious developers need to be made aware of, such as the ability and amount of data able to be downloaded.

Page Settings

Each page in an APEX application has its own, distinct set of attributes. While a couple of these attributes may defer to an application attribute, most of them are unique and specific to the page. Of the page attributes, most of the ones that have to do with the security of a page are grouped under the Security region. However, there are a couple of them in other sections that are worth considering.

Read Only

Items in APEX contain an attribute called Read Only. When the condition associated with this attribute returns a TRUE, then the associated item will render in "read-only" mode, making it uneditable to all users. If the Read Only attribute returns a FALSE, then the item will render as normal, and any user will be able to change the value of the item.

Traditionally, the Read Only attribute has been associated with each individual item. Making a 30-item form conditionally read-only was an arduous and time-consuming task because each item had to be configured individually. In APEX 4.2, there is now a page-level Read Only attribute available. Identical in mechanics and functionality to the item-level attribute, the page-level Read Only attribute will control all items on a specific page. However, if an individual item has its Read Only attribute set to Never, then that value will override the page-level Read Only attribute. Additionally, each region has a similar setting, making the task of creating a read-only form much easier and straightforward.

This attribute can be very useful for when an entire page should be rendered in read-only mode for a specific set of users. Since it's a best practice to control user access to APEX components via authorization schemes and not conditions, the same practice should be also applied to Read Only conditions. The APEX_UTIL.PUBLIC_CHECK_AUTHORIZATION API can be used to easily determine whether the currently logged on user is a member of a specific authorization scheme.

Keep in mind that if the user does pass the API check, it will return a TRUE, which when applied to a Read Only attribute will render the page with all items as read-only. It may be necessary to include a NOT before calling the API, as illustrated in Figure 6-14, to achieve the desired result.

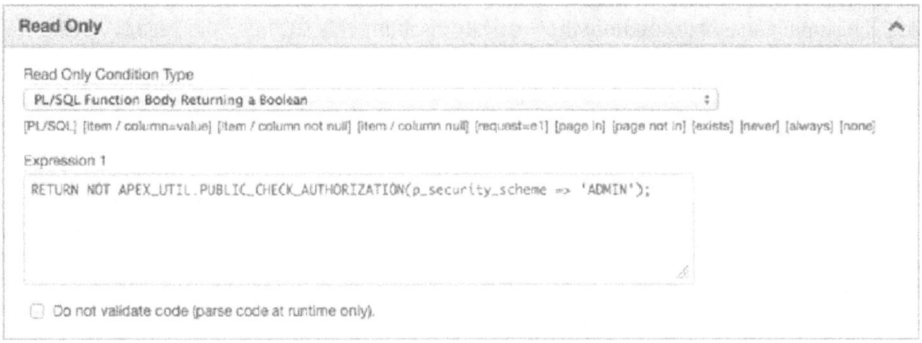

Figure 6-14. Configuring the page-level Read Only attribute to call the APEX_UTIL.PUBLIC_CHECK_AUTHORIZATION API

To summarize, when using the read-only page-level attribute, it is best to use an API to reference an authorization scheme. This way, all management of which users are mapped to which authorization scheme can be done outside the application itself, allowing for a more centrally administered system.

Authorization Scheme

Each page can also have an authorization scheme associated with it. Authorization schemes are used to determine which authorized users can have access to which APEX components. If the currently signed on user is a member of the specified authorization scheme, then that user can run the corresponding page. If not, then the page will not render, and an error message will be displayed.

By default, APEX will not assign an authorization scheme with freshly created pages. It is totally up to the developer to create and assign these schemes manually. This task should not be saved for the end of the development cycle but rather done as early as possible.

All pages should have an authorization scheme associated with them. Even if there is only a single scheme associated with an application, adding that scheme early on will be beneficial if the application requires multiple schemes in the future. Chapter 9 discusses the specifics of authorization schemes in more detail.

Authentication

The Authentication page attribute determines whether a user must be authenticated. There are two options for this attribute: Page Requires Authentication and Page is Public. When Authentication is set to the first option—which is also the default—the user will have to be successfully authenticated before the page is rendered. It does not matter which user or which authorization schemes pass or not; the check here is simply for a valid authenticated user. When Authentication is set to Page is Public, anyone who can access the server and enter the URL will be able to view this page.

If a page's Authentication attribute is set to Page is Public, the associated authorization scheme may or may not apply, based on the application-level attribute Run on Public Pages, as discussed earlier in this chapter.

More often than not, this attribute should be set to Page Requires Authentication. However, there are cases where pages within an application are intended to be public. When this is the case, ensure that all other sensitive components on the page are properly secured with an authorization scheme so that they do not inadvertently render for public users.

Deep Linking

The Deep Linking attribute of a page determines whether users will be able to bookmark that specific page and be able to return to that page successfully. The page-level attribute is identical to the application-level Deep Linking attribute discussed earlier in this chapter.

At the page level, there are three options for Deep Linking: Enabled, Disabled, and Application Default. Enabled and Disabled function the same as the application-level options do. Application Default will defer to the value defined for the application-level Deep Linking attribute. Unless there is a specific requirement for deep linking, the Deep Linking option should be disabled because it may not work correctly in all places within an application, causing confusion among the users.

Page Access Protection

Page Access Protection is designed to prevent the user from altering or tampering with the URL and resubmitting it, which could result in sensitive data being displayed on the page. There are four settings for Page Access Protection, and they are listed from the least restrictive to the most restrictive:

- *Unrestricted*: Unrestricted is the default setting for newly created pages in APEX. Any parameter can be passed to any portion of the URL, and the APEX engine will simply accept it as valid.

- *Arguments Must Have Checksum*: When any parameters or values are passed through the URL, this option requires the URL to contain an additional checksum value. The APEX engine will compare that checksum value to what it expects, and if there is any discrepancy, the page will not be rendered. This option is the most commonly used when adding security to an APEX page.

- *No Arguments Allowed*: This option prohibits any parameters from being passed via the URL. This includes not only item and value pairs but also request, clear cache, and pagination directives.

- *No URL Access*: This is the most restrictive of the group; when this is set to No URL Access, the only way to access that specific page is to end up there as the result of an APEX branch. Trying to get to that page by changing the URL to reflect the corresponding page number will fail.

Every page in an application should have its Page Access Protection attribute set to at least Arguments Must Have Checksum. This will trigger any link to this page from a declarative APEX component to automatically include a checksum as part of the link. Even for pages that do not contain items, it is important to set them to Arguments Must Have Checksum as well, since any page can be used to set any item in APEX. For instance, if only the page with the form on it is configured to use Arguments Must Have Checksum, a malicious user could always use a page that is set to Unrestricted to set the item and simply change the URL to return to the page that contains the form to see the potentially unauthorized data.

If any links to this page are produced in a PL/SQL region or as part of a SQL statement, they will need to be modified so that the checksum is included. This is done by passing the URL to the APEX_UTIL.PREPARE_URL API. This API will return a URL that includes the session state protection checksum, starting with the f?p portion. For example, if the URL in Listing 6-4 were passed into the APEX_UTIL.PREPARE_URL API, the result would look similar to that in Listing 6-5.

Listing 6-4. An APEX URL That Passes a Value to P2_EMPNO

```
f?p=150:2:31029755:::::P2_EMPNO:7499
```

Listing 6-5. An APEX URL That Includes a Checksum Value Appended Automatically or by Calling the APEX_UTIL.PREPARE_URL Function

```
f?p=150:2:31029755:::::P2_EMPNO:7499&cs=314C4BD3626E0E3A29B1FB0
```

Without the additional checksum or with a manipulated or absent checksum, the page will simply not render, and an error message will be displayed.

Enabling Page Access Protection is a layer of protection that is APEX-specific. Given that it is quick and easy to do, it should be set up for every page within an application. However, it is also worth considering using a database-level data security mechanism as well, such as virtual private database or secure views. These approaches are also relatively simple to set up and will work across platforms, whereas Page Access Protection is APEX-specific. Taking the dual-layer approach is best and ensures that all data is protected from inside and outside of APEX.

You can find more details about Page Access Protection and Item Protection in Chapter 7.

Form Auto Complete

The Form Auto Complete attribute controls whether an APEX page will remember previous values input into the page item and display them in a drop-down list the next time the page is rendered, as illustrated in Figure 6-15.

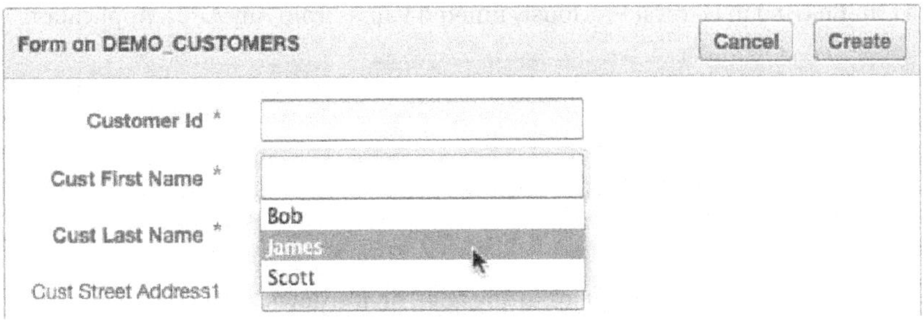

Figure 6-15. *An APEX item displaying previous values, as Form Auto Complete is enabled*

By default, Form Auto Complete is set to On, which can be extremely dangerous. First, if sensitive data such as account or credit card numbers is being collected, the values will be stored on the local PC. This data is not well protected because it can be easily harvested using a tool like Form History Control (https://addons.mozilla.org/en-us/firefox/addon/form-history-control), as illustrated in Figure 6-16.

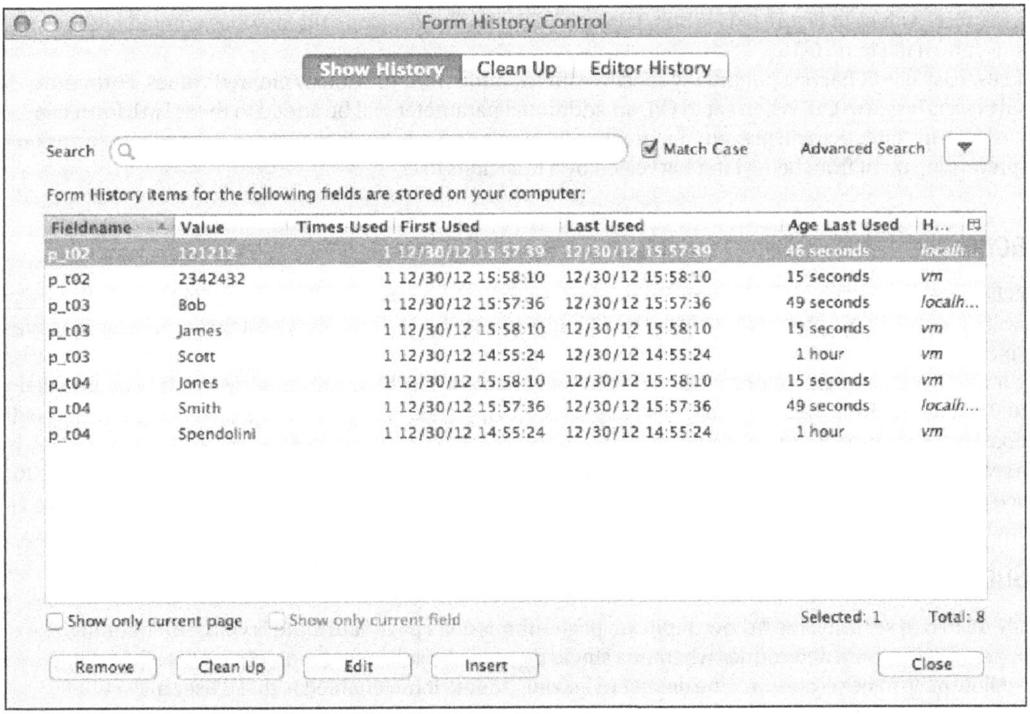

Figure 6-16. *Using Form History Control, any previously entered value can be easily viewed*

Second, since at the HTML form level all APEX item names are the same (p_t01 through p_t200), it would be simple to create a static HTML page using those names and harvest all previously entered values without the need for a particular tool. Listing 6-6 illustrates a simple HTML file that can be loaded into any browser.

Listing 6-6. A Simple HTML File That Can Be Used to Harvest Previously Entered Values from Any APEX Application

```
<form action="none">
t01<input name="p_t01">
t02<input name="p_t02">
t03<input name="p_t03">
t04<input name="p_t04">
</form>
```

When this file is run from a browser, the user can place the cursor in any field, hit the down arrow key, and see previously entered values, as shown in Figure 6-17.

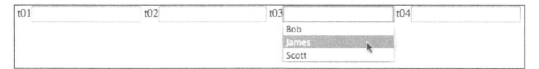

Figure 6-17. *Using a simple HTML file, previous values entered into an APEX application can be displayed*

Notice that the three values in Figure 6-17—Bob, James, and Scott—are the same three values entered in the APEX applications shown in Figure 6-15.

Because of how easy it is to harvest potentially sensitive information from previously entered values, Form Auto Complete should always be set to Off. When set to Off, an additional parameter will be added to the HTML form tag: `autocomplete="off"`. This directive will prevent the browser from remembering values that are entered into forms on that page, thus preventing them from being later harvested by a malicious user.

Browser Cache

The Browser Cache page-level attribute is the same as the Cache application-level attribute. Essentially, it controls whether pages will be stored in the browser's local cache. While enabling the user to use the back button, enabling the Browser Cache may also store sensitive data in the browser's local cache.

At the page level, there are three options for Browser Cache: Enabled, Disabled and Application Default. Enabled and Disabled function the same as the application-level options do. Application Default will defer to the value defined for the application-level Cache attribute.

At the page level, Browser Cache should always be disabled—either by setting the application-level attribute Cache to Disabled and each page-level attribute to Application Default or by setting each page-level attribute to Disabled directly.

Duplicate Submissions

While not directly related to security, the "Allow duplicate page submissions page" attribute is worth mentioning. As the name implies, this attribute determines whether a single page can be submitted more than once. By default, it is set to "Yes—Allow page to be re-posted." The danger of leaving this attribute enabled is that a user may either accidentally or intentionally try to submit the same form twice. The results of a duplicate submission can vary widely, from nothing at all to charging a user's credit card twice. Therefore, in most cases this attribute should be disabled by setting it to "No—Prevent page from being re-posted."

Server Cache

APEX offers a very basic caching feature at the page and region levels. When enabled, APEX will cache the HTML from either the page or the region that was just rendered. On each subsequent page view, if the cache duration has not expired, APEX will use the cached version of the page or region instead of dynamically rendering either.

This feature is useful for poorly performing pages or regions that contain data that does not need to be updated frequently. For example, a page that contains summary reports from yesterday's data that takes ten seconds to render would be a good candidate for caching.

Since the cache is handled automatically and transparently by APEX on the server side, there is no danger of any users accessing it directly. However, there is one option that could potentially open up a security vulnerability. The Cache by User option determines whether the page cache is created for each individual user or is shared among all users.

By default, this attribute is set to No, meaning that a single cache will be shared among all users. The drawback to this is that if any region or report on the page contained data that was specific to a user, other users would see that data. For example, if one of the cached regions were a report that detailed a specific user's salary, all users who accessed that page would see the original user's details because the cache would be created for the first user who accessed the page and then shared with all other users.

If enabling a server cache on a page that contains regions with data specific to individual users, be sure to set the Cache by User option to Yes. This way, each user will have to create their own specific cache that will not be shared with any others.

▨ **Note**   Enkitec eSERT can also provide insight as to which page settings have been secured properly and which have not, allowing the developer to spend time with only those that present a potential vulnerability. Figure 6-18 shows an example summary.

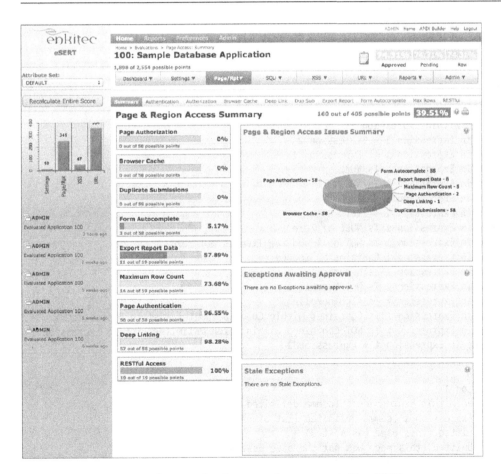

Figure 6-18. *A summary of page and region access issues generated by eSERT*

Region Settings

All regions—regardless of their type—share some basic security controls. Each region contains a condition, an authorization scheme, and, new in APEX 4.2, a read-only attribute. As each region is generated, each of these attributes is checked to determine whether the region is rendered and, if so, whether to render it in read-only mode.

Conditions

Like most components in APEX, each region contains a condition attribute. When the condition specified returns a TRUE, then that region, as well as any items, buttons, and subregions associated with that region, is rendered on the page. Conversely, when the condition returns a FALSE, that region and any items, buttons, and subregions associated with it do not render.

Many types of conditions are available, as outlined in Listing 6-7. Some are simple and straightforward, whereas others are more complex and require additional data elements. Despite the long list of potential conditions, most developers find that they utilize only a small subset of conditions when building applications.

Listing 6-7. All Available APEX Conditions

```
- No Condition -
Exists (SQL query returns at least one row)
NOT Exists (SQL query returns no rows)
SQL Expression
PL/SQL Expression
PL/SQL Function Body Returning a Boolean
Request = Expression 1
Request != Expression 1
Request Is Contained within Expression 1
Request Is NOT Contained within Expression 1
Value of Item / Column in Expression 1 = Expression 2
Value of Item / Column in Expression 1 != Expression 2
Value of Item / Column in Expression 1 Is NULL
Value of Item / Column in Expression 1 Is NOT NULL
Value of Item / Column in Expression 1 = Zero
Value of Item / Column in Expression 1 != Zero
Value of Item / Column in Expression 1 Is NULL or Zero
Value of Item / Column in Expression 1 Is NOT null and the Item Is NOT Zero
Value of Item / Column in Expression 1 Contains No Spaces
Value of Item / Column in Expression 1 Is Numeric
Value of Item / Column in Expression 1 Is Not Numeric
Value of Item / Column in Expression 1 Is Alphanumeric
Value of Item / Column in Expression 1 Is Contained within Colon Delimited List in Expression 2
Value of Item / Column in Expression 1 Is NOT Contained within Colon Delimited List in Expression 2
Value of User Preference in Expression 1 = Expression 2
Value of User Preference in Expression 1 != Expression 2
Current page = Expression 1
Current page != Expression 1
Current Page Is Contained Within Expression 1 (comma delimited list of pages)
Current Page Is NOT in Expression 1 (comma delimited list of pages)
Current Page = Page Submitted (this page was posted)
Current Page != Page Submitted (this page was not the page posted)
Current Page Is in Printer Friendly Mode
```

```
Current page is NOT in Printer Friendly Mode
Text in Expression 1 Is Contained in Value of Item / Column in Expression 2
Text in Expression 1 Is Contained within the Text in Expression 2
Text in Expression 1 Is NOT Contained within the Text in Expression 2
Text in Expression 1 = Expression 2 (includes &ITEM. substitutions)
Text in Expression 1 != Expression 2 (includes &ITEM. substitutions)
Page/Region is Read Only
Page/Region is NOT Read Only
User is Authenticated (not public)
User is the Public User (user has not authenticated)
Inline Validation Errors Displayed
No Inline Validation Errors Displayed
SQL Reports (OK to show the forward button)
SQL Reports (OK to show the back button)
Client Browser: Mozilla, Netscape 6.x/7x or higher
Client Browser: Microsoft Internet Explorer 5.5, 6.0 or higher
Client Browser: XHTML / CSS capable browser
Client Browser: Other browsers (or older version)
Current Language Is Contained within Expression 1
Current Language Is NOT Contained within Expression 1
Current Language != Expression 1
Current Language = Expression 1
When CGI_ENV DAD_NAME = Expression 1
When CGI_ENV DAD_NAME != Expression 1
When CGI_ENV SERVER_NAME = Expression 1
When CGI_ENV SERVER_NAME != Expression 1
When CGI_ENV HTTP_HOST = Expression 1
When CGI_ENV HTTP_HOST != Expression 1
Never
Always
```

Despite the lengthy list, all conditions at their core essentially make a PL/SQL call to determine whether the condition is met. This is important to understand because in some cases the business rule at hand may not be able to be evaluated with a single condition. In that case, a condition of type PL/SQL Function Body Returning a Boolean can be used. In the function, multiple checks can be made, and if all checks are successful, the function can return TRUE.

Conditions were designed to facilitate business rules in an APEX application, not security. However, many developers will use them for both. While this does not present any security risk, security rules should be mapped to authorization schemes and conditions should be reserved for business rules as much as possible.

There are multiple benefits for this approach. First, if a condition is used for a security role and later that region needs a business rule associated with it, there is no place to put that business rule. The condition will have to be either moved to an authorization scheme or rewritten to accommodate both business rules and security roles.

Second, consistently using authorization schemes for security roles provides an easier-to-manage and more declarative approach. A developer can query the APEX views to determine which components are associated with which authorization scheme quite easily. It would be a lot more difficult to query the conditions of all components and determine which role they mapped to, because there is no declarative way to do so.

Lastly, using authorization schemes over conditions for security roles makes it a lot easier to map to an external role repository. This enables the role management to occur outside of APEX at a centralized source, such as an LDAP directory, ensuring that all identity management occurs at the same place.

Authorization Schemes

Authorization schemes are used to determine which APEX components an authorized APEX user has access to. They can be associated with every APEX component, from the application itself to a specific column in a report. If the Authorization Scheme setting passes or evaluates to TRUE, then the corresponding APEX components will execute or render. Otherwise, a FALSE is returned, and the corresponding APEX components do not execute or render.

Each region in APEX can have an authorization scheme associated with it. The results of the authorization scheme will determine whether to render the region. The authorization scheme is evaluated independent of the condition, but if either returns a FALSE, the region will not render.

As mentioned in the previous section, security should be mapped to authorization schemes rather than conditions when possible. The benefits of this approach were discussed when discussing the previous attribute, Conditions. For more details on authorization schemes, please refer to Chapter 9.

Read Only

Much like the new page-level attribute, regions in APEX 4.2 also now have a Read Only attribute. When the region-level Read Only attribute returns TRUE, all items within that region will render in read-only mode. When the region-level Read Only attribute returns FALSE, then all items in that region will render normally.

The value for Read Only determined at the region level will override any value determined at the page level. For example, if the page-level Read Only attribute returned TRUE and the region-level Read Only attribute returned FALSE, the items within that region would be editable.

Furthermore, any item that has its Read Only setting set to Never will never render in read-only mode, regardless of what the region or page setting is. You can find more details about the Read Only attribute and how to use the APEX_UTIL.PUBLIC_CHECK_AUTHORIZATION API earlier in this chapter.

Caching

Similar to page-level caching, an APEX region can also be cached. When enabled, APEX will cache the HTML from the corresponding region the first time it is rendered. On each subsequent view, the cache will be used until it expires, thus increasing performance of that region.

When using region caching with a report, only the first set of rows displayed in the region is cached. For example, if the report contains 10,000 records displayed in sets of 15, only those first 15 records are cached. As soon as the user clicks the pagination controls, APEX will have to dynamically fetch the next set of records.

When enabling the region cache, there are two options to choose from: Cached and Cached by User. Selecting Cached will create a single cached region that will be reused among all users of an application. This can have security implications if the data in the region is specific and private to the end user. The Cached by User option is much more secure but potentially less efficient because a new cache will be created for each individual user who renders the region. However, with this option, data specific to a user will not be shared among other users of the application. Thus, when caching regions, ensure that the Cached by User option is selected.

Report Settings

The four region settings in the previous section are available in any and all types of regions in APEX. When using reports, there are a few additional attributes that need to be secured as well. Most of them have to do with being able to download the contents of a report to a CSV or other type of file. While this feature does add convenience for the developer and takes just seconds to enable, it does so at a potentially great cost. Chapter 10 outlines some techniques to apply to applications to make downloading data much more secure and regulated.

Mobile Applications

The adoption rate of mobile applications is off the charts. From Facebook to banking and from video games to travel planning, virtually every facet of our lives can be planned, purchased, and monitored from a mobile platform. As smartphones become cheaper and more common, this adoption rate will continue to skyrocket.

Hesitancy Toward Corporate Adoption

Despite the explosive growth on the personal side, corporations have been a little more hesitant to adopt mobile applications. There are a couple of major reasons for this. First, corporations are always concerned about security. Let's face it: you're far more likely to leave your mobile phone than you are your laptop at a restaurant or on a plane. Because of this risk, many have been reluctant to extend their enterprise to a device that they have little direct control over.

Second, custom native mobile application development is not cheap. Before even starting to develop a native application, a choice needs to be made as to which platform or platforms to develop on—Android, iOS, Windows Mobile, or BlackBerry. Each additional platform will obviously require more resources and take more time to develop, not to mention the additional associated maintenance costs. To further complicate this approach, many organizations are allowing employees to bring their own device (BYOD). This will guarantee a mix of different platforms, making it impractical to support all of them natively.

Another approach to mobile development is to build an HTML-based application that runs on the smartphone's browser. With this approach, a single application can run on any popular device, regardless of the platform. This greatly reduces the time and cost to develop and maintain each application. As new devices are introduced, it matters little as which operating system they run on, so as long as they have a modern, standards-compliant browser.

This is the approach that APEX has taken—HTML-based mobile applications that will run on virtually any modern smartphone. To achieve this, APEX incorporates the jQuery Mobile framework. This framework is designed to work properly and securely on all modern mobile browser platforms. Since APEX utilizes it, any APEX application that uses jQuery Mobile will also be able to run on all modern mobile browsers. While APEX 4.1 introduced loose integration with jQuery Mobile, APEX 4.2 is the first release that is truly mobile-ready right out of the box. With APEX 4.2 and absolutely no knowledge of jQuery mobile or HTML, it is possible to build robust, fully functional mobile applications that run on all popular smartphones.

The beauty of this approach is that as an APEX developer, there is almost nothing additional to learn. APEX mobile applications are designed in the same development environment as their desktop counterparts. They can call the same PL/SQL packages, write to the same tables, and be deployed on the same server because they are technically an APEX application with a different set of mobile-optimized templates. Because of this, nearly every single concept and technique discussed in this book also applies to mobile development. The few that differ are highlighted in the next few paragraphs.

Mobile Considerations for Security

Without getting into the specifics of mobile application development design techniques, there are a few high-level concepts that are important to consider from a security point of view. First, there are a couple of different methods to build a mobile application. One method, which is used in some of the Oracle packaged applications, is to include both a desktop and mobile interface in a single application. Another method is to use a separate application for mobile entirely.

On the surface, the integrated approach may seem like the better choice. A single application is perfectly capable of running in either desktop or mobile mode, thanks to a new feature introduced in APEX 4.2. One application is also less to manage over two applications. But dig a little deeper, and some of the flaws of this approach become apparent.

First, the users of a desktop application may or may not be the same as the users of a mobile application. In many cases, it is a subset of users. If that is the case, additional care must be taken to ensure that both the mobile and desktop pages have the proper authorization scheme associated with them so that each is secured based on the corresponding group of authorized users. It is much easier to manage two distinct user lists—desktop and mobile—and associate one with the corresponding application. This way, as either application is expanded, there is less work to do in order to ensure that new pages are associated with the corresponding authorization scheme.

Second, most mobile applications offer a subset of transactions of their desktop counterparts. Given that, mobile applications will typically need to access less of the schema as their desktop applications. In fact, some mobile applications may be largely read-only, with only a screen or two that can update the database. By creating a separate mobile application, a different, much more limited parse-as schema can be associated with it. This will ensure that even if a user discovers a vulnerability, the potential damage that can be done will be mitigated by the limited privilege schema. Chapter 13 discussed this technique, called a *shadow schema*, in more detail.

Third, having the mobile application separate from the desktop application allows the developer to adjust the session idle time and duration. For desktop application, it is common to allow the length of a session to span eight hours, or a typical workday. This way, a user can sign in to the application in the morning and potentially not have to sign in again all day. Additionally, the session idle time is typically set to around one hour. For mobile applications—which have much more brief use patterns—these values should be greatly reduced. Depending on specific security requirements and the sensitivity of the data, the total session time may span only 20 or 30 minutes, while the idle time may be set to as low as 5 minutes. This guarantees that if a phone is in fact lost, by the time someone finds it and potentially accesses the browser, the duration of the session idle time will have been exceeded, and the user will automatically be logged out of the application.

Lastly, and perhaps the least related to security, is the overall maintenance of the mobile application. If the mobile application is separated from the desktop application, then bugs and enhancements in each can be made independent of one another. An issue in the mobile application can quickly be fixed and deployed, regardless as to what is currently being worked on in the desktop application.

Both methods of supporting mobile can be properly secured and managed. The integrated approach often requires more work and maintenance but also allows for a single application that supports both mobile and desktop applications. If the users for each interface are the same, then this method works well. However, the second method offers a strong case, especially when looking at it from a security point of view. No matter which one is used, at the end of the day, they are both APEX applications, and the same secure best practices and techniques should be applied to either.

It is worth repeating that requiring mobile applications to run over HTTPS is absolutely essential. Keep in mind that many users of mobile devices will jump onto a WiFi hotspot when they can in order to get better performance. In most cases, these hotspots are completely unencrypted. Using HTTPS is essential in these cases because being connected to the hotspot over HTTP only means network packets that are sent in the clear can easily be viewed by others.

Summary

Configuring application, page, and regions settings is one of the easier phases of securing APEX applications because most of the attributes have a finite list of values to choose from. Despite this, these settings are also critical to be secured. If any number of application- or page-level attributes are configured incorrectly, the results could be disastrous because these attributes apply to either the application itself or the contents of a specific page or pages.

Using an automated tool such as Enkitec eSERT is also recommended because it will not skip anything and will save a great deal of time in evaluating an application for improper application and page settings. eSERT will also provide guidance as to why an attribute is important and also how to fix it if a vulnerability is detected.

CHAPTER 7

Application Threats

If only it were as simple as configuring a few application-level options to completely secure your application. This is clearly not the case because there are many attack vectors that a malicious user will attempt to take in order to compromise your application. Typically, these attacks involve passing malicious values or strings to an otherwise valid component of an application, such as a form or the URL. The malicious user then relies on the fact that the developer did not take enough precautions to ensure that the malicious code is properly neutralized. If that is the case, then the attack is successful, and the malicious user has succeeded.

This chapter covers how to protect against three types, or classifications, of attacks: SQL injection, cross-site scripting, and URL tampering. *SQL injection* is when a malicious user enters a snippet of SQL into a form and, in turn, that snippet is executed by the database. While not a simple attack to implement, when there is a risk for such an attack, the malicious user can run almost any SQL statement that the database will execute, making this type of attack extremely dangerous.

Cross-site scripting is similar to SQL injection, in that a malicious user attempts to insert or inject code that is executed, but the difference is that the code is JavaScript, not SQL. On the surface, this may not seem as dangerous because the data is protected by the controls implemented in the database. However, cross-site scripting attacks typically attempt to steal sensitive data and send it back to the malicious user, making them every bit as dangerous as SQL injection attacks. APEX contains a number of constructs that assist with sanitizing data or ensuring that malicious code has been removed or rendered useless. These constructs and techniques are covered in this chapter as well.

The last type of attack is called *URL tampering*. The easiest to execute, URL tampering is when a malicious user changes the values passed via the URL and causes the application to display otherwise-restricted records. URL tampering also includes attempting to modify values that are stored in hidden items to gain access to restricted data.

SQL Injection

Simply put, a SQL injection attack is when a malicious user passes in, or *injects*, a malicious value into a form on a web page. That value is then sent back to the server where it is used to modify the SQL that is subsequently executed. Depending on the type of the SQL injection attack, it may cause the server to return data that would otherwise be restricted, to execute a DDL command that drops or alters database objects, or simply to delete data from a table.

Recently, these types of attacks have been on the rise and in many cases have caused damage to organizations by harvesting data from their sites. Perhaps one of the most recognized SQL injection attacks occurred in 2011 when the group called LulzSec attacked Sony's web site and claimed to have downloaded more than 1 million user names and passwords. While Sony claimed that the number of accounts compromised was closer to 37,000, this attack got Sony a tremendous amount of negative press for failing to adequately protect personal information.

There are many reasons for the rise in popularity of SQL injection attacks. First, they are getting a lot easier to employ. There are a number of automated tools that assist in scoping out a site for SQL injection vulnerabilities, tremendously reducing the amount of time it takes a malicious user to find a weakness with a site. As SQL injection attacks receive more and more media attention, they also attract more and more malicious users willing to attempt them, thus increasing the number of attacks.

SQL injection attacks have a much higher likelihood of succeeding when a malicious user finds a server that has not been either properly patched or configured. With regard to the Oracle Database and APEX, a general rule of thumb is the older the release, the more security vulnerabilities that exist. As security vulnerabilities are discovered in both the database and APEX, Oracle typically addressed them by way of patches. If these patches are not applied, then the vulnerability will persist, giving the malicious user an easy in. Keeping up with the latest patches is critical when securing your environment—from the web server to the database to APEX itself.

■ **Tip**   To keep informed of Oracle's Critical Patch Updates (CPU) and security alerts, please visit www.oracle.com/technetwork/topics/security/alerts-086861.html.

On the other hand, developers are quite often at fault for introducing SQL injection vulnerabilities into applications. Most often, this is done because of a lack of education of secure APEX best practices on a developer's part. Developers simply don't realize that some of the code that they are writing could lead to a SQL injection attack. On a similar note, developers who are aware of secure APEX best practices don't always follow them. The daily demands placed on them force them to cut corners many times, and often the corners cut are the security reviews of their applications. Thus, easy-to-remedy vulnerabilities go undetected and make it to the production server.

Anatomy of an Attack

To succeed, SQL injection attacks rely on developers improperly handling variables that users can influence in their code. The key here is how a developer incorporates variables provided by the user in their actual SQL or PL/SQL code. In cases that are susceptible to SQL injection attacks, this is done by concatenating the static portion of the query with the values provided by the user. What this does is give a malicious user the opportunity to provide a snippet of SQL as a value rather than an expected value, such as a name or ID. Rather than be used as part of the predicate, this snippet will be used to restructure the actual SQL statement before it executes.

Let's start with a simple example that can be illustrated with SQL*Plus. The code in Listing 7-1 takes in a single input parameter, p_ename. This input parameter will be used when constructing the SQL that will be executed. For this example to work, be sure that the EMP demonstration table is installed in the schema.

Listing 7-1. A Simple PL/SQL Procedure That Is Susceptible to SQL Injection

```
CREATE OR REPLACE PROCEDURE sqli_example
  (
  p_ename IN VARCHAR2
  )
AS
  l_sql VARCHAR2(100);
  type emp_t IS TABLE OF emp%ROWTYPE;
  emp_r emp_t := emp_t();
BEGIN
-- Concatenate the SQL statement, including quotes
l_sql := 'SELECT * FROM emp WHERE ENAME = '''
  || p_ename || '''';

-- Print the SQL statement about to be executed
DBMS_OUTPUT.PUT_LINE(l_sql);

-- Execute the SQL statement
EXECUTE IMMEDIATE l_sql BULK COLLECT INTO emp_r;
```

```
-- Loop through the results and print the name of the employee
FOR x IN emp_r.FIRST..emp_r.LAST
LOOP
  DBMS_OUTPUT.PUT_LINE('Emp: ' || emp_r(x).ename
    || ' - Dept:' || emp_r(x).deptno);
END LOOP;
END sqli_example;
/
```

Entering any valid name of an employee in the EMP table will result in printing part of that employee record. For example, if the value KING is passed in, the results would resemble those in Listing 7-2, which is to be expected.

Listing 7-2. The Results of the Procedure Using the Value KING for p_ename

```
SQL> BEGIN
  2  sqli_example(p_ename => 'KING');
  3  END;
  4  /
SELECT * FROM emp WHERE ENAME = 'KING'
Emp: KING - Dept:10

PL/SQL procedure successfully completed.
```

However, if a snippet of SQL were entered instead of just a value—specifically, 'KING'' OR ''X'' = ''X'—the results would be very different, as shown in Listing 7-3.

Listing 7-3. The Results of the Same Procedure Using a SQL Injection Attack

```
SQL> BEGIN
  2  sqli_example(p_ename => 'KING'' OR ''X'' = ''X');
  3  END;
  4  /
SELECT * FROM emp WHERE ENAME = 'KING' OR 'X' = 'X'
Emp: KING - Dept:10
Emp: BLAKE - Dept:30
Emp: CLARK - Dept:10
Emp: JONES - Dept:20
Emp: SCOTT - Dept:20
Emp: FORD - Dept:20
Emp: JONES - Dept:20
Emp: ALLEN - Dept:30
Emp: WARD - Dept:30
Emp: MARTIN - Dept:30
Emp: TURNER - Dept:30
Emp: ADAMS - Dept:20
Emp: JAMES - Dept:30
Emp: MILLER - Dept:10

PL/SQL procedure successfully completed.
```

It is very clear that in the SQL that is about to be executed that the input provided added an additional portion to the WHERE clause of the query, namely, OR 'X' = 'X'. This caused the logic of the SQL to change, and since a literal always equals the same literal, the right half of the OR clause evaluates to TRUE, thus triggering all records to be returned versus just the one that matches the input parameter.

The reason that this is possible is that the SQL is altered before the database has a chance to parse it. Parsing is one of the first steps to occur when the database attempts to run a SQL statement. During this phase, the database examines the SQL and ensures that it is syntactically correct and all objects that it references are accessible and valid. In some sense, the database is "stupid" because it is unable to make a distinction between an unaltered and an altered SQL statement. It simply parses what is passed to it.

Fortunately, there is a simple solution to this problem: bind variables. As their name implies, bind variables are evaluated during the bind phase of processing a query. During the bind phase, any placeholder in the SQL statement is replaced with the corresponding value. Since the structure of the SQL has already been processed, it can no longer be influenced with a SQL injection attack during the bind phase.

■ **Note**　Oracle Database 10g Release 2 and newer implements a DBMS_ASSERT package containing functions to help fight SQL injection. One such function is ENDQUOTE_LITERAL. Use of bind variables is a more robust protection, however, and is what I recommend whenever possible.

Therefore, with a small alteration to the code, the previously vulnerable PL/SQL procedure can be made safe by using bind variables, as outlined in Listing 7-4.

Listing 7-4. A Simple PL/SQL Procedure That Uses Bind Variables and Is Not Susceptible to SQL Injection Attacks

```
CREATE OR REPLACE PROCEDURE sqli_fixed_example
  (
  p_ename IN VARCHAR2
  )
AS
  l_sql VARCHAR2(100);
  type emp_t IS TABLE OF emp%ROWTYPE;
  emp_r emp_t := emp_t();
BEGIN
-- Assemble the SQL statement with a bind variable
l_sql := 'SELECT * FROM emp WHERE ENAME = :ename';
-- Print the SQL statement about to be executed
DBMS_OUTPUT.PUT_LINE(l_sql);
-- Execute the SQL statement
EXECUTE IMMEDIATE l_sql BULK COLLECT INTO emp_r USING p_ename;
-- Loop through the results and print the name of the employee
IF emp_r.COUNT > 0 THEN
  FOR x IN emp_r.FIRST..emp_r.LAST
  LOOP
    DBMS_OUTPUT.PUT_LINE('Emp: ' || emp_r(x).ename
      || ' - Dept:' || emp_r(x).deptno);
  END LOOP;
ELSE
  DBMS_OUTPUT.PUT_LINE('No Data Found');
```

```
END IF;
END sqli_fixed_example;
/
```

There are three main changes to this version of the procedure. First, the string assembled into the l_sql variable is no longer concatenated; rather, a bind variable reference called :ename is included. Second, when the EXECUTE IMMEDIATE line is run, it will bind the value passed into the parameter p_ename to the query stored in l_sql. Bind variables are positional when called from an EXECUTE IMMEDIATE statement, so it will simply use the :ename reference when binding in the value from p_ename. Third, a simple check to ensure that there is at least one record present before entering the loop was added. Otherwise, the procedure would throw an error when no matching records were found.

Now, if the same SQL injection attack is implemented against the updated procedure, very different results occur, as shown in Listing 7-5.

Listing 7-5. Results of a SQL Injection Attempt Against a Secure Procedure

```
SQL> begin
  2   sqli_fixed_example(p_ename => 'KING'' OR ''X'' = ''X');
  3  end;
  4  /
SELECT * FROM emp WHERE ENAME = :ename
No Data Found
```

Since APEX will call named PL/SQL program units quite frequently, it is important to ensure that any use of EXECUTE IMMEDIATE or DBMS_SQL with SQL that contains variables does so properly by using bind variables. In addition to being more secure, bind variables are a much more performant way to write SQL. So, as a side benefit, secure SQL will typically run faster.

SQL Injection in APEX

Let's take a look at an example SQL injection attack on an APEX application. This example also requires the EMP table to be installed in your parse-as schema. To start, create a report on a page using the SQL in Listing 7-6. Next, create a page item of type text field called P1_ENAME, as well as a button that will submit the page.

Listing 7-6. SQL Statement for the Report

```
SELECT * FROM emp WHERE deptno = 10 AND ename LIKE '&P1_ENAME.'
```

The SQL used in the report will do two things to limit the records retrieved. First, it will return only those records that have a value of 10 for the DEPTNO column. Next, it will filter the ENAME column with the value of the user's input in the item P1_ENAME. The operator used to filter the records is LIKE, so it is possible for the user to enter a %, which will act as a wildcard.

Running the page with the report on it returns no records, as shown in Figure 7-1.

Figure 7-1. *Results of running the report with no value in P1_ENAME*

This is because no value was entered into P1_ENAME, causing the LIKE operator to not find any matches. The fact that only records where DEPTNO is 10 was irrelevant. Now, rerun the report, but this time, enter the name of a valid employee in the EMP table who has a DEPTNO of 10, such as KING. The report behaves as expected, returning only a single record, as shown in Figure 7-2.

Figure 7-2. *Results of running the report where P1_ENAME is set to KING*

Since the SQL uses the LIKE operator, it is possible to execute a fuzzy search by using the % character. In fact, entering just a single % into P1_ENAME should return all records that have a DEPTNO of 10, as illustrated in Figure 7-3.

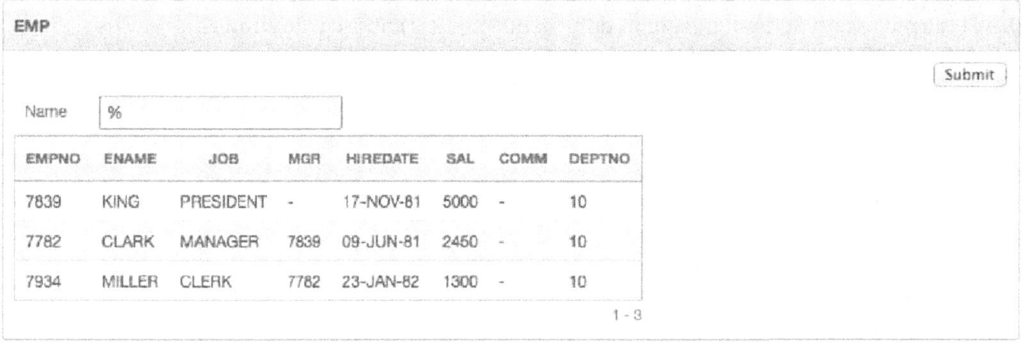

Figure 7-3. *Results of running the report where P1_ENAME is set to %*

Even though a wildcard character was entered, the first half of the predicate ensured that only those employees who have a DEPTNO of 10 were returned.

So far, the report has behaved exactly as expected, returning the corresponding records based on the values passed in to P1_ENAME. Remember, SQL injection attacks use a value that will modify the SQL that will be executed rather than be used to actually filter the results. You can see an example of such a string in Listing 7-7.

Listing 7-7. Value to Enter to Implement a SQL Injection Attack

```
KING' or 'x' = 'x
```

Entering this string into P1_ENAME and running the report would return all of the records in EMP, as shown in Figure 7-4.

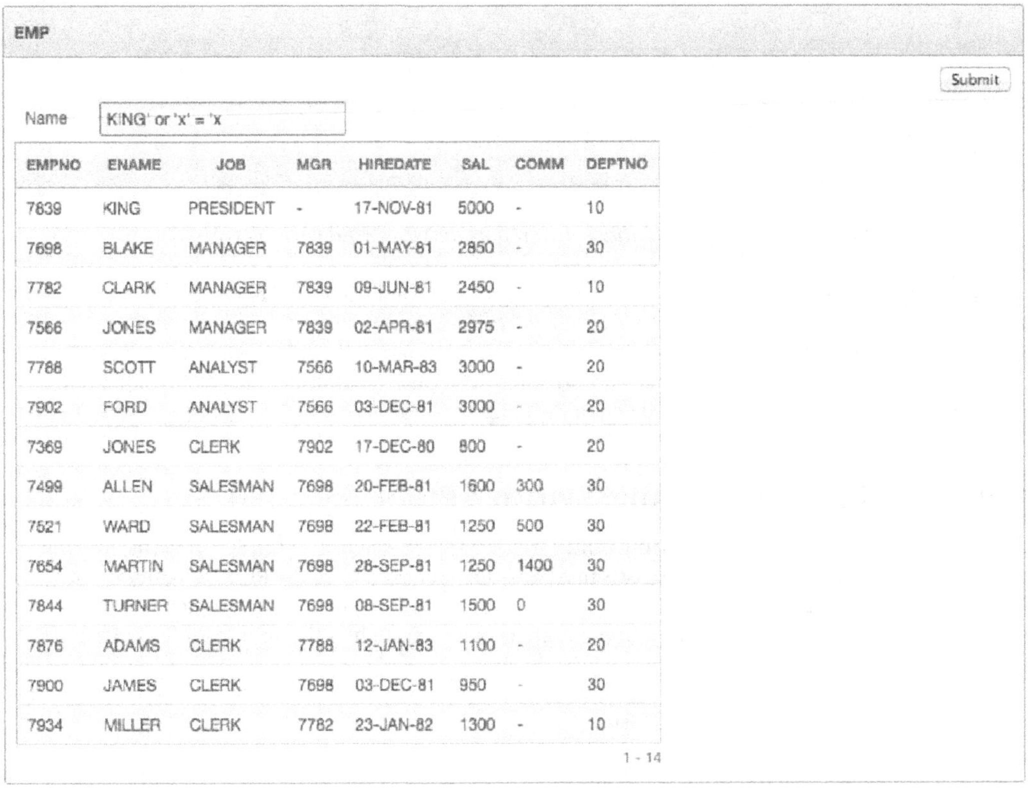

EMP								Submit

Name: KING' or 'x' = 'x

EMPNO	ENAME	JOB	MGR	HIREDATE	SAL	COMM	DEPTNO
7839	KING	PRESIDENT	-	17-NOV-81	5000	-	10
7698	BLAKE	MANAGER	7839	01-MAY-81	2850	-	30
7782	CLARK	MANAGER	7839	09-JUN-81	2450	-	10
7566	JONES	MANAGER	7839	02-APR-81	2975	-	20
7788	SCOTT	ANALYST	7566	10-MAR-83	3000	-	20
7902	FORD	ANALYST	7566	03-DEC-81	3000	-	20
7369	JONES	CLERK	7902	17-DEC-80	800	-	20
7499	ALLEN	SALESMAN	7698	20-FEB-81	1600	300	30
7521	WARD	SALESMAN	7698	22-FEB-81	1250	500	30
7654	MARTIN	SALESMAN	7698	28-SEP-81	1250	1400	30
7844	TURNER	SALESMAN	7698	08-SEP-81	1500	0	30
7876	ADAMS	CLERK	7788	12-JAN-83	1100	-	20
7900	JAMES	CLERK	7698	03-DEC-81	950	-	30
7934	MILLER	CLERK	7782	23-JAN-82	1300	-	10

1 - 14

Figure 7-4. *Results of a successful SQL injection attack*

Displaying records that have a DEPTNO equal to anything other than 10 was not the developer's intention when this report was created. But clearly when the illicit value was passed in to P1_ENAME, that is exactly what happened.

The SQL injection attack succeeded for one simple reason: the wrong APEX item syntax was used in the SQL query. Taking another look at Listing 7-6, the &ITEM. syntax was used when referring to P1_ENAME. When using the &ITEM. syntax, APEX will evaluate and replace all variables before it parses the SQL statement. So, much like the previous example, it is possible to pass in a SQL snippet and have that snippet rewrite the SQL statement before it gets parsed, thus allowing for a SQL injection attack to succeed.

Fortunately, the same solution that worked for the sample PL/SQL procedure can be applied in APEX as well. By using bind variable syntax instead of the &ITEM. syntax, APEX will bind in the value for P1_ENAME during the bind phase as it runs the query. This way, the structure of the query will remain intact, and only the value passed in will be able to be influenced by the user.

To do this, simply change the way that the P1_ENAME item is referred to in the SQL for the report, as shown in Listing 7-8.

Listing 7-8. Updated SQL for the Report, Using Bind Variable Syntax

```
SELECT * FROM emp WHERE deptno = 10 AND ename LIKE :P1_ENAME
```

When the report is rerun with the same value for P1_ENAME, very different results will occur, as shown in Figure 7-5.

Figure 7-5. *The results of an attempted SQL injection attack on a report that uses bind variables*

Since the SQL is using the bind variable syntax now, attempting to change the SQL will fail, and unless there is an employee whose name is actually KING' or 'x' = 'x, no data will be found.

Therefore, the bind variable syntax should be used anytime a variable needs to be referenced within any SQL or PL/SQL region in APEX. This also includes conditions, authorization schemes, dynamic actions, or any other place within the APEX tool itself that SQL or PL/SQL is used with a variable.

Bind Variable Notation and Dynamic SQL in APEX

There is one exception to the approach of always using bind variables in APEX SQL and PL/SQL regions, and it is applied when using dynamic SQL. Dynamic SQL reports in APEX—also referred to as the PL/SQL Function Body Returning SQL Query report—essentially allow the developer to assemble a SQL statement and then use that as the source of a report. Dynamic SQL can also be utilized in other areas of APEX, such as the source for lists of values and lists.

Dynamic SQL statements consist of two components: the static component and the variable component. You can see a simple example of a dynamic SQL statement in Listing 7-9.

Listing 7-9. A Simple Example of a Dynamic SQL Statement

```
DECLARE
  l_sql VARCHAR2(255);
BEGIN
-- Start the SQL statement
l_sql := 'SELECT * FROM emp';
-- If P1_ITEM is set to Y, include the WHERE clause
IF :P1_ITEM = 'Y' THEN
  l_sql := l_sql || ' WHERE deptno = 10';
END IF;
-- Return the SQL
RETURN l_sql;
END;
```

This snippet can produce two different SQL queries, based on the value of the APEX item P1_ITEM. If P1_ITEM is set to Y, then the SQL returned will be SELECT * FROM emp WHERE deptno = 10. Otherwise, the SQL returned will be SELECT * FROM emp. The APEX report that this SQL is returned to will then use either of those statements when producing the report. There is also no inherent SQL injection risk with this example, because no variables are used in the construction of the SQL.

The next example uses a variable using bind variable syntax when constructing the SQL statement. If the user enters a value into the item P1_DEPTNO, the code will then incorporate that value into the WHERE clause of the query, as shown in Listing 7-10.

Listing 7-10. An Example of Dynamic SQL That Incorporates a Bind Variable

```
DECLARE
  l_sql VARCHAR2(255);
BEGIN
-- Start the SQL statement
l_sql := 'SELECT * FROM emp';
IF :P1_DEPTNO IS NOT NULL THEN
  -- Apply the filter if a value is provided
  l_sql := l_sql || ' WHERE deptno = ' || :P1_DEPTNO;
ELSE
  -- Otherwise, force the query to return no rows
  l_sql := l_sql || ' WHERE 1=2';
END IF;
-- Print the SQL
htp.p(l_sql);
-- Return the SQL
RETURN l_sql;
END;
```

When this page is run and a valid department number is passed in to P1_DEPTNO, the reports adjusts its results accordingly, returning only those records that match the corresponding department, as shown in Figure 7-6.

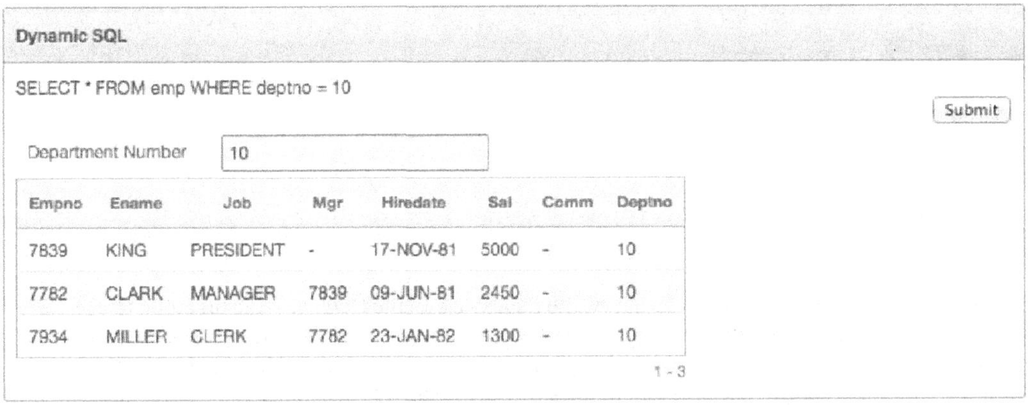

Figure 7-6. Results of the dynamic SQL-based report for DEPTNO = 10

However, when a SQL injection attack is attempted on this report—which, remember, uses bind variable syntax—the results may be a bit surprising, as illustrated in Figure 7-7.

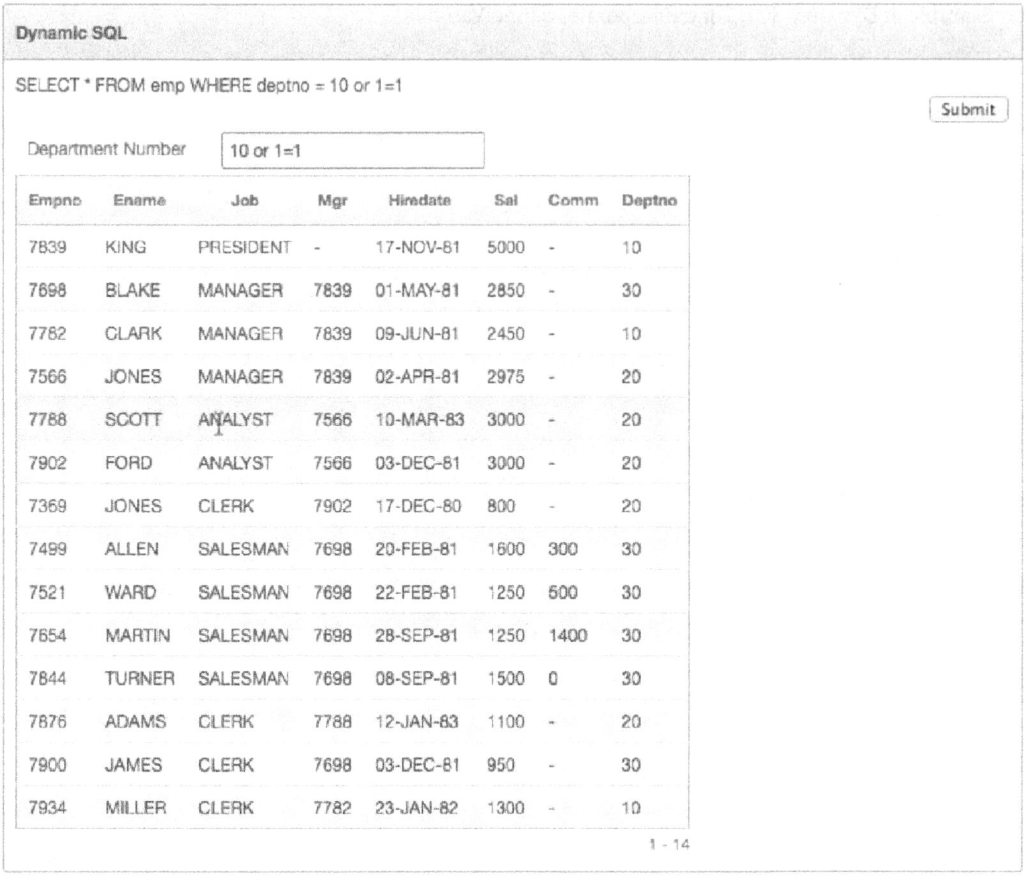

Empno	Ename	Job	Mgr	Hiredate	Sal	Comm	Deptno
7839	KING	PRESIDENT	-	17-NOV-81	5000	-	10
7698	BLAKE	MANAGER	7839	01-MAY-81	2850	-	30
7782	CLARK	MANAGER	7839	09-JUN-81	2450	-	10
7566	JONES	MANAGER	7839	02-APR-81	2975	-	20
7788	SCOTT	ANALYST	7566	10-MAR-83	3000	-	20
7902	FORD	ANALYST	7566	03-DEC-81	3000	-	20
7369	JONES	CLERK	7902	17-DEC-80	800	-	20
7499	ALLEN	SALESMAN	7698	20-FEB-81	1600	300	30
7521	WARD	SALESMAN	7698	22-FEB-81	1250	500	30
7654	MARTIN	SALESMAN	7698	28-SEP-81	1250	1400	30
7844	TURNER	SALESMAN	7698	08-SEP-81	1500	0	30
7876	ADAMS	CLERK	7788	12-JAN-83	1100	-	20
7900	JAMES	CLERK	7698	03-DEC-81	950	-	30
7934	MILLER	CLERK	7782	23-JAN-82	1300	-	10

Figure 7-7. *The results of a SQL injection attack on a dynamic SQL-based report*

What happened? Because this is a dynamic SQL query, the database executes it twice—the first time to concatenate and return the SQL query and the second time to execute it. During the first time it is run, the value of `P1_DEPTNO` is evaluated, replaced, and then concatenated with the rest of the `l_sql` string. If a snippet of SQL is passed in via `P1_DEPTNO`, it will simply get concatenated as part of the string before the PL/SQL block is parsed. Thus, a SQL injection attack can still be achieved, despite that bind variable notation was used.

The proper way to use dynamic SQL in APEX is to ensure that variables that should be part of the SQL are not evaluated while concatenating the string but are instead included as part of the string in their bind variable syntax form. In the case of the previous example, this would be achieved simply by moving in the reference to `:P1_DEPTNO` into the string rather than concatenating it with the string. You can see the correct version of the line in question in Listing 7-11.

Listing 7-11. The correct way to concatenate bind variables into dynamic SQL in APEX

```
-- Apply the filter if a value is provided
l_sql := l_sql || ' WHERE deptno = :P1_DEPTNO';
```

With the reference to `:P1_DEPTNO` moved back into the string, any SQL injection attack on the report will fail with an invalid number error message, as shown in Figure 7-8.

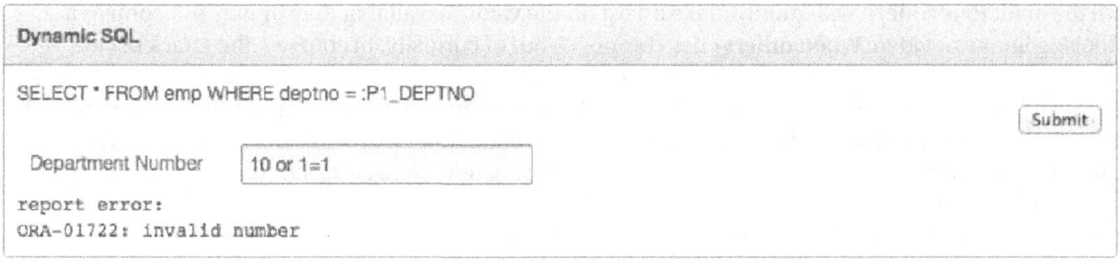

Figure 7-8. *The results of a SQL injection attack on a properly secured dynamic SQL report*

Getting the hang of where to include references to APEX items in dynamic SQL can be tricky. There is a technique that you can use to assist in understanding it better. First, the end goal when using a dynamic SQL statement is to produce a sound, secure SQL statement that makes use of bind variables where needed. It may help to try to visualize or even write down what the expected end result looks like and then instrument your code to produce that.

To assist with the visualization, run the page in debug mode, and then search through the debug information. APEX will automatically insert a record that includes the SQL that it used for dynamic SQL reports, as shown in Figure 7-9.

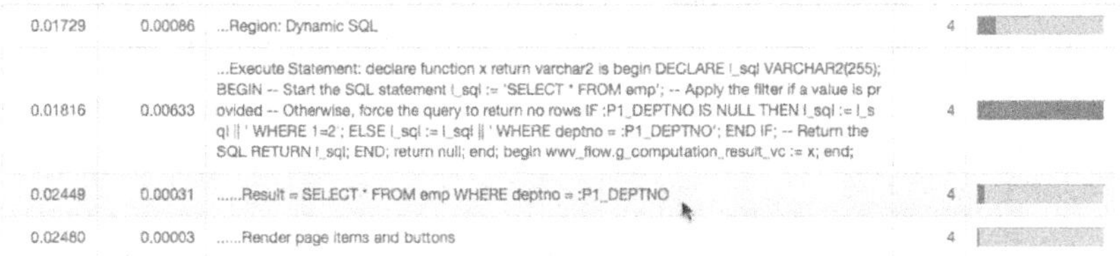

Figure 7-9. *Using debug mode to display the query used in a dynamic SQL report*

Alternatively, you can add a simple line such as `htp.p(l_sql)` that prints the variable used to store the SQL statement, as was done in the examples. If any variables are evaluating too early, they will be evident on the page where the query prints. This technique is a bit quicker but more intrusive than debug mode because the results of the SQL are displayed right above the report as soon as it is generated. Be sure to remove code to display the SQL before deploying to production.

SQL injection is a real risk for APEX and any web application. Fortunately, most APEX developers are already in the habit of using the bind variable syntax to represent APEX items, which is the recommended best practice. Bind variables alone are not the entire answer because attention also needs to be paid when using dynamic SQL in APEX or concatenating strings in named PL/SQL program units that will be passed to `EXECUTE IMMEDIATE`.

Cross-Site Scripting

A cross-site scripting (XSS) attack is similar to a SQL injection attack because they both are carried out by a user inserting malicious code into a web page. The main difference between SQL injection and XSS is the underlying technology that the attacks are targeting. While SQL injection attacks inject malicious SQL or PL/SQL code, XSS attacks inject JavaScript. Given that JavaScript is almost always a client-side language, most XSS attacks occur directly in the browser and oftentimes never need to connect to the back-end database to be successful.

Like SQL injection attacks, the number of cross-site scripting attacks has also seen a surge in recent times. Fortunately, the most common forms of XSS attacks tend to be the most benign. An example of this type of XSS attack is any number of the fake Facebook wall spam posts. If you have been a Facebook user for any amount of time, there's a good chance that one of your friends has fallen victim to these types of attacks. Typically, when the victim comes across a site with the malicious code, it will quietly make a post on the victim's wall that may or may not contain a seedy or illicit-looking image or video. When others click this post—out of curiosity, of course—the attack occurs again, and a new post is made on that user's wall. Given the amount of time people spend on social networking sites these days, this type of attack can spread extremely quickly. Similar attacks have also been reported on Twitter as well.

While making an illicit post of a friend's Facebook wall may be nothing more than embarrassing, the level of sophistication of these types of attacks is on the rise. And as the sophistication increases, one can only assume the severity of the attacks will do so as well.

One of the more dangerous traits of an XSS attack is that it has the capability to go unnoticed for potentially long periods of time. A properly executed XSS attack makes no indication to the user that an attack has occurred. It will silently work in the background, doing whatever it was designed to do. In attack scenarios that do not connect to the web server or database, no log entries are generated, making it that much harder to detect.

In the context of APEX, XSS vulnerabilities are much more common than SQL injection because many database developers simply do not know how to protect against them. Most database developers understand bind variables and the danger of not using them because their benefits are not unique to APEX. Because these database developers transition from older, client-server environments where XSS is simply not possible, they need to become better educated as to what XSS attacks are and how to prevent them.

Furthermore, applications that were originally developed in earlier versions of APEX may have more vulnerabilities than those built in more recent versions because some of the security features aimed at combatting XSS vulnerabilities simply did not exist then. Even today's advanced APEX developer was once a beginner, and that time was likely a few years back, when the product simply did not have the controls to prevent XSS that it does today. So, it is quite likely that applications written in the past by today's advanced APEX developers have quite a few XSS vulnerabilities that need to be addressed.

Anatomy of an Attack

XSS attacks involve passing in a snippet of malicious JavaScript that is then executed by the browser. Since the browser cannot tell the difference between JavaScript that was intended to be on a page from illicit JavaScript, anything that gets passed to it without being properly handled will execute. Thus, in order to implement an XSS attack, you need to have at least an intermediate understanding of JavaScript. When executed, the malicious JavaScript can do any number of things: alter hidden values on a form, open up an iFrame that contains a different site, steal session or cookie values and pass them back to the malicious user's server, or even try to initiate transactions from other parts of the site that the victim is authenticated to. The severity of an XSS attack is limited only by the malicious user's imagination and technical capabilities.

One of the best defenses against any type of XSS attacks is to escape all data before rendering it on the page. When data is escaped, the browser will not try to execute the code but rather harmlessly render it on the page. You can find more details on how to escape data later in this section.

XSS attacks can mostly be categorized into a couple different categories: reflexive and persistent. While both types are equally as dangerous, the methods in which they are implemented do differ. In an APEX environment, it is much more likely to see a persistent attack.

Reflexive Attacks

Reflexive XSS attacks—sometimes referred to as *nonpersistent attacks*—rely on user input being displayed or rendered on the very next page of a web site. In APEX, an example of this would be an error message that contained a reference to a page or application item or a search page that displayed the search term alongside the results. If the page is not properly secured, a malicious user can inject some JavaScript code into a form, and when the resulting page is rendered, the JavaScript will execute.

In APEX 4.0 and older, reflexive attacks were a lot easier to pull off, since values passed to application items via the URL were not escaped. Consider this example: a page contained a region that had a title that included reference to an application item, such as `Transactions for &G_USER.`. If a malicious user altered the URL to include a value for G_USER, as shown in Listing 7-12, the attack would be successful.

Listing 7-12. Passing Illicit JavaScript to the G_USER Item via the URL

```
f?p=139:2:3628920663345303:::::G_USER:<script>alert('Hello');</script>
```

You can see the result of this attack in Figure 7-10 because the JavaScript alert function executes and produces a dialog box.

Figure 7-10. *Passing JavaScript to an application item in APEX 4.0 could result in the JavaScript being executed*

Clearly there is no harm in displaying a dialog box. However, if this simple JavaScript code can be executed, more sophisticated and damaging code could also be executed. Fortunately, this vulnerability was fixed in APEX 4.1 so that any subsequent release is protected against such an attack. The fix involved ensuring that any value passed through the URL is escaped before it is rendered. Using the same syntax illustrated in Listing 7-12 in APEX 4.2, the result is very different, as shown in Figure 7-11.

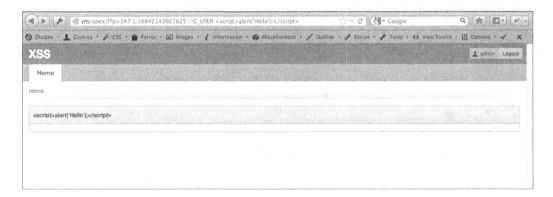

Figure 7-11. *Passing JavaScript to an application item in APEX 4.1 or newer results in the item value being escaped and harmlessly rendered*

This time, instead of the JavaScript code being executed, it was harmlessly rendered as the title of the region. This example is just one of many that underscores the importance of keeping current with the release of APEX. With each release, more and more potential security vulnerabilities are fixed.

APEX has long since automatically escaped page items when they are rendered on the page using the &ITEM. syntax. Thus, if the previous example tried to pass a value to a page item instead of an application item via the URL, there would be no chance that the XSS attack would succeed.

But what if the value of the item is not passed through the URL but rather set via a page computation? The next example does just that—incorporates the value of a page item in the region title. When a snippet of JavaScript is passed in, it is safely escaped and rendered, as shown in Figure 7-12.

Search Results for <script>alert('Hello');</script>

Search   <script>alert('Hello');</script>

no data found

Figure 7-12. *Passing in a value to a page item and rendering it as part of the region title*

APEX doesn't care how the page item got its value; it will always escape any page item before rendering it regardless as to whether it was set via the URL or a computation.

On the other hand, application items are never escaped before being rendered. If an application item is used in part of a region title and that item contains malicious JavaScript, that code will execute, not render harmlessly on the page. This can occur by using a computation that sets the value of an application item to the value of a page item that contains malicious code or by fetching unescaped data from a table or view and assigning it to the application item.

In the next example, the user can input a string into an item called P1_SEARCH. On the same page, there is an after submit computation that sets an application item called G_SEARCH to the value of P1_SEARCH. The region title on the page contains a reference to G_SEARCH using the &ITEM. syntax, with the intent being to alter the region title based on what the user searched for.

Since G_SEARCH is being set from an APEX computation, not via the URL, the string passed to it is not escaped by default. If a bit of malicious JavaScript—<script>alert('Hello');</script>—is entered, it will in turn be used to set G_SEARCH and, then when the page renders, execute and display an alert, as shown in Figure 7-13.

Figure 7-13. *A successful XSS attack using a computation that sets an application item*

This risk exists in all versions of APEX, up to and including APEX 4.2. Therefore, it is recommended that you be cautious when setting values of application items that will be used as part of a static component of an application such as the region title, breadcrumb, tab, list item, and so on. When this is necessary, the value passed to the application item should be escaped by using the apex_escape.html function (more on this later in this chapter) so that any malicious scripts that may be embedded in the item are rendered harmless.

Persistent Attacks

Persistent XSS attacks are similar to reflexive XSS attacks, in that they inject JavaScript code in hopes of it getting executed. The main difference between the two is that a reflexive attack is carried out and impacts only a single user, whereas a persistent attack is carried out by a single user but is designed to impact many. It does this by storing the malicious script in the database rather than simply manipulating a single page. This way, many users can potentially fall victim to the attack over and over again. If undetected, a persistent XSS attack can remain active indefinitely, doing a tremendous amount of damage as more and more users fall victim to it.

Persistent XSS attacks rely on a developer fetching and displaying data from the database without first escaping the data. When this is the case, any malicious code that is stored within the data will be executed rather than displayed. Every time that the record that has been injected with the malicious code is displayed, the attacks occur. When implemented properly, there will be no evidence to the end user that an attack is occurring. Any malicious code will silently execute, giving the user no indication that there may be a problem.

To illustrate a persistent XSS attack, let's consider an example of a simple contact management system. When a malicious user wants to launch a persistent XSS attack, the user would update their own record and embed the malicious JavaScript within one of their fields, as illustrated in Figure 7-14.

Figure 7-14. *A user using a persistent XSS attack to store malicious JavaScript in the Job field of their own employee record*

The intent here is that anyone who searches for the malicious user's record and views it as part of a report will fall victim to the attack because that is where the malicious code would be executed. Every time their record came up as part of a report, the code would execute again, as shown in Figure 7-15. In a real attack, it would be unlikely that the malicious code made any indication as to its existence by displaying an alert. Rather, the attack would likely attempt to steal session values or other sensitive information and send it back to the malicious user.

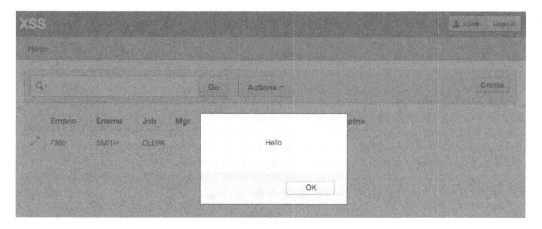

Figure 7-15. *The result of a persistent XSS attack*

In more modern versions of APEX, a developer would have to go out of their way to enable the persistent XSS attack to occur because report columns are now created with built-in escaping routines by default. Applications written in older versions of APEX may also still be susceptible to this type of attack, even if upgraded to APEX 4.1 or 4.2.

Persistent XSS attacks do not have to be limited to the same application in which they were implemented. It is possible to launch the persistent attack through one application and have it manifest itself through a completely different application written in a completely different technology, making them that more dangerous.

Sanitizing Data

To prevent any type of cross-site scripting attack, you must ensure that all output that can be influenced by a user at any point in time is properly escaped. As previously mentioned, escaping a string of HTML will cause the browser to harmlessly render that string rather than interpret any tag within it. To illustrate this concept, let's consider a simple example. If the string <b>hello</b> was included in an HTML document, the word *hello* would be rendered on the page in bold text. The <b> and </b> tags were interpreted by the browser not as text to render but rather as a directive to apply a bold font to the text placed in between them. The same holds true for any valid HTML markup tag, including <script>, which denotes that the contents is code and may be executed.

Thus, escaping any data that may contain illicit tags is the best defense mechanism against XSS attacks. Within an APEX application, escaping data is done differently, depending on what component is being secured. In some cases— such as report columns—there are options that can be configured to ensure that when APEX renders data, it will be first escaped. In other cases, such as PL/SQL regions, no such declarative controls exist, and it is up to the developer to instrument the code so that all output is properly escaped.

Instead of relying on escaping data as it comes out of the database, why not simply escape it before it goes into the database? While that sounds like a good idea, it does have a couple of potentially fatal flaws. In many systems, there is no way to ensure that data that will be displayed has been properly escaped. Perhaps there is an older client-server system that interfaces with the same database that the APEX application is built on. Since it is unlikely the client-server application is sanitizing input at all, developers have to assume that any data could contain malicious code and ensure that it is escaped.

On the other side of the fence, if all inputs are purely escaped, that may cause issues with other systems that also use the data. Consider the following string that a user may have input: Scott Spendolini. If escaped, this string would now look like this: Scott Spendolini. If this value had to be printed on a legal document or other contract, there may be issues because the escaped version of a space is now rendering as   in between the first and last names. There may also be cases when a form needs to capture HTML so that it can in turn be rendered on another page or from another application.

Unfortunately, there is no single correct way to sanitize data. Some values should be escaped, whereas others may simply have specific tags, such as `<script>`, removed. It all depends on the specific use case of the form in question. Any data that needs to be validated before being inserted into the database is going to create extra work for the developer. Developers will need to create either table APIs or validation rules built into database triggers to facilitate the type of sanitization required. In many cases, the APEX automated row processes will need to be replaced with a call to a table API to ensure that data is handled properly. Validations may also be required to ensure that specific strings are simply rejected and not allowed to be inserted into the database at all.

Restricted Characters

New in APEX 4.2, the Restricted Characters attribute allows the developer to choose which characters are allowed on a per-item basis. There are five different options for this attribute:

- All Characters Allowed

- Whitelist for a–Z, 0–9 and Space

- Blacklist HTML command characters (<>")

- Blacklist &<>";,*|=% and --

- Blacklist &<>"/;,*|=% or -- and new line

By restricting which characters are allowed, the risk of a malicious user executing an XSS attack is greatly reduced. APEX will validate the values entered in an item as the page processes, and if an invalid character is discovered, APEX will produce an error message, as shown in Figure 7-16.

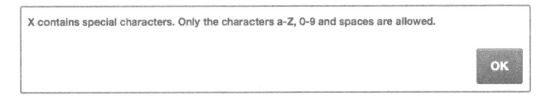

X contains special characters. Only the characters a-Z, 0-9 and spaces are allowed.

OK

Figure 7-16. *Error message generated when a restricted character is submitted*

As previously mentioned, while useful in some cases, simply escaping all input fields may not be the most effective strategy to prevent XSS attacks.

APEX_ESCAPE

The guidelines as to when to sanitize output are a little more cut and dry. If the data is going to be rendered as part of an HTML page, it needs to be sanitized. Fortunately, there are relatively simple ways to do this within APEX. While many components within APEX offer declarative controls that enable escaping, any regions that contain code that produces output need to handle this via calling the proper API. This includes any region that contains a SQL query—such as a report, chart, or calendar—as well as PL/SQL regions. Traditionally, APEX used a function called `htf.escape_sc`. Part of the Oracle Web Toolkit, `htf.escape_sc` would return an escaped version of the string passed to it, replacing instances of <, >, ", and & with their escaped counterparts.

New in APEX 4.2, an API called apex_escape was introduced. This API is designed to take the place of the older htf.escape_sc by providing more functionality and utilities for different contexts, such as JavaScript and LDAP. The apex_escape API was designed exclusively for use with APEX, so the level of integration is strong. Depending on the escaping mode, which can be set at the application level, apex_escape can behave the same way as htf.escape_sc does, or it can escape all four characters that htf.escape_sc does as well as the , and /.

When rendering HTML from a PL/SQL region or applying a function to a SQL query, ensure that the output string is passed to apex_escape.html. This will ensure that the values rendered are properly escaped, thus neutralizing any potential XSS attacks. For example, consider a PL/SQL region that loops through some records and prints the name and job of each record, as shown in Listing 7-13.

Listing 7-13. Code for a PL/SQL Region That Prints Unescaped Text

```
BEGIN
FOR x IN (SELECT ename, job FROM emp ORDER BY ename)
LOOP
  htp.prn(x.ename || ' (' || x.job || ')<br />');
END LOOP;
END;
```

When this region renders, it will display any data stored in the EMP and JOB columns without escaping it. If there is malicious code in either of those columns, it will be executed rather than rendered on the page. Adding a call to apex_escape.html, as shown in Listing 7-14, will ensure that any data output from this region will get properly escaped and rendered harmlessly.

Listing 7-14. Code for a PL/SQL Region That Includes a Call to apex_escape.html

```
BEGIN
FOR x IN (SELECT ename, job FROM emp ORDER BY ename)
LOOP
  htp.prn(apex_escape.html(x.ename || ' (' || x.job)
    || ')<br />');
END LOOP;
END;
```

Thus, be sure that anytime a PL/SQL region is used to render data on the page that the data gets properly escaped beforehand using the apex_escape.html function.

Column Formatting

Oftentimes, developers will intersperse HTML markup or references to images within a SQL query in order to include it as part of a report. While this practice does allow a lot of flexibility in the look and feel of a report, it could introduce the potential for a cross-site scripting attack. For example, take the SQL query in Listing 7-15.

Listing 7-15. A SQL Query That Embeds Image References

```
SELECT
  e.ename,
  CASE
    WHEN e.deptno = 10 THEN '<img src="/i/green_flag.gif"> '
      || d.dname
    WHEN e.deptno = 20 THEN '<img src="/i/red_flag.gif"> '
      || d.dname
    WHEN e.deptno = 30 THEN '<img src="/i/grey_flag.gif"> '
      || d.dname
```

```
    WHEN e.deptno = 40 THEN '<img src="/i/yellow_flag.gif"> '
      || d.dname
    ELSE '<img src="/i/white_flag.gif"> ' || d.dname
  END icon
FROM
  emp e,
  dept d
WHERE
  e.deptno = d.deptno
```

In the recent few releases of APEX, all report columns in any report are configured by default so that their output will be escaped. Therefore, the data in the report that is based on the SQL query from Listing 7-15 will initially be escaped and render the HTML tags rather than interpret them. The result would look similar to Figure 7-17.

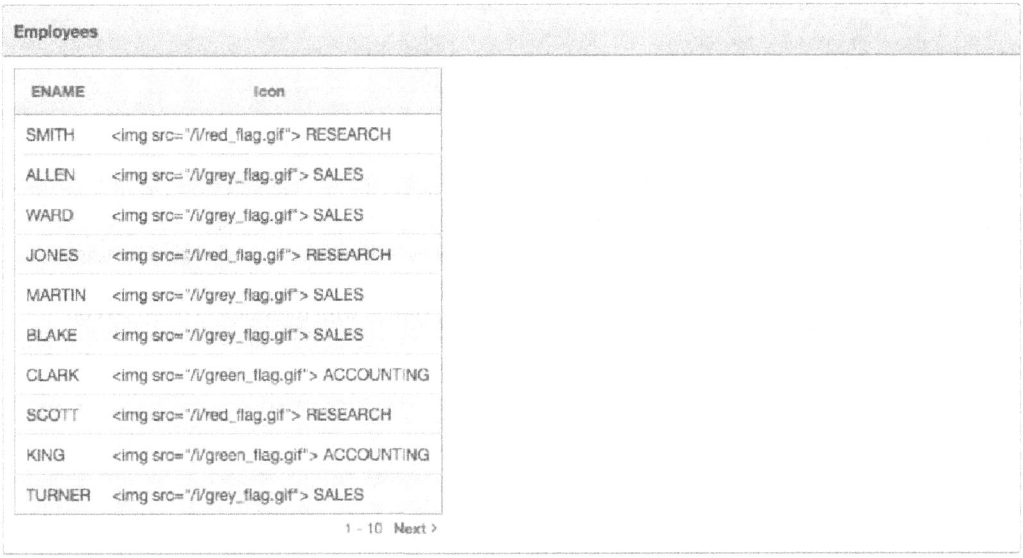

ENAME	Icon
SMITH	<img src="/i/red_flag.gif"> RESEARCH
ALLEN	<img src="/i/grey_flag.gif"> SALES
WARD	<img src="/i/grey_flag.gif"> SALES
JONES	<img src="/i/red_flag.gif"> RESEARCH
MARTIN	<img src="/i/grey_flag.gif"> SALES
BLAKE	<img src="/i/grey_flag.gif"> SALES
CLARK	<img src="/i/green_flag.gif"> ACCOUNTING
SCOTT	<img src="/i/red_flag.gif"> RESEARCH
KING	<img src="/i/green_flag.gif"> ACCOUNTING
TURNER	<img src="/i/grey_flag.gif"> SALES

1 - 10 Next >

Figure 7-17. *The results of running a report based on the previous SQL statement*

Each column in any APEX report—standard or interactive—contains a Display As attribute. This attribute determines how that column will be rendered when the report is run. By default, it will be set to "Display as Text (escape special characters, does not save state)," as shown in Figure 7-18.

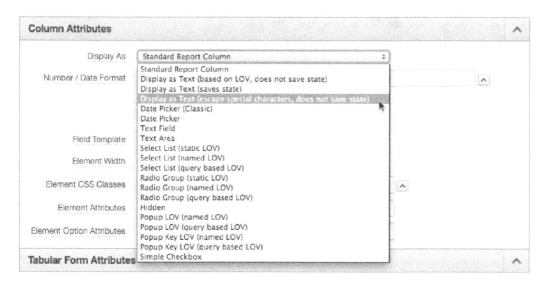

Figure 7-18. *The Display As attribute of a column in a standard report*

As its name implies, this option will ensure that all data that is output is first escaped before being displayed on the page. The first option on the list—Standard Report Column—does not have nearly as obvious a name. When selected, data in this column will not be escaped and rendered on the page as is. If malicious code exists for data in this column, it will be executed as the page renders.

In keeping with the example, if the desired result is to render the image inline with the value in the ICON column, the Display As needs to be set to Standard Report Column. If the report is run now, the date in the ICON column is not escaped, and the image renders inline with the data, as shown in Figure 7-19.

ENAME	Icon
SMITH	RESEARCH
ALLEN	SALES
WARD	SALES
JONES	RESEARCH
MARTIN	SALES
BLAKE	SALES
CLARK	ACCOUNTING
SCOTT	RESEARCH
KING	ACCOUNTING
TURNER	SALES

Employees

1 - 10 Next >

Figure 7-19. *The same report, this time with escaping disabled for the ICON column*

Finally, the report works as desired because the icon renders just before the department name. However, since the ICON column is no longer being escaped, it is wide open to a XSS attack. If a user was able to set the value of Department Name to a snippet of malicious JavaScript—such as ACCOUNTING<script>alert('Hello');</script>—that code will be executed, as shown in Figure 7-20.

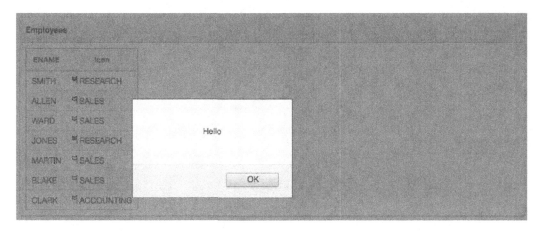

Figure 7-20. Again, the same SQL statement, this time falling victim to an XSS attack

Wrapping the entire CASE statement in apex_escape.html will of course escape the data returned from it, but the result will look exactly like Figure 7-17. This is clearly not what the developer intended because the images are still not rendering. In many instances, developers will simply just give up trying to secure this report the proper way and disable escaping on the ICON column. This does not have to be the case because there is a viable and secure alternative.

Instead of embedding the HTML code in the SQL, it is better to simply select the data and use the HTML Expression attribute at the column level to apply the HTML code needed. With this approach, the SQL query can be rewritten to simply return the name of the employee, department, and corresponding image, as illustrated in Listing 7-16.

Listing 7-16. A SQL Query That Will Be Used to Display an Image but Contains No HTML

```
SELECT
  e.ename,
  d.dname,
  CASE
    WHEN e.deptno = 10 THEN 'green_flag.gif'
    WHEN e.deptno = 20 THEN 'red_flag.gif'
    WHEN e.deptno = 30 THEN 'grey_flag.gif'
    WHEN e.deptno = 40 THEN 'yellow_flag.gif'
    ELSE 'white_flag.gif'
  END icon
FROM
  emp e,
  dept d
WHERE
  e.deptno = d.deptno
```

Instead of including the `img` tag in the SQL, it will be placed in the HTML Expression attribute in the Column Formatting region. Column aliases surrounded by a # can be used to represent their corresponding column values from the SQL query. As shown in Figure 7-21, the `img` tag referencing the `ICON` column as well as a reference to the `DNAME` column is included in the HTML expression.

Figure 7-21. *The HTML Expression attribute for the ICON column*

Now, when the report is run again, the result that the developer was after is finally achieved in a secure fashion. In a standard report, there is an option in the report attributes called Strip HTML. When selected, APEX will automatically strip any HTML tags from the original column value fetched from the database. HTML that is entered via the HTML expression of column link will still be applied. Since this option is enabled by default, APEX will automatically remove the `<script>` tags before rendering the data. Thus, only part of the malicious string that was added is displayed in Figure 7-22.

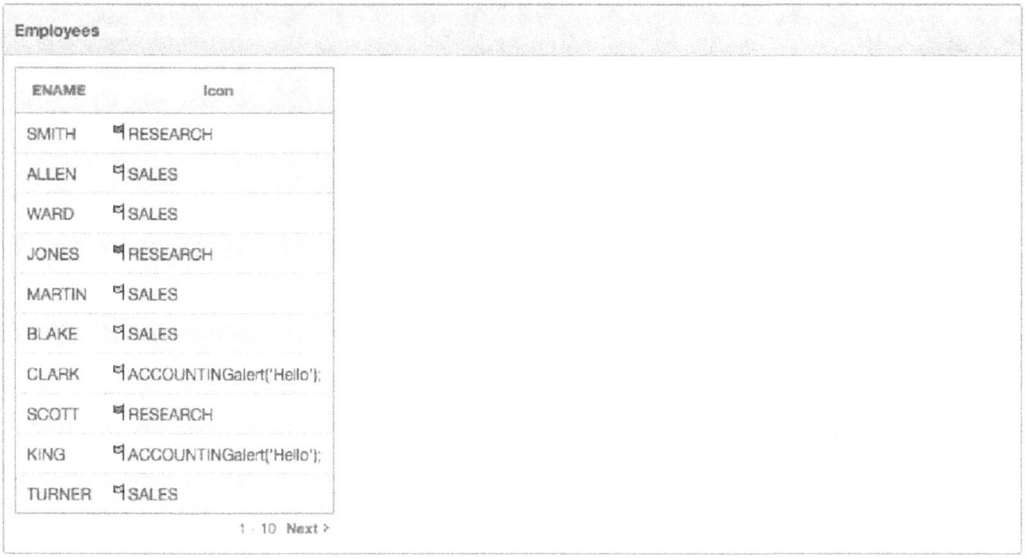

Figure 7-22. *The report when the HTML is applied through the HTML Expression attribute*

In an interactive report, the `<script>` tag is not removed from the HTML expression; rather, it is escaped with the rest of the string, as shown in Figure 7-23.

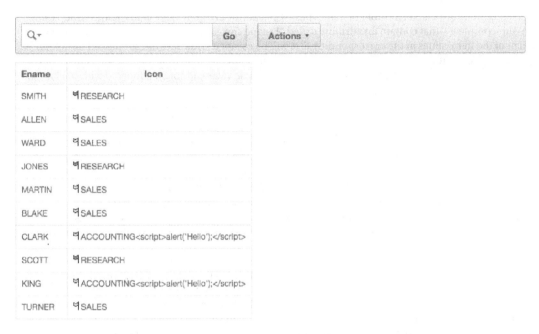

Figure 7-23. *An interactive report where the HTML is applied through the HTML Expression attribute*

Escaping data programmatically can be tricky because it is not as simple as always passing any column that will be displayed through a function. Take adequate time to secure output rendered from either SQL or PL/SQL regions in your application by ensuring that the Display As attribute is set to escape the data and any HTML is entered in the HTML Expression attribute.

Escaping Regions and Items

Similar to report columns, a number of other components in APEX can have their output escaped, so as long as the proper attribute is set. These component types include HTML regions, some item types, cookies, and frames. Be sure to ensure that any output rendered within these components is escaped.

First, consider HTML regions. There are actually three subtypes of HTML regions: HTML Text, HTML Text (with shortcuts) and HTML Text (escape special characters). These regions are often used simply as containers for items, and text is rarely entered in them, so the need to ensure that their contents are escaped is typically low. Given that more recent versions of APEX automatically escape any value stored in page items, the need to worry about HTML regions is even lower.

However, if the HTML region contains reference to an application item using the &ITEM. syntax, then the "HTML Text (escape special characters)" region type should be selected so that any malicious code in the application item is escaped rather than executed.

Next, it is important to reiterate how page items differ from application items when rendered on the page. APEX will automatically escape any output from a page item when it is referred to with the &ITEM. syntax. There is no option to enable for this to occur; it happens automatically. Application items, on the other hand, do not automatically get escaped when referred to with the &ITEM. syntax. For example, developers will often reference a page or application item in a region title so that it reflects the name of the customer being edited. If the name of the customer is stored in a page item, then no additional precautions need to be taken. However, if the name of the customer is stored in an application item, be sure to escape that value before assigning it to the application item so that any malicious code is neutralized.

Speaking of items, there are a small number of item types—Checkboxes, Display Only items, Radio Groups, and Text Fields with Autocomplete—that contain an attribute called "Escape special characters." When enabled, the value of the item itself or of the item values in the corresponding lists will be escaped. This attribute is enabled by default and should be always be left that way unless there is a specific need to render an item or items in a list using HTML tags. If this is the case, then great care should be taken to ensure that those vales cannot be tampered with or altered.

Protecting Cookies

Cookies are nothing more than text files that a browser reads and writes to in order to maintain a value-attribute pair that can persist longer than a single page view. Developers have long used cookies to store session-specific information so that as a user goes from one page view to another, the value of the cookie can be used to determine whether their session is valid. Many web sites, regardless of their underlying technologies, also use cookies in this manner.

APEX uses cookies for both the application development environment as well as any user-developed applications. The APEX development team made it a point to store very little information in the cookies because any data stored there is not very secure. This best practice is a good model for any developer or any web application. Chapter 9 discusses how APEX uses cookies in much more detail.

Most APEX application developers elect to use preferences to store user-specific values that need to persist across sessions for a number of reasons. First, preferences are automatically stored in the database. This way, there is no local trace of them and their associated values are not left on the user's workstation. Second, since preferences are stored in the database, they are available no matter which physical device the user uses to log in. Cookies, on the other hand, are available only when the user is using the application from the same physical device. And lastly, there is a robust set of APIs that APEX provides that easily is called to manage preferences. This set of APIs can also be used by developers to set default preferences, for instance.

Should cookies still be needed, there are a couple of security concerns that need to be reviewed. One of the attributes used when setting a cookie is called HttpOnly. When enabled, this attribute prevents any client-side script from accessing the values of the cookie, essentially blocking it from a potential XSS attack. The downside is that this value is also blocked from legitimate code. Thus, if sensitive, session-based information needs to be stored in a cookie, the HttpOnly parameter should be enabled.

Unfortunately, the version of owa_cookie that comes with APEX does not support the HttpOnly parameter. The attribute is simply not part of the SEND procedure, making it impossible to enable. Oddly enough, the version of owa_cookie that is part of Fusion Middleware does support this option. Short of creating a custom version of owa_cookie that supports HttpOnly or copying the version that ships with Fusion Middleware, there is no cut-and-dry solution to setting cookies with the HttpOnly attribute via APEX until the version of owa_cookie is updated to support it.

Second, when setting cookies in APEX, the secure flag should always be set to Y. By enabling the secure attribute, it will ensure that the web session is running over SSL before the cookie is allowed to be set. If the session is running over just HTTP and is not encrypted, the cookie will simply not be set because there is a risk that someone would be able to see the value passed back by sniffing the network traffic. For this to work, the associated APEX web listener needs to be configured to work with SSL first. You can find more details about secure cookies in Chapter 14.

Frames

As mentioned in Chapter 6, there is a new setting in APEX 4.2 called Embed in Frames. Depending on the setting, this attribute controls whether an APEX application will be allowed to run within an iFrame. A specific type of XSS attack called *clickjacking* attempts to trick the user into clicking one link, when in reality they are clicking a malicious link set up by the malicious user. The Embed in Frames option is designed to prevent such an attack from occurring. You can find details of how to securely set Embed in Frames properly in Chapter 6.

URL Tampering

Last, but definitely not least, is URL tampering. This type of attack is perhaps one of the most dangerous because unlike the others, it requires zero programming knowledge and can be launched by even the most nontechnical user. Furthermore, many APEX developers who come from a nonweb environment are typically not familiar with URL tampering and take no steps to protect against it.

URL tampering involves a user changing a parameter or value in the URL and reloading the page with the new value. When the page with the new value is submitted, there is a potential that the user will see data or components that he would otherwise not see. Since many APEX applications make use of the URL as a mechanism to pass values to items, APEX can be particularly vulnerable to this type of attack, if not properly secured.

Authorization Inconsistencies

One of the most common security vulnerabilities in APEX applications is when a developer forgets to secure a page or group of pages from unauthorized users. Oftentimes this occurs as an application grows in size and sophistication. For example, a simple application based on a few tables may at some point require a couple of pages used to manage the application itself. These pages contain forms on somewhat sensitive data. To protect users from accessing these pages, the developer may add an authorization scheme to the tab that leads to the admin pages but forget to protect the page itself. Thus, if a malicious user tampers with the URL and happens to enter the ID of one of the administrative pages, he will be able to run those pages as if he were an admin user.

This type of vulnerability in APEX is known as an *authorization inconsistency*. An authorization inconsistency can be defined as when a component—such as a list entry, tab, or process—is restricted by an authorization scheme but the page or other component that it is associated with is not. In some cases, both the component and target page may have different authorization schemes. This may be acceptable, depending on the criteria of each scheme. Also, any on-demand process that does not have a corresponding authorization scheme is at risk because a malicious user could reference and execute that process via the URL.

Keep in mind that once a user authenticates to an APEX application, that user can tamper with the URL and change the current page and/or pass values to attempt to set items or execute processes. Therefore, if there is not adequate protection on the target pages or components, a malicious user may gain access to them.

Authorization inconsistencies are difficult to protect against because there is no easy way or single report to determine whether and where they exist within APEX. In fact, they tend to be more common in larger, more sophisticated applications that have been developed by more advanced developers because the sheer size and complexity of such applications is ripe for these types of vulnerabilities. Fortunately, tools like Enkitec eSERT has such a report, as shown in Figure 7-24.

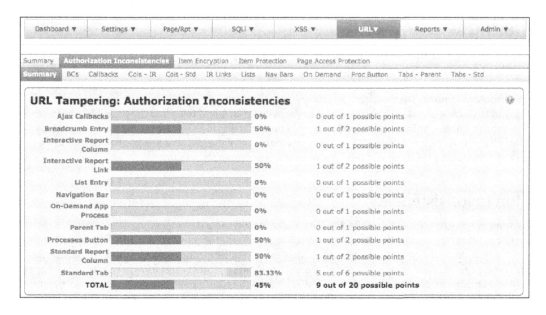

Figure 7-24. *The Authorization Inconsistencies report in eSERT*

Once eSERT identifies any potential authorization inconsistency, it is up to the developer to inspect and either mitigate the risk by securing the corresponding component or determine that there is no risk based on the specific instance.

Page and Item Protection

Consider a report based on the simple SQL statement SELECT * FROM emp WHERE deptno = 30. When the report is run, only those employees in department 30 will be returned, as shown in Figure 7-25.

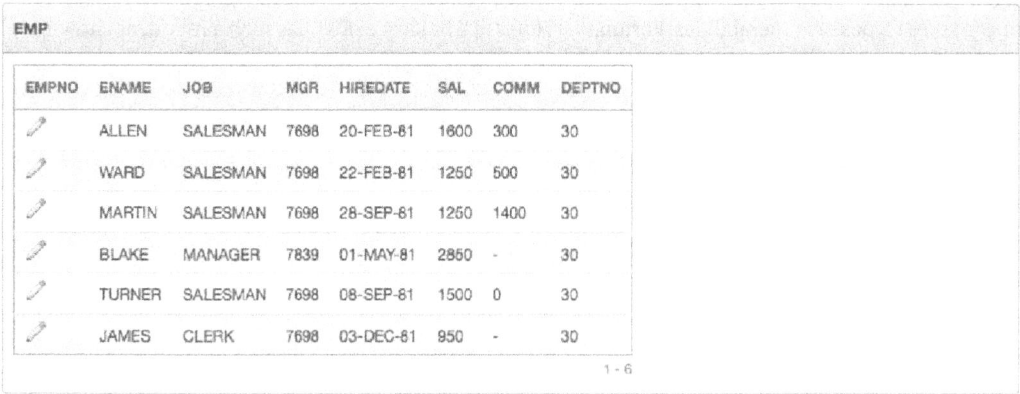

EMP							
EMPNO	ENAME	JOB	MGR	HIREDATE	SAL	COMM	DEPTNO
🖉	ALLEN	SALESMAN	7698	20-FEB-81	1600	300	30
🖉	WARD	SALESMAN	7698	22-FEB-81	1250	500	30
🖉	MARTIN	SALESMAN	7698	28-SEP-81	1250	1400	30
🖉	BLAKE	MANAGER	7839	01-MAY-81	2850	-	30
🖉	TURNER	SALESMAN	7698	08-SEP-81	1500	0	30
🖉	JAMES	CLERK	7698	03-DEC-81	950	-	30

1 - 6

Figure 7-25. *The results of a report on the EMP table for DEPTNO = 30*

This report also has a link to a form that allows the user to edit any of the records returned in the report. After clicking the edit link for the user WARD, there is a new URL displayed in the browser, as shown in Listing 7-17.

Listing 7-17. The URL When Editing the Record for WARD from the EMP Table

```
http://server/apex/f?p=149:2:233212876525::::P2_EMPNO:7521
```

This URL—and the link that leads to it—uses APEX's ability to pass a value-attribute pair through the URL. In Listing 7-17, the item P2_EMPNO is passed the value 7521 using the seventh and eighth positions in the parameterized string. When page 2 loads, the automatic row fetch process will incorporate the value of P2_EMPNO when it fetches a row to be displayed on the form.

If a malicious user took note of how the mechanics of processing this value worked, he may be inclined to pass a different value to P2_EMPNO through the URL. If the malicious user changed the value from 7521 to 7782 and submitted that URL to the page, APEX would in turn fetch the record for CLARK, as shown in Figure 7-26.

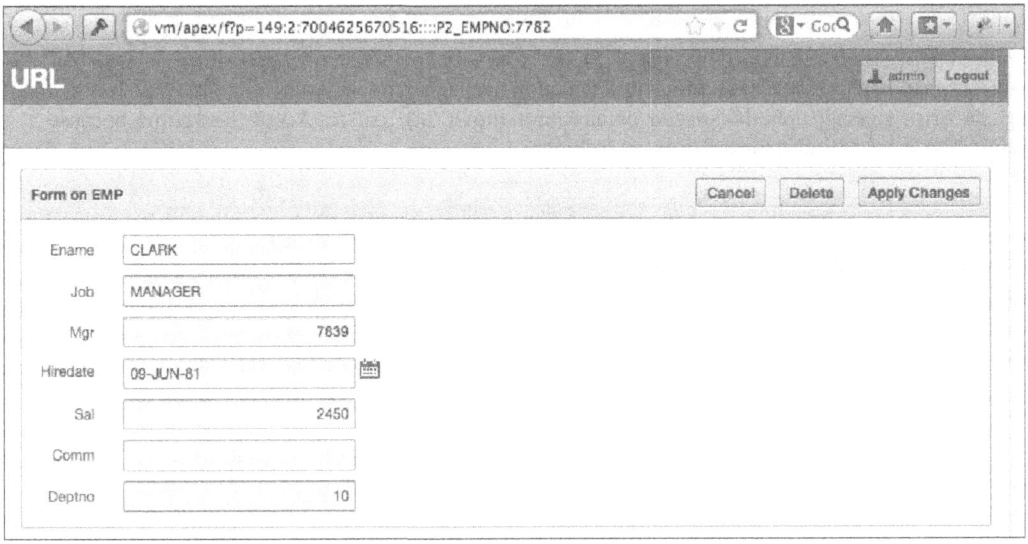

Figure 7-26. A record where P2_EMPNO = 7782, after the URL was tampered with

How would the user guess which value was used? It all depends. Perhaps the IDs are nothing more than employee IDs, which are easy to find by other means. Or perhaps the IDs are all sequential, so that all a user would have to do is take theirs and add or subtract 1 to see someone else's record. It is even possible that the malicious user was skilled enough to use an automated tool, such as URL Flipper, to quickly cycle through many IDs with the tap of a key. It really doesn't matter how the user found data they were not supposed to see or how long it took for them to find it. At the end of the day, there was a data breach that could have easily been prevented.

APEX provides a feature called Page Access Protection, which is part of APEX's Session State Protection mechanism. When enabled, this feature will prevent a malicious user from manipulating the values passed via the URL. It does this by appending an additional checksum to the end of the URL. If the any portion of the URL is modified, then the checksum will no longer equal what the APEX engine expects, and an error message will be displayed, as shown in Figure 7-27. Chapter 6 discusses Page Access Protection and its different options.

Session state protection violation: This may be caused by manual alteration of a URL containing a checksum or by using a link with an incorrect or missing checksum. If you are unsure what caused this error, please contact the application administrator for assistance.

Contact your application administrator.

OK

Figure 7-27. *Error message displayed when an improper checksum or tampered URL is passed to a page with Page Access Protection enabled*

When running an application and logged into the APEX development environment, a more detailed error message will be displayed when a session state protection violation occurs, as shown in Figure 7-28. There is little risk here, even though the error message includes specific details about the PL/SQL call stack and checksums, because this will occur only when the user is also logged in as a developer.

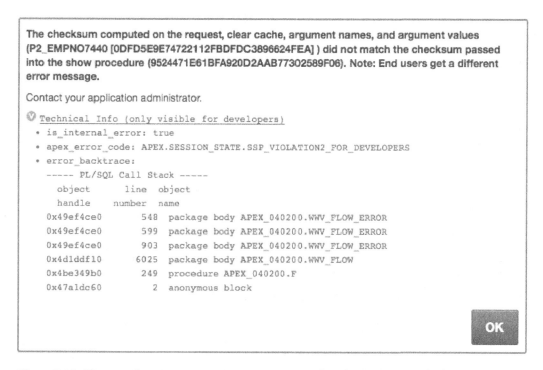

The checksum computed on the request, clear cache, argument names, and argument values (P2_EMPNO7440 [0DFD5E9E74722112FBDFDC3896624FEA]) did not match the checksum passed into the show procedure (9524471E61BFA920D2AAB77302589F06). Note: End users get a different error message.

Contact your application administrator.

ⓥ Technical Info (only visible for developers)
- is_internal_error: true
- apex_error_code: APEX.SESSION_STATE.SSP_VIOLATION2_FOR_DEVELOPERS
- error_backtrace:
  ----- PL/SQL Call Stack -----
    object   line object
    handle   number name
  0x49ef4ce0   548 package body APEX_040200.WWV_FLOW_ERROR
  0x49ef4ce0   599 package body APEX_040200.WWV_FLOW_ERROR
  0x49ef4ce0   903 package body APEX_040200.WWV_FLOW_ERROR
  0x4d1ddf10   6025 package body APEX_040200.WWV_FLOW
  0x4be349b0   249 procedure APEX_040200.F
  0x47a1dc60   2 anonymous block

OK

Figure 7-28. *The same Page Access Protection error message when the developer is also logged into the APEX development environment*

Enabling Page Access Protection essentially puts a "shield" around a specific page, protecting it based on the level of protection applied. In the case of the Arguments Must Have Checksum setting, any attempt to set values while accessing that page will require a proper checksum as part of the URL. If the checksum is modified or absent, then they page will simply not render, and an error message will be displayed.

What is deceiving to many developers is that Page Access Protection does nothing to directly protect the individual items on that page. Rather, it simply determines what level of security is applied when a user attempts to access that page. Consider this example: if an application had page 1 set to Arguments Must Have Checksum and page 2 set to Unrestricted, a clever, malicious user would be able to set the value of an item on page 1—or any other page, for that matter—by passing its name and value to page 2. The fact that page 1 is protected at the page level is irrelevant and does not protect against any individual item on page 2 from being set from the URL.

Fortunately, there is a feature that prevents such an attack from occurring: Item Protection. Item Protection is part of APEX's Session State Protection mechanism and is applied at the item level. Item Protection can be set to five values. The number of settings available depends on whether Session State Protection is enabled at the application level. If it is disabled, then only Unrestricted and "Restricted—may not be set from browser" will be available. If it is enabled, then all five options will be available. The details of each option are outlined here:

- *Unrestricted*: When set to Unrestricted, item values may be set either by using a form or by passing values through the URL. This is the default setting when creating new items.

- *Restricted—may not be set from browser*: As the name of this option implies, values for the associated item cannot be set from the browser—either by using a form or by passing a value through the URL. This option can be associated only with items of type Display Only (save state = no), Text Field (Disabled, does not save state) and Start and Stop Grid Layout.

- The next three options are available only when Session State Protection is enabled at the application level. All of them require that an additional checksum be present when attempting to change the value of the item. The only difference is the scope at which each option is applied.

  - *Checksum Required—Application Level*: The value of the item may be set via the URL provided that a checksum common to the application is passed along with it.

  - *Checksum Required—User Level*: The value of the item may be set via the URL provided that a checksum common to the user is passed along with it.

  - *Checksum Required—Session Level*: The value of the item may be set via the URL provided that a checksum common to the session is passed along with it.

While the difference between the latter three options is subtle, only the last one, Checksum Required—Session Level, should be used because it offers the most security, preventing the same checksum from being used in a different session by any other user. Always enabling Item Protection on hidden primary key items is a good best practice to adopt. This way, a malicious user cannot modify these values by passing them through the URL of a page that is not properly protected.

Unfortunately, enabling Item Protection on items that are modified through an Ajax call will result in an error. The APEX engine cannot distinguish how a value was changed. It can tell only if a value was changed, based on the current and expected checksum. Thus, if a value is altered by an Ajax call, the checksum that APEX expects will not match what was originally sent with the page. In this case, it may be necessary to disable Item Protection in order to preserve the intended functionality. When this is necessary, it is recommended you provide an additional layer of validation via an APEX validation to ensure that the value passed in is, in fact, a legitimate one.

Virtual Private Database and Secure Views

Enabling session state protection is a critical step in securing any APEX application because it prevents malicious users from tampering with the URL and manipulating item values. However, session state protection is but one layer in a multilayered approach that should be used to secure the application data. Also important to consider is that while session state protection does offer adequate protection for APEX applications, it does nothing to protect applications that access the same data using a technology other than APEX.

Chapter 11 discusses how to use a standard Oracle view combined with an application context to secure what data is available to the application. These "secure views," as they are called, are used in the place of any reference to a table in the APEX application. The security embedded in the view automatically limits what data is exposed through the application without having to rely on the developer to add a sophisticated WHERE clause to each query. The benefit of applying this security at the data layer is that it will be available regardless of what technology is used to access it. This allows for a more centralized data security model to be built, which is easier to manage over time.

Chapter 12 expands on the idea of securing data at the database but does so using Virtual Private Database (VPD). VPD is a no-cost supported feature of the Oracle Database Enterprise Edition. It can be managed either through Oracle Enterprise Manager or via SQL*Plus and is completely compatible with APEX applications. VPD essentially dynamically rewrites the WHERE clause of a query before it executes, based on rules specified in a function. It is also more robust and offers more features than a secured view.

Summary

Protecting against SQL injection, cross-site scripting, and URL tampering attacks is one of the most difficult tasks when it comes to securing an APEX application, largely because of the large number of possible attack vectors. However, it is one of the most critical tasks because malicious users are well aware of how to attempt to exploit these types of weaknesses in web applications.

One of the best ways to ensure that all application code adheres to these best practices is to ensure that regular peer code reviews occur. This way, a second set of eyes will be able to evaluate the code and usually identify potential risks that the original developer may not have noticed. As Tom Kyte has said, for the best results when doing peer reviews, be sure you pick someone who does not like you. Using an automated tool such as eSERT will also assist in identifying the obvious mistakes.

■ ■ ■

CHAPTER 8

User Authentication

Before users can access APEX applications, they have to log in. This is typically done by providing a user name and corresponding password. If the credentials match, then a user becomes authenticated and can proceed to use the application. If not, then the user will be prompted to try again. Too many invalid attempts, and the account may become disabled, requiring an administrator to intervene.

The mapping of a user repository to an APEX application is called an *authentication scheme*. Each application can have multiple authentication schemes embedded within it, but only one can be set as the current authentication scheme or the one that APEX will actually use when running the application.

■ **Caution** APEX is not an identity management solution and should never, ever be used as one. User credentials for all APEX applications should be stored in a centrally managed repository, such as an LDAP server. This way, as users are hired and fired, all of their access to any systems are immediately also activated or revoked by the administrator.

Since no two organizations are alike—or since, in many cases, no two departments within any single organization are alike—APEX provides a wide range of authentication options. Each option has its own settings that can be altered to meet the specific needs of the user repository. If one of the prebuilt authentication schemes still won't cut it, there is a Custom authentication scheme that can be configured to do virtually anything.

This chapter will start by reviewing the different types of authentication schemes. It will then cover attributes that are specific to all types of authentication scheme. Since the type of authentication scheme does not change how APEX manages sessions, that process is identical no matter which scheme is used. The last part of this chapter will cover both the login and logout events in APEX in detail.

Types of Authentication Schemes

In most cases, organizations do not want to create another set of credentials for use with APEX—or any other technology, for that matter. A good identity management strategy has its core a centralized user repository for use across the entire enterprise. APEX subscribes to this strategy in that it is extensible enough to be integrated with virtually any type of user repository. This ensures that all credentials are managed outside of APEX yet allows developers to easily integrated with it for both authentication and authorization.

Out of the box, APEX provides a number of preconfigured authentication schemes. Some of these will work right out of the box, while others may take a little bit of configuration. When none of the preconfigured authentication schemes meets your business needs, the Custom scheme should be used. This scheme is extensible enough that virtually any external repository can be integrated with APEX.

When creating a new scheme in an application, that scheme will automatically become the current scheme. It is possible to later change which scheme is the current scheme. Simply edit the scheme that should be the current one, and click Make Current Scheme, as shown in Figure 8-1.

Figure 8-1. *Setting the current authentication scheme*

Application Express Users

As described in Chapter 5, APEX contains its own internal repository of users. These users are specific and unique to a workspace and can be managed by either the workspace or instance administrator. APEX manages these credentials internally, and they are subject to the password complexity, longevity, and login attempt rules as defined at the workspace level.

On the surface, using APEX users seems like an attractive option, since there is zero work required to do so. The table and associated methods in which to manage the users are already created and integrated into their own API set as well as available in the application development environment. However, most organizations do not use APEX users for production applications, simply because it is another user repository that would have to be updated and maintained alongside others. Furthermore, APEX users' restriction to a single workspace presents problems for an organization that uses applications across multiple workspaces.

For training exercises or even small, simple applications, using the Application Express Accounts scheme is acceptable. Be cautious when using this scheme for small applications, though, because small applications tend to grow into larger ones, and if Application Express Accounts are still being used, there could be potential issues with managing the access to those applications.

Enabling the Application Express Accounts scheme is quite simple. Typically, it is installed and set as the default scheme when creating a new application. If for any reason it needs to be re-added to an application, there is nothing at all to configure. Simply create a new authentication scheme or select one based on a preconfigured scheme from the gallery, and set the scheme type to Application Express Accounts.

Database Accounts

As its name implies, the Database Accounts authentication scheme will use database schema user names and passwords when authenticating to an APEX application. Like with APEX users, no additional settings need to be configured; simply add the Database Accounts scheme to your application, ensure that it is set as the current scheme, and that's it.

The Database Accounts authentication scheme can be used when migrating an application from Oracle Forms because the end users in many Oracle Forms applications are database schemas. In this case, it is best that a migration strategy be put in place to move the end users to a more centralized repository, such as an LDAP server. Using Database Accounts will suffice for the short term, but most organizations are reluctant to give end users access to database schemas.

HTTP Header Variable

The HTTP Header Variable authentication scheme allows APEX to use a value in the HTTP header for the currently authenticated user. This type of authentication is typically used in conjunction with a single sign-on server that sets an HTTP header variable to the value of the currently authenticated user.

When configuring this authentication scheme, a few additional options also need to be set, as outlined in Figure 8-2.

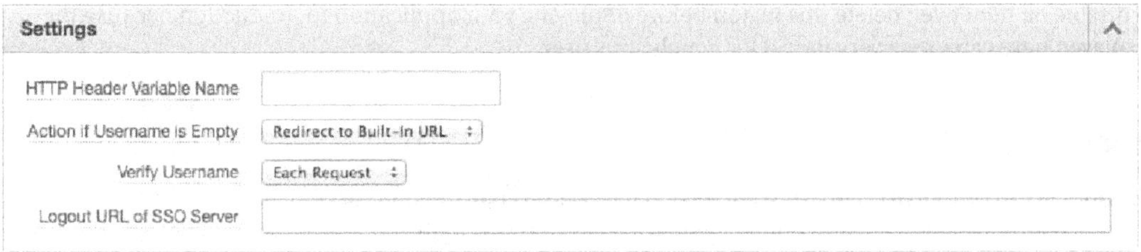

Figure 8-2. *Settings for the HTTP Header Variable authentication scheme*

When using HTTP headers, it is useful to be able to see a list of all the currently set variables for a session. This can be achieved by adding a PL/SQL region to the page that contains the following snippet: owa_util.print_cgi_env;. This will render a region that contains all HTTP header variables and their current settings, as illustrated in Figure 8-3.

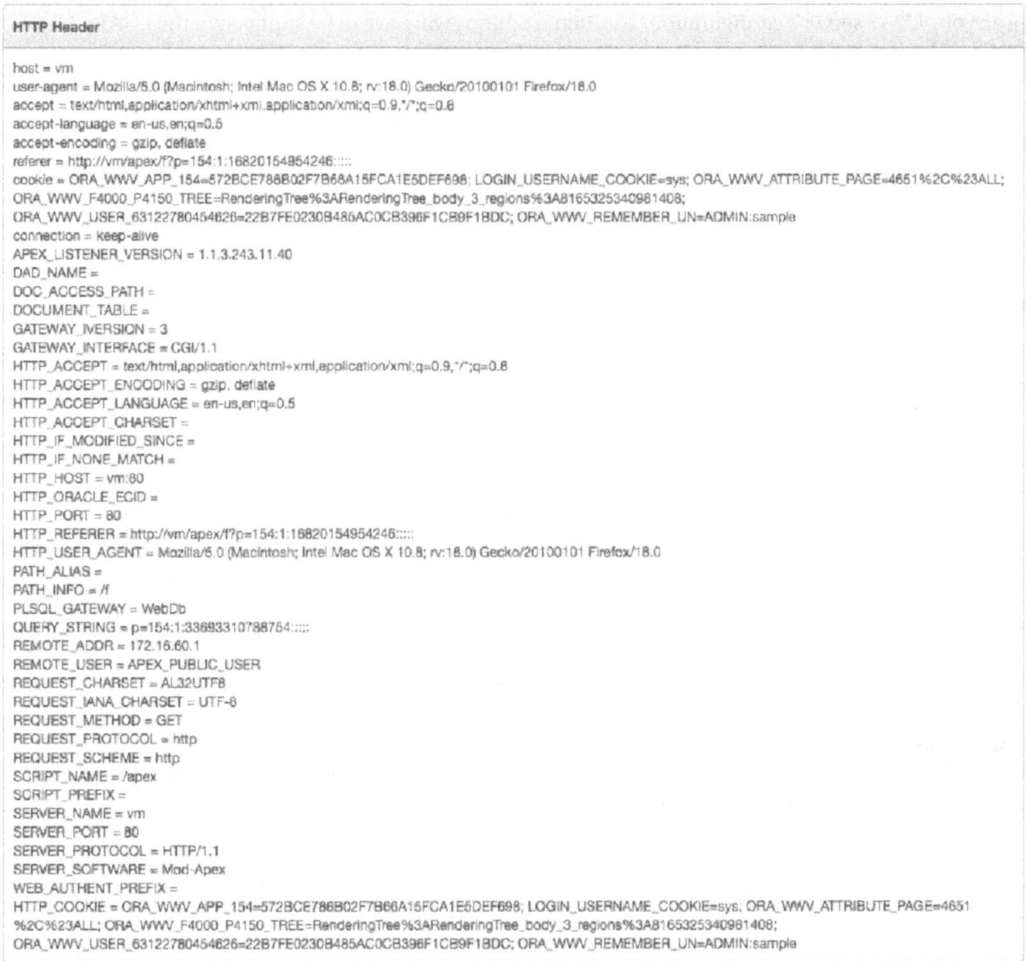

Figure 8-3. *The result of calling owa_util.print_cgi_env*

Be sure to disable or, better yet, delete this region before deploying your application to production because the information displayed here can prove very useful for a malicious user.

LDAP Directory

Lightweight Directory Access Protocol (LDAP) is what most organizations have standardized on for a centrally managed user repository. All account management and options—such as password strength and reuse—are managed by the LDAP server, not by APEX. This provides a solid approach with regard to identity management because all credentials are in a single, centrally managed place.

By using an LDAP directory for authentication in an APEX application, the task of user management can be safely delegated to the designated people who manage the LDAP server. This way, when a user is either hired or fired from the organization, it is done centrally and will be respected by any application that uses LDAP credentials. Another benefit of using LDAP is that the specific LDAP vendor should not matter much. The LDAP Directory authentication scheme has been proven to work with almost any LDAP server, such as Oracle Internet Directory, Active Directory, and OpenLDAP, to name a few.

Depending on your LDAP server's configuration, additional options will have to be supplied to the LDAP authentication scheme by way of the Settings region, as shown in Figure 8-4.

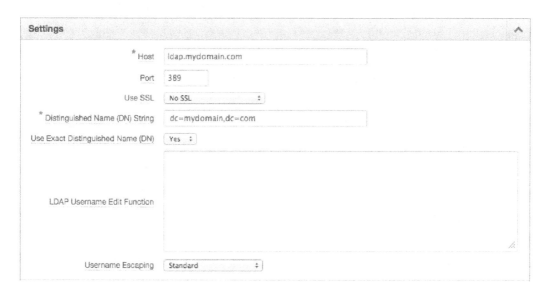

Figure 8-4. *The settings for the LDAP Directory authentication scheme*

Despite these attributes, there are scenarios with some LDAP servers that require more functionality than can be declaratively defined. When that is the case, the Custom authentication scheme can be used, and the logic can be handled in a PL/SQL function that uses the DBMS_LDAP APIs.

No Authentication (Using DAD)

The No Authentication scheme will reuse whatever database user is defined in the database access descriptor (DAD). By default, the DAD for APEX will be set to use the user APEX_PUBLIC_USER for all connections. Thus, using this authentication method with a DAD that already contains a predefined user name and password is not very practical.

If no user name and password are defined in the DAD, then the user will be prompted to enter a valid set of database schema credentials. APEX will then use basic authentication to set the user to whatever the end user provided, if the credentials are valid. In other words, it will behave almost identically to how the Database Accounts authentication scheme does.

Open Door Credentials

The Open Door Credentials scheme has a unique purpose: to allow a developer to become any user by simply entering the user name. This authentication scheme was designed to simplify testing an application as different users without their respective credentials. Clearly, it has no place in a production environment but can prove quite useful during development.

Oracle Application Server Single Sign-On

When using the Oracle Application Server Single Sign-On (OASSSO) authentication scheme, there are a few extra steps that are required before this scheme will work. Either your specific application or APEX itself will need to be registered as a partner application with the OASSSO server. You can find specific details on how to configure APEX and OASSSO in Oracle Support Note #562807.1. According to the note, it has been tested with versions 2.0 through 4.1.1 of APEX and versions 9.0.4.2 through 10.1.2.*x* of Oracle Application Server.

OASSSO delegates all credential verification to the OASSSO server. This means that any application that uses this authentication scheme will not use the APEX login page but rather redirect and use the OASSSO login page. Upon successful authentication, the user will be redirected to the APEX application's home page and can use the application without any other special considerations.

Custom

The Custom authentication scheme is the most versatile of the group because it can be tailored to meet almost any specific business rule or user repository. It is often used when the preconfigured authentication schemes fall short of being able to properly integrate with an existing user repository. In some cases, the Custom scheme is used to store user credentials in a database table, often for applications on the public Internet or where no centralized user repository is available.

The Custom authentication scheme contains a few attributes that are unique to it, as shown in Figure 8-5. Not all of these attributes are required for a Custom authentication scheme to work properly. In fact, many implementations of the Custom authentication scheme provide only an authentication function and nothing else.

Figure 8-5. *Settings specific to the Custom authentication scheme*

The Custom authentication function's premise is simple: return either TRUE or FALSE, based on whether the user successfully authenticated. The only restriction for the custom authentication function is that it must return a Boolean and contain exactly two input parameters: p_username and p_password.

When referring to the custom function, only the name of the function needs to be entered in the Authentication Function Name attribute. APEX will automatically use the user name and password items from the login page to pass the corresponding values to the custom function.

The sentry function is similar to the authentication function in that it also returns a Boolean, but that's where the similarities end. The purpose of the sentry function is to ensure that a user's session is still valid. It will be called before every page view and asynchronous transaction in an application. If a FALSE is returned, then APEX will kill the session and run the invalid session procedure, also specified here. It will then redirect to the location specified in the Session Not Valid section of the authentication scheme. A TRUE returned to the sentry function will mean business as usual, and the application will continue to function as intended.

If no function is specified for the sentry function, APEX will simply revert to its own built-in session management engine to determine whether a session is valid. If a custom sentry function is specified, then great care must be taken to ensure that it works properly and cannot be easily compromised or hacked. In most cases, leaving this field blank and relying on the internal APEX session management is sufficient.

The Invalid Session Procedure will execute when APEX detects an invalid session. This procedure can perform any task, such as logging the event or notifying an administrator. Lastly, the Post Logout Procedure will execute after a user logs out of an application. It will get called only if the user explicitly logs out by clicking the Logout link in the navigation bar. Simply closing or quitting the browser will not trigger this event from firing.

There is one more option that allows the user to enable legacy authentication values. When legacy authentication values are enabled, an additional group of attributes will appear, as shown in Figure 8-6.

Figure 8-6. *The Legacy Attributes section of a Custom authentication scheme*

These attributes are included for backward compatibility with authentication schemes that were created in APEX 4.0 and previous versions. Starting with APEX 4.1, all authentication schemes were migrated so that they could fit into APEX's plug-in architecture. As a result, many of the options that were embedded with each type of scheme are now available only with schemes where they make sense. For example, options that have to do with LDAP are exposed only when using the LDAP authentication scheme.

Since all of these options used to be available to any type of scheme, the Enable Legacy Authentication Attributes option allows a developer to view them, if needed. At some point, it is best to create a new authentication scheme and migrate any settings there.

APIs for Custom Authentication

When using a custom authentication scheme, a few APIs will come in handy. They are, alphabetical order, as follows:

- APEX_AUTHENTICATION
- APEX_CUSTOM_AUTH
- APEX_LDAP
- APEX_UTIL

Each of these APIs can provide a range of common functionality that will be needed for almost any Custom authentication scheme.

APEX_AUTHENTICATION

The first API—APEX_AUTHENTICATION—is designed to be used by an authentication scheme to perform common authentication actions, such as logging in and out, checking to see whether a session is valid, and getting the APEX session cookie, among other things. When a new application is created, APEX will automatically reference APEX_AUTHENTICATION as part of the login and get and set cookie processes on the login page and when logging out of an application.

The APEX_AUTHENTICATION API was introduced in APEX 4.1 to provide support for authentication schemes as plug-ins. It was not available in versions prior to 4.1. Applications that were created in APEX 4.0 or previous versions may still contain direct references to APEX_CUSTOM_AUTH instead of APEX_AUTHENTICATION. While they should continue to function normally, replacing calls to APEX_CUSTOM_AUTH with calls to APEX_AUTHENTICATION where possible should be considered but is currently not a critical task that needs to be performed.

APEX_CUSTOM_AUTH

Many of the functions and procedures in APEX_AUTHENTICATION are simply wrappers that will ultimately call APEX_CUSTOM_AUTH. One of the older APIs, APEX_CUSTOM_AUTH, can do most everything that APEX_AUTHENTICATION can do and then some. Also, many of the APIS in APEX_CUSTOM_AUTH offer more parameters than their counterparts in APEX_AUTHENTICATION. As your custom authentication scheme grows in complexity, you will find yourself making more references to APEX_CUSTOM_AUTH.

APEX_LDAP

If the built-in LDAP authentication scheme will not meet your needs, then a custom authentication scheme will have to be created. In almost all cases, the custom scheme will use the APEX_LDAP API. This API is a wrapper to the DBMS_LDAP API that is specifically designed to work in an APEX environment. Direct calls to DBMS_LDAP are still possible from a Custom authentication scheme but should be considered only when the APEX_LDAP does not have a suitable API.

APEX_LDAP provides commonly needed APIs, such as a call to verify LDAP credentials, a call to determine whether a user is a member of a specific LDAP group, and calls to get either a specific or all user attributes.

APEX_UTIL

Lastly, the APEX_UTIL API contains quite a number of procedures and functions that are typically used in conjunction with Custom authentication schemes. In addition to those procedures used for managing authentication, there are several that can be used to create, modify, and delete APEX users, too.

There are too many to describe all of them in detail, but there are a couple worth mentioning. First, there are a pair of APIs that can be used to override the maximum session length and idle time parameters defined at the application level. By calling either SET_SESSION_LIFETIME_SECONDS or SET_SESSION_MAX_IDLE_SECONDS, the value of the session duration and session idle time, respectively, can be changed. An example of this would be altering these values for a specific user as part of the post-authentication procedure.

The next API that is critical to understand is SET_AUTHENTICATION_RESULT. When called as part of a Custom authentication scheme, this API will set the authentication result in the Login Attempts report accordingly. Unfortunately, the API documentation is quite misleading because it claims that any value can be passed to this API. While technically that is true, there are specific values that will record specific events, as shown in Table 8-1.

Table 8-1. *Codes and their corresponding authentication results for the SET_AUTHENTICATION_RESULT API*

Code	Authentication Result
0	Normal, Successful Authentication
1	Unknown User Name
2	Account Locked
3	Account Expired
4	Incorrect Password
5	Password First Use
6	Maximum Login Attempts Exceeded
7	Unknown Internal Error

It is critical when using a Custom authentication scheme to call SET_AUTHENTICATION_RESULT for each and any of the events listed in Table 8-1. Failure to do so will produce erroneous data in the Login Attempts report, such as recording a Normal, Successful Login when an invalid user or password was entered.

Common Authentication Scheme Components

Despite the wide variety of authentication schemes available in APEX, all schemes do share some common attributes that function the same. These attributes control the basics of the authentication scheme—where to go when a session is invalid, when a user logs out, and settings for cookies. There is also a place to embed any PL/SQL functions and/or procedures that may be required in support of the different components of the authentication scheme.

Source

The Source region is used to enter an anonymous block of named PL/SQL code that will be referenced only from within the authentication scheme. This differs from all other PL/SQL regions in APEX, in that named functions and procedures need to be entered here versus a true anonymous block of PL/SQL.

Using this method is not required or recommended because any code embedded within the authentication scheme cannot be accessed from anywhere else, including similar authentication schemes in different applications. It is a much better idea to refer to named PL/SQL packages from within an authentication scheme because all the benefits of using PL/SQL packages are extended in this case. Additionally, multiple applications can call the same PL/SQL packages, making them more reusable and manageable should a change be required.

Session Not Valid

The Session Not Valid settings, as shown in Figure 8-7, are designed to provide a landing page for when a user attempts to access an application with an invalid session. There are essentially three options: the application's login page, the built-in APEX login page, or a URL. In almost all cases, it is best to use the login page as defined in your application. However, there are times when a specific URL—such as an application that is used to allow only users to log in—is acceptable.

Figure 8-7. *The Session Not Valid settings*

There is an additional option in the Session Not Valid section: Verify Function Name. This function is called after the page sentry function is called. While that seems redundant, it has a slightly different purpose. First, in most cases, the page sentry function is the internal APEX session management function and is not specified. Therefore, in most authentication schemes, the verify function is the only place that the session can be manually enforced.

The intended purpose of the verify function is also different from that of the page sentry function. The verify function is intended to check a business rule to determine whether the application should be available, whereas the page sentry function is intended to check the integrity of the actual session. They are intended to work in concert with one another, not be redundant. An easy-to-understand application that differentiates the use of the verify function would be one that checks the time of day and allows a user to access an application only during business hours.

Login Processing

The Login Processing settings, as illustrated in Figure 8-8, provide the developer with the ability to call a PL/SQL procedure both before and after the user attempts to log in to the applications. These can be used for any type of event, such as auditing the login attempt or calling a procedure to initialize the environment.

Figure 8-8. *The Login Processing settings*

The Pre-Authentication event will not occur when using the HTTP Header Variable or Oracle Application Server Single Sign On authentication schemes because the authentication event occurs outside of APEX in those cases.

Post Logout URL

The Post Logout URL specifies where APEX will branch to after the user logs out of an application by explicitly clicking the Logout link. It is a little counterintuitive to set this to the home page because that page typically requires that the user be authenticated. However, if it is set to the home page, APEX will first check to see whether a valid session is present. In this case, there will not be a valid session present, so APEX will then redirect to the page specified in the Session Not Valid section. If the Post Logout URL is set to a URL, then APEX will branch to that URL upon logout.

Session Cookie Attributes

The last common section across all authentication schemes is Session Cookie Attributes. These attributes control how the APEX session cookie for an application is created. There are four options, as shown in Figure 8-9.

Figure 8-9. *The Session Cookie Attributes section*

By default, APEX will assign the cookie used for an application a standard name in the format ORA_WWV_APP_NNN, where NNN is the application ID. The developer does not need to specify anything for this to occur; it is completely automated. This allows APEX to keep track of and keep session isolated for any number of distinct applications, given that the cookie associated with each is different and easily identifiable.

The Cookie Name attribute can be set to any value that the developer chooses. If, for instance, the developer set this value to MONSTER, when a user authenticates to the application, the name of the cookie set by APEX will be MONSTER. If the cookie name of a suite of applications is set to MONSTER, then as soon as the user authenticates to any one of them, they will be authenticated to all of them. All that would need to be added to each application is a way to refer to one another using the same session ID.

In fact, the APEX development environment uses this same technique so that when you authenticate to the Application Builder, your session is also valid in the SQL Workshop, Team Development, and Administration because each of those modules is a separate APEX application that happens to share the same cookie name.

Lastly, the Secure attribute is used to determine whether to allow the session cookie to be created when running over HTTP. If it is set to No, then APEX will permit the session cookie to be set when using HTTP. This is extremely dangerous and opens up your application to a great deal of risk because anyone who can view network packets can eavesdrop and grab the session cookie values and session ID as they are sent to your PC. Armed with these two values, it is possible for a malicious user to hijack your APEX session by constructing a fake cookie on their PC.

Therefore, this attribute should always be set to Yes, which will restrict APEX from sending a session cookie to the client when the connection is done over HTTPS. If this attribute is set to Yes and the user attempts to connect via HTTP, they will simply not be able to log in, despite that the correct credentials have been provided.

Mechanics of Authentication

Authenticating in APEX is actually quite simple. When an unauthenticated user attempts to access an application, that user must provide their credentials. If successful, the credential verification function will return a TRUE, and the user will be authenticated. If a FALSE is returned, it can mean only that there was an error if verifying the user's credentials. APEX does not particularly care how the credentials are verified or what type of repository is used. It only cares that either a TRUE or FALSE is returned and knows what to do in either case.

Thus, the mechanics of authenticating to an APEX application are largely identical, aside from the specifics of how the credentials are verified. This is true across all types of authentication schemes—LDAP, HTPP Header, Application Express Accounts, and so on. The next session steps through the mechanics of what APEX does when a user logs in. For simplicity, the authentication scheme that will be used is the Application Express Accounts. Keep in mind that the mechanics would be the same regardless of the specific authentication scheme used.

The Login Page

When users attempt to access an APEX application, they typically do so by either typing in the URL or using a bookmark that contains at least a reference to the application ID. This request is sent to the APEX engine, which in turn begins to process it. Before the page is even rendered, one of the first checks to occur is to determine whether the user's session is valid. This is done by the page sentry function. It will check both the session ID and session cookie values with those stored in the database and determine whether the session is, in fact, valid.

Since in this example you are starting from scratch, the page sentry function will immediately determine that the session is not invalid and take action. The action it will take is to look up where to go next in the Session Not Valid section of the corresponding authentication scheme. Assuming that you are using the APEX application login page, you will then be redirected to that page. Since that page is a public page, it will be allowed to render, even though you have not yet successfully authenticated.

By default, APEX will assign page 101 as the login page and page 1 as the home page when a new application is created. While it is possible to change this, it is best to keep with the de facto standards of 101 for login and 1 for home so that other developers will know where to look for them.

APEX will also assign a page alias of LOGIN_DESKTOP to page 101. This alias is used when defining the login page for a specific user interface. If the page alias is changed, the reference in the user interface attributes section will also have to be updated to match it. New in APEX 4.2, a user interface determines which set of pages to use when running an application based on whether the device is a desktop PC or a mobile browser. It is possible to create an application that contains a user interface for both desktop and mobile, each with their own separate login and home page. The User Interfaces section can be found under an application's shared components, as shown in Figure 8-10.

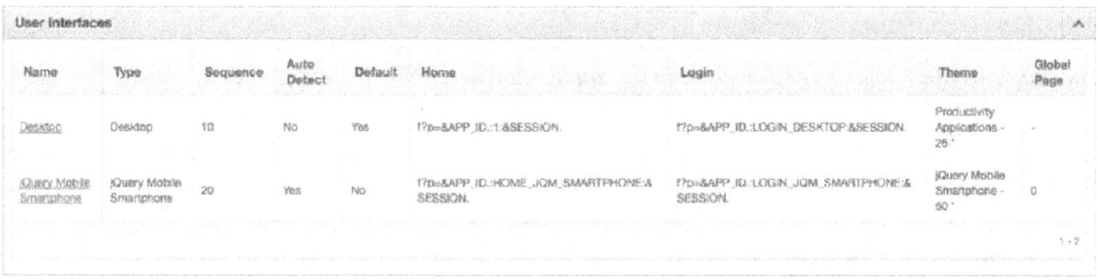

Name	Type	Sequence	Auto Detect	Default	Home	Login	Theme	Global Page
Desktop	Desktop	10	No	Yes	f?p=&APP_ID.:1:&SESSION.	f?p=&APP_ID.:LOGIN_DESKTOP:&SESSION.	Productivity Applications - 26	-
jQuery Mobile Smartphone	jQuery Mobile Smartphone	20	Yes	No	f?p=&APP_ID.:HOME_JQM_SMARTPHONE:&SESSION.	f?p=&APP_ID.:LOGIN_JQM_SMARTPHONE:&SESSION.	jQuery Mobile Smartphone - 50	0

1 - 2

Figure 8-10. *The User Interfaces section of an application*

Editing the Desktop user interface will reveal where the home and login pages of an application are defined in APEX 4.2 for that specific user interface, as illustrated in Figure 8-11. In previous versions of APEX, the login and home page were defined in the Security Attributes section.

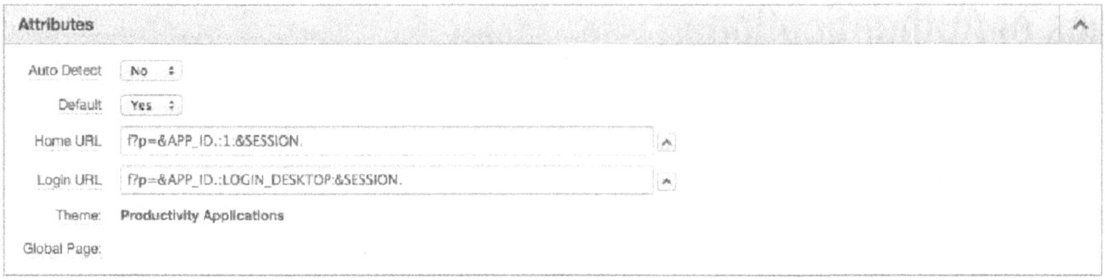

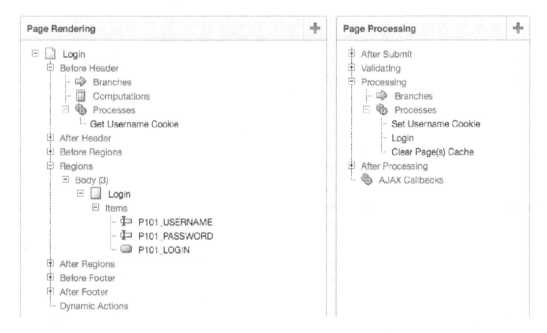

Figure 8-11. *The attributes of the Desktop user interface, including home and login pages*

When created, the application login page will contain a number of precreated processes, as shown in Figure 8-12. In most cases, there is no need to modify these processes. In fact, altering or disabling them may cause APEX's login mechanism to stop working.

Figure 8-12. *The standard APEX login page as viewed in the application development environment*

Login Page Processes

The first process that gets executed when the login page runs is called Get Username Cookie. This process will attempt to read a value from a cookie called LOGIN_USERNAME_COOKIE, which contains the last used user name for this application. Using the Web Developer add-on, it is simple to view this and any another cookies, as shown in Figure 8-13.

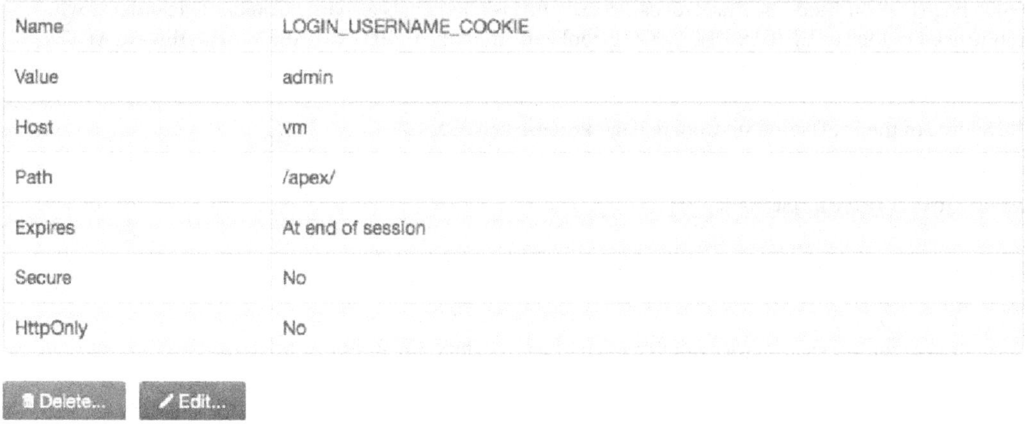

Name	LOGIN_USERNAME_COOKIE
Value	admin
Host	vm
Path	/apex/
Expires	At end of session
Secure	No
HttpOnly	No

🗑 Delete...   ✎ Edit...

Figure 8-13. *The LOGIN_USERNAME_COOKIE, as shown with the Web Developer add-on*

Cookies are nothing more than text files that a browser reads and writes to in order to maintain a value-attribute pair that can persist longer than a single page view. Developers have long used cookies to store session-specific information so that as a user goes from one page view to another, the value of the cookie can be used to determine whether their session is valid. Many web sites, regardless of their underlying technologies, also use cookies in this manner.

APEX uses cookies for both the application development environment as well as any user-developed applications. The APEX developers made it a point to store very little information in the cookies because any data stored there is not terribly secure. This best practice is a good model for any developer or any web application.

If the LOGIN_USERNAME_COOKIE cookie exists, then the process will set the value of the page item P101_USERNAME to the value of the cookie. In APEX 4.1 and 4.2, this is done via the APEX_AUTHENTICATION API, as shown in Listing 8-1.

Listing 8-1. The Source of the Get Username Cookie Process in APEX 4.2

```
:P101_USERNAME := apex_authentication.get_login_username_cookie;
```

Prior to APEX 4.1, a call to owa_cookie had to be made, similar to how the Set Username Cookie setting worked. You can see this call in Listing 8-2.

Listing 8-2. The Source of the Get Username Cookie Process in APEX 4.1 and Prior Releases

```
declare
    v varchar2(255) := null;
    c owa_cookie.cookie;
begin
    c := owa_cookie.get('LOGIN_USERNAME_COOKIE');
    :P101_USERNAME := c.vals(1);
exception when others then null;
end;
```

Once the value of the last user name used is fetched from the cookie, the user is presented with the login page, where they are prompted to enter their credentials. There is nothing proprietary about the user name and password fields because they are standard APEX items. The only consideration is that the password field has an attribute called "Does not save state." This attribute will be set to Yes by default and should left that way. By doing so, it will prevent the password from ever being written to APEX's session state, where it could be viewed by an administrator or DBA. The value of the password will be available in memory for only the page-processing phase of this page so that it can be checked against the stored password.

Once the login page is submitted, the first process to execute is called Set Username Cookie. This process will store the user name used in the LOGIN_USERNAME_COOKIE cookie by making a call to the APEX_AUTHENTICATION API, as shown in Listing 8-3.

Listing 8-3. The Source of the Set Username Cookie Page Process in APEX 4.2

```
apex_authentication.send_login_username_cookie (
    p_username => lower(:P1001_USERNAME) );
```

Versions prior to APEX 4.1 set the same cookie with the same value but made calls directly to the owa_cookie package, as shown in Listing 8-4.

Listing 8-4. The Source of the Set Username Cookie Page Process in APEX 4.0 and Prior Releases

```
begin
owa_util.mime_header('text/html', FALSE);
owa_cookie.send(
    name=>'LOGIN_USERNAME_COOKIE',
    value=>lower(:P101_USERNAME));
exception when others then null;
end;
```

The user name will be stored only as long as the browser session is valid. If the user logs out of an application, the user name will be fetched and automatically entered into the user name field when redirected to the login page. If the user quits the browser and then restarts it later and attempts to access the application, the user name will no longer be stored, and the corresponding field on the login page will be blank.

Next, the actual authentication event occurs when the login process is executed. Regardless of which authentication scheme is being used, APEX will call the same API and pass in two parameters: the user name and password supplied by the user via the login page. In APEX 4.1 and 4.2, the APEX_AUTHENTICATION API is called with only two parameters, as shown in Listing 8-5.

Listing 8-5. The Source of the Login Page Process in APEX 4.2

```
apex_authentication.login(
    p_username => :P101_USERNAME,
    p_password => :P101_PASSWORD
    );
```

In APEX 4.0 and prior versions, a different API—wwv_flow_custom_auth_std—is called. Not only are the user name and password passed to this API, but so are the application session and home page, as shown in Listing 8-6.

Listing 8-6. The Source of the Login Page Process in APEX 4.0 and Previous Releases

```
wwv_flow_custom_auth_std.login(
    P_UNAME      => v('P101_USERNAME'),
    P_PASSWORD   => :P101_PASSWORD,
    P_SESSION_ID => v('APP_SESSION'),
    P_FLOW_PAGE  => :APP_ID||':1'
    );
```

Once the API in the login process is called, APEX will look up and call the current authentication scheme, passing in the credentials provided by the user. That authentication scheme will do the actual authentication check—be it at an LDAP server or HTTP header value or a custom function—and return either a TRUE or FALSE to the API. If successful, the APEX session and corresponding cookie will be created.

At this point, APEX will write a row to the WWV_FLOW_SESSIONS$ table, which is in the APEX_040200 schema, as shown in Figure 8-14.

	ID	SESSION_ID_HASHED	SECURITY_GROUP_ID
1	14788437140955	6D00617EE8BE733D38FA400674074C08	3010820895725282

Columns | Data | Constraints | Grants | Statistics | Triggers | Flashback | Dependencies | Details | Partiti
Sort.. | Filter:

Figure 8-14. *A row from WWV_FLOW_SESSIONS$, showing the session ID and hashed session ID*

The value in the ID column corresponds to the APEX session ID and should match the value found in the URL. The SESSION_ID_HASHED value is stored in the APEX session cookie, which is used to check the validity of that user's session. Its name will vary based on the application that the user is running. In Figure 8-15, the cookie's name is ORA_WWW_APP_157 because the ID of the application running is 157.

Name	ORA_WWV_APP_157
Value	4DF257EBCF75A216713A961B4D7250E3
Host	vm
Path	/apex/
Expires	At end of session
Secure	No
HttpOnly	Yes

🗑 Delete...   ✏ Edit...

Figure 8-15. *The main APEX session cookie*

Lastly, the value in the SECURITY_GROUP_ID column maps to the PROVISIONING_COMPANY_ID in the WWV_FLOW_COMPANIES table, as shown in Figure 8-16.

	ID	PROVISIONING_COMPANY_ID	SHORT_NAME	DISPLAY_NAME	SOURCE_IDENTIFIER
1	3011029421725366	3010820895725282	SAMPLE	SAMPLE	SAMPLE

Columns | Data | Constraints | Grants | Statistics | Triggers | Flashback | Dependencies | Details | Partitions | Indexes | SQL
Sort.. | Filter:

Figure 8-16. *A row from WWV_FLOW_COMPANIES, showing how the PROVISIONING_COMPANY_ID maps to the SECURITY_GROUP_ID column in the WWV_FLOW_SESSIONS$ table*

Back when Oracle APEX was called Oracle Flows, workspaces were referred to as *companies*. Hence, the name of the base table matches the old name. This table is, of course, used to store information about the workspace. Thus, the value stored in the APEX session cookie can be tracked to the sessions table and then to the workspace table, providing APEX with all the details it needs to securely manage sessions.

After the session cookie is set, one last process will clear the page cache for the login page. This is done to ensure that the user name and password values do not remain in session state, where a workspace administrator or DBA could compromise them. Once the session state for the login page is cleared, the user is directed to the home page of the application as defined in the user interface section and will officially be authenticated, as shown in Figure 8-17.

Figure 8-17. *A successfully authenticated APEX session*

Notice that the session ID in Figure 8-17 is set to 14788437140955. Back in Figure 8-14, the value of the ID column was also set to 14788437140955. Again, this is how the APEX session ID is linked to the APEX session cookie.

If the credentials that the user supplied are invalid, then the user will be redirected to the login page and given the opportunity to try again. Depending on the instance settings, each additional attempt at logging in may result in a delay. This is done to combat a malicious user who is trying to guess what a user's password is by brute force.

Logging Out

Once the user is authenticated, the session associated with them will remain valid until one of the following events occurs:

- The session duration is exceeded.

- The session idle time is exceeded.

- The session is purged by the ORACLE_APEX_PURGE_SESSIONS job.

- The session is purged by an APEX administrator.

- The session ID in the URL is altered/removed.

- The session cookie is altered/removed.

- The user quits the browser.

- The user clicks the logout link.

Any of these events will cause the session to be invalidated and cause APEX to redirect to the URL as specified in the Session Not Valid section of the current authentication scheme. It doesn't really matter which event occurs, because once a session is terminated, there is no way for the user to rejoin that session. All they can do is log in again with their credentials and establish a new session.

By default, every APEX application will contain a navigation bar entry called Logout. The target of this navigation bar entry is set to &LOGOUT_URL., which is a built-in item that will be replaced with a call to the APEX_AUTHENTICATION API, as shown in Listing 8-7.

Listing 8-7. The URL Associated with the Logout Navigation Bar Entry

```
http://servername.com/apex/apex_authentication.logout?p_app_id=154&p_session_id=11260269600710
```

When the Logout navigation bar is clicked, the user's session will be terminated, and any values stored in session state will be deleted. If the user instead quits the browser without clicking the Logout link, only the session state will be terminated. The values stored in session state will persist in the internal APEX tables until they are purged by the ORACLE_APEX_PURGE_SESSIONS job, which runs every eight hours by default. All session cookies will also be deleted in the event that the user bypasses clicking Logout and quits the browser.

It is important to note that if a user simply closes the browser tab and other tabs are open, the associated APEX session is not terminated. When a browser tab is closed, the APEX session cookie does not get removed and is still valid. A user could search though their browser history and find a URL that contains the previously used session ID and rejoin that session. This is not cause for alarm because only the user who previously mapped to that session can rejoin it if a browser tab is closed. Another user on another PC—or even the same user on the same PC in a different browser—will be unable to rejoin that session, even when using a URL that contains the session ID.

Summary

APEX authentication schemes are both simple and sophisticated at the same time. Their simplicity lies in the fact that all they do is return a Boolean value. Their sophistication comes from the virtually limitless procedures and functions that can influence the value returned. With just a little configuration, the needs of most organizations can be met by one of the built-in authentication schemes. If this is not the case, the capabilities of the Custom authentication scheme can be used.

CHAPTER 9

■ ■ ■

User Authorization

Once users are authenticated to APEX applications, they will be able to run any page and see all components, unless there are restrictions put in place. Most often, these restrictions will be implemented using authorization schemes or conditions. Authorization schemes are APEX components that act like roles. They are associated with an APEX component on one side and then map to a user or group of users on the other, thus allowing a developer to secure their applications using a standard, structured approach.

This chapter will cover APEX authorization schemes, both what they are and how they should be implemented. It will review the core features of authorization schemes and discuss which ones are most optimal for a secure application. It will then discuss where to store user-to-role mappings and summarize the benefits and drawbacks of each approach. It will also cover different use cases of authorization schemes and how to protect against authorization inconsistencies. It will conclude with a brief review of the built-in Access Control feature.

Authorization Schemes

As just mentioned, an authorization scheme in APEX is a component that returns either a TRUE or a FALSE when evaluated. Authorization schemes can be associated with almost every single component in APEX, from the application itself to a specific column in a report. They differ from authentication schemes in that they determine which components of an application a user can access or execute, whereas an authentication scheme determines whether a user's credentials are valid.

When an authorization scheme is created, APEX will automatically create a second authorization scheme that will be the opposite of the one just created. For example, if an authorization scheme for admin users was created, a second scheme called {Not Admin Users} would also be created. This second scheme can be associated with any APEX component and will evaluate to TRUE when the result of the original authorization scheme is FALSE, or vice versa. No additional option needs to be selected for the second, opposite authorization scheme to be created.

Authorization schemes are shared components and can be referenced from almost any other component. Despite their power and utility, authorization schemes are one of the simplest components in APEX, containing only four editable attributes, as shown in Figure 9-1.

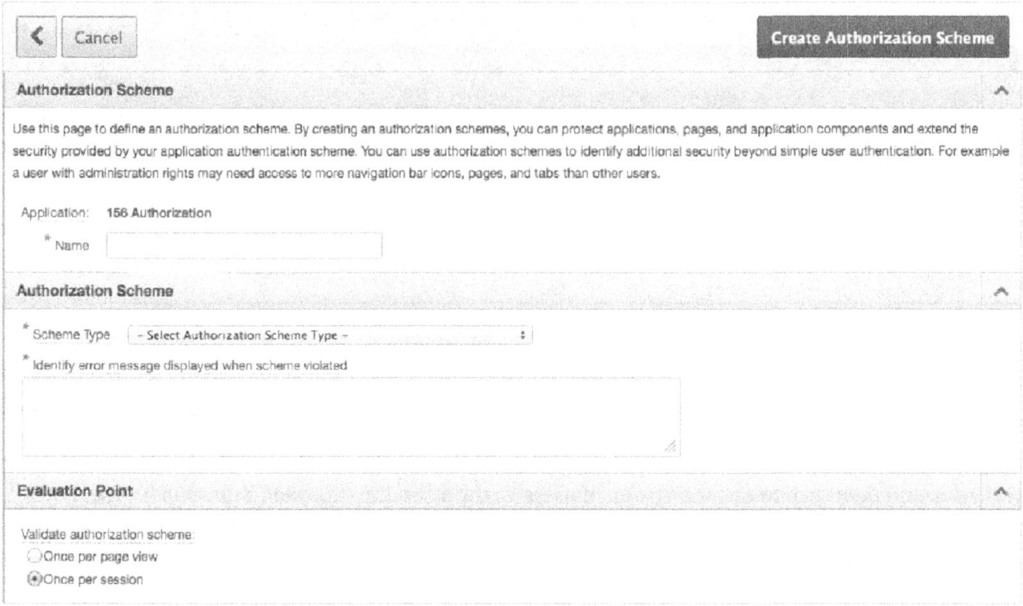

Figure 9-1. *The attributes of an authorization scheme*

While the name of the authorization scheme may seem cosmetic, several APIs make reference to it. For example, the APEX_UTIL.PUBLIC_CHECK_AUTHORIZATION API takes in a single parameter: the name of an authorization scheme. Thus, the name of an authorization scheme should not be altered once it is created, especially if APIs that make reference to it are being used. Unfortunately, there is no way to enforce this in APEX because the name field is always editable.

A number of different methods can be used when determining the result of an authorization scheme. Regardless of the authorization scheme's type, the end result is still a Boolean. The following are the possible authentication schemes:

- Exists SQL Query

- Item in Expression 1 is NULL

- Item in Expression 1 is NOT NULL

- NOT Exists SQL Query

- PL/SQL Function Returning Boolean

- Value of Item in Expression 1 Does NOT Equal Expression 2

- Value of Item in Expression 1 Equals Expression 2

- Value of Preference in Expression 1 Does NOT Equal Expression 2

- Value of Preference in Expression 1 Equals Expression 2

Most types are self-explanatory as to what they do and should be familiar to experienced APEX developers because conditions utilize similar constructs. Depending on the type selected, additional attributes may be required.

The last attribute of an authorization scheme is the evaluation point. There are two possible settings for this attribute: once per page view and once per session. The former will evaluate the authorization scheme each and every page view, whereas the latter will evaluate the authorization scheme only once per session.

While setting the value of this attribute to "once per page view" will certainly introduce a small amount of additional overhead, it does provide the most secure implementation of authorization schemes because a user's association with a scheme can immediately be revoked on the very next page view. Setting this attribute to "once per session" is much more efficient because all authorization schemes will be evaluated only when the user logs in, and the results are used throughout the duration of their session.

Authorization schemes are one of the few shared components that work with subscriptions. A subscription in APEX allows any number of components to "subscribe" to a master copy. A developer can then either publish the master to all subscribers or refresh the subscription on a per-component basis. This allows for better centralized control of components because if an update is required, only the master needs to be updated and then republished versus editing many individual components. In addition to authorization schemes, you'll find that authentication schemes, lists of values, shortcuts, and templates work with subscriptions.

While the intended purpose of conditions in APEX is to facilitate business rules, sometimes they need to be used for security. A typical example of this is when a condition is used to determine whether the user is authenticated. While this practice should be avoided if possible, there is no inherent risk in applying it.

Implementing Authorization Schemes

Implementing an authorization scheme is typically as simple as associating it with the corresponding APEX components that need to be secured. Once done, those components will render only when the associated authorization scheme returns a TRUE. While that sounds simple enough, properly adding authorization schemes to your application is one of the most critical parts of developing a secure application and should be planned carefully from the beginning of the design phase.

Role Location

The first decision that needs to be made is where the mapping of users to roles will be stored. In some organizations, these mappings are done via LDAP groups. If this is the case, then an authorization scheme can easily check a user's membership in an LDAP group by calling the APEX_LDAP.IS_MEMBER API. If the user is in fact a member of the associated group, then the authorization scheme will return a TRUE, and any component associated with it will be available to the user.

In many organizations, it is nearly impossible to gain access to the LDAP server so that user-to-group mappings can efficiently be managed. Rather than fight the political battle to gain these rights to the LDAP server, many choose to manage user-to-group mappings locally via a set of database tables. In this case, it is still possible to use LDAP for an authentication scheme, ensuring that user management is still done at the LDAP server, not in APEX. As long as the authentication scheme is associated with a centrally managed user repository, there is little risk to this hybrid approach.

Table-Based Roles

Storing roles in a local set of tables is relatively simple to implement and manage. A basic solution can be achieved with only two tables: one for the role definition and one for the user-to-role mappings. Like any development project, building a locally managed role management infrastructure is something that should be properly designed and developed, not something that is thrown together in a couple of hours. For example, when securing pages, it makes much more sense to have a single authorization scheme that is aware of the page and its associated users versus one authorization scheme per page.

The tables that manage the roles and role mappings should be stored in a separate schema from any schema that is mapped to an APEX workspace. This is done for security purposes because a simple read-only view accessible to any parse-as schema can be built and referenced in any APEX application to determine whether a user has any role.

A simple APEX application can also be built for the specific purpose of managing the role and role mappings. This application would need access to a set of APIs that securely allow the management of role and mappings. Care should be taken to ensure that any activity in this application is audited.

Gatekeeper Authorization Scheme

The most important component to associate an authorization scheme with is the application itself. If this is not done, then any user who can authenticate will be able to run your application. Consider an organization with 1,000 employees. Each of those employee's credentials will be stored in an LDAP server that will be associated with all applications via an authentication scheme. If a developer wanted to build an application for a specific subset of the employees, having an authentication scheme is simply not enough because any of the 1,000 employees will be able to log in.

Thus, a "gatekeeper" authorization scheme should be created and associated with the application. A gatekeeper scheme is slightly different from other authorization schemes in that its goal is to determine whether the current user has at least one valid role or group in the associated application. How it does this all depends on where the user-to-role mappings are stored. If they are in LDAP, then the APEX_LDAP.MEMBER_OF or MEMBER_OF2 API can be called to determine whether the user has at least one valid group. If roles are stored in a table, then a simple EXISTS query can be run to ensure that the user has at least one valid role.

To associate an authorization scheme with the application, edit the application's shared components. Next, click Security Attributes, and in the Authorization region, select an authorization scheme, as shown in Figure 9-2.

Figure 9-2. *Associating an authorization scheme with an application*

Page-Level Authorization Schemes

Ensuring that sensitive pages have an authorization scheme associated with them is another important step to take when building your applications. Every page—aside from the global pages—can and should have an associated authorization scheme. To associate an authorization scheme with a page, edit the page properties, and then in the Security region, select an authorization scheme, as shown in Figure 9-3.

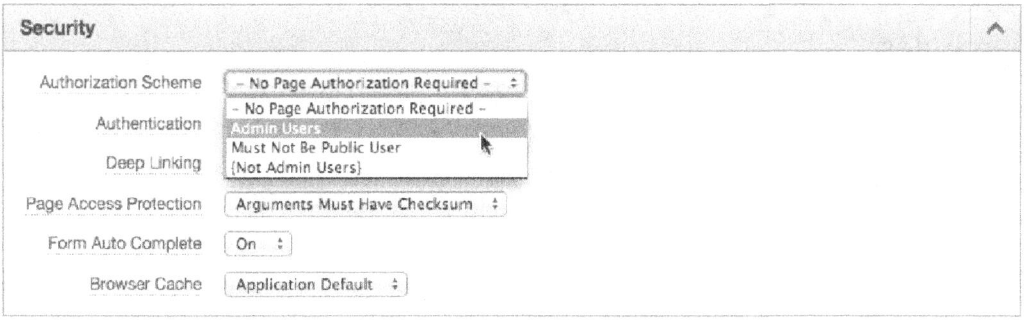

Figure 9-3. *Associating an authorization scheme with a page*

While this approach would be effective for a small number of pages, it would get quite tedious when the application has 20 or more pages. Fortunately, there is an updatable report that allows some page attributes—including authorization scheme—to be updated in batch. This report is buried within the Application Utilities section of the Application Builder. To access it, navigate to the application home page. From there, click the Utilities icon. Next, select Cross Page Utilities from the Page Specific Utilities region, which can be found in the lower-right side of the page. Lastly, select Grid Edit of All Pages. The resulting updatable report will list the first 15 pages of your application, as shown in Figure 9-4.

Figure 9-4. *Editing multiple page attributes at once*

One thing to note when using this report is that changes must be saved before clicking the next or previous set of records icon. APEX 4.2 will display a reminder if there are unsaved changed, but previous versions of APEX will not.

Using a security tool such as Enkitec's eSERT can help when it comes to keeping track of which page is mapped to which authorization scheme. One of eSERT's attributes inspects every page and produces a report based on which pages are mapped to an authorization scheme and which are not, as illustrated in Figure 9-5.

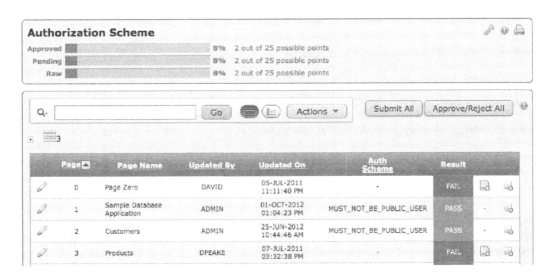

Figure 9-5. *The page authorization scheme report from eSERT*

From this report, it is clear to the developer which pages have authorization schemes and which do not. Additionally, a developer can click the edit link and immediately edit the corresponding page, allowing them to quickly remedy any issue.

Authorization Inconsistencies

Associating authorization schemes with other APEX components—items, regions, buttons, charts, and so on—is relatively straightforward. Simply edit the component in question, navigate to the Security region, select the corresponding authorization scheme, and then save your changes.

At some point, it can become overwhelming to mentally keep track of which authorization scheme is associated with which APEX component. Fortunately, there is a report that does just that. Simply edit the authorization scheme in question, and then select the Utilization tab, as shown in Figure 9-6. This report will detail all the components in APEX that are associated with either all authorization schemes or a specific one, based on the value selected.

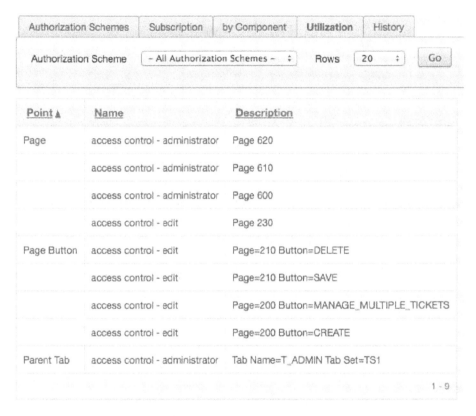

Figure 9-6. *An authorization scheme utilization report*

As your applications grow in size and complexity, the chance that they will contain at least one authorization inconsistency will increase. An authorization inconsistency is when a developer has associated an authorization scheme with a button or tab but neglected to associate the same scheme with the target page. This would allow the user to access the page by simply editing the URL. Authorization inconsistencies can also be defined as insecure Ajax callbacks or unsecured processes associated with secured buttons.

There is no report built in to APEX that details these authorization inconsistencies. Fortunately, there is a section in Enkitec eSERT that does this. The Authorization Inconsistencies category covers a wide range of issues, as shown in Figure 9-7.

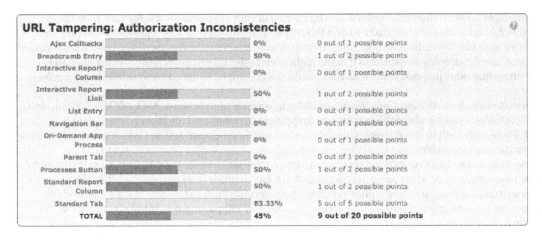

Figure 9-7. The Authorization Inconsistencies report in Enkitec eSERT

Even experienced APEX developers are not immune from authorization inconsistencies because they are extremely simple to overlook. Thus, care should be taken to ensure that all pages are properly secured not only with any authorization scheme but with the proper one.

APEX Access Control

APEX actually does contain a built-in role management feature called Access Control. When installed in your application, this feature creates three roles—administrator, edit, and view—each mapped to an authorization scheme. Users can then be mapped to a role via an administration page. The corresponding authorization schemes are then mapped to different APEX components.

Access Control is installed into an application by creating a new page of type "access control." Once installed, Access Control will create a management page in your application, as shown in Figure 9-8. This page will facilitate the user-to-role mappings, as well as configure the Access Control application mode.

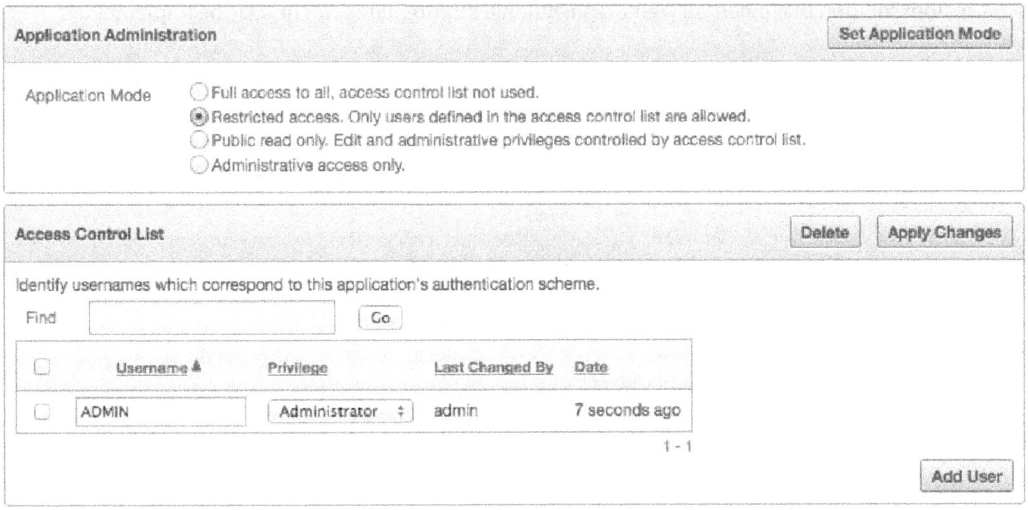

Figure 9-8. The main Access Control management page

Additionally, three authorization schemes will also be created in your application—one for each role. These authorization schemes are quite sophisticated and don't simply look at the role that they represent. First, they will check the application mode. The mode that is set will depend on what result will be returned. The three roles included with Access Control are hierarchical in nature, in that the higher-level roles inherit the privileges of the lower-level roles. Thus, anything that users mapped to the read role can do, users mapped to the edit and administration roles can do, too.

On the database side, Access Control will create two tables in your parse-as schema: APEX_ACCESS_CONTROL and APEX_ACCESS_SETUP. The former is where the user-to-role mappings are stored, and the latter is where the application mode is stored. These tables will be created only if they do not already exist because Access Control stores information for all applications in the same table.

While it may seem convenient to use the Access Control feature, there are a number of reasons it is less than optimal. First, only three roles are available when using Access Control. If a fourth role is required, then additional coding will be required to construct the corresponding authorization scheme. Second, the functionality of the three available roles is quite specific. In some applications, they should suffice. But many applications require roles outside of the three available in Access Control.

Since Access Control is embedded within an application, it is not possible to have a single place where roles for all applications can be managed. Each application would end up having its own role management facility. This presents the problem of a distributed role management system without any central oversight or auditing. In such an environment, any user who has access to the Access Control administration pages would be able to grant access to any other user and not be held accountable.

Because of its numerous shortcomings and drawbacks, it is best to avoid APEX's Access Control feature in most cases. The amount of effort that would need to be done to remedy its issues is about the same as the amount of effort required to develop a custom solution that overcomes these drawbacks.

Summary

Authorization schemes are a powerful tool when it comes to controlling who gets to see what in an application. However, like most facets of application development, they need to be considered early on in the design phase and not implemented hastily right before an application goes live. It matters little where the roles are defined—an LDAP server or a local table. What does matter is that the assignment and management of roles is centralized and audited so that all activity can be recalled, if necessary.

While APEX does provide an Access Control tool, it falls short of what many organizations need. With just a small amount of effort, a custom solution that meets all your organizational requirements can quickly be implemented.

CHAPTER 10

Secure Export to CSV

Consider this: when you enable export to CSV on an APEX report, you're allowing any user to export all rows of any report with a single click. Think about that for a second. Enabling this feature may make users' lives extremely convenient and solve a lot of their problems. But the security implications of enabling it are massive and definitely outweigh any convenience that it brings.

This chapter will start by discussing options in APEX that can be configured to control some aspects of the report exports that APEX provides. It will also introduce a more secure method for allowing users to export report data to a CSV file. While this method is not a core component of APEX, it is very unobtrusive and requires only a couple of additional components be added to an application for it to work. It is also flexible enough that it can be configured for a specific application's security and auditing needs.

APEX Export Options

Although the feature which allows APEX to export reports is quite powerful, it is also quite rudimentary in nature. The ability to export cannot be conditionally enabled based on a security role or other business rule; it is either on for everyone or off for everyone. APEX will log a page view event upon export and record the date, time, username, and page (and if from an interactive report, the report ID) that the event occurred on, but it does not provide any additional information as to which report was downloaded. Thus, in the case of multiple standard reports on the same page, it remains unclear which one was exported in the logs.

Despite these drawbacks, you can configure some features of the export to make them more secure. For example, you can set a limit on how many records can be exported for any report, whether interactive or standard. In addition, columns can be displayed in the browser but excluded in an export.

These basic features may be more than enough for your needs and security requirements. However, if they fall short of your requirements, there is another option: you can build a custom export to CSV routine from scratch. While this approach requires some additional components and custom code, it is very lean and can be implemented once and used everywhere within an application.

Maximum Row Count

Every report in APEX has a parameter called Maximum Row Count. This parameter will control the maximum number of rows presented in a report in APEX, regardless of the size of the underlying data set. You can find the Maximum Row Count parameter on the Report Attributes page for both standard and interactive reports. Figure 10-1 illustrates its location in standard reports, whereas Figure 10-2 illustrates its location in interactive reports.

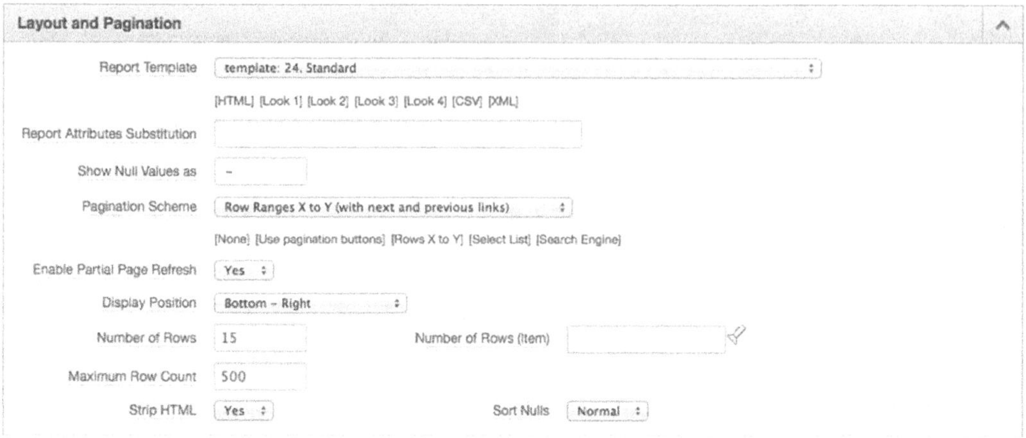

Figure 10-1. *The Maximum Row Count parameter on the standard report attributes screen*

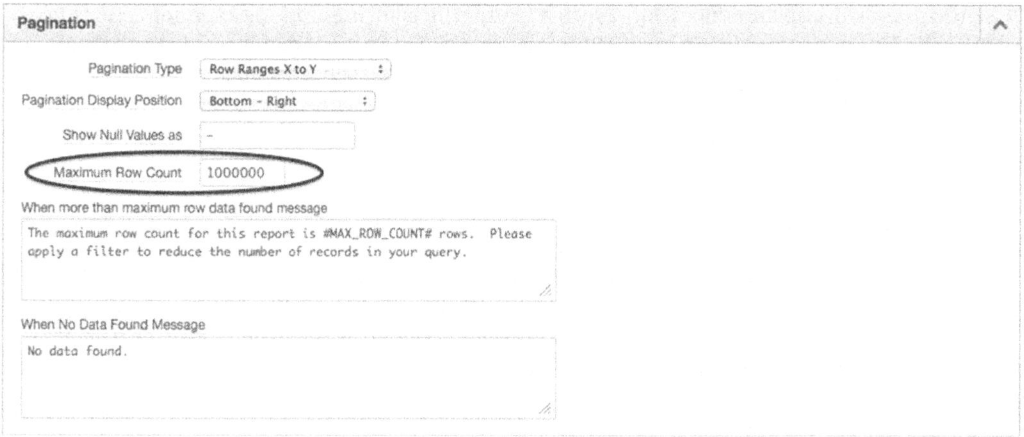

Figure 10-2. *The Maximum Row Count parameter on the interactive report attributes screen*

In standard reports, this parameter defaults to 500, even when left blank. Often developers will set this value to something unnecessarily high, such as 999,999. This is not recommended for two major reasons: first, performance will be negatively impacted, and second, if users can view all the records, they can also export all records to CSV.

In interactive reports, this value is set considerably higher by default: 10,000 or even higher for larger data sets. Not altering this value for interactive reports is much more dire than in standard reports because instead of a default setting of just 500, thousands of records can be exported.

Therefore, you should set the Maximum Row Count parameter as low as possible based on your business requirements. Use item-based filters or an interactive report to allow users to slice and dice the data to find what they are looking for. If your data set contains 1,000 or more records, there is no user who will want to paginate through all of those records 15 at a time. Thus, the use of smart filters will help them get to the records they need to see quickly and securely.

Column Restrictions: Standard Reports

Another method used to protect sensitive data is to restrict which columns can be exported. This comes in handy when you need a user to search by account number and display that column on the screen but do not want that user to be able to export all account numbers; you may want the user to be able to export just the name and address, for example. While it's obvious how to configure restrictions for standard reports, it takes a bit more work for interactive reports.

To restrict a column from being exported in a standard report, simply edit the column's attributes and set the Include in Export parameter to No, as shown in Figure 10-3. This approach will still allow the column to be displayed in the report normally. It will restrict the column only when exporting to CSV.

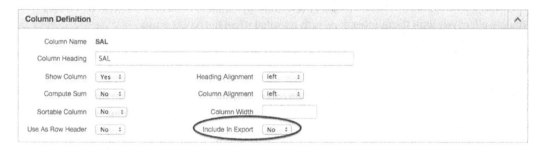

Figure 10-3. *Disabling a column from being exported in a standard report*

Column Restrictions: Interactive Reports

Unfortunately, there is no such declarative option for interactive reports. Despite this limitation, you can achieve the same functionality using a simple condition at the column level. As illustrated in Figure 10-4, simply set the condition to Request is NOT Contained within Expression 1, and then set Expression 1 to the following: CSV:HTMLD:XLS:PDF:RTF.

Figure 10-4. *Setting the condition of a column to prevent it from being exported*

The string entered in Expression 1 ensures that the column will not be included in any native APEX export, regardless of the format selected by the user. This list can obviously be changed to allow the column to be included in the PDF but not the other formats, for example.

Custom Export to CSV

Although there are a few declarative ways to control and restrict the ability to export report data in APEX, they often do not provide a comprehensive enough solution for more secure or sophisticated requirements. The built-in export function offers an "all-or-nothing" approach. Either it is enabled and all users can export all of the records or it is disabled and no one can export anything.

Restricting Records with ROWNUM

Since there is no facility within APEX to augment this procedure, you need to do it in the SQL that constructs an APEX report. By wrapping the SQL with a WHERE clause that selectively limits the number of records returned based on a business rule, you can effectively limit the number of records returned when the report is run.

To implement this technique, you need to create an application item called G_MAX_ROWS. This item will be populated with the maximum number of records a user is allowed to export. When creating this item, be sure to set the Session State Protection parameter to Restricted – May not be set from browser. Failure to do so will allow a savvy user to set this item by simply passing a value through the URL.

The value for G_MAX_ROWS can be determined by a function call, a SQL query, or even a fixed amount. This item can even be set differently for each user-page combination. Regardless of how it is set, it should be set in an application computation that fires before each page is rendered.

When APEX calls the built-in export routine, it does so by passing a specific value to the request parameter of the URL. For a standard report, APEX will pass FLOW_EXCEL_OUTPUT_RXXX_en to the request parameter, where XXX refers to the corresponding region ID. For an interactive report, APEX will pass in CSV, HTMLD, XLS, PDF, or RTF, depending on what type of report was exported. Thus, if any of these values are passed to the request parameter, you can assume that a report is being exported by the built-in APEX export function and instrument the SQL to take that into consideration.

■ **Caution**   When using interactive reports, this technique will *not* work when selecting e-mail as a download format or when using e-mail subscriptions. Both options should be disabled in the interactive report to ensure that data is not exported using that method.

For example, a simple SQL statement like the one in Listing 10-1 can be augmented to restrict the maximum number of records in a standard report, as shown in Listing 10-2, or in an interactive report, as shown in Listing 10-3.

Listing 10-1. A Simple SQL Statement

```
SELECT
  ename,
  empno,
  sal
FROM
  emp
```

Listing 10-2. *The Same SQL Statement Wrapped to Restrict the Maximum Number of Records Returned for a Standard Report*

```
SELECT
  ename,
  empno,
  sal
FROM
  (
  SELECT
    ename,
    empno,
    sal
  FROM
    emp
  )
WHERE
  rownum <= CASE
  WHEN :REQUEST LIKE 'FLOW_EXCEL_OUTPUT%' THEN
    TO_NUMBER(:G_MAX_ROWS)
  ELSE rownum END
```

Listing 10-3. *The Same SQL Statement Wrapped to Restrict the Maximum Number of Records Returned for a Standard Report*

```
SELECT
  ename,
  empno,
  sal
FROM
  (
  SELECT
    ename,
    empno,
    sal
  FROM
    emp
  )
WHERE
  rownum <= CASE
  WHEN :REQUEST IN ('CSV','HTMLD','XLS','PDF','RTF') THEN
    TO_NUMBER(:G_MAX_ROWS)
  ELSE rownum END
```

While this technique is a bit intrusive, in that you have to add an additional WHERE clause to your SQL, it is effective and does not require any additional components, save for an application item and its associated computation.

Restricting Records with PL/SQL

If modifying the SQL to restrict the number of rows returned is not sufficient, then the only alternative is to build your own custom export routines by hand. While this sounds a bit daunting at first, the code and mechanism required here are not sophisticated and are very repeatable and nonintrusive to your applications.

■ **Note**   The core code for this approach can be traced back to one of my blog posts from April 2006 (`http://spendolini.blogspot.com/2006/04/custom-export-to-csv.html`). Using the techniques described in that blog post and expanding upon them, you can create a custom export routine that offers as much auditing and control as you need.

Since there is no way to modify the core APEX components, the solution will have to sit just outside the APEX framework. The solution should be both reusable and as minimally intrusive as possible, thus making it almost seamless to enable whenever and wherever needed. The core of the solution will reside in a PL/SQL package. The actual generation of the export files, as well as all security and audit routines, will occur there. The rest of the solution will be based on built-in APEX components. It is important to note that despite this being a custom solution, it relies on 100 percent supported functionality of APEX and the Oracle Database.

The following example uses the standard Oracle EMP table. Both EMP and DEPT should be installed by default in an APEX workspace (as long as the option to install demonstration applications is enabled). Create a new application, and make sure that it has a page 1. On this page, simply create two reports, one classic and the other interactive. The SQL for these reports is quite simple, as illustrated in Listing 10-4.

Listing 10-4. SQL Statement Used for Both Types of Reports

```
SELECT * FROM EMP
```

Step 1: Disable Built-in Export Controls

The first step to implementing a custom download procedure is to disable the built-in export or download controls. Since custom controls will be added later, there is no longer a need to display the built-on ones. Depending on the type of report, the steps will vary. For Standard standard Reportsreports, edit the report attributes and simply set the **Enable CSV Output** option in the Report Export region to **No**, as illustrated in Figure 10-5.

Figure 10-5. *Disabling the export function in a standard report*

> **Note** When using classic reports, disabling the Report Export function is not enough. A clever, malicious user can easily get the region ID of a classic report and pass that through the URL, thus triggering the built-in export mechanism, even if it is disabled. The only way to truly protect against this type of attack is to ensure that each column in a classic report has its Include in Export option set to No. Failure to properly secure each column in a classic report puts the data in that column at risk.

For interactive reports, this is a two-step process. First, edit the report attributes. Next, uncheck the Download option in the Search Bar region of a report's attributes, as illustrated in Figure 10-6.

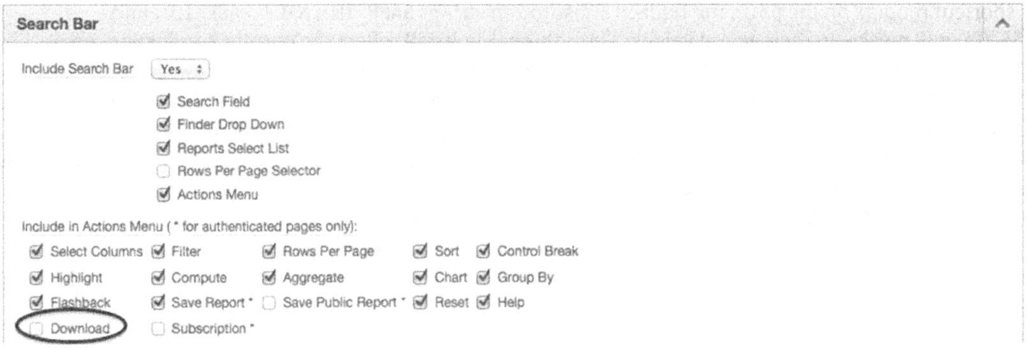

Figure 10-6. *Disabling the export function for an interactive report*

Unchecking the Download option simply removes that option from the interactive report menu. It does not prevent a user from using the URL to download the contents of the interactive report. Thus, all Download Formats options also need to be unchecked, as per Figure 10-7. Failure to uncheck all these options will allow a malicious user to use the URL to harvest information from any interactive report.

Figure 10-7. *Be sure to also uncheck all Download Formats options in an interactive report*

Step 2: Create a Shortcut

Once the built-in export mechanism is disabled and columns are restricted, the next step is to create a shortcut. Shortcuts in APEX are shared components that can be assigned a value by a developer. When used throughout the application, the shortcut will simply render as the value to which it is set. They are quite useful if you need to reuse the same snippet or code in multiple places.

The shortcut used in this solution will call an APEX URL that is generic enough that it can be referenced from any report on any page using built-in APEX substitution strings. Thus, only a single shortcut for any number or reports is required for this solution. Creating a single shortcut also provides the ability for the URL references to be changed in a single place and impact the entire application, should it be necessary to do so.

To create a shortcut, navigate to the shared components of your application. Create a new shortcut from scratch, name it DOWNLOAD, and set its type to HTML Text. Next, enter the code from Listing 10-5 into the Shortcut region and create the shortcut.

Listing 10-5. The DOWNLOAD Shortcut URL

```
<a href="f?p=&APP_ID.:&APP_PAGE_ID.:&APP_SESSION.
:EXPORT::: G_REGION_ID:#REGION_ID#">Download</a>
```

When the shortcut renders on the page, the built-in substitution strings &APP_ID., &APP_PAGE_ID., and &APP_PAGE_SESSION. will resolve to their actual values. Thus, this snippet will reflect the current application, page, and session ID associated with a specific user. When referred to in a region header or footer, #REGION_ID# will be replaced with the corresponding region's internal ID. This will help to get a "handle" on the region and determine which export link was clicked if there is more than one region on a page. The value of region ID will be passed to an application item called G_REGION_ID, which will also be passed to the PL/SQL package.

The value EXPORT will be passed to the request parameter of the URL. An application process will be added later and conditionally set to call the PL/SQL export routine if the request value is set to EXPORT.

Figure 10-8 shows the shortcut page.

Figure 10-8. *The type and source of the DOWNLOAD shortcut*

Once the shortcut is created, it will have to be added to any region that will call the custom export procedure. Simply edit any report (standard or interactive), and paste the shortcut name enclosed in double quotes into the Region Footer area, as illustrated in Figure 10-9.

***Figure 10-9.** Associating the shortcut with a region footer*

When users run the page, the Download link will look identical to the built-in Export to CSV link that they are accustomed to seeing. Keeping the link title consistent will alleviate the need for additional user training.

Step 3: Associate a Static ID

One more slight modification needs to be made to the region before it will work with the custom export procedure: a static ID must be associated with it. All APEX regions have an associated region ID that can be determined by inspecting the #REGION_ID# built-in item from within a region. APEX region IDs are surrogate keys and will consequentially be changed when moving the application from one instance to another. Therefore, they do not make good references if you want to look for a specific region from a PL/SQL package.

The static ID is a place to supply a natural primary key for a region so that if it is programmatically referred to in the PL/SQL package in one instance, it will still retain that same ID in any other instance. The static ID in APEX can be set to any value at all. Unfortunately, APEX does not check to see whether it is unique within a page, so extra attention needs to be paid when creating static IDs to ensure that they are unique on a page.

Oftentimes, the static ID will already be set for use in jQuery or JavaScript. That will not interfere with the purposes of the custom export routine. As long as it's defined to some value and is unique within an APEX page, there should be no conflicts.

To set the static ID of any region, simply edit the region and enter a value for Static ID, as illustrated in Figure 10-10.

***Figure 10-10.** Setting the static ID of a region*

A consistent naming convention may combine the page number that the region resides on with the title or a portion of the title of the region. For this example, the static ID of the classic report will be set to p1EmpClassic, and the static ID of the interactive report will be set to p1EmpInteractive.

Step 4: Set an Application Item

To capture the region ID of the corresponding region that was clicked, an application item is needed. The value of this item can easily be inspected within a PL/SQL package to determine which export procedure to execute. The Session State Protection attribute for this item must be set to Unrestricted. Typically, the best practice is to set application items to at least some variant of Checksum Required, as illustrated in Figure 10-11. However, in this case, it is safe to leave this application item set to Unrestricted, because additional security checks will be implemented within the PL/SQL package. Since this application item will be unrestricted, it should never be referred to by using &G_REGION_ID. within a static region of APEX.

Figure 10-11. *Creating the application item to store the region ID*

Alternatively, a hidden item on Page 0 can be used in lieu of an application item. Technically, there is little difference between the two. Page 0 items, of course, require that page 0 and at least one region be created, whereas application items have no such requirement.

Any APEX item must be associated with a region, so you may want to create a placeholder HTML region on page 0 and associate P0_REGION_ID with that region. This region should not have a condition on it so that P0_REGION_ID is available on all pages of the application.

Step 5: Create an Application Process

The final APEX component needed is an application process. This process should be a PL/SQL anonymous block set to fire On Load: Before Header and be given a sequence of 0 so that it executes before anything else. Figure 10-12 provides an example of the settings for the application process.

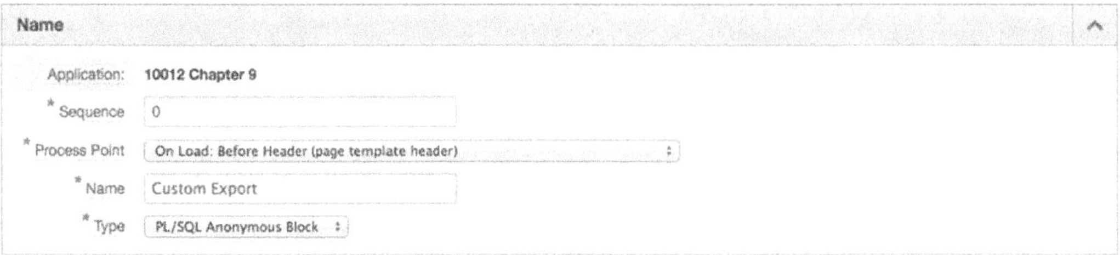

Figure 10-12. *Application process settings used to call the custom export package*

Next, enter the code in Listing 10-6 for the source or process text of the application process.

Listing 10-6. The Source for the Custom Export Application Process

```
custom_export.export_data
  (
  p_app_id                     => v('APP_ID'),
  p_app_page_id                => v('APP_PAGE_ID'),
  p_app_session                => v('APP_SESSION'),
  p_app_user                   => v('APP_USER'),
  p_region_id                  => :G_REGION_ID
  );
```

The process will evaluate and determine the application ID, page, session, and user by calling the v function and passing in the corresponding parameter. It will use G_REGION_ID as the final parameter, thus identifying which link in which report was clicked.

Finally, the process should be conditional and set to fire only on Request = Expression 1, and Expression 1 should be set to EXPORT, as illustrated in Figure 10-13. This will limit the process to fire only when the custom link is clicked rather than before every page view.

Figure 10-13. *Setting the condition of the application process*

Step 6: Create the PL/SQL Package

Now that all of the APEX components are configured, the PL/SQL package that will facilitate the actual export routine needs to be created. The complete listing for this package as well as the supporting database objects can be found in the source code download for this book. (Snippets of the package are referred to in this chapter for illustrative purposes only.)

This package also assumes that the EMP and DEPT tables installed in the schema. If these tables are not installed, then the contents of the procedures p1_emp_classic and p1_emp_interactive can be modified to refer to tables that are present.

Once the database objects and package from the source code are installed, the custom export routine is ready to go. Clicking the custom export link in either the classic or interactive report region can test the custom export procedure, as depicted in Figure 10-14.

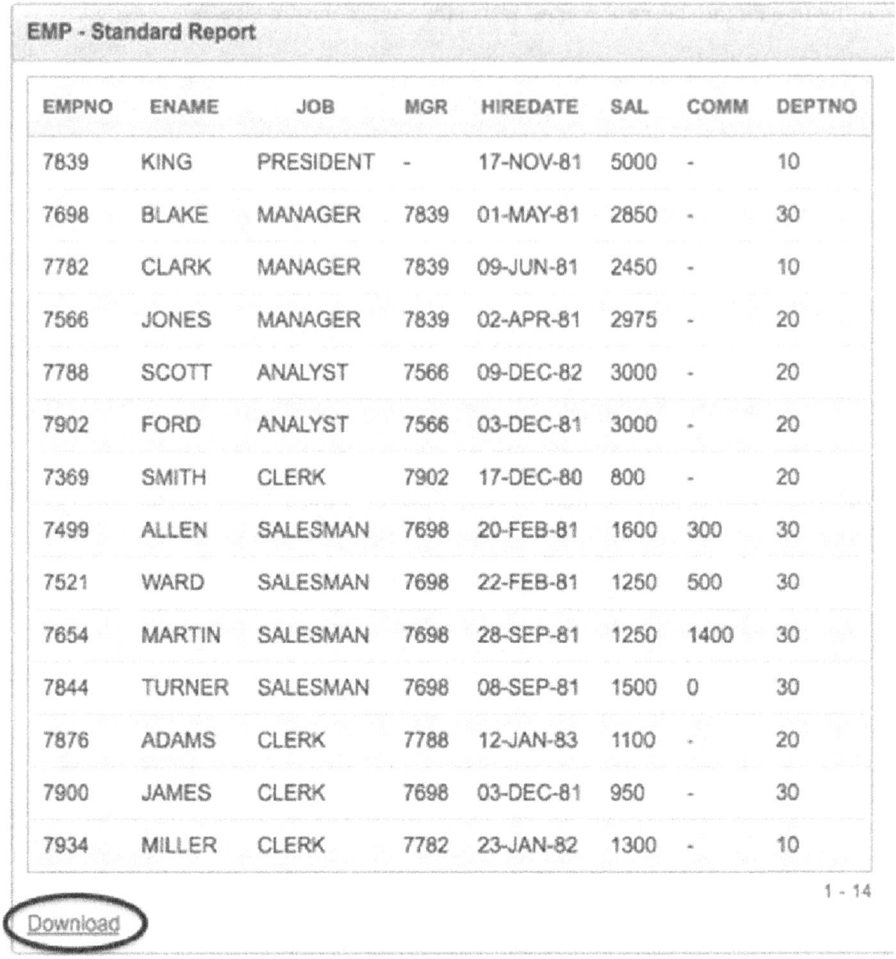

EMPNO	ENAME	JOB	MGR	HIREDATE	SAL	COMM	DEPTNO
7839	KING	PRESIDENT	-	17-NOV-81	5000	-	10
7698	BLAKE	MANAGER	7839	01-MAY-81	2850	-	30
7782	CLARK	MANAGER	7839	09-JUN-81	2450	-	10
7566	JONES	MANAGER	7839	02-APR-81	2975	-	20
7788	SCOTT	ANALYST	7566	09-DEC-82	3000	-	20
7902	FORD	ANALYST	7566	03-DEC-81	3000	-	20
7369	SMITH	CLERK	7902	17-DEC-80	800	-	20
7499	ALLEN	SALESMAN	7698	20-FEB-81	1600	300	30
7521	WARD	SALESMAN	7698	22-FEB-81	1250	500	30
7654	MARTIN	SALESMAN	7698	28-SEP-81	1250	1400	30
7844	TURNER	SALESMAN	7698	08-SEP-81	1500	0	30
7876	ADAMS	CLERK	7788	12-JAN-83	1100	-	20
7900	JAMES	CLERK	7698	03-DEC-81	950	-	30
7934	MILLER	CLERK	7782	23-JAN-82	1300	-	10

EMP - Standard Report

1 - 14

Download

Figure 10-14. *The download link that will call the custom export routine*

When the Download link is clicked, APEX will redirect to the same page, but this time, it will pass the value EXPORT to the request parameter. This, in turn, will trigger the application process that calls custom_export.export_data. Let's step through what happens inside custom_export.export_data, one chunk at a time.

The very first thing that happens is that a check is performed to determine whether the click came from a classic or interactive report, and then the details of that event get logged, as outlined in Listing 10-7. Since the APEX views for these are different, this determination needs to be made right away. Once this determination is made, then the download event is logged to the export_audit table. Slightly different parameters are required based on the type of report used. These values will be used by triggers on the table to ensure that the correct data for the report is logged.

Listing 10-7. Code to Determine and Log What Type of Report Was Downloaded

```
-- Determine if the report is Classic or Interactive
SELECT COUNT(*) INTO l_count FROM apex_application_page_ir
  WHERE region_id = l_region_id;
-- Log the download
```

```
IF l_count = 1 THEN
  INSERT INTO export_audit (region_id, report_type)
    VALUES (p_region_id, 'Interactive');
ELSE
  INSERT INTO export_audit (region_id) VALUES (p_region_id);
END IF;
```

Once the type of report is determined and the download event is logged, the next task is to determine the static ID based on the region ID that was passed to G_REGION_ID. The value of the static ID will be used to determine which download procedure to run. This needs to be transformed in this manner because the region ID of any APEX region is a surrogate key and will change when exported from one instance to another. Listing 10-8 illustrates the loop used to capture the static ID.

Listing 10-8. Fetching the Static ID Based on the Region ID

```
 -- Fetch the Static ID
FOR x IN (SELECT static_id FROM apex_application_page_regions
  WHERE region_id = l_region_id)
LOOP
  l_static_id := x.static_id;
END LOOP;
```

If the static ID is found, the process will continue, as outlined in Listing 10-9. However, if it is not found, then the process will fail and produce a basic error message, indicating to the user that no corresponding static ID exists for the region. More sophisticated error handling could be added here, but to keep things simple, the error message will simply be printed on the page.

Listing 10-9. Error Handling for When the Static ID Is Not Found

```
IF l_static_id IS NOT NULL THEN
  ...
ELSE
  -- Static ID not found
    htp.p('There is no Static ID defined for this region.'
      || '<br /><a href="f?p=' || p_app_id || ':'
      || p_app_page_id || ':' || p_app_session
      || '">Back to Report</a>');
    mime_footer;
END IF;
```

Assuming that a static ID was found, two security checks will be made, which are outlined in Listing 10-10. The first will determine whether the user can run the page that the report is on. The second will check to see whether the user can run the actual report. It does this by calling the built-in APEX APIs to check the authorization scheme for the page and region.

This step is required because the URL is being used to pass the region ID to an unprotected application or page item. Thus, it would be very easy for malicious users to look up or even brute-force attack with a range of other region IDs and pass them to the procedure, thus allowing them to see data from reports that they do not have access to. Adding these additional security checks will prevent such an attack from occurring and allow only authorized users to run the custom export procedure.

Listing 10-10. Authorization Checks for Both the Page and Region

```
-- Determine if the user can run the page that the region is located on
FOR x IN
  (
  SELECT
    pr.authorization_scheme region_auth,
    p.authorization_scheme page_auth
  FROM
    apex_application_page_regions pr,
    apex_application_pages p
  WHERE
    pr.page_id = p.page_id
    AND p.application_id = pr.application_id
    AND pr.region_id = TO_NUMBER(l_region_id)
    AND p.application_id = p_app_id)
  )
LOOP
  l_page_auth := x.page_auth;
  l_region_auth := x.region_auth;
END LOOP;
-- Check to see that the user has access to the page
IF l_page_auth IS NOT NULL THEN
  l_page_auth_res := APEX_UTIL.PUBLIC_CHECK_AUTHORIZATION(l_page_auth);
ELSE
  l_page_auth_res := TRUE;
END IF;
-- Check to see that the user has access to the region
IF l_region_auth IS NOT NULL THEN
  l_region_auth_res := APEX_UTIL.PUBLIC_CHECK_AUTHORIZATION(l_region_auth);
ELSE
  l_region_auth_res := TRUE;
END IF;
```

If either of the checks failed (meaning that an APEX authorization scheme would prevent this user from viewing either this page or this specific region), then the procedure will display an error message and not continue, as illustrated in Listing 10-11. For additional security, this event could be logged and an administrator notified because ending up here would almost always be the result of a malicious attempt to view the export.

Listing 10-11. Error Message Displayed When the User Is Not Authorized to View the Page or Region

```
-- If the user can't see either the region of page,
-- then do not allow the download to start
IF l_region_auth_res = FALSE OR l_page_auth_res = FALSE THEN
  -- User cannot export this report
  htp.p('You are not Authorized to export this report.'
    || '<br /><a href="f?p=' || p_app_id || ':'
    || p_app_page_id || ':' || p_app_session || '">Back</a>');
  mime_footer;
```

In the case that both checks returned a TRUE, the next step is to call the corresponding export procedure. Additional checks can also be made at this point, such as ensuring that only a specific user or set of users can export a report. The possibilities of what else can be checked here are limitless.

In this example, p1_emp_classic and p1_emp_interactive are procedures that will be called based on which export link was clicked. The custom export package can have several additional procedures added to it, based on how many reports need custom export routines. For more reusability, you could even use the APEX views and dynamically create the SQL statements that will be run for the export. Listing 10-12 shows how the custom_export procedure determines which export procedure to run.

Listing 10-12. Determining Which Procedure to Run Is Based on the Static ID

```
ELSE
  -- Determine which export procedure to run
  CASE
    WHEN l_static_id = 'p1EmpClassic' THEN p1_emp_classic;
    WHEN l_static_id = 'p1EmpInteractive' THEN p1_emp_interactive;
  ELSE
    -- No procedure for Static ID
    htp.p('There is no procedure for the static ID'
    || l_static_id
    || '<br /><a href="f?p=' || p_app_id || ':'
    || p_app_page_id || ':' || p_app_session
    || '">Back to Report</a>');
    mime_footer;
  END CASE;
END IF;
```

Let's assume that the Export link in the classic report on page 1 in the application was clicked. In that case, the procedure p1_emp_classic, as illustrated in Listing 10-13, would be called. p1_emp_classic will first call mime_header, which sets up the MIME type so that the browser will download a file rather than display a page. Next, it simply loops through a subset of the columns in the EMP table. For each row, it produces a line of CSV output followed by a carriage return. Upon completion of the loop, it will call mime_footer, which will indicate that the CSV stream is complete and prevent any additional APEX processes from executing.

Listing 10-13. The Procedure p1_emp_classic, Which Generates the Custom CSV File

```
PROCEDURE p1_emp_classic IS
BEGIN
mime_header(p_filename => 'emp.csv');
-- Loop through all rows in EMP
FOR x IN (SELECT e.ename, e.empno, d.dname FROM emp e, DEPT d
  WHERE e.deptno = d.deptno)
LOOP
  -- Print out a portion of a row, separated by commas
  -- and ended by a CR
  htp.prn(x.ename ||','|| x.empno ||','|| x.dname || chr(13));
END LOOP;
mime_footer;
END p1_emp_classic;
```

This is an extremely simple example of what could be exported. Additional rules could be checked here to limit how many rows or which columns would be exported based on who is logged in. The entire file could also be stored in a CLOB so that there is a record of specifically what was downloaded and by whom. A notification could be sent to an administrator if the data set exceeded 500 rows or a sensitive report was exported. Again, the possibilities of additional checks and functionality here is limitless.

Summary

The ability to export data from an APEX application is a powerful feature. Yet it has a dark side that too often goes undetected because any user can export almost any data set and easily take ownership of potentially sensitive data.

APEX offers some controls as to limiting what columns can be exported. However, those controls are somewhat limited and not very specific. Implementing a custom export mechanism involves a little bit of time and thought, but it can be specifically tailored to meet almost any security requirement imaginable. If done properly, a custom export mechanism will be transparent to both users and developers alike.

CHAPTER 11

Secure Views

While APEX offers a number of controls to limit user access to its components, it offers few components to protect the data itself. That may seem like a shortcoming on the surface, but it is not. Protecting data at the application layer can be potentially short-sighted because it protects only that single avenue to the data. If developers spent all of their time building in controls to their APEX application to restrict what users could see, then users could circumvent those controls by accessing the data via another application or directly.

Thus, data is best secured at the database layer, not within the application. Oracle provides a couple of features to assist with this task: Oracle Virtual Private Database and Oracle Label Security. Both of these tools require the Enterprise Edition of the Oracle Database, and Oracle Label Security is a for-cost option. Fortunately, if you're running Oracle Standard Edition One or Standard Edition, you can still secure your data at the database layer using nothing more than a smartly designed view.

This chapter will outline the benefits of using such views as a layer of security in your APEX and other Oracle applications. It will illustrate some techniques for where and how to use secured views and their associated components. It concludes with a summary of the benefits and potential drawbacks to using this approach.

The View

In general, most Oracle developers are quite familiar with views. Views are very powerful and are often an underappreciated and underused construct in any database. They allow developers to mask the complexity of a sophisticated SQL statement in a much easier-to-use format. Additionally, they can obfuscate columns or data that should not be seen by specific applications. If the definition of the view needs to change, it can do so without any application code changes in many cases, thus making applications easier to manage over the course of their lifetime.

All of the traditional benefits of views are good for nothing if they don't get used in APEX applications. And chances are, most APEX applications are built to interact directly with tables and make little, if any, use of views at all.

The use of views in your application should be something that is considered during the design phase. Designing an application based on views from the ground up is a lot faster than trying to retrofit an existing application with views. Like most facets of application development, a little bit of planning will go a long way.

Using a view in APEX is quite simple. Simply create the view in the same schema that the APEX application parses as and then reference that view in a report, form, chart, and so on, just as if it was a table. That's all there is to it! Take, for example, the view in Listing 11-1.

Listing 11-1. SQL to Create a simple Simple view View on the EMP tableTable

```
CREATE OR REPLACE VIEW emp_v
AS
SELECT
  empno,
  ename,
```

```
  job,
  deptno
FROM
  emp
/
```

This simple view will return the EMPNO, ENAME, JOB, and DEPTNO columns from all the rows from the EMP table. To use this view when creating a component in APEX, simply select from EMP_V instead of EMP, and your component will be based on the rows and columns referenced in the view. If business conditions dictated a change in how this view were constructed, the definition of the view could be rewritten, and little to no code changes in the application would be required.

If a simple APEX application were created using the EMP_V view, the results would look similar to Figure 11-1.

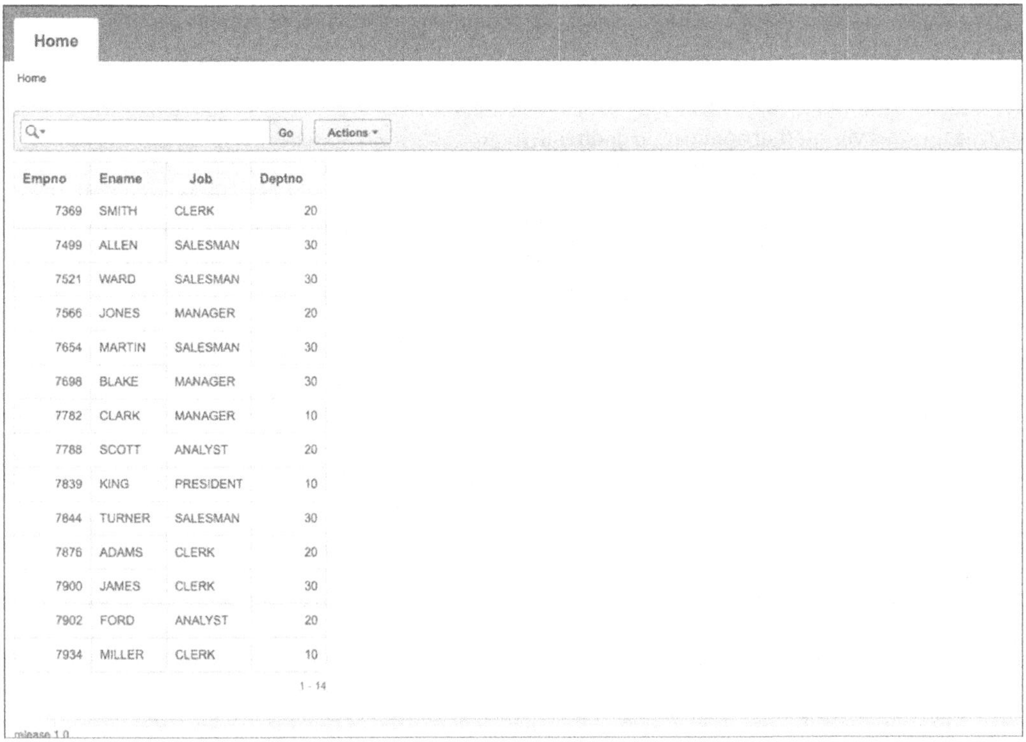

Figure 11-1. *A simple APEX report based on EMP_V*

Secure View Components

A secure view is not an actual database object or APEX component type but rather a term used to describe the techniques of using a view to provide data security for an application. Secure views provide both the traditional benefits of views combined with an added layer of both data security and functionality that can be used in any application – APEX or otherwise.

In the following example, you will create a secure view based on the EMP table that restricts users from seeing records from other departments. When you build the APEX report on top of this view, you will pay little to no attention to data security there because it will all be addressed via the secure view. Not only does this decrease the time it takes to develop applications, but it also makes them a lot easier to manage over time because of their minimalistic design and sparse use of sophisticated SQL queries.

Because secure views are not an actual object type, there are a few components that need to be in place before they will actually work. Secure views rely on application contexts to act as the filter in their predicate. Application contexts are the most efficient and effective way to create a secure view, because their values are stored in memory and take almost no measurable time to reference.

The values of application contexts can be set only by a specific PL/SQL procedure, so you will have to create one of them. And since application contexts are based on database sessions, not APEX sessions, you need to augment your APEX application with some PL/SQL code to call both before and after a page is rendered.

Application Contexts

An *application context* is a database object type that simply stores name-value pairs in memory. Setting the values of an application context is controlled by a specific procedure, not by the user. Furthermore, the values stored in an application context can be modified or removed only by this same procedure.

In APEX, application items are also components that can store a value that can be referenced throughout the APEX session. Application items can be configured to either allow or prohibit users from directly making changes to their values. Application contexts work in a similar fashion but are applied to a database session, not an APEX session.

To create an application context, a database user needs to have the CREATE ANY CONTEXT system privilege. Alternatively, an alternate schema with DBA privileges and the CREATE ANY CONTEXT system privilege can create a context that references a procedure from any schema. Listing 11-2 outlines the SQL required to create a simple application context that is secured by a procedure called SET_CTX that is owned by SCOTT

Listing 11-2. SQL Used to Create an Application Context

```
CREATE CONTEXT emp_ctx USING SCOTT.emp_ctx_pkg;
```

It is important to note that when an application context is created, there is no verification as to whether the associated procedure used to secure it exists. Thus, the order in which you create the application and corresponding procedure does not matter.

PL/SQL Procedure

The PL/SQL package referenced in Listing 11-2 needs to be created next. The purpose of this package is to set and unset a value or set of values associated with the EMP_CTX application context. The methods or business rules used to set these values are up to the developer and will be vastly different from application to application. Despite this, they will all reference the same API used to set the application context values: DBMS_SESSION.SET_CONTEXT.

As outlined in Listing 11-3, the SET_CTX procedure simply looks up the department number of the currently logged in user. It then uses that value to set the DEPTNO attribute of the EMP_CTX application context. This value will be used later in the actual SQL of the secure view. The UNSET_CTX procedure clears all values of the context so that they do not get inadvertently reused by another APEX session.

Listing 11-3. The Procedure SET_CTX, Which Is Used by the EMP_CTX Application Context

```
CREATE OR REPLACE PACKAGE emp_ctx_pkg
AS
PROCEDURE set_ctx
  (
  p_user_name                IN VARCHAR2
  );
```

```
PROCEDURE unset_ctx;
END emp_ctx_pkg;
/


CREATE OR REPLACE PACKAGE BODY emp_ctx_pkg
AS
PROCEDURE set_ctx
  (
  p_user_name                 IN VARCHAR2
  )
IS
  l_deptno                    NUMBER;
BEGIN

-- Fetch the DEPTNO based on the currently signed on APP_USER
SELECT deptno INTO l_deptno FROM emp
  WHERE ename = p_user_name;

-- Set the Context
dbms_session.set_context(
  namespace => 'EMP_CTX',
  attribute => 'DEPTNO',
  value     => l_deptno);

EXCEPTION
WHEN no_data_found THEN
  -- If no data is found, then clear the context
  dbms_session.clear_context('EMP_CTX');
END set_ctx;

PROCEDURE unset_ctx
IS
BEGIN
-- Clear the context
dbms_session.clear_context('EMP_CTX');
END unset_ctx;

END emp_ctx_pkg;
/
```

Secure View SQL

Now that you have your application context and associated PL/SQL package in place, you can re-create the EMP_V view with a reference to the application context. The SYS_CONTEXT procedure is provided by Oracle to return the value of an application context namespace and parameter. It can be used in the predicate of a SQL statement in the same manner as a bind variable or literal can be.

Listing 11-4 outlines the updated EMP_V SQL. There is only one difference between this version and the one used in Listing 11-1: the WHERE clause in this version is used and refers to the application context. The rest of the SQL is identical between the two versions.

Listing 11-4. SQL for the EMP_V Using the SYS_CONTEXT Procedure

```
CREATE OR REPLACE VIEW emp_v AS
SELECT
  empno,
  ename,
  job,
  deptno
FROM
  emp
WHERE
  deptno = SYS_CONTEXT('EMP_CTX', 'DEPTNO')
/
```

Back in the APEX application, if you were to rerun your report, you would get the results illustrated in Figure 11-2.

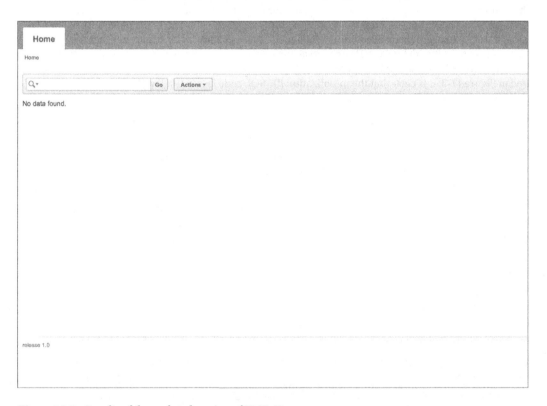

Figure 11-2. *Results of the updated version of EMP_V*

The reason that no records are returned is that the application context has not been properly set for the APEX application. Remember, the only way to set the value of an application context is to call the procedure that was associated with it when it was created. Since no such call to that procedure has been made, the value of the application context is not set, and thus the report does not return any records.

Security Attributes

Setting, as well as unsetting, the application context is a critical step in creating a secure view. Setting an application context is as simple as calling the procedure associated with it. In a stateful environment, such as SQL*Plus, the context can be set one time and remain set for the duration of that session. Since APEX sessions are stateless and distinct from database sessions, setting the application context once is not sufficient. It must be set for each and every distinct page view in an APEX application.

To do this, many developers will instinctually gravitate towards using either a page or an application PL/SQL process to set the application context. While this would technically work, it is not an ideal place to set our the application context, as because the application context should be set before any application or page process executes. Furthermore, application and page processes will not fire when using asynchronous components such as dynamic actions.

Fortunately, APEX provides a process point designed for just such a scenario. It's called the **Initialization PL/SQL Ccode**, and can be found in the **Database Session** region of the **Security Attributes**, one of APEX's shared components. This attribute will execute whatever PL/SQL code is entered there before any other APEX component is executed. This ensures that when using application contexts, they will be set before any business rules execute.

To prove this, a simple test case was set up that compared three execution points: Initialization PL/SQL code, an application process, and a page process. All three execution points were set with a call to the procedure named apex_debug_message.log_message. When called from within an APEX session, the apex_debug_message.log_message call will write a message to the APEX debug log. Those messages can be viewed inline with all of the other built-in debug entries that APEX records during a debug capture.

As illustrated in Figure 11-3, it is clear that the initialization PL/SQL code is executed well before either the application or page process.

0.01811	0.00049	...Check for session expiration:	4	
0.01860	0.00145	Session: Fetch session header information	4	
0.02006	0.00088	...Execute Statement: begin apex_debug_message.log_message('DEMO: Init PL/SQL Code'); end;	4	
0.02093	0.00054	Branch point: Before Header	4	
0.02147	0.00149	Fetch application meta data	4	
0.02296	0.00028	...metadata, fetch computations	4	
0.02323	0.00029	...metadata, fetch buttons	4	
0.02352	0.00004	...http header processing	4	
0.02356	0.00026	...set mime type: text/html	4	
0.02382	0.00011	...set additional http headers	4	
0.02392	0.00008	Process point: BEFORE_HEADER	4	
0.02401	0.00007	Processes - point: BEFORE_HEADER	4	
0.02407	0.00022	...Process "On Load - Page Process" - Type: PLSQL	4	
0.02429	0.00033	...Execute Statement: begin apex_debug_message.log_message('DEMO: On Load - Page Process'); end;	4	
0.02462	0.00013	...Process "On Load - Application Process" - Type: PLSQL	4	
0.02475	0.00028	...Execute Statement: begin apex_debug_message.log_message('DEMO: On Load - Application Process'); end;	4	
0.02503	0.00004	...close http header	4	
0.02507	0.00040	...metadata, fetch item type settings	4	
0.02548	0.00112	...metadata, fetch items	4	
0.02660	0.00231	Show page template header	4	
0.02890	0.00059	Rendering form open tag and internal values	4	

Figure 11-3. *The APEX debug report highlighting the execution points of the initialization PL/SQL code, an application process, and a page process*

This test case reinforces the recommendation that application contexts should be set via the Initialization PL/SQL Code attribute, not an application or page process. Thus, in this example, you need to make a simple call to both set and unset the application context so that it will be set for the application.

To configure the application to set the application context, navigate to the shared components, and under Security, click Security Attributes. In the last region on the page called Database Session are the two attributes required for setting the application context, as illustrated in Figure 11-4.

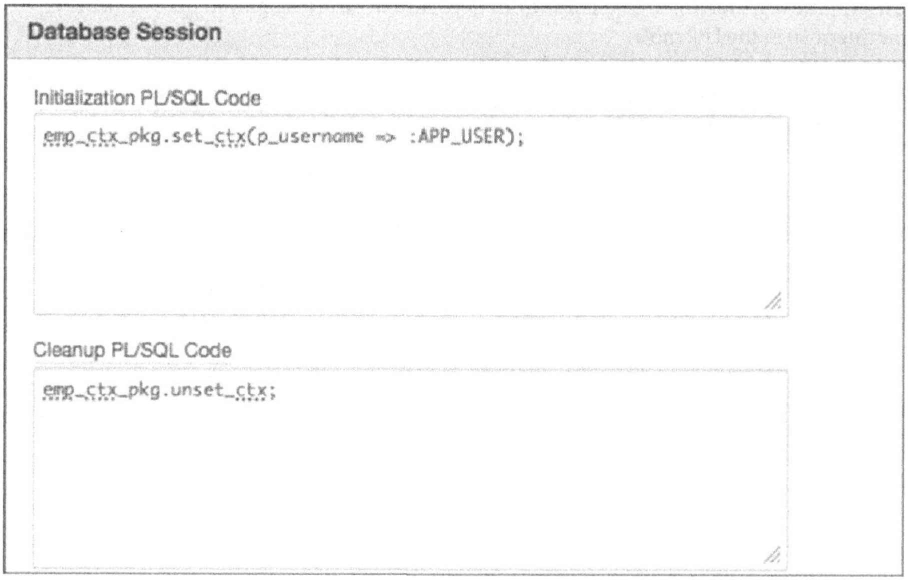

Figure 11-4. *The Initialization PL/SQL Code and Cleanup PL/SQL Code attributes*

Enter the code in Listing 11-5 into the Initialization PL/SQL Code box, and enter the code in Listing 11-6 into the Cleanup PL/SQL Code box. Then save your changes.

Listing 11-5. PL/SQL Call to Set Application Context

```
emp_ctx_pkg.set_ctx(p_username => :APP_USER);
```

Listing 11-6. PL/SQL Call to Unset Application Context

```
emp_ctx_pkg.unset_ctx;
```

■ **Note** The attribute Initialization PL/SQL Code was called *Virtual Private Database call to set security context* in APEX 4.0 and previous versions. Despite the reference to Virtual Private Database in the old title, you do not need to use that feature or have a version of the database that even supports it to use this attribute to execute PL/SQL code before any application process or computation.

Now that the application context is being properly set, when you run the APEX application, you should see some records (as long as you log in to the APEX application with a username that has the same username as any value of ENAME in the EMP table does). Remember, the set_ctx procedure is fetching the DEPTNO associated with a record in EMP that matches ENAME to the currently signed on APEX user. If your username does not yield a match, then you will continue to see no records returned from the report.

To ensure that your secure view is working, simply create a user whose username is the same as any value of ENAME in the EMP table, and run your application while logged in as that user. In Figure 11-5, the report was run while logged on as a user with the username of KING. All three records from department 10 are displayed because KING is directly associated with department 10 in the EMP table.

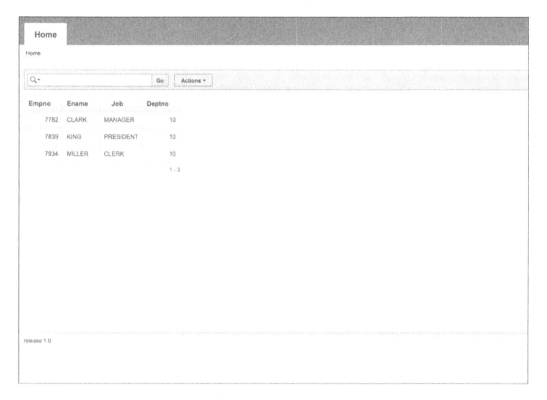

Figure 11-5. *Results of the report on EMP_V when logged in as KING*

Benefits and Drawbacks

One of the biggest benefits of using secure views in an APEX environment is that they will neutralize most types of URL tampering attacks. Since the view itself is filtering the data at the data layer, it matters little if a user passes a different ID via the URL to an APEX page. In fact, if a malicious user does pass an ID that he does not have access to see, a "no data found" message will be displayed, which may lead users to believe that the record they are trying to access simply does not exists.

It is important to keep in mind that any Automated Row Fetch and Get Next/Previous Primary Key processes also reference the secure views, not the base tables. Failure to reference the secure view will allow a user to see records that they are not supposed to see by manipulating the URL or simply clicking the Next/Previous Record buttons, if they exist on a form.

Another benefit of using secure views is that the total time to develop an application will decrease. If all the data security is taken care of at the data level, then developers don't need to be concerned with ensuring that all queries are secured with the proper predicates. This will also simplify the SQL used in reports, thus making it easier to understand and maintain over the life cycle of the application.

Centralizing the data security also makes it a lot easier to change the business rules, should the need arise. Making a change to the application context procedure will impact any view that references that application context instantly. If the rule for determining which department a user is associated with changes, a single change to the procedure would instantly change how the entire application worked without making a single change to the application itself. This obviously saves a great deal of time and money and makes the application much more flexible.

Lastly, secure views also carry with them all of the benefits of standard views. Complex joins between multiple tables can easily be masked by a view. Columns that are not necessary for an application can be omitted, providing the developer with just those columns that are needed for a specific application. And if core business rules change, the definition of the view itself can be changed without impacting the application in many cases.

Nothing comes without a cost, and secure views are no exception. While they are quite robust and can be configured in a number of ways, they do have their shortcomings and potential drawbacks.

Secure views protect data only from a SELECT. They do nothing when it comes to INSERTs, UPDATEs, and/or DELETEs. In some scenarios, this drawback does not make much of a difference because the requirement is to simply filter data in reports and forms. However, if additional controls are required to also prevent users from updating or deleting specific records, then secure views may not offer enough functionality, and you should consider Virtual Private Database, which provides protection for all DML transactions.

If a secure view is created with the READ ONLY option enabled, either a separate set of PL/SQL APIs or INSTEAD OF triggers will have to be developed to facilitate any DML transaction. While there is no additional risk with using either of these approaches, it will take extra time to design and develop the extra code required versus using the APEX built-in DML processes.

Summary

Using secure views, you can easily and affordably secure the data in your APEX application, no matter which version of the Oracle Database you are running on. The techniques described in this chapter use both core APEX and database functionality and can be set up and configured quickly and easily. In addition to the benefits of the secure views, using views in general will result in a more manageable and easier-to-understand application.

Although secure views provide an adequate layer of security in many cases, they may not provide enough. Carefully consider your security requirements before starting any development to ensure that your application won't soon outgrow what secure views can provide.

■ ■ ■

CHAPTER 12

Virtual Private Database

Using the secure views technique outlined in Chapter 10 can go a long way with quickly and affordably securing data in APEX applications and other applications. However, it does have some limitations that cannot be easily overcome.

Virtual Private Database (VPD) is a no-cost feature of the Oracle Database Enterprise Edition that dynamically adds WHERE clauses to any SQL statement used against a table or view. Managed by a simple PL/SQL function, VPD is a robust way to restrict which rows and columns a given user can view. In addition to restricting SELECT statements, VPD can be configured to also restrict INSERT, UPDATE, and DELETE statements, offering a full breadth of data protection.

Despite that it uses its own session management, APEX is fully compatible with VPD and can easily and quickly be configured to work with it. This chapter will provide a general overview of VPD and how to configure it to work in an APEX environment.

The Evolution of Data

Take a moment and think about what technologies were used to build applications 15 or 20 years ago. It was likely some sort of host-based system, possibly even a mainframe. Chances are really good that it was a character-based application because the mouse was not as commonplace then as it is today. Many of these systems were written in COBOL, ADA, or even C. Regardless of which language was used, many had no choice but to deal with data security within the application itself.

Now, think about systems from 10 or so years ago. Many systems of that time were mostly client-server, where the data resided on a server and the client was installed on each individual workstation. While these systems looked better than their character-mode forefathers, they still had the same fundamental security architecture; data security was mostly built into the client.

Fast-forward to today's web-based and even smartphone-based systems. These systems are, in a way, a hybrid of host-based and client-server computing, because processing does occur on both the client and the server. The main difference between the two is that any code that is executed on the client is easily and seamlessly distributed from the application or web server. And much like with the older systems, data security is almost always managed from within the application itself.

It's not too difficult to spot the trend in application development over the last 20 or so years. Time after time, data security gets folded into the application code. And since it seems that the longevity of any specific technology is just a few years, all of that work eventually gets scrapped and rebuilt in the next technology.

Consider a payroll system that is 20 years old. While there have been numerous tax law changes over the years, the basic business and security rules of almost any payroll system have remained constant. However, as the technologies used to build the payroll system have changed, the same data security rules have had to be rewritten in the new technology every time, with few changes to the basic security rules themselves. These changes not only are costly but also introduce risk that the rules are not properly migrated to the new technology.

Wouldn't it make more sense to apply data security to tables and views rather than to the application? This way, once the security rules are defined and applied, it no longer matters which technology is being used to access the data because the security occurs at the database layer, not within the application. This is exactly the premise that VPD takes when it comes to securing your data: do it once at the database layer and never have to do it again. The data is what lives forever, not the application code.

VPD Basics

VPD—sometimes referred to as *fine-grained access control*—essentially will automatically append conditions to a SQL query's WHERE clause as it executes, thus dynamically changing the results returned. How and what changes when a query is executed is determined by a VPD policy, which is essentially a PL/SQL function that returns the WHERE clause to be appended to the query.

Developers can create policies that have different business rules for SELECTs, INSERTs, UPDATEs, and DELETEs. Alternatively, they can create a single policy that handles all four DML transaction types at once, or any combination thereof. Policies can also be grouped together and applied all at once.

While the most common use of VPD is to filter rows based on some value or business rule, VPD can also be applied to columns within a query. Column-level policies can be applied in one of two ways: show only those records that match predefined criteria or show all records but mask data in columns that don't match a defined criteria.

For example, if a VPD policy were created that allowed them to see only records in their department, a simple query on the EMP table would return only the rows where the DEPTNO column value was the same as the currently logged in user. Thus, only a subset of all records would ever be returned. If the VPD policy was created and set to show all records but obfuscate the SAL and COMM columns for records that had a different DEPTNO than the user who was logged in, all rows would be returned, but those with a different DEPTNO would simply have NULLs displayed in the SAL and COMM columns.

VPD quite often uses application contexts as a parameter in the dynamic WHERE clause that it generates. This is done for both security and performance reasons. As discussed in Chapter 10, APEX can work perfectly fine with application contexts, provided they are set properly in the Initialization PL/SQL Code region in an application's Security Attributes section. Refer to the previous chapter for more details.

While there are more features and information about implementing VPD, they are out of scope for this book. To learn more, take a look at Chapter 7 of the Oracle Database Security Guide (Part #B28531-06).

Integration with APEX

Configuring VPD to work with APEX is relatively simple. Essentially the steps are the same as they are for implementing VPD outside of an APEX environment. In fact, if an application context is not used, then the steps are the same as they would be for a non-APEX implementation.

To illustrate VPD in an APEX environment, you'll go through a simple example that filters queries on the EMP table to show only the record associated with the currently logged in APEX user. As a first step, create a simple APEX application with one page. On that page, create a report—interactive or standard—that contains the SQL illustrated in Listing 12-1.

Listing 12-1. A Simple SQL Statement on the EMP Table

```
SELECT * FROM EMP
```

When running this APEX application, all 14 records will be returned because there is not yet any WHERE clause or VPD function to restrict the report.

VPD Policy Function

Next, the VPD policy function needs to be created. To add an additional layer of security, the VPD policy function can be created in a separate schema. This is done namely to prevent a developer from maliciously altering the business rules of the policy function, assuming that the developer does not have DBA rights or access to the schema in which the policy function is created in. For this example, the policy function will be created in the same schema that the EMP table resides in.

One more important point about VPD policy functions is that they must have two IN parameters of type VARCHAR2 that will be passed the schema and object name to which the policy function will be applied. These parameters can be called anything at all but must be the first and only two parameters passed to the function.

Listing 12-2 illustrates a VPD policy function that restricts the result based on the currently signed on APEX user. Note how double quotes had to be used when making reference to the APEX v function. This is done so that the quotes are included in the string rather than being treated as delimiters.

Listing 12-2. A VPD Policy Function Used to Limit Results by User Name

```
CREATE OR REPLACE FUNCTION limit_by_username
  (
  p_schema      IN VARCHAR2 DEFAULT NULL,
  p_objname     IN VARCHAR2 DEFAULT NULL
  )
RETURN VARCHAR2
AS
BEGIN

-- Return the SQL
RETURN 'ename = v(''APP_USER'')';

END limit_by_username;
/
```

At this point, running the report will still yield the same results because the VPD policy function must be associated with the EMP table by using the DBMS_RLS packages. Access to the DBMS_RLS packages are not granted by default, so a DBA will need to grant EXECUTE to your APEX parse-as schema before the policy can be registered. The grant can be done via a simple SQL statement, as illustrated in Listing 12-3.

Listing 12-3. SQL Executed as a DBA Used to Grant Access to DBMS_RLS to a Schema

```
GRANT EXECUTE ON SYS.DBMS_RLS TO MY_SCHEMA
/
```

Once the grant has been made, the policy can be registered using the DBMS_RLS.ADD_POLICY API, as outlined in Listing 12-4.

Listing 12-4. Using DBMS_RLS.ADD_POLICY to Register the VPD Policy Function

```
BEGIN
DBMS_RLS.ADD_POLICY
  (
  object_schema   => 'ENKITEC',
  object_name     => 'EMP',
  policy_name     => 'LIMIT_BY_APP_USER',
```

```
  policy_function => 'LIMIT_BY_APP_USER',
  function_schema => 'ENKITEC'
  );
END;
/
```

Once the policy is applied, let's take a look at the results of the report in the APEX application. If you log in as the user KING and run the report in the APEX application, you see only your own row, as illustrated in Figure 12-1.

Empno	Ename	Job	Mgr	Hiredate	Sal	Comm	Deptno
7839	KING	PRESIDENT	-	17-NOV-81	5000	-	10

Figure 12-1. *Report on EMP after the VPD policy function has been applied*

If you log in as any user who does not have a corresponding record in the EMP table, you will see no rows, because the VPD policy function does not yield any matches based on the dynamic WHERE clause. Also, if you run the same query—SELECT * FROM EMP—in SQL*Plus connected to the database as any user, there will also be no rows returned. This is because the APEX v function does not return a valid value outside of APEX, which causes the WHERE clause to filter out all records.

A simple alteration to the policy function will allow it to work both inside and outside of APEX. Instead of comparing ENAME to the result of v('APP_USER') only, an NVL can be used to first check to see whether APP_USER has a value and, if it does not, default to the currently signed on database user. Listing 12-5 shows the updated line of the policy function.

Listing 12-5. Updated Line of the Policy Function to Enable It to Work Both with and Without APEX

```
-- Return the SQL
RETURN 'ename = NVL(v(''APP_USER''),user)';
```

Once the policy function is modified, there is no need to reregister it with the DBMS_RLS package. The changes will take place immediately without any further action on the part of the developer. In APEX, there should be no difference in results. However, in SQL*Plus, there may or may not be a row returned. This will depend on whether your schema name has a corresponding ENAME record in the EMP table. If it does, then that record will be returned. If not, then no records will be returned.

Chances are that no records will be returned in SQL*Plus. If this is indeed the case, adding or even altering a record in SQL*Plus will also be blocked by the VPD policy function because when the policy function was created, it was applied to all types of DML transactions—INSERTs, UPDATEs, DELETEs, and SELECTs.

Attempting to update the EMP table directly with SQL*Plus will not yield an error but rather simply state that no rows were updated, as illustrated in Listing 12-6.

Listing 12-6. Attempting to Update a Table Protected by a VPD Policy Function

```
SQL> update emp set ename = 'ENKITEC';

0 rows updated.
```

Thus, the VPD policy function needs to be disabled for any type of transaction to occur. This is also done via the DBMS_RLS packages, specifically the DROP_POLICY API. Calling DROP_POLICY does not drop the corresponding policy function but rather disassociates it from the object that it was originally associated with. Listing 12-7 shows an example of how to disable or drop a VPD policy function.

Listing 12-7. Dropping a VPD Policy Function

```
BEGIN
DBMS_RLS.DROP_POLICY
  (
  object_schema => 'ENKITEC',
  object_name   => 'EMP',
  policy_name   => 'LIMIT_BY_APP_USER'
  );
END;
/
```

Once the policy is disabled, normal DML operations on the EMP table can resume. Reenabling the VPD policy is done by simply calling the DBMS_RLS.ADD_POLICY API, as referenced in Listing 12-4. There is no need to re-create the policy function itself.

Column Masking and Obfuscation

In addition to filtering which records are returned from a query, VPD can also filter or obfuscate data in a column or columns. There are two types of column masking: the first type will simply remove the specified column or columns entirely from the query, whereas the second type will display NULLs in place of values that meet the policy function's criteria. When using column masking and VPD, the policy function used can be associated only with a SELECT statement. An error will occur if the policy function is registered with either INSERT, UPDATE, or DELETE.

For the next example, a new policy will be added to the EMP table that will be used to illustrate the column relevance feature of VPD. This policy will be applied only when either the SAL or COMM column is present in a query on the EMP table.

To illustrate this example, create a new APEX page. On that page, create two standard reports side-by-side. Both of these reports will contain simple queries based on the EMP table. The first report should use the SQL from Listing 12-8, and the second report should use the SQL from Listing 12-9.

Listing 12-8. SQL for the First Report

```
SELECT ename, sal, comm FROM emp
```

Listing 12-9. SQL for the Second Report

```
SELECT ename, deptno FROM emp
```

Notice that in both SQL statements there is no WHERE clause. The VPD policy function and the application context will take care of that for you. When the new APEX page is run, each report should show all selected columns of all records in the EMP table, as illustrated in Figure 12-2.

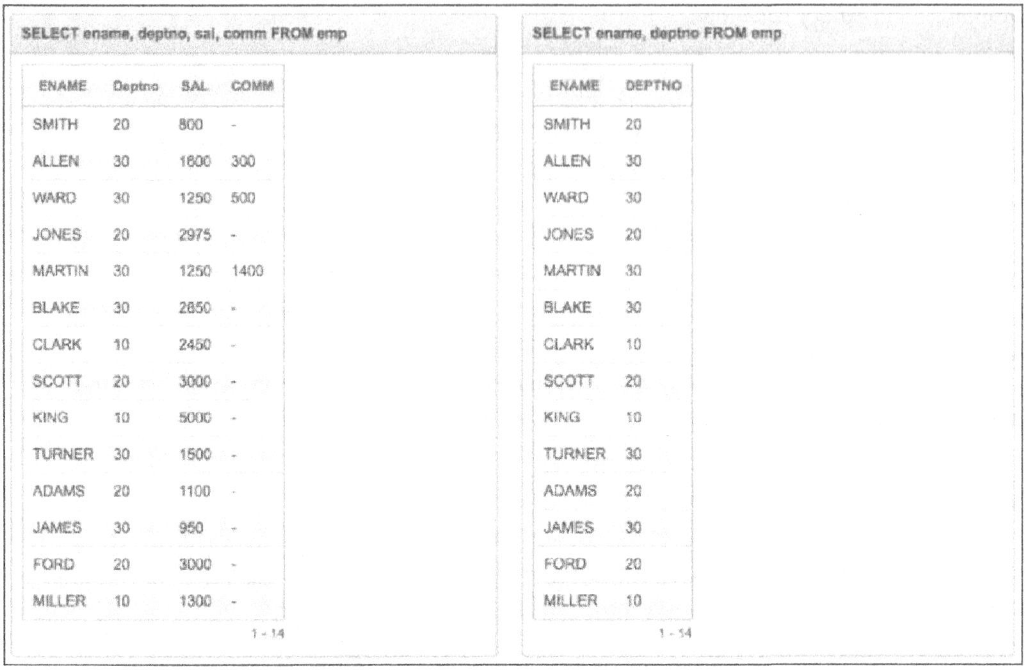

ENAME	Deptno	SAL	COMM
SMITH	20	800	-
ALLEN	30	1600	300
WARD	30	1250	500
JONES	20	2975	-
MARTIN	30	1250	1400
BLAKE	30	2850	-
CLARK	10	2450	-
SCOTT	20	3000	-
KING	10	5000	-
TURNER	30	1500	-
ADAMS	20	1100	-
JAMES	30	950	-
FORD	20	3000	-
MILLER	10	1300	-

SELECT ename, deptno, sal, comm FROM emp — 1 - 14

ENAME	DEPTNO
SMITH	20
ALLEN	30
WARD	30
JONES	20
MARTIN	30
BLAKE	30
CLARK	10
SCOTT	20
KING	10
TURNER	30
ADAMS	20
JAMES	30
FORD	20
MILLER	10

SELECT ename, deptno FROM emp — 1 - 14

Figure 12-2. *The results of two simple SQL statements on the EMP table*

Once the APEX reports are created, the next step is to create a new VPD policy function. The new function will act similar to the first but with a slight change. Initially, it will remove the entire record if the corresponding DEPTNO does not match that of the current user. Then, with a slight alteration to how you register the policy function, it will show all of the records but display NULLs for the SAL and COMM columns where the corresponding DEPTNO does not match that of the current user. This policy will also use an application context, which will be configured a little later. Listing 12-10 shows the new policy function, limit_by_deptno.

Listing 12-10. *The limit_by_deptno Policy Function*

```
CREATE OR REPLACE FUNCTION limit_by_deptno
  (
  p_schema     IN VARCHAR2 DEFAULT NULL,
  p_objname    IN VARCHAR2 DEFAULT NULL
  )
RETURN VARCHAR2
AS
  l_sql        VARCHAR2(255);
BEGIN

-- Set the SQL to compare DEPTNO to the application context
l_sql := 'deptno = SYS_CONTEXT(''EMP_VPD_CTX'',''DEPTNO'')';

-- Return the SQL
RETURN l_sql;

END limit_by_deptno;
/
```

The next step is to register the policy function, as illustrated in Listing 12-11. This is done by calling the same API as in the previous exercise, with one minor difference. By passing in a list of columns to the sec_relevant_cols parameter, you can tell the VPD function that it needs to execute only when either of those columns is present in the query. Thus, if a simple SELECT ename FROM EMP query was issued against the table, the VPD policy function would not execute, and all records would be returned.

Listing 12-11. Setting the limit_by_deptno VPD Policy Function

```
BEGIN
DBMS_RLS.ADD_POLICY(
  object_schema      => 'ENKITEC',
  object_name        => 'EMP',
  policy_name        => 'LIMIT_BY_DEPTNO',
  policy_function    => 'LIMIT_BY_DEPTNO',
  function_schema    => 'ENKITEC',
  sec_relevant_cols => 'SAL,COMM');
END;
/
```

At this point, the VPD policy function is created and registered. Because the policy is now triggered only when either the SAL or COMM column is present in the query, it is being applied only to the first report. And because the application context it uses is neither created nor set in APEX, the first report returns no data, as illustrated in Figure 12-3. The second report, on the other hand, is not impacted by the policy because it includes only the ENAME and DEPTNO columns.

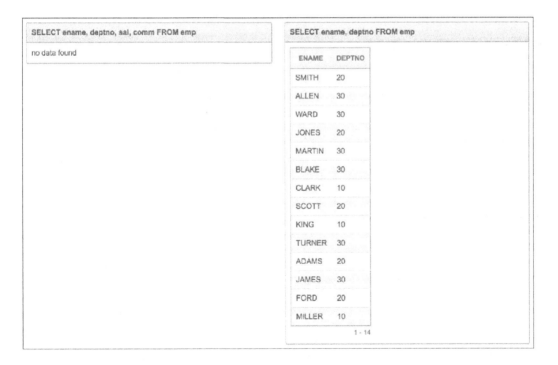

Figure 12-3. *Running the reports without setting the application context*

As your business rules and corresponding policy functions get more sophisticated, it is a good idea to consider using an application context to store values used in the function itself. As outlined in Chapter 10, an application context is a server-side component designed to securely and efficiently store value-attribute pairs in memory. These value-attribute pairs can easily and efficiently be accessed by calling the SYS_CONTEXT API within a SQL query.

Application contexts are typically set at the beginning of a database session and then last throughout the duration of that session. Since APEX sessions are distinct from database sessions, the application context must be set before every page view and asynchronous transaction. While this seems redundant and inefficient, it is the only way to properly instrument APEX to work with application contexts. Fortunately, it is quite easy to do.

As mentioned in the previous chapter, a schema needs to have the CREATE ANY CONTEXT system privilege be able to create an application context. Alternatively, a schema with DBA privileges can create the context but must refer to the associated procedure with the SCHEMA.PROCEDURE notation. In this example, it is assumed that the ENKITEC schema does have CREATE ANY CONTEXT and can use the SQL in Listing 12-12 to create the application context. Oracle will not report an error if an application context is created that references a package or procedure that does not yet exist, as in this case.

Listing 12-12. SQL Used to Create an Application Context

```
CREATE CONTEXT emp_vpd_ctx USING emp_vpd_ctx_pkg;
```

Next, the package—shown in Listing 12-13—that will set and unset the application context must be created. The set_ctx procedure will set the DEPTNO attribute of the EMP_VPD_CTX context based on the currently logged in user. That value is then in turn referenced in the limit_by_deptno VPD policy function and is used to filter the results based on the currently signed on user's DEPTNO. The unset_ctx procedure will simply remove any value stored in the EMP_VPD_CTX context.

Listing 12-13. The emp_vpd_ctx_pkg Package, Which Is Used to Manage the Application Context

```
CREATE OR REPLACE PACKAGE emp_vpd_ctx_pkg
AS
PROCEDURE set_ctx
  (
  p_user_name                 IN VARCHAR2
  );

PROCEDURE unset_ctx;

END emp_vpd_ctx_pkg;
/

CREATE OR REPLACE PACKAGE BODY emp_vpd_ctx_pkg
AS
PROCEDURE set_ctx
  (
  p_user_name                 IN VARCHAR2
  )
IS
  l_deptno                    NUMBER;
BEGIN

-- Fetch the DEPTNO based on the currently signed on APP_USER
SELECT deptno INTO l_deptno FROM emp
  WHERE UPPER(ename) = UPPER(p_user_name);
```

```
-- Set the Context
dbms_session.set_context(
  namespace => 'EMP_VPD_CTX',
  attribute => 'DEPTNO',
  value     => l_deptno);

EXCEPTION
WHEN no_data_found THEN
  -- If no data is found, then clear the context
  dbms_session.clear_context('EMP_VPD_CTX');
END set_ctx;

PROCEDURE unset_ctx
IS
BEGIN
-- Clear the context
dbms_session.clear_context('EMP_VPD_CTX');
END unset_ctx;

END emp_vpd_ctx_pkg;
/
```

As a final step, the APEX application must set and unset the context before every page view, whether the page view is done traditionally or asynchronously. This can be done by editing the security attributes of your application, which can be found in the Shared Components section. At the bottom of that page, there is a section called Database Session. In that section, there are two fields where you can call PL/SQL before and after an APEX session.

To reference the package that manages the application context, set the value of the Initialization PL/SQL Code option to emp_vpd_ctx_pkg.set_ctx(p_user_name => :APP_USER); and the value of Cleanup PL/SQL Code to emp_vpd_ctx_pkg.unset_ctx;, as illustrated in Figure 12-4. Then apply your changes.

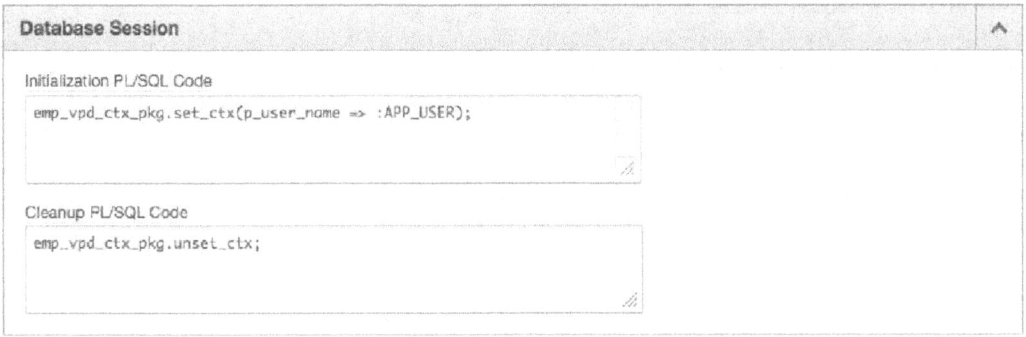

Figure 12-4. *Setting the Initialization SQL Code and Cleanup PL/SQL Code options to enable an application context*

Now that all the required components are in place, run the APEX application, and make sure to sign on with a user name that has a corresponding entry in the ENAME column of the EMP table. For this example, a user called KING was created and used. Based on which user you log in as, the results will vary. In all cases, the only records that show up in the first report will be those that have the same DEPTNO as the user account that you are logged in to, as illustrated in Figure 12-5.

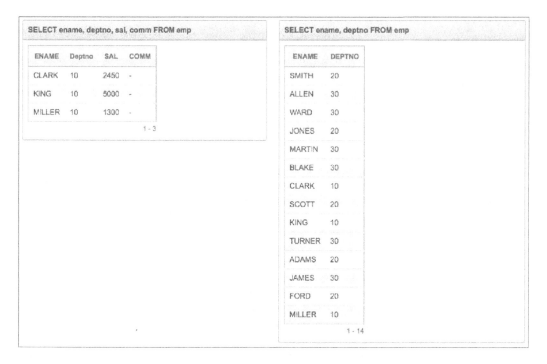

Figure 12-5. Running the APEX application as KING with VPD column relevance rules applied

Now that everything is working with the VPD and application context, you can alter the way you register the policy function slightly to change how it behaves. Instead of removing rows that don't meet the criteria, you can choose to include those rows with the columns specified set to NULL. This would prove useful if you needed a system that showed customer data but did not want to expose Social Security numbers to a specific group of users.

To do this, first drop the policy function as per Listing 12-14.

Listing 12-14. SQL Used to Drop the limit_by_deptno VPD Policy

```
BEGIN
DBMS_RLS.DROP_POLICY
  (
  object_schema => 'ENKITEC',
  object_name   => 'EMP',
  policy_name   => 'LIMIT_BY_DEPTNO'
  );
END;
/
```

Next, all that is required is to reregister the policy function like before but this time using an additional parameter, as illustrated in Listing 12-15. By passing DBMS_RLS.ALL_ROWS to the sec_relevant_cols_opt parameter of DBMS_RLS.ADD_POLICY, the way that the policy function is applied changes. All rows will be returned for all records, but values in the SAL and COMM columns will appear only if the rule set in the policy is met. No code needs to change anywhere else in the policy or package required to manage the application context.

Listing 12-15. SQL for Adding a VPD Policy Function That Returns All Records but Obfuscates Sensitive Data

```
BEGIN
DBMS_RLS.ADD_POLICY
  (
  object_schema         => 'ENKITEC',
  object_name           => 'EMP',
  policy_name           => 'LIMIT_BY_DEPTNO',
  policy_function       => 'LIMIT_BY_DEPTNO',
  function_schema       => 'ENKITEC',
  sec_relevant_cols     => 'SAL,COMM',
  sec_relevant_cols_opt => DBMS_RLS.ALL_ROWS
  );
END;
/
```

Once the new VPD policy is added, rerun the APEX application. Now, both reports should show all records. The first report will show only SAL and COMM values for records that have the same DEPTNO as the user who is logged in, as illustrated in Figure 12-6.

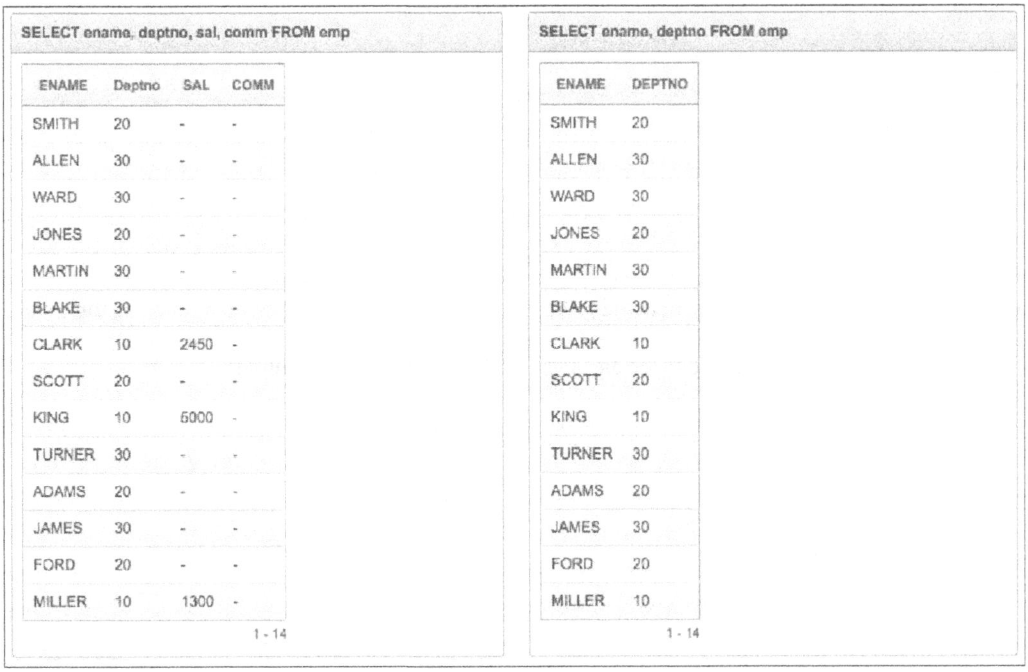

SELECT ename, deptno, sal, comm FROM emp

ENAME	Deptno	SAL	COMM
SMITH	20	-	-
ALLEN	30	-	-
WARD	30	-	-
JONES	20	-	-
MARTIN	30	-	-
BLAKE	30	-	-
CLARK	10	2450	-
SCOTT	20	-	-
KING	10	5000	-
TURNER	30	-	-
ADAMS	20	-	-
JAMES	30	-	-
FORD	20	-	-
MILLER	10	1300	-

1 - 14

SELECT ename, deptno FROM emp

ENAME	DEPTNO
SMITH	20
ALLEN	30
WARD	30
JONES	20
MARTIN	30
BLAKE	30
CLARK	10
SCOTT	20
KING	10
TURNER	30
ADAMS	20
JAMES	30
FORD	20
MILLER	10

1 - 14

Figure 12-6. *Results of the new VPD policy where sensitive data is hidden*

Managing VPD in Oracle Enterprise Manager

If the command line is not for you, you can configure and manage Oracle VPD via Oracle Enterprise Manager (OEM). OEM provides a GUI interface that masks most of the complexity of registering policy functions. Policies can be quickly created and removed by simply filling in the blanks, reducing the potential for error and decreasing the time it takes to manage VPD. The policy functions themselves still have to be created using an external tool, such as SQL*Plus or SQL Developer. In addition to managing VPD from OEM, the creation and management of application contexts can be done here, too.

By centralizing the management of VPD, a DBA can take ownership of the task of managing the components of VPD all through a familiar interface. This not only simplifies the DBAs job but also decreases the potential for error because the GUI will provide more guidance and error checking than the command line.

To manage either the application contexts or VPD, simply click the Server tab on the home page of the database that you are managing in OEM. On the next page, there will be several options in the Security region, as illustrated in Figure 12-7. Your list may vary, depending on which options are installed in your database.

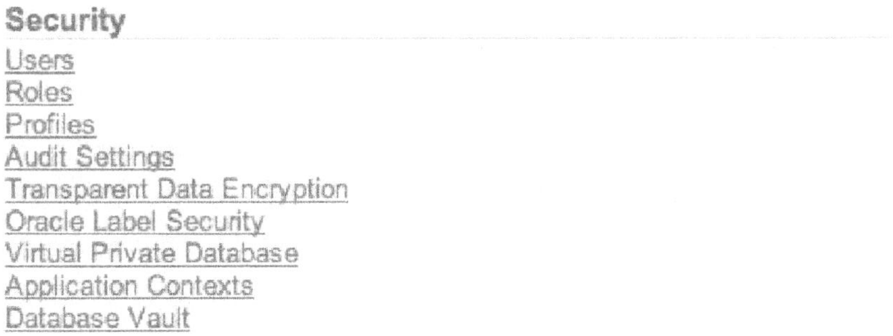

Security

Users
Roles
Profiles
Audit Settings
Transparent Data Encryption
Oracle Label Security
Virtual Private Database
Application Contexts
Database Vault

Figure 12-7. *The Security options on the Oracle Enterprise Manager Server page*

To register a VPD policy function, click Virtual Private Database. From this page, any registered function can be queried based on its schema name, object name, or owner. VPD functions can also be registered by clicking the Create button and filling out the corresponding details. Figure 12-8 shows the parameters required to replicate the most recent example in this section. Note that in some fields the SCHEMA.OBJECT notation is required.

General

* Policy Name   LIMIT_BY_DEPTNO

* Object Name   ENKITEC.EMP

Policy Type   STATIC   ⬩

☑ Enabled
Check this box to enable the policy after creation

Policy Function

Specify a policy function to return a predicate for filtering the data. The function can also reside in a package.

* Policy Function   ENKITEC.LIMIT_BY_DEPTNO
Example: Schema.Policy Function

☐ Long Predicate
Check this box to allow policy function to return a predicate with a length up to 32k.
Default is 4k.

Overview Of Policy Types

STATIC - For this type of policies the policy function is executed once and then the predicate is cached in the SGA (System Global Area) for fast performance. Applies to only one object.

SHARED_STATIC - Same as STATIC except that the server first looks for a cached predicate generated by the same policy function of the same policy type. Shared across multiple objects.

CONTEXT_SENSITIVE - For this type of policies, the server re-evaluates the policy function at statement execution time if it detects context changes. Server always executes the policy function on statement parsing and does not cache the value returned by the function. Applies to only one object.

SHARED_CONTEXT_SENSITIVE - For this type of policy the policy function is executed when the object to which it is associated is referenced for the first time in a database session. Predicates (WHERE clauses) are then cached in the private session memory UGA (User Global Area). Server first looks for a cached predicate and does not execute the policy function until session private application context changes occur. Shared across multiple objects.

DYNAMIC - For this type of policy server assumes the predicate may be affected by any system or session environment at any time. So the policy function is executed every time a policy protected database object is accessed. Applies to only one object.

Enforcement

Select operation types to which the policy applies. It can be any combination of SELECT, INSERT, UPDATE, INDEX and DELETE.

☐ INSERT
☐ UPDATE
☐ DELETE
☑ SELECT
☐ INDEX
☐ Insert/Update Check (CHECK OPTION)
Check this to allow changes to the row if they are still visible to the user after update. Can be specified only if INSERT or UPDATE options are specified.

Security Relevant Columns

Specify security relevant columns if the policy being created is meant to apply Column-Level Virtual Private Database (VPD).

☑ Enable Column Masking Behavior
Check this box to enable Column Masking Behavior of Column-Level Virtual Private Database.

(Add)

(Remove)
Select Name
○ SAL
○ COMM

Overview of Column Level VPD and Column Masking

Column-Level Virtual Private Database (VPD) enforces row level security policies only when a particular column or columns are accessed in the user's query. These columns containing sensitive information are marked as Security Relevant Columns. Column-level VPD applies to tables and views, but not to synonyms.

It can be configured to produce two distinct behaviors as follows:

- Default Behavior which restricts the number of rows returned for a query that references columns containing sensitive information.

- Column-Masking Behavior of Column-Level VPD displays all rows including those that reference sensitive columns unlike the default behavior of Column-Level VPD which restricts the number of rows returned. However, the sensitive columns display as NULL values.

Figure 12-8. Registering a VPD policy function with Oracle Enterprise Manager

Summary

While there's no way to tell just how long APEX will be a viable application development platform, it is almost certain that your data will outlive it. Therefore, taking the time to implement access control rules at the lowest level possible—the database—makes the most sense. Virtual Private Database provides a secure, easy-to-use construct that allows developers to ensure that data access rules are always applied, regardless of the technology used to access the data. VPD rules are also flexible and can easily be adapted to fluid business rules. VPD can easily be configured to work with APEX's session state constructs, making it an ideal complement to APEX.

CHAPTER 13

Shadow Schema

Two approaches can control access when it comes to security: blacklisting and whitelisting. *Blacklisting* involves building an application with any number of features and functions and then restricting a specific user from accessing a subset of those features. *Whitelisting* is just the opposite: building an application with any number of features and functions and then granting access on a subset of those features to a specific user. While the end result with either approach is the same, the overall manageability and liability with each differs.

A major drawback with the blacklisting approach is that as new features and functions are added, it must be determined which users can have access to those features and functions. For example, if a new sensitive column was added to a table, that column would need to have the appropriate authorization scheme associated with it anywhere it appears in any APEX application, including reports, forms, charts, calendars, PL/SQL regions, and so on. While this may not be difficult to do with a small system, the level of involvement and potential for error both increase with the size and complexity of the system.

Using the whitelisting approach, several smaller APEX applications could be built, each specifically for a group of users who have the same level of access. This way, when a new column is added, little attention needs to be paid to most of the system, because the applications that should see the new column will, and the ones that don't need to see it won't. Thus, if the sensitive column were based on an employee's salary, it would be added to the core HR application but not the employee lookup application.

This concept of whitelisting can also be applied at the database level to achieve the same results: easier-to-manage access control. If your application has no need to ever create a table or execute any DDL for that matter, then why should the underlying schema have those privileges? Removing privileges from a schema or creating a set of views that interacts with a subset of data greatly enhances the security of any application, because the list of potential features and functions is built from the ground up, not secured from the top down.

Overview

A *shadow schema* is not a feature but rather represents a methodology that utilizes several features of both APEX and the Oracle Database. When properly followed, APEX applications designed using this methodology offer a higher level of security than those developed the traditional way. However, as stated, security is hard, and this method does involve a little bit more work. Be sure to review the previous two chapters to become familiar with both secure views and virtual private databases (VPDs), because either of those techniques can be used to augment data security when using the shadow schema methodology.

The core concept of the shadow schema is to both strip the APEX parse-as schema of all system privileges and allow only views and synonyms to be created there. The synonyms will reference only those APIs that reference packages that reside in the data schema. These APIs will be used to facilitate all DML processes required in the application, and they contain even more security checks within them. This way, if your application is somehow compromised through SQL injection or a cross-site scripting attack, most, if not all, attempts to access data will be mitigated because the schema has no or little privilege to do anything at all, and the database will simply not execute the nefarious code. An attacker who does manage to compromise the shadow schema will not be able to escalate their privileges beyond that of the shadow schema, greatly mitigating the potential damage that the attacker can inflict.

By whitelisting the privileges and objects that the parse-as schema has access to, the number of components that must be secured is not only small but also fixed as the complexity of the system increases.

Either a secure view or a VPD can be used to filter which records are displayed based on who is logged onto the system. This technique, which was described in the previous two chapters, is implemented in the shadow schema in the same way. An application context is also required in support of either the secure views or VPD policy functions.

Lastly, on the APEX side, a couple things must be done. First, the application context must be set as in the previous chapters. Second, instead of using the built-in DML processes, APIs need to be written for any DML transaction that needs to be supported. While this represents more work than using the built-in APEX components, it does offer a lot more flexibility, because each DML operation can be tightly controlled and only columns that need to be included can be added to the API. There is also a little-known API generator in APEX that can greatly reduce the time required to complete this task.

Components

The shadow schema approach actually involves two schemas: the data schema, which is where all tables and PL/SQL packages are, and the shadow schema, which contains nothing more than read-only views and synonyms that point at the data schema. The corresponding APEX application is set to parse as the shadow schema, thus effectively limiting what it can and can't do at the database level.

Every APEX application must have a corresponding "parse-as" schema associated with it at design time. This mapping is fixed, and once the application is deployed, there is no way to change it. When an APEX application is run, all SQL and PL/SQL executed is as if the application were connected directly to database as the parse-as schema. APEX handles this session alteration securely and transparently behind the scenes. What many don't realize is that when you set an application to parse as a particular schema, the application inherits all of the system privileges and grants made to that schema.

When building an APEX application with the shadow schema methodology, most of the configuration will take place in three places: the shadow schema, the data schema, and the APEX application itself. To set up the example that will be used to illustrate this concept, the next section provides scripts to create and populate the data schema and create the shadow schema. Note that there is nothing specific or proprietary in how these schemas are created. In fact, if you already have a schema associated with an existing APEX application, you can easily refer to it and use it as the data schema. A shadow schema that has read-only views and synonyms that point to the existing schema can easily be created and configured using this methodology.

The example discussed in this chapter will require SYS access, because two new schemas as well as application contexts need to be created.

Database: Schema and Object Creation

To start, the two schemas and corresponding tables need to be created. Listing 13-1 will create the DATA and SHADOW schemas, and Listing 13-2 will create and populate objects in the DATA schema, specifically, the familiar EMP and DEPT tables. A trigger will also be added to EMP so that as new rows are added, they will be automatically given a new EMPNO.

Listing 13-1. Script to Create the DATA and SHADOW Schemas (Run as SYS)

```
CREATE USER DATA IDENTIFIED BY ENKITEC;

CREATE USER SHADOW IDENTIFIED BY ENKITEC;

GRANT CONNECT, RESOURCE, CREATE VIEW TO DATA;
```

Listing 13-2. Script to Create and Populate Objects in the DATA Schema (Run as DATA)

```
CREATE TABLE EMP
  (
  EMPNO    NUMBER(4) NOT NULL,
  ENAME    VARCHAR2(10),
  JOB      VARCHAR2(9),
  MGR      NUMBER(4),
  HIREDATE DATE,
  SAL      NUMBER(7, 2),
  COMM     NUMBER(7, 2),
  DEPTNO   NUMBER(2),
  CONSTRAINT EMP_PK PRIMARY KEY (EMPNO)
  );

INSERT INTO EMP VALUES
  (7369, 'SMITH', 'CLERK', 7902,
  TO_DATE('17-DEC-1980', 'DD-MON-YYYY'), 800, NULL, 20);
INSERT INTO EMP VALUES
  (7499, 'ALLEN', 'SALESMAN', 7698,
  TO_DATE('20-FEB-1981', 'DD-MON-YYYY'), 1600, 300, 30);
INSERT INTO EMP VALUES
  (7521, 'WARD', 'SALESMAN', 7698,
  TO_DATE('22-FEB-1981', 'DD-MON-YYYY'), 1250, 500, 30);
INSERT INTO EMP VALUES
  (7566, 'JONES', 'MANAGER', 7839,
  TO_DATE('2-APR-1981', 'DD-MON-YYYY'), 2975, NULL, 20);
INSERT INTO EMP VALUES
  (7654, 'MARTIN', 'SALESMAN', 7698,
  TO_DATE('28-SEP-1981', 'DD-MON-YYYY'), 1250, 1400, 30);

INSERT INTO EMP VALUES
  (7698, 'BLAKE', 'MANAGER', 7839,
  TO_DATE('1-MAY-1981', 'DD-MON-YYYY'), 2850, NULL, 30);
INSERT INTO EMP VALUES
  (7782, 'CLARK', 'MANAGER', 7839,
  TO_DATE('9-JUN-1981', 'DD-MON-YYYY'), 2450, NULL, 10);
INSERT INTO EMP VALUES
  (7788, 'SCOTT', 'ANALYST', 7566,
  TO_DATE('09-DEC-1982', 'DD-MON-YYYY'), 3000, NULL, 20);
INSERT INTO EMP VALUES
  (7839, 'KING', 'PRESIDENT', NULL,
  TO_DATE('17-NOV-1981', 'DD-MON-YYYY'), 5000, NULL, 10);
INSERT INTO EMP VALUES
  (7844, 'TURNER', 'SALESMAN', 7698,
  TO_DATE('8-SEP-1981', 'DD-MON-YYYY'), 1500, 0, 30);
INSERT INTO EMP VALUES
  (7876, 'ADAMS', 'CLERK', 7788,
  TO_DATE('12-JAN-1983', 'DD-MON-YYYY'), 1100, NULL, 20);
```

```
INSERT INTO EMP VALUES
  (7900, 'JAMES', 'CLERK', 7698,
  TO_DATE('3-DEC-1981', 'DD-MON-YYYY'), 950, NULL, 30);
INSERT INTO EMP VALUES
  (7902, 'FORD', 'ANALYST', 7566,
  TO_DATE('3-DEC-1981', 'DD-MON-YYYY'), 3000, NULL, 20);
INSERT INTO EMP VALUES
  (7934, 'MILLER', 'CLERK', 7782,
  TO_DATE('23-JAN-1982', 'DD-MON-YYYY'), 1300, NULL, 10);

CREATE SEQUENCE emp_seq START WITH 8000;

CREATE OR REPLACE TRIGGER bi_emp
BEFORE INSERT ON emp
FOR EACH ROW
BEGIN
  SELECT emp_seq.NEXTVAL INTO :NEW.empno FROM dual;
END;
/

CREATE TABLE DEPT
  (
  DEPTNO NUMBER(2),
  DNAME  VARCHAR2(14),
  LOC    VARCHAR2(13)
  );

INSERT INTO DEPT VALUES (10, 'ACCOUNTING', 'NEW YORK');
INSERT INTO DEPT VALUES (20, 'RESEARCH', 'DALLAS');
INSERT INTO DEPT VALUES (30, 'SALES', 'CHICAGO');
INSERT INTO DEPT VALUES (40, 'OPERATIONS', 'BOSTON');

COMMIT
/
```

Data Schema: Views

The data schema is where all tables, indexes, views, and procedural components will be stored. Views may also be created in the data schema, especially when it is necessary to prevent specific columns from being accessed by the shadow schema or to employ row-level security. In the case of existing applications that don't make use of a shadow schema, the data schema is typically the parse-as schema. The data schema will never be accessed directly by an APEX application, so it is safe to store tables and procedures there.

The script in Listing 13-1 not only created the DATA schema but also populated it with the standard EMP and DEPT tables. If all columns of the EMP needed to be exposed in the APEX application, then a simple view that selected all columns from EMP could be created. However, if not all columns of a table are required in an application, then there is no reason to add them to a view.

In our example, let's assume that the APEX application being built is a simple employee management system. Since the requirements don't call for salary or bonus information to be included in the system, there is no reason to even make those columns available to the shadow schema. Thus, you can create a view in the data schema—DATA.EMP_V—that includes only the columns you need, eliminating any chance of someone accessing the SAL and/or COMM columns from your APEX application. You can then create a second view in the shadow schema—SHADOW.EMP_V—that references the view in the data schema rather than the EMP table. This will limit which columns are available to the shadow schema to those included in the SHADOW.EMP_V view.

In Listing 13-3, the EMP_V read-only view is created in the DATA schema, referencing only the EMPNO, ENAME, JOB, and DEPTNO columns. These will be the only columns that are eventually made available to the APEX application. A grant is also required so that the shadow schema can SELECT from the EMP_V view.

Listing 13-3. Script to Create the EMP_V View and Corresponding Grant in the DATA Schema (Run as DATA)

```
CREATE OR REPLACE VIEW emp_v AS
SELECT
  empno,
  ename,
  job,
  deptno
FROM
  EMP
WITH READ ONLY
/

GRANT SELECT ON emp_v TO shadow
/
```

Next, a similar view needs to be created in the SHADOW schema. This view will directly reference the view from the DATA schema, as illustrated in Listing 13-4. Since the shadow schema does not have create session privileges, this script needs to be run as SYS or SYSTEM.

Listing 13-4. Script to Create the EMP_V View in the SHADOW Schema (Run as SYS)

```
ALTER SESSION SET CURRENT_SCHEMA = SHADOW;

CREATE OR REPLACE VIEW emp_v AS
SELECT
  empno,
  ename,
  job,
  deptno
FROM
  data.EMP_V
/
```

Revoke Privileges

Most parse-as schemas associated with APEX applications have the same default system privileges in production as they do in development. While necessary to have in a development environment, these system privileges are often unnecessary and actually a liability in a production system. If an APEX application's parse-as schema has a system privilege, then if an exploit is successful, the hacker will have that same privilege. Thus, revoking access to any privilege that is not required in production is a simple yet highly effective step that should be taken.

For example, a schema created as part of an APEX workspace typically has about 14 system privileges (depending on the version of APEX) that permit the schema to create most common object types. Most applications do not perform any DDL statements during runtime, so all of these unnecessary system privileges are actually a liability. Therefore, any of them that are not required in support of the application should be revoked in production. There is no need for any of them to be there, and any DDL needed to develop or upgrade the system can be executed as SYS or another schema with DBA privileges. Listing 13-5 illustrates a series of revokes that will remove various privileges from the SHADOW schema.

Listing 13-5. Sample SQL That Can Be Used to Revoke System Privileges (Run as SYS)

```
REVOKE CREATE VIEW FROM SHADOW;
REVOKE CREATE CLUSTER FROM SHADOW;
REVOKE CREATE ANY CONTEXT FROM SHADOW;
REVOKE CREATE PROCEDURE FROM SHADOW;
REVOKE CREATE MATERIALIZED VIEW FROM SHADOW;
REVOKE CREATE DIMENSION FROM SHADOW;
REVOKE CREATE TYPE FROM SHADOW;
REVOKE CREATE SEQUENCE FROM SHADOW;
REVOKE CREATE TABLE FROM SHADOW;
REVOKE CREATE SYNONYM FROM SHADOW;
REVOKE CREATE JOB FROM SHADOW;
REVOKE CREATE OPERATOR FROM SHADOW;
REVOKE CREATE TRIGGER FROM SHADOW;
REVOKE CREATE INDEXTYPE FROM SHADOW;
REVOKE CREATE SESSION FROM SHADOW;
```

It is important to note that the code in Listing 13-5 is just an example, and the revoke statements required to limit system privileges on your system may vary. To determine which system privileges a schema has, run the SQL in Listing 13-6 while connected to that schema.

Listing 13-6. SQL Used to Determine System Privileges for the Connected User

```
SELECT * FROM user_sys_privs
```

To determine which roles a schema has, run the SQL in Listing 13-7 while connected to that schema.

Listing 13-7. SQL Used to Determine Role Privileges for the Connected User

```
SELECT * FROM user_role_privs
```

Based on the results of the previous two queries, determine which system privileges and/or roles can be revoked depending on the needs of your specific application.

System and User Event Trigger

Revoking CREATE privileges prevents any additional objects from being created in the shadow schema. However, it does little to prevent objects from being dropped. Many SQL injection attacks will attempt to do this, forcing a DBA to recover the dropped table, which at best translates to downtime for the system and, at worst, data loss. Fortunately, there is a simple way to prevent a user from dropping their own objects: system and user event triggers.

System and user event triggers function much like their table-based counterparts, except they listen for events that occur at the system or user level, not the table level. System triggers can execute when the database is started or stopped, and user-level triggers can execute when users log in or log out or before or after DDL statements. Thus, a user-level trigger can be added that prevents the SHADOW schema from dropping any object at all, thus further protecting the schema.

The code in Listing 13-8 will execute before any object in the database is dropped. If the owner of the object is SHADOW and the currently logged-in user is not SYS or SYSTEM, then the trigger will fire, thus preventing the object from being dropped. Thus, once again, giving the database the final say when it comes to security is often the best approach.

Listing 13-8. Adding a User-Level Trigger to Prevent SHADOW from Dropping Any Object (Run as SYS)

```
CREATE OR REPLACE TRIGGER prevent_shadow_drop
BEFORE DROP ON SHADOW.SCHEMA
BEGIN
IF ORA_DICT_OBJ_OWNER = 'SHADOW'
  AND ORA_LOGIN_USER NOT IN ('SYS','SYSTEM')
THEN
  RAISE_APPLICATION_ERROR(-20000, ORA_DICT_OBJ_OWNER
    || ' can not drop ' || ORA_DICT_OBJ_TYPE || 'S.');
END IF;
END;
/
```

The syntax and specifics of this trigger should be modified to meet your requirements and match your specific schema names. Additional triggers can be created for more granular control, if needed.

APEX: Simple Form and Report

At this point, the SHADOW schema has been stripped of all privileges and is ready for a simple APEX application. If you have not done so already, create a new APEX workspace that parses as the SHADOW schema. Once connected to that workspace, browse to the SQL Workshop and notice that there are no tables in the SHADOW schema, only a single view: EMP_V. At this point, all rows from all columns are visible from the SQL Workshop and any APEX application. Also, any attempt to query the EMP table in the DATA schema will also fail because there are no direct privileges on DATA.EMP granted to SHADOW.

Next, create a simple APEX application that contains a report and form based on the EMP_V view. This application can be created any number of ways—using the Create Application Wizard, creating a blank page and then using the Create Form & Report Wizard, or even creating it by hand. It doesn't matter which method is used to create the application, because the underlying view will act the same for all. This example will assume that the Create Application Wizard was used.

■ **Note** If the application is created with the Create Application Wizard, the name of the EMP_V view will need to be entered by hand because the pop-up list lists only tables. Simply enter **EMP_V** for the table name and click Add Page to continue.

Once the application is built, run the application. After logging in, the page with the report on EMP_V should look similar to Figure 13-1.

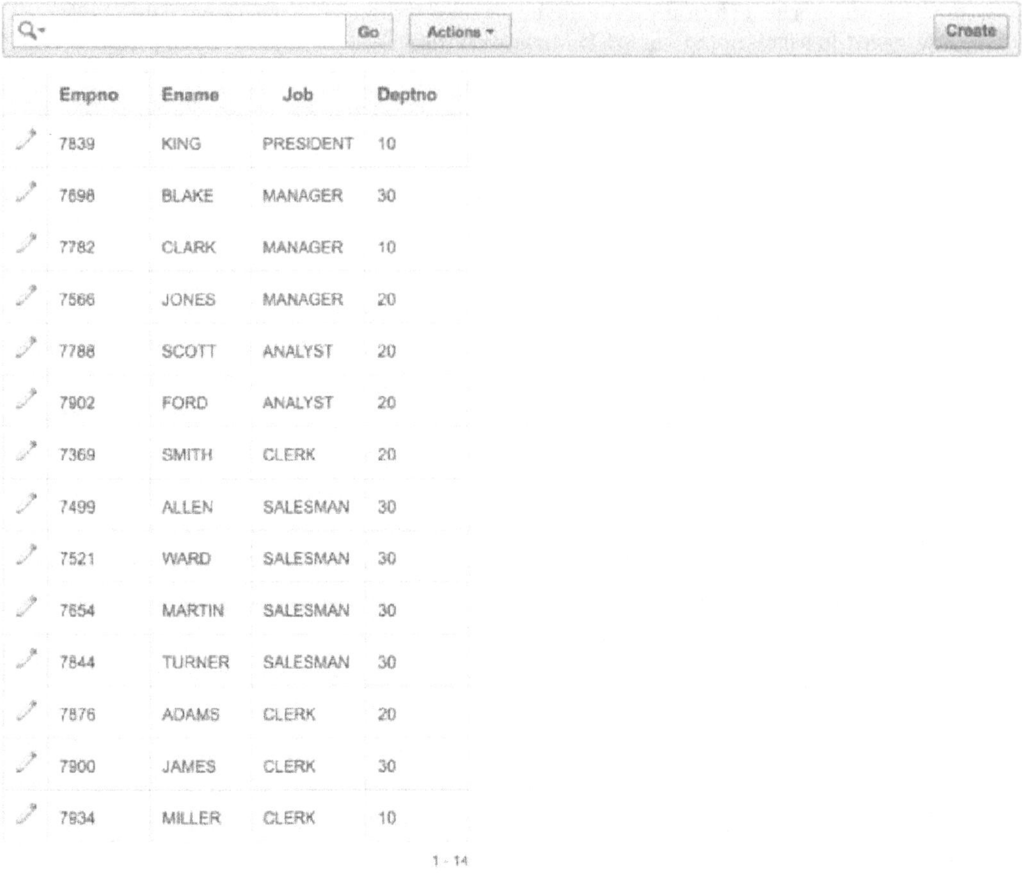

Empno	Ename	Job	Deptno
7839	KING	PRESIDENT	10
7698	BLAKE	MANAGER	30
7782	CLARK	MANAGER	10
7566	JONES	MANAGER	20
7788	SCOTT	ANALYST	20
7902	FORD	ANALYST	20
7369	SMITH	CLERK	20
7499	ALLEN	SALESMAN	30
7521	WARD	SALESMAN	30
7654	MARTIN	SALESMAN	30
7844	TURNER	SALESMAN	30
7876	ADAMS	CLERK	20
7900	JAMES	CLERK	30
7934	MILLER	CLERK	10

***Figure 13-1.** A simple report on the EMP_V view*

Your application may look slightly different, depending on the version of APEX used and theme selected. What is important to understand is that your application is able to see all of the rows from the `DATA.EMP` table by querying the `SHADOW.EMP_V` view. Any attempt to drop `EMP_V` or create additional objects will ultimately fail, because either the user-level trigger or the lack of privilege will prevent both from happening.

DML APIs and Processes

Upon editing a record, nothing seems out of the ordinary. However, if any change is attempted—whether it's adding a new record, modifying an existing record, or deleting an existing one—it will result in the following error: `ORA-01031: insufficient privileges`. This is because the `SHADOW` schema has access only to a read-only view and nothing else. Even though it seems that any DML transaction is possible, the database has the final say here and prevents any updates from occurring. Therefore, the built-in APEX DML processes are essentially useless in this scenario, and an alternative needs to be implemented.

A common approach when managing data is to use table APIs, which are a set of PL/SQL procedures that facilitate all inserts, updates, and deletes on a specific table. Technically speaking, the APEX built-in DML processes can be considered APIs themselves, because they take in parameters by way of page items and use those values to insert, update, or delete data. In addition to the core operations performed, the APEX DML processes also checks for lost updates before committing an update.

Table APIs offer a number of benefits over directly manipulating data in a table. First, a single API can be called from anywhere in the system, thus centralizing the business rules. A table API may have to insert records into multiple tables for a single transaction. Centralizing that call in a single place makes for a system that is easier to manage over time. Table APIs can also be called from different platforms, ensuring that business rules are consistent as platforms and technologies change.

Table APIs also offer security. As part of their business rules, a table API can restrict which user can perform which operation. For instance, perhaps only a specific set of users can even delete records based on their membership in a group. A table API can easily enforce this rule by restricting the delete procedure to only those authorized to call it. Table APIs also limit what type of access needs to be granted to the parse-as schema. In this example, the only grant that is required is one on the table API package to the parse-as schema. No direct access by way of inserts, updates, or deletes needs to be granted to the parse-as schema, resulting in a more secure system.

Given all of the benefits, creating a table API may seem like a complex undertaking. Fortunately, there is a quick and easy way to create robust table APIs right within APEX's SQL Workshop. This little known feature is also named "create a package with methods on database tables" and can be found in the Object Browser. When started, a wizard will step through the different options for creating the table APIs. Once they are created, they are nothing more than a PL/SQL package that can be further modified to suit business rules and requirements.

Using the shadow schema methodology, no objects aside from views and synonyms can reside in the SHADOW schema. Therefore, the table APIs should be created in the DATA schema. To do this easily and with the APEX wizard, a new workspace that has a parse-as schema of DATA needs to be created. Once created, the table APIs are easy to create.

Navigate to the SQL Workshop and then select the Object Browser. From there, click the Create button. A list of object types should appear. Click Package. At this point, the next screen will look like Figure 13-2. Select "Package with methods on database table(s)," and click Next.

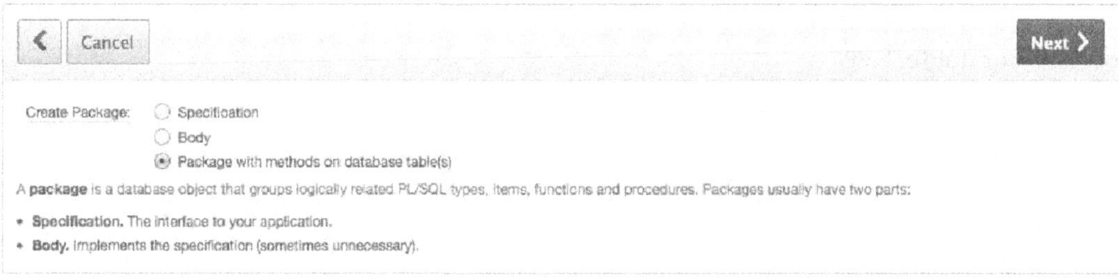

Figure 13-2. *Creating a package with methods on database tables*

On the next screen, enter **EMP_DML** for the package name, and click Next. While the package can be named anything, it is best to adhere to a naming standard, especially if multiple packages will be used in your application. The one used here was table name followed by _DML. Any naming scheme will work, as long as it is easy to remember and used by everyone.

This wizard provides the ability to create APIs for up to ten tables at once. In this example, only one is needed, so enter **EMP** in the field for Table 1 and click Next. Confirm the creation of the package on the next page by clicking Create Package. At this point, a new package—EMP_DML—will be created in the DATA schema. Listing 13-9 shows the specification of the EMP_DML package.

Listing 13-9. The Specification of the EMP_DML Package

```
create or replace package "EMP_DML" is
----------------------------------------------------------------
-- create procedure for table "EMP"
   procedure "INS_EMP" (
       "P_EMPNO"    in number,
       "P_ENAME"    in varchar2  default null,
       "P_JOB"      in varchar2  default null,
       "P_MGR"      in number    default null,
       "P_HIREDATE" in date      default null,
       "P_SAL"      in number    default null,
       "P_COMM"     in number    default null,
       "P_DEPTNO"   in number    default null
   );
----------------------------------------------------------------
-- update procedure for table "EMP"
   procedure "UPD_EMP" (
       "P_EMPNO" in number,
       "P_ENAME"    in varchar2  default null,
       "P_JOB"      in varchar2  default null,
       "P_MGR"      in number    default null,
       "P_HIREDATE" in date      default null,
       "P_SAL"      in number    default null,
       "P_COMM"     in number    default null,
       "P_DEPTNO"   in number    default null,
       "P_MD5"      in varchar2  default null
   );
----------------------------------------------------------------
-- delete procedure for table "EMP"
   procedure "DEL_EMP" (
       "P_EMPNO" in number
   );
----------------------------------------------------------------
-- get procedure for table "EMP"
   procedure "GET_EMP" (
       "P_EMPNO" in number,
       "P_ENAME"    out varchar2,
       "P_JOB"      out varchar2,
       "P_MGR"      out number,
       "P_HIREDATE" out date,
       "P_SAL"      out number,
       "P_COMM"     out number,
       "P_DEPTNO"   out number
   );
----------------------------------------------------------------
-- get procedure for table "EMP"
   procedure "GET_EMP" (
       "P_EMPNO" in number,
       "P_ENAME"    out varchar2,
       "P_JOB"      out varchar2,
       "P_MGR"      out number,
```

```
        "P_HIREDATE" out date,
        "P_SAL"      out number,
        "P_COMM"     out number,
        "P_DEPTNO"   out number,
        "P_MD5"      out varchar2
    );
-----------------------------------------------------------------
-- build MD5 function for table "EMP"
    function "BUILD_EMP_MD5" (
        "P_EMPNO" in number,
        "P_ENAME"    in varchar2  default null,
        "P_JOB"      in varchar2  default null,
        "P_MGR"      in number    default null,
        "P_HIREDATE" in date      default null,
        "P_SAL"      in number    default null,
        "P_COMM"     in number    default null,
        "P_DEPTNO"   in number    default null,
        "P_COL_SEP"  in varchar2  default '|'
    ) return varchar2;

end "EMP_DML";
```

Notice that in the package specification, all columns are referenced. In the view EMP_V, only a subset of the columns is referenced. Thus, only the columns that you want to be able to be updated should be exposed in the EMP_DML package. Any reference to the MGR, HIDEDATE, SAL, and COMM columns should be stripped from the package specification and body. This will ensure that those columns that were not included as part of the view can never be updated by an undiscovered security hole or malicious code. It will also ensure that the package will work properly, because it will no longer rely on values that are not passed to it.

Entire procedures can also be removed from the package, effectively limiting the API as to which DML transactions it supports. In this example, the insert and delete procedures are not part of the business requirements and thus should be removed from the package entirely. Again, this prevents even the most remote possibility that either of these procedures could be executed maliciously.

Listing 13-10 shows a modified package specification for EMP_DML.

Listing 13-10. Modified Package Specification for EMP_DML

```
create or replace package "EMP_DML" is
-----------------------------------------------------------------
-- update procedure for table "EMP"
    procedure "UPD_EMP" (
        "P_EMPNO" in number,
        "P_ENAME"    in varchar2  default null,
        "P_JOB"      in varchar2  default null,
        "P_DEPTNO"   in number    default null,
        "P_MD5"      in varchar2  default null
    );
-----------------------------------------------------------------
-- get procedure for table "EMP"
    procedure "GET_EMP" (
        "P_EMPNO" in number,
        "P_ENAME"    out varchar2,
        "P_JOB"      out varchar2,
```

```
      "P_DEPTNO"   out number,
      "P_MD5"      out varchar2
   );
----------------------------------------------------------------
-- build MD5 function for table "EMP"
   function "BUILD_EMP_MD5" (
      "P_EMPNO" in number,
      "P_ENAME"    in varchar2  default null,
      "P_JOB"      in varchar2  default null,
      "P_DEPTNO"   in number    default null,
      "P_COL_SEP"  in varchar2  default '|'
   ) return varchar2;

end "EMP_DML";
/
```

Since the package specification was changed, the body will also have to be updated to reflect the modifications. A similar approach will be taken, and all references to the MGR, HIDEDATE, SAL, and COMM columns will be removed. Also, the insert and delete routines are removed. Listing 13-11 details the updated version of EMP_DML.

Listing 13-11. Modified Package Specification for EMP_DML

```
create or replace package body "EMP_DML" is
----------------------------------------------------------------
-- update procedure for table "EMP"
   procedure "UPD_EMP" (
      "P_EMPNO" in number,
      "P_ENAME"    in varchar2  default null,
      "P_JOB"      in varchar2  default null,
      "P_DEPTNO"   in number    default null,
      "P_MD5"      in varchar2  default null
   ) is

      "L_MD5" varchar2(32767) := null;

   begin

      if "P_MD5" is not null then
         for c1 in (
            select * from "EMP"
            where "EMPNO" = "P_EMPNO" FOR UPDATE
         ) loop

            "L_MD5" := "BUILD_EMP_MD5"(
               c1."EMPNO",
               c1."ENAME",
               c1."JOB",
               c1."DEPTNO"
            );

         end loop;

      end if;
```

```
        if ("P_MD5" is null) or ("L_MD5" = "P_MD5") then
            update "EMP" set
                "EMPNO"       = "P_EMPNO",
                "ENAME"       = "P_ENAME",
                "JOB"         = "P_JOB",
                "DEPTNO"      = "P_DEPTNO"
            where "EMPNO" = "P_EMPNO";
        else
            raise_application_error (-20001,'Current version of data in database has changed since user
initiated update process. current checksum = "'||"L_MD5"||'", item checksum = "'||"P_MD5"||'".');
        end if;

    end "UPD_EMP";
-------------------------------------------------------------
-- get procedure for table "EMP"
    procedure "GET_EMP" (
        "P_EMPNO" in number,
        "P_ENAME"    out varchar2,
        "P_JOB"      out varchar2,
        "P_DEPTNO"   out number,
        "P_MD5"      out varchar2
    ) is

    begin

        for c1 in (
            select * from "EMP"
            where "EMPNO" = "P_EMPNO"
        ) loop
            "P_ENAME"    := c1."ENAME";
            "P_JOB"      := c1."JOB";
            "P_DEPTNO"   := c1."DEPTNO";
            "P_MD5" := "BUILD_EMP_MD5"(
                c1."EMPNO",
                c1."ENAME",
                c1."JOB",
                c1."DEPTNO"
            );
        end loop;

    end "GET_EMP";
-------------------------------------------------------------
-- build MD5 function for table "EMP"
    function "BUILD_EMP_MD5" (
        "P_EMPNO" in number,
        "P_ENAME"    in varchar2  default null,
        "P_JOB"      in varchar2  default null,
        "P_DEPTNO"   in number    default null,
        "P_COL_SEP"  in varchar2  default '|'
    ) return varchar2 is
```

```
  begin

      return sys.utl_raw.cast_to_raw(sys.dbms_obfuscation_toolkit.md5(input_string=>
          "P_ENAME"     ||"P_COL_SEP"||
          "P_JOB"       ||"P_COL_SEP"||
          "P_DEPTNO"    ||"P_COL_SEP"||
          ''
      ));

  end "BUILD_EMP_MD5";

end "EMP_DML";
/
```

As additional business rules need to be applied, they can easily be added to any of the procedures in the EMP_DML package. For example, either the insert or delete procedure can be added back if a future business requirement necessitates that type of transaction. Additional checks may be added before any transaction to ensure that only specific users or specific values are present.

Grants and Synonyms

It may seem intuitive to use a grant and synonym to access the EMP_V in the DATA schema versus creating a separate view. While this would work in many other environments, the APEX wizards do not work well with synonyms for views and tables. Thus, by adding the view in the SHADOW schema, the APEX wizards can be used to create reports and forms, speeding up the development process significantly and, at the same time, reducing the chance of errors.

Using a grant and synonym works just fine for packages, procedures, and functions in APEX. The next step is to grant access on the EMP_DML API to the SHADOW schema. This can be achieved by running two simple commands as SYS, shown in Listing 13-12.

Listing 13-12. Grant and Synonym for the EMP_DML Package (Run as SYS)

```
GRANT EXECUTE ON data.emp_dml TO shadow;

CREATE OR REPLACE SYNONYM shadow.emp_dml FOR data.emp_dml;
```

The example application that parses as the SHADOW schema should now be able to execute the EMP_DML package, which of course resides in the DATA schema. Any additional PL/SQL call can be configured in a similar manner, ensuring that only what is needed is exposed to the SHADOW schema via a synonym.

Table API Processes

Once the grant and synonym are created, the built-in DML processes in APEX need to be replaced with calls to the EMP_DML table API for both fetching and processing records. Since the built-in APEX DML processes no longer work, they can safely be removed from the application. To do this, edit the page that contains the form on the view EMP_V. In the Page Rendering column, look for the process called Fetch Row from EMP. Edit that process by double-clicking it. On the next page, click the Delete button and confirm the delete. Repeat these steps for the Process Row of EMP process, which is in the Page Processing column.

At this point, the form is relatively useless because it can neither fetch nor insert, update, or delete data. Creating new processes that reference the EMP_DML API calls will return the form to its original functionality—save for the bits that you leave out on purpose. To add the fetch process back, right-click the Processes node under Before Header, as shown in Figure 13-3.

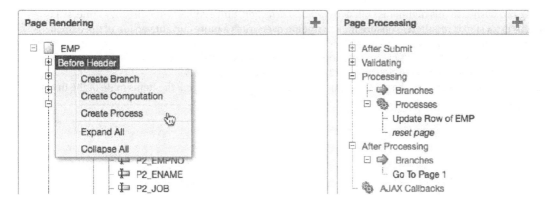

Figure 13-3. *Creating a new fetch process*

On the next page, select PL/SQL as the process type, and click Next. Enter **Fetch Row from EMP** for the name of the process, and click Next, as shown in Figure 13-4.

Figure 13-4. *Naming the fetch DML process*

Next, enter the code in Listing 13-13 into the field Enter PL/SQL Page Process, and click Create Process.

Listing 13-13. PL/SQL to Be Entered in the Enter PL/SQL Page Process Text Area

```
emp_dml.get_emp
  (
  p_empno  => :P2_EMPNO,
  p_ename  => :P2_ENAME,
  p_job    => :P2_JOB,
  p_deptno => :P2_DEPTNO,
  p_md5    => :P2_MD5
  );
```

Sharp readers will note that the previous PL/SQL block made reference to an item called P2_MD5, and no such item exists on the page. This item is used to store an MD5 hash of the value of the row being edited. This hash is generated by the get_emp procedure as part of the EMP_DML API. Before an update occurs, the hash will be recalculated on the current value stored in the database. If the two hashes do not match, then the value in the database is newer than the value in the web browser, and APEX will not let any change be saved until the web browser is refreshed with the current version of the data.

Comparing two hashes in this manner is called *lost update detection*. Since APEX is not directly connected to the database, this extra step is required to ensure that an update overwrites a more current version of the data in the database. APEX's built-in DML processes automatically handle lost update detection, and no additional item is required to use it with them. Unfortunately, this solution requires you to manage and compare the hashes on your own, and thus you need an additional hidden item—P2_MD5—to help facilitate this.

Creating an item is simple and can be done in almost no time. To start, right-click the Items node of the tree, just below the EMP region, and select Create Page Item, as illustrated in Figure 13-5.

Figure 13-5. *Creating a new item in the EMP region*

On the next page, select Hidden, and click Next. Enter **P2_MD5** for the item name on the next page, and click Next. Ensure that Value Protected is set to Yes, and click Next on the next page. This will prevent a malicious user from tampering with the value of this item using a tool such as Firebug. Take all of the defaults on the final page, and click Create Item to complete the wizard and create the item for the MD5 hash.

Speaking of items, a small tweak must be made to the remaining items on the page. Because they were created with the Report and Form Wizard, they anticipate that an APEX built-in process will be providing their values. Since this is no longer the case, a small change to the Source attribute of the items must be made.

The Source attribute of an item determines whether to use the value stored in session state or to use the value defined in the Source Type field when rendering the page. Since the wizard created all items on the page, the value of this attribute is initially set to "Always, replacing any value in session state." This option is used almost exclusively for when Source Type is set to Database Column to ensure that the value from the database overwrites any stale values in session state.

To retrofit the items on page 2, first edit the item P2_EMPNO by double-clicking it. Next, scroll down to the Source region. Change the value of Source Used to "Only when current value in session state is null." Change the Source Type value to "Static Assignment (values equals source attribute)." Lastly, delete any value for the source value or expression. Your region should now resemble Figure 13-6. When finished, scroll to the top of the page, and click Apply Changes. Repeat these steps for each item on the page—P2_ENAME, P2_JOB, and P2_DEPTNO.

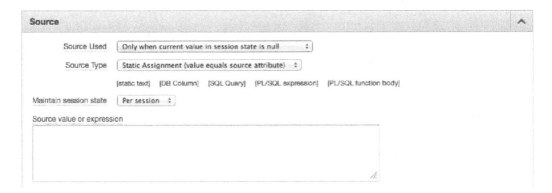

Figure 13-6. *Changing the Source attributes of an item*

Next, a reference to the EMP_DML API needs to be added to the page-processing portion of the page. This reference will call the UPD_EMP procedure, which is used to update a record of EMP.

To create a new process in the page-processing column, right-click the Processes node and select Create, as illustrated in Figure 13-7.

Figure 13-7. *Creating a new page-processing process*

On the next page, select PL/SQL, and click Next. Enter **Update EMP** for the name, take the rest of the defaults, and click Next. Enter the SQL in Listing 13-14 for the Enter PL/SQL Page Process region, and click Next.

Listing 13-14. SQL to Update a Record of EMP via the EMP_DML.UPD_EMP Procedure

```
emp_dml.upd_emp
  (
  p_empno  => :P2_EMPNO,
  p_ename  => :P2_ENAME,
  p_job    => :P2_JOB,
  p_deptno => :P2_DEPTNO,
  p_md5    => :P2_MD5
  );
```

For the Success Message text area, enter **Record Updated**, and click Next. On the next page, set When Button Pressed to SAVE (Apply Changes), as illustrated in Figure 13-8, and click Create Process. This will ensure that the process is executed only when the corresponding button—in this case, Save (Apply Changes)—is clicked by the user.

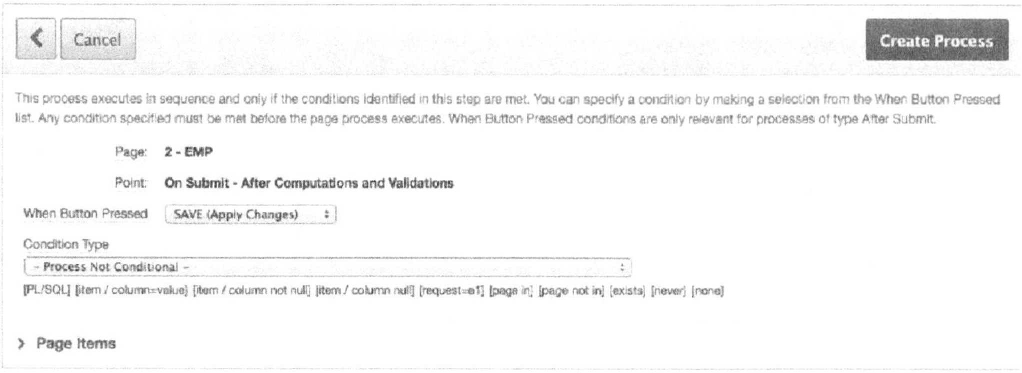

Figure 13-8. *Setting the Update Record process to execute only when the Save button is clicked*

There still may be a process on the page that is no longer necessary for the application: reset page. The reset page process was created by the wizard, and its purpose was to clear the cache of page 2 when the Delete button was clicked. Since the example business rules do not allow for deletes, there is no reason to keep this process in place. Simply edit the process by double-clicking it and delete it. If support for deleting records is added later, care should be taken to either add this process back or ensure that the cache for page 2 is cleared within the table API call.

Lastly, two buttons from the form need to be removed: CREATE and DELETE. Since the example business requirements allow only for updates, there is no reason to present these buttons to the end user, because they will simply not work when clicked. Thus, they should each be removed. To delete either button, double-click the button name, and then click Delete. Confirming the delete action will complete the removal process. The same holds true for the CREATE button on page 1.

At this point, the application should be functional and allow any user to edit—but not delete—any record in the EMP table. Also, there is no way to create a new record from this application, because the API simply does not support it. End users will notice no difference between applications built with the shadow schema methodology versus applications built using the traditional approach.

Securing Data

Securing data with a shadow schema is still possible using the same techniques discussed in Chapters 11 and 12. The only difference is that the procedure used to set the application context would reside in the data schema, much the same way the API package does. Since views are already created in the shadow schema, they need be modified only slightly to accommodate the call to SYS_CONTEXT.

The next three sections will illustrate how to secure the data in the EMP_V view based on DEPTNO. You can find more in-depth discussion of application contexts, secure views, and virtual private databases in Chapters 11 and 12.

Application Context

First, a package to set and unset the application context must be created. This package will be created in the DATA schema, and then a grant and synonym will be added so that the SHADOW schema can execute it. The package will determine the DEPTNO of the currently signed-on user and set the application context accordingly. Listing 13-15 shows the deptno_ctx_pkg package.

Listing 13-15. The deptno_ctx_pkg Package, Which Will Set and Unset the DEPTNO_CTX Application Context (Run as DATA)

```
CREATE OR REPLACE PACKAGE deptno_ctx_pkg
AS
PROCEDURE set_ctx
  (p_user_name              IN VARCHAR2,
   p_app_session            IN VARCHAR2);

PROCEDURE unset_ctx
  (p_app_session            IN VARCHAR2);

END deptno_ctx_pkg;
/

CREATE OR REPLACE PACKAGE BODY deptno_ctx_pkg
AS

PROCEDURE set_ctx
  (p_user_name              IN VARCHAR2,
   p_app_session            IN VARCHAR2)
IS
  l_deptno                  NUMBER;
BEGIN

-- Fetch the DEPTNO based on the currently signed on APP_USER
SELECT deptno INTO l_deptno FROM emp
  WHERE UPPER(ename) = UPPER(p_user_name);

-- Set the Context
dbms_session.set_context(
  namespace => 'DEPTNO_CTX',
  attribute => 'G_DEPTNO',
  value     => l_deptno,
  username  => p_user_name,
  client_id => p_app_session);

EXCEPTION
WHEN no_data_found THEN
  -- If no data is found, then clear the context
  dbms_session.clear_context('DEPTNO_CTX', p_app_session);
END set_ctx;

PROCEDURE unset_ctx
  (p_app_session            IN VARCHAR2)
IS
BEGIN
  dbms_session.clear_context('DEPTNO_CTX', p_app_session);
END;

END deptno_ctx_pkg;
/
```

Next, the application context and grant on deptno_ctx_pkg to shadow need to be created in the SYS schema, as illustrated in Listing 13-16.

Listing 13-16. Creating the Application Context and Granting Execute to the Shadow Schema (Run as SYS)

```
CREATE CONTEXT deptno_ctx USING deptno_ctx_pkg;

GRANT EXECUTE ON DATA.deptno_ctx_pkg TO shadow;
```

The deptno_ctx_pkg package will be called from the APEX application each time a page is rendered, thus ensuring that it is always set to the proper value.

Views

To simplify application development, the view in the DATA schema can be modified rather than the one in the SHADOW schema. This way, no code changes need to be made to the APEX application. At this point, there is only a single reference to EMP_V in the application, but for larger, more mature systems, the number of references may be much higher. Thus, changing the view in the DATA schema limits the impact on the application. The updated SQL for EMP_V is identical to the original, save for the WHERE clause that makes reference to the application context, as shown in Listing 13-17. Additional data security measures can be implemented in a similar manner.

Listing 13-17. SQL for emp_v, which Incorporates the DEPTNO_CTX Application Context (Run as DATA)

```
CREATE OR REPLACE VIEW emp_v AS
SELECT
  empno,
  ename,
  job,
  deptno
FROM
  emp
WHERE
  deptno = SYS_CONTEXT('DEPTNO_CTX', 'G_DEPTNO')
WITH READ ONLY;
```

Running the APEX application now will yield no records, because the application context is being applied in the view, but it not yet being set in the APEX application.

Synonym

Only a single change needs to be made to the SHADOW schema; a new synonym must be created that references the deptno_ctx_pkg package so that the application context can be properly set. The grant was already created as part of Listing 13-16, so only the synonym needs to be created. Listing 13-18 shows code for this.

Listing 13-18. Creating the Synonym for set_ctx (Run as SYS)

```
CREATE SYNONYM SHADOW.deptno_ctx_pkg FOR data.deptno_ctx_pkg;
```

At this point, all that's left to add is the call to deptno_ctx_pkg from the APEX application.

PL/SQL Initialization Code

Lastly, to execute the deptno_ctx_pkg package—which will, in turn, set the value of the DEPTNO_CTX—it needs to be called before each and every page view. APEX has a special attribute that is designed just for this called PL/SQL Initialization Code, which can be found in the Security Attributes portion of an application's shared components. By placing the call to deptno_ctx_pkg here, APEX will be sure to execute it before every page view, including those that are called asynchronously via dynamic actions.

To set the PL/SQL Initialization and Cleanup code, edit the application's shared components and then click Security Attributes. Scroll to the Database Session region, and copy the SQL from Listing 13-19 into the Initialization PL/SQL Code text area.

Listing 13-19. PL/SQL Call to Set the DEPTNO_CTX Application Context

```
deptno_ctx_pkg.set_ctx
  (p_user_name              => :APP_USER,
   p_app_session            => :APP_SESSION);
```

Next, copy the SQL from Listing 13-20 into the Cleanup PL/SQL Code text area.

Listing 13-20. PL/SQL Call to Unset the DEPTNO_CTX Application Context

```
deptno_ctx_pkg.unset_ctx
  (p_app_session            => :APP_SESSION);
```

Scroll to the top of the page, and click Apply Changes. Now, when the application is run—and the user name matches any user names from the EMP table—the report will show only those records from the same department as the logged-in user. For instance, if the user KING signs on to the application, the results will look like those in Figure 13-9.

Figure 13-9. *Results of the report with the DEPTNO_CTX application context applied*

Logging on as different users from the EMP table will yield potentially different results, depending on the associated DEPTNO of that user. If a user does not have a corresponding record in the EMP table, then no records will be displayed, because the set_ctx procedure will clear the DEPTNO_CTX when no records are returned. The way that the application context is set is of course completely configurable based on specific business rules and needs.

Summary

Granting access to a small set of components is much easier to manage than restricting access to a much larger set. The whitelist approach will remain unaltered as new components are added, which ensures that users do not accidentally get privileges added as new components are introduced. Whitelisting can be achieved with an APEX application, but it does take a little bit of work. It is also far easier to design your application with a shadow schema in mind versus trying to retrofit it later.

Using a shadow schema, developers can ensure that their APEX applications present only a small, finite number of components to their users. Combined with some flavor of data security—either secure views or virtual private databases—this approach offers the most security for applications that demand it.

CHAPTER 14

Encryption

If you have read every other chapter in this book, you should have a relatively good grasp on what needs to be done to properly secure an APEX application. Each previous chapter focused on proper settings, planning, or techniques that, when implemented, will provide a solid and secure foundation for your applications. These techniques include things such as authentication, authorization, data security, and tamper-proofing an application. The common thread with these techniques is that they are designed to manage the day-to-day, normal, secure operations of your applications.

The last component of security in this book—encryption—has a different purpose. Encryption is a mathematical formula that, when applied to data in combination with a key, renders the data unreadable. Only those who possess the key can reverse the process and reveal the original data. Encryption should be applied to sensitive data so that if the data ends up in the wrong hands, it cannot be read. This applies to both while the data is in transit and when the data is at rest.

This chapter revisits and emphasizes using HTTPS, highlighting specific places in APEX that are designed to enforce its use. It then covers how to encrypt APEX item vales that are stored in session state, illustrating how other users can see these values when encryption is not applied. Next, it covers different techniques and technologies that can be used to encrypt data as it is stored in the database, APEX collections, and even backup files. It concludes with a summary of the Advanced Security Option and the benefits that that feature brings when it comes to securing your data.

Encryption

The path that data takes in a web-based application is quite predictable. Most data originates at the end user's PC and then travels over some sort of network to the web server. From there, the web server will pass the data back to the database, where in an APEX environment, it will initially be stored in a user's session state. Upon a commit, the data will then be written to both the redo logs and the database files. Finally, the redo logs will occasionally be copied to archive log files. Each time the data travels from one point to another, it is susceptible to being intercepted, as shown in Figure 14-1.

Web Browser　　　**Web Server**　　　**APEX**　　　**Database**　　　**Redo Logs**　　　**Archive Logs**

Figure 14-1. *Points at which unencrypted data can be vulnerable*

As developers, it is our responsibility to ensure that all precautions are taken so that the data is encrypted not only while it's in transit but also when it arrives at its final destination. Unfortunately, there is no single technology or feature that can be enabled that will ensure that data is encrypted from end to end. Instead, a combination of features and techniques must be implemented and configured to provide end-to-end encryption of the data, as illustrated in Figure 14-2.

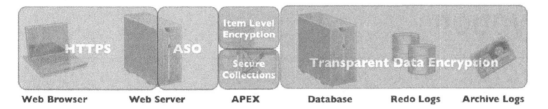

Figure 14-2. *Different technologies and features are used to encrypt data at different points of its journey*

Each of these features or techniques is covered in this chapter, starting with HTTPS and concluding with Transparent Data Encryption. In some cases, the specifics on how to implement a feature are out of scope for this book. In those cases, references to other documents with more specifics are provided.

One final point about encryption: it is not a substitute for data access control but rather a mechanism put in place to protect data that may be stolen. It is important to manage data access control with either a secure view, VPD, or Oracle Label Security combined with authorization schemes to limit what a specific user can do. Relying on encryption to provide data access control is a bad design decision.

HTTPS

The importance of using HTTPS in each and every APEX environment—development, test, QA, and production—simply cannot be overstated. HTTPS ensures that all data sent from your browser to the web server is encrypted. This way, anyone who is sniffing the network packets will not be able to read the data sent. When running over only HTTP, it is possible that a malicious user could intercept the data that is being sent either to or from the web server.

Packet Peeper is an open source network packet sniffer available for Mac OS X. (For an open source alternative that runs on all popular platforms, take a look at Wireshark.) Within seconds of downloading and installing Packet Peeper, it is possible to begin capturing and analyzing network packets, all with just a single click of the mouse. The results are simple text files that can easily be saved and searched at any time.

After capturing some network traffic, Packet Peeper will display a list of the captured data, as shown in Figure 14-3. In this example, a simple authentication to an APEX workspace was captured. Simply click any of the rows to see a snippet of that specific capture. Data can also be sorted by length, making it easier to identify potentially valuable packets by their larger sizes.

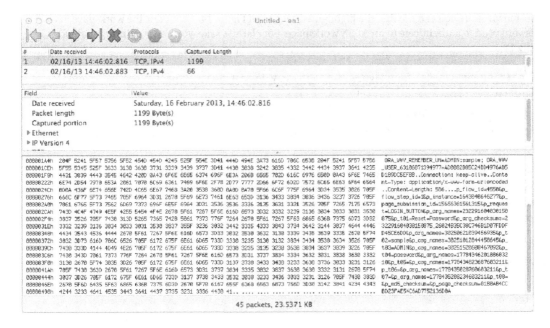

Figure 14-3. *A packet capture from Packet Peeper*

By right-clicking any element and selecting Reassemble TCP Stream, a much easier-to-read version of the packet will be displayed, as shown in Figure 14-4.

```
 4   Accept: text/html,application/xhtml+xml,application/xml;q=0.9,*/*;q=0.8
 5   Accept-Language: en-us,en;q=0.5
 6   Accept-Encoding: gzip, deflate
 7   Referer: http://servername.com/apex/f?p=4550:1:
 8   Cookie: ORA_WWV_REMEMBER_UN=ADMIN:sample; ORA_WWV_USER_63106871394977=AD0082B85C248D4976A85D189DC5EFB8
 9   Connection: keep-alive
10   Content-Type: application/x-www-form-urlencoded
11   Content-Length: 586
12
13   p_flow_id=4550&p_flow_step_id=1&p_instance=1643040646277&p_page_submission_id=15656361561315&p_request=
14      LOGIN_BUTTON&p_arg_names=2322916040301508758&p_t01=Reset+Password&p_arg_checksums=
15      2322916040301508758_26024B35C38C745B1D07FDDFD45CE6DD&p_arg_names=30250621039456935
16      &p_t02=sample&p_arg_names=30251012844458645&p_t03=ADMIN&p_arg_names=30251520608467092
17      &p_t04=password&p_arg_names=1778434620188603210&p_t05=&p_arg_names=1778434823687603211
18      &p_t06=&p_arg_names=1778435028760603211&p_t07=&p_arg_names=1778435208234603211&p_t08=
19      &p_md5_checksum=&p_page_checksum=0180AB4CC8D23FAE54C6AD7752136D0AHTTP/1.1 302 Moved Temporarily
20   X-Powered-By: Servlet/3.0 JSP/2.2 (Oracle GlassFish Server 3.1.1 Java/Oracle Corporation/1.7)
21   Server: Oracle GlassFish Server 3.1.1
22   X-ORACLE-IGNORE: IGNORE
23   X-ORACLE-IGNORE: IGNORE
24   X-ORACLE-IGNORE: IGNORE
25   X-ORACLE-IGNORE: IGNORE
26   Set-Cookie: ORA_WWV_REMEMBER_UN=ADMIN:sample; expires=Thu, 15-Aug-2013 22:46:02 GMT; path=/apex; HttpOnly
27   Set-Cookie: ORA_WWV_USER_63106871394977=9E98E4208DBF365D93254501347C6F86; path=/apex; HttpOnly
28   Location: http://servername.com/apex/f?p=4550:1:1643040646277&notification_msg=Invalid%20Login%20Credentials%3C
29   Content-Type: text/html;charset=UTF-8
30   Content-Language: en-US
31   Content-Length: 457
32   Date: Sat, 16 Feb 2013 19:46:03 GMT
33
34 ▼ <html>
35   <head><title>Document moved</title></head>
36 ▼ <body><h1>Document moved</h1>
37   This document has moved <a href="http://servername.com/apex/f?p=4550:1:1643040646277&amp;notification_msg=Inval
38 ᴸ </body>
39 ᴸ </html>
40   GET /apex/f?p=4550:1:1643040646277&notification_msg=Invalid%20Login%20Credentials%3Cdiv%20id%3D%22apex_login_th
```

Figure 14-4. *The raw text from a Packet Peeper capture of traffic over HTTP, with the reference to APEX credentials highlighted*

After a closer inspection, you can see that the highlighted section of Figure 14-4 contains the workspace, user name, and password used to authenticate to an APEX workspace. For clarity's sake, you can see the highlighted snippet in Listing 14-1.

Listing 14-1. *The Highlighted Region from Figure 14-4, with the Values of the Workspace, User Name, and Password Underlined*

```
&p_t02=sample&p_arg_names=30251012844458645
&p_t03=ADMIN&p_arg_names=30251520608467092
&p_t04=password&p_arg_names=17784346201888603210
```

If this were a real attack, the perpetrator would have all they needed to log into this APEX workspace as the ADMIN user. Fortunately, this problem is quite simple to solve: use HTTPS. When the same actions are taken over HTTPS, the results are dramatically different. No longer is any identifiable information captured, but rather a bunch of garbage characters is the only result in Packet Peeper, as shown in Figure 14-5.

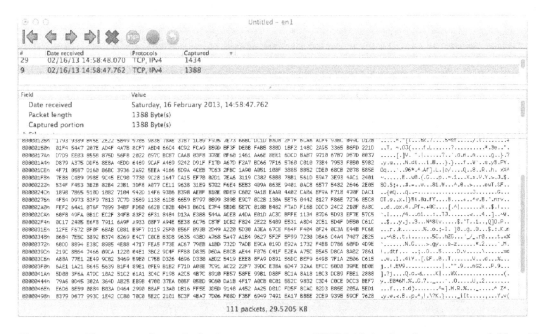

Figure 14-5. *The raw text from a Packet Peeper capture over HTTPS. Notice that there are no readable or identifyable strings in the raw text*

This time, since all the data sent across the network is encrypted, Packet Peeper is unable to capture anything meaningful. The only data that it did capture is simply a bunch of garbage characters that cannot be read by anyone.

HTTPS should be installed and enforced on every APEX instance, no matter what its purpose. All too often, developers will use the same credentials on a development instance as they will on a QA or even production instance. Thus, if the development instance is not using HTTPS, user credentials can be sniffed there and simply reused on the QA or even production instances.

APEX HTTPS Settings

HTTPS needs to be installed and configured at the web server tier, not from within APEX. Depending on the web server used, the specific instructions on how to configure HTTPS will vary slightly. All of the supported web listeners are capable of running HTTPS, with the exception of the APEX Listener in Standalone mode. Once HTTPS is installed and configured, there are a few places within APEX that can be configured to ensure that the user is coming over a secured connection.

Instance Admin Console and Application Development Environment

The entire instance can be configured so that any attempt to access the instance administration console or application development environment over HTTP will be refused. This setting must be managed by an instance administrator and can be found in the Security section of Instance Settings, as illustrated in Figure 14-6. A similar setting exists for outbound communications, such as calls to web services. These settings have no impact on applications developed with APEX. Refer to the next section for information about requiring a developed application to require HTTPS.

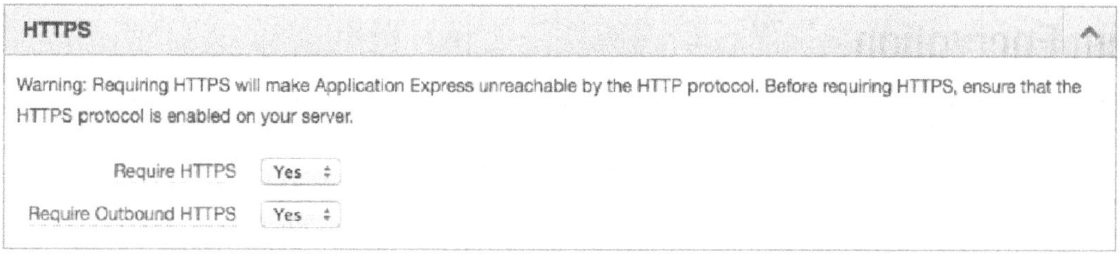

HTTPS

Warning: Requiring HTTPS will make Application Express unreachable by the HTTP protocol. Before requiring HTTPS, ensure that the HTTPS protocol is enabled on your server.

Require HTTPS   [Yes ÷]

Require Outbound HTTPS   [Yes ÷]

Figure 14-6. *Configuring an instance of APEX to require HTTPS for both inbound and outbound transactions*

Before enabling either of these settings, be sure to test and ensure that your instance of APEX and any associated web service can be reached over HTTPS. If the Require HTTPS setting is enabled and the instance of APEX cannot be accessed over HTTPS for some reason, it can be reverted by calling the APEX_INSTANCE_ADMIN.SET_PARAMETER API, as illustrated in Listing 14-2.

Listing 14-2. Resetting the Require HTTPS Parameter via the APEX_INSTANCE_ADMIN API

```
APEX_INSTANCE_ADMIN.SET_PARAMETER
    (
    p_parameter => 'REQUIRE_HTTPS',
    p_value => 'N'
    );
```

Calling APEX_INSTANCE_ADMIN must be done from SYS, SYSTEM, or any other schema that has been granted the APEX_ADMINISTRATOR_ROLE role.

Applications

Each application has a setting that will require that it be accessed over HTTPS, similar to the workspace-level Require HTTPS attribute. However, the name and the location of that setting are anything but obvious. Called simply Secure, this setting can be found embedded within an authentication scheme in the Secure Cookie Attributes section, as shown in Figure 14-7.

Figure 14-7. *The Secure attribute, which, when enabled, will require application to run over HTTPS*

When set to Yes, the corresponding application can be accessed only over HTTPS. This ensures that a network sniffer cannot compromise the session cookie that APEX sends to the client. Additionally, by running over HTTPS, any sensitive information displayed via an APEX form or report will also be encrypted. Most browsers also will prevent pages run over HTTPS from being cached, too.

APEX Item Encryption

APEX has a robust session state management component that is completely integrated into both APEX itself as well as any application developed with APEX. It does not require any code or configuration to enable it; it simply works. In fact, most developers will quickly learn how to use and take advantage of it within their own applications by using the associated APIs.

One of the major benefits of APEX's session state is that it keeps values from one session completely isolated from all other sessions. Therefore, there is no chance that one user in an application can view the values set by another user in the same or even different application. Again, this level of security is automatically enabled, and nothing special needs to be done to take advantage of it.

However, it is possible for others to see the data stored in APEX session state. Any workspace administrator or developer can run the Active Sessions report from the Administration section of a workspace, which will display all information about all active sessions. It will also allow the user to inspect that session's page views, browser details, and item values. When the Monitor attribute is set to Session State Details, as it is in Figure 14-8, all currently set items in that session state will be displayed.

Figure 14-8. *The Active Sessions report, as viewed by an APEX developer*

While there is no similar report available to the instance administrator, they can easily create an account in any workspace, log in to that, and then view any session details in any application within the instance of APEX.

Additionally, all values for APEX session state are stored in a table called WWV_FLOW_DATA, which can be found in the APEX_040200 schema. This table is adequately secured so that other schemas cannot view it. However, SYS, SYSTEM, and schemas that have been granted DBA can still view all data stored there and potentially see sensitive information. Listing 14-3 shows a simple SQL query that will return the value of an APEX item called P3_SAL from application 159, if run by SYS, SYSTEM, or any schema with the DBA role.

Listing 14-3. A SQL Statement That Will Display the Value of an APEX Session State Item

```
SELECT
  flow_id application_id,
  item_name,
  is_encrypted,
  item_value
FROM
  wwv_flow_data
WHERE
  item_name = 'P3_SAL'
SQL> /

APPLICATION_ID ITEM_NAME       IS_ENCRYPTED ITEM_VALUE
-------------- --------------- ------------- ----------
           159 P3_SAL          N                   5500
```

To combat this threat, there is an item-level attribute in APEX that, when enabled, will store all session state values in an encrypted format. To enable this attribute, edit any item in your application, and in the Security region, set the value of "Store value encrypted in session state" to Yes, as shown in Figure 14-9; then save your changes.

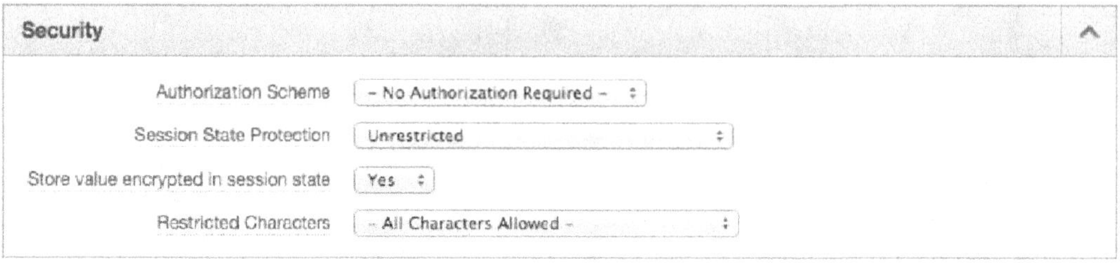

Security	∧
Authorization Scheme	– No Authorization Required – ⬧
Session State Protection	Unrestricted ⬧
Store value encrypted in session state	Yes ⬧
Restricted Characters	– All Characters Allowed – ⬧

Figure 14-9. *Enabling item-level encryption*

Once enabled, APEX will store any value associated with that item in an encrypted format. As a developer, there is nothing at all that needs to be changed in code that refers to that item, regardless of how it is done. APEX will automatically decrypt the value when the item is referenced anywhere within a report or programmatically via one of the APIs.

If the same Active Sessions report is run after item encryption is enabled on P3_EMP, the value of that item is no longer displayed. Rather, the Item Value column for P3_EMP is set to *****, denoting that the value of this item has been encrypted, as shown in Figure 14-10.

Item Name	Item Value	Status	Application
P101_USERNAME	-	RESET_TO_NULL	159
P3_ROWID	AAAdtAAAZAAAAHrAAI	Inserted	159
P3_EMPNO	7839	Inserted	159
P3_ENAME	KING	Inserted	159
P3_JOB	PRESIDENT	Inserted	159
P3_MGR	-	Inserted	159
P3_HIREDATE	17-NOV-81	Inserted	159
P3_SAL	*****	Inserted	159
P3_COMM	-	Inserted	159
P3_DEPTNO	10	Inserted	159

Figure 14-10. *The Active Sessions report, after item-level encryption has been enabled for P3_SAL. Notice that the value of P3_SAL is displayed as *****, denoting that it is encrypted*

Also, the same SQL statement in Listing 14-3 will return the raw encrypted value of the item P3_EMP, as shown in Listing 14-4. Once encrypted in APEX session state, sensitive values will always be encrypted as they are written to redo logs, then written to database files, and ultimately backed up, ensuring that no one will be able to view sensitive data at any point in the chain of ownership of an application's data.

Listing 14-4. The Same SQL Statement as Listing 14-3, This Time Returning the Raw Encrypted Value of P3_SAL

```
SELECT
  flow_id application_id,
  item_name,
  is_encrypted,
  item_value
FROM
  wwv_flow_data
WHERE
  item_name = 'P3_SAL'
SQL> /

APPLICATION_ID ITEM_NAME  IS_ENCRYPTED  ITEM_VALUE
-------------- ---------- ------------- ----------------
           159 P3_SAL                N  9839BEFE425E74DX
                                        5C0318373DE67FCD
                                        C8B66BEF97B13AB3
```

Enabling item encryption is a simple, unobtrusive feature that should be done for any item that could store sensitive data. Even though APEX has plenty of safeguards to ensure that data is protected from other users, a malicious APEX developer or DBA could still easily view any data stored unencrypted in APEX session state.

Data Encryption

Encrypting sensitive data in APEX session state is sufficient protection against curious APEX developers and even DBAs, but at the end of the day, that data will eventually end up in a regular table outside of the APEX schema. Sensitive data that must be stored in a more permanent manner—such as credit card numbers, account numbers, and Social Security numbers—should also be encrypted so that if the database itself is compromised, it will be protected. In fact, in some industries, there are laws that dictate what type of data must be encrypted.

With Oracle, there are a couple of different mechanisms that can be used to facilitate the actual encryption. Which one you use will largely depend on one thing: how much money you want to spend.

DBMS_CRYPTO

The DBMS_CRYPTO package is included with all editions of the database—Standard One, Standard, and Enterprise. Prior to Oracle 10g, this package was referred to as DBMS_OBFUSCATION_TOOLKIT. DBMS_CRYPTO contains a number of API calls that can be used to both encrypt and decrypt your data before it is stored in a table. No matter how it is implemented, there will be three challenges when using DBMS_CRYPTO: how to integrate it into your applications, where to store the key, and what performance impacts using it will have.

First, implementing DBMS_CRYPTO requires some planning because calling the API to encrypt and decrypt the data will be the sole responsibility of the developer. Each time before sensitive data is written to a table, a separate call must be made to encrypt the data. And on the other side, each time encrypted data is fetched from the table and used in any way—be it a report, form, chart, or procedure—another call must be made to decrypt the data.

Encrypted data is always returned in a binary format. Therefore, to store it, either a RAW or BLOB column must be used. If the base tables of your applications do not have a RAW or BLOB column—and they probably don't—then one must be added. If adding such a column is simply not possible, then the encrypted data can be converted back to text and stored in a VARCHAR or VARCHAR2 format, but this takes yet another procedure call and additional code to facilitate.

The second challenge when using DBMS_CRYPTO is where to store the key. Encryption is a two-way algorithm—anything that can be encrypted can also be decrypted, so as long as you have the key used to encrypt it in the first place. Thus, when calling your procedure to either encrypt or decrypt your data, the key must be retrieved and used as part of that procedure. If that key were compromised, a malicious user would be able to decrypt all of the data, making the encryption a mere inconvenience.

One recommendation is to store the key in a separate schema that is otherwise completely locked down. That schema could have a single procedure that, when called by an authorized application, either encrypts or decrypts the data and returns the corresponding value. The key could be embedded in that procedure and then that procedure could be wrapped for an added level of protection. However, if a competent malicious user were able to somehow access that schema, they may still be able to gain access to the key. Even if the key is stored outside of the database, it would still need to be accessed and retrieved every time that encrypted data was used in the application, making the management of external keys difficult.

Lastly, and probably the least critical of the three drawbacks of using DBMS_CRYPTO, is the performance impact it may have. Calling additional APIs each time encrypted data is accessed is going to add to the total amount of processing required for your application, as compared to using Transparent Data Encryption. How much it impacts performance will of course depend on a number of factors, such as size of data, number of page views, and number of times DBMS_CRYPTO is referenced.

Using DBMS_CRYPTO definitely comes with some baggage. In some cases, this baggage may cause a developer to consider an alternative approach. One such approach is to use the Advanced Security Option (ASO), which is a for-cost option of the Enterprise Edition of the database. ASO can transparently encrypt data in either a column or an entire tablespace and protect the network connection between the web server and database, among other things. It can do all of this transparently, without changing a single line of code, and uses Oracle Wallet to store keys securely outside of the database.

However, ASO does come at a cost—the list price is $11,500 USD per processor as of early 2013. While that may seem excessive and even unaffordable, consider the cost of implementing the same or similar solution on your own. It can quickly seem like a better deal when approached from the "what if I were to build that" angle, especially when it comes to something that *has* to be correct like security.

As discussed in the first couple of chapters, there is no hard formula that can be applied to determine whether ASO is required. It is a combination of a number of factors, one of which includes the associated security budget. If purchasing ASO is simply not possible, then a solution built using DBMS_CRYPTO should be considered because despite its drawbacks, it is much better to deploy than no encryption.

Encrypted Collections

Since APEX sessions do not map directly to a database session, it is simply not possible to use a construct such as a global temporary table to store data temporarily. Thus, the developers of APEX created a feature called *collections*. Collections are essentially temporary tables that are mapped to and secured by an APEX session. While data in a collection can be seen by querying the view APEX_COLLECTIONS, all inserts, updates, and deletes are facilitated by the APEX_COLLECTION API.

APEX_COLLECTIONS, which is actually a public synonym for the view APEX_040200.WWV_FLOW_COLLECTIONS, contains a number of generic columns, namely, fifty VARCHAR2, five NUMBER, five DATE, and one of each of a CLOB, BLOB, and XMLTYPE. Developers can use any of these columns to temporarily store and retrieve data from within their applications. An example of APEX collections is an application that uses a shopping cart. Items placed in the shopping cart are associated with the user's specific session. Only when the user actually checks out are the rows in the collection copied to a table in the parse-as schema of the application.

The WWV_FLOW_COLLECTIONS view joins the two collections base tables—WWV_FLOW_COLLECTIONS$ and WWV_FLOW_COLLECTION_MEMBERS$—together so that the only data returned is the data associated with that APEX session. All data stored in a collection is done so in an unencrypted fashion. Thus, any data that ends up in a collection in an APEX application will persist in that collection unencrypted for up to a day, when the collections are typically purged. Additionally, collection data will also be written to redo logs, database files, and backups, where it may remain unprotected permanently.

Therefore, if an application is going to use a collection to store sensitive information, steps should be taken to ensure that the data is first encrypted. In this case, DBMS_CRYPTO may be the only practical option. Ideally, column encryption—a feature of the Advanced Security Option discussed in the next section—would be used. However, column encryption requires that the base tables used for collections be altered, which could jeopardize the support status of your instance of APEX. Transparent Data Encryption may also seem like an option, but that would need to have been decided when installing APEX, because it would encrypt the data files used in the tablespace that APEX is associated with.

When using DBMS_CRYPTO with collections, the three drawbacks previously outlined still exist, but none of them is nearly as severe. Manipulating APEX collections requires calls to APIs. Thus, the burden of additional code is already there when using collections. Adding a line or two to ensure that data is encrypted to an existing procedure is a lot easier than having to create the procedures from scratch.

The problem of key management is also a bit easier when it comes to collections. Since collections are temporary data structures, their associated keys can also be temporary. For instance, the key associated with a collection can be created and stored as an APEX application page item with encryption enabled and used through that specific session. Once the session is terminated, so is the collection and APEX item value; thus, the key is no longer needed.

Only the issue with performance still exists, and unfortunately, there is no way to mitigate or change this. Each time a value needs to be encrypted or decrypted, a call to DBMS_CRYPTO will still be necessary. There is simply no way to avoid this, but in most cases, the performance impact will be minimal, if noticeable at all.

Example

To illustrate how encrypted collections could be implemented, a simple application with an encrypted collection based on the EMP table will be created. To encrypt and decrypt the data, a package with calls to DBMS_CRYPTO is required. The package in Listing 14-5 contains two functions—encrypt_data and decrypt_data—which are used to encrypt and decrypt data, respectively. Be sure that the schema in which this package will be created has been granted EXECUTE on DBMS_CRYPTO prior to creating it.

Listing 14-5. The encrypt_collection_pkg Package

```
CREATE OR REPLACE PACKAGE encrypt_collection_pkg
AS
FUNCTION encrypt_data
  (
  p_data IN VARCHAR2
  )
RETURN RAW;

FUNCTION decrypt_data
  (
  p_data IN RAW
  )
RETURN VARCHAR2;

END encrypt_collection_pkg;
/
```

```
CREATE OR REPLACE PACKAGE BODY encrypt_collection_pkg
AS
   g_character_set     VARCHAR2(10)  := 'AL32UTF8';
   g_encryption_type  PLS_INTEGER   :=
     dbms_crypto.encrypt_aes256 +
     dbms_crypto.chain_cbc +
     dbms_crypto.pad_pkcs5;
   g_key               RAW(32)       :=
     UTL_I18N.STRING_TO_RAW(v('P1_EMP_KEY'));

FUNCTION encrypt_data
  (p_data IN VARCHAR2)
RETURN RAW
IS
BEGIN

RETURN dbms_crypto.encrypt
  (
  src => utl_i18n.string_to_raw
    (
    data       => p_data,
    dst_charset => g_character_set
    ),
  typ => g_encryption_type,
  key => g_key
  );

END encrypt_data;

FUNCTION decrypt_data
  (p_data IN RAW)
RETURN VARCHAR2
IS
BEGIN

RETURN utl_i18n.raw_to_char
  (
  data       => dbms_crypto.decrypt
    (
    src => p_data,
    typ => g_encryption_type,
    key => g_key
    ),
  src_charset => g_character_set
  );
EXCEPTION
WHEN OTHERS THEN
  raise_application_error(-20000,'Invalid Key.');
END decrypt_data;

END encrypt_collection_pkg;
/
```

The functions in `encrypt_collection_pkg` are little more than calls to `DBMS_CRYPTO`, with a couple of exceptions worth noting. First, the key will be stored in a page item called `P1_EMP_KEY`. Putting the key in a page item versus an application item allows for it to be itself encrypted, because only page items have that ability. Second, the encryption type used is stored in the package constant `g_encryption_type`. This can be altered as needed, depending on the specific needs of the application.

Once the package is created, create a new APEX application with a single blank page. On that page, create a report based on the SQL in Listing 14-6.

Listing 14-6. The SQL for the Report on Page 1 of the Application

```
SELECT
  c001,
  c002,
  encrypt_collection_pkg.decrypt_data(blob001) sal
FROM
  apex_collections
WHERE
  collection_name = 'EMP_E'
```

This SQL will query the `APEX_COLLECTIONS` view for the collection called `EMP_E`. It will also use the `decrypt_data` function on the `BLOB` column, which will decrypt any data stored there and display it in the report.

Next, create a hidden page item in the report region called `P1_EMP_KEY`, which will be used to store the key that is referenced by the `encrypt_collection_pkg` package. This item should have its value both protected and encrypted. The item protection will prevent the user from modifying it, while the encryption will prevent the user from being able to view the key.

At some point in your application, there will be code to populate the collection with data. This may be done as items are added to a shopping cart or as the users select rows in a report. No matter how the collection gets populated, it can be done so only by calling either the APEX_COLLECTION.ADD_MEMBER or ADD_MEMBERS API. In this example, you will simulate this event by creating and calling an application process that executes after a button has been clicked.

Next, create a button in the report region that will submit the page and name it Seed Collection or something similar. The name and layout position of the button are not important. After the button is created, create a page process by right-clicking the Processing node in the Page Processing region, as shown in Figure 14-11.

Figure 14-11. Creating a page process to seed the encrypted collection

For the process type, select PL/SQL. On the next screen, give the process a name, such as seed encrypted collection, and click Next. Copy the code from Listing 14-7 into the region labeled Enter PL/SQL Page Process, and click Next.

Listing 14-7. The Source for the Page Process Used to Seed the Encrypted Collection

```
apex_collection.create_or_truncate_collection
  (
  p_collection_name => 'EMP_E'
  );

FOR x IN (SELECT * FROM emp)
LOOP
  apex_collection.add_member
  (
    p_collection_name => 'EMP_E',
    p_c001 => x.empno,
    p_c002 => x.ename,
    p_blob001 => encrypt_collection_pkg.encrypt_data(x.sal)
  );
END LOOP;
```

There is no need to enter a value for the success or failure messages, so simply click Next. Finally, ensure that the value of the attribute When Button Pressed is set to the button created in the previous step. Click Create Process to finish.

One last component needs to be created before the example will function properly. Navigate to the shared components of your application, and click Application Computations. Create a new application computation by clicking the Create button. Set Computation Item to P1_EMP_KEY, ensure that Computation Point is set to On New Instance (new session), set the computation type to SQL Query (return single value), and then copy the code from Listing 14-8 into the Computation region.

Listing 14-8. The Source of the Application ComputationUsed to Calculate P1_EMP_KEY

```
SELECT dbms_random.string('A',32) FROM dual
```

Click Create Computation when done. This computation will set the key with a random value each time the user logs in. Because the key is going to be used only to secure collections—which are also session-based—there is no need to store the key permanently anywhere because each session will get its own unique key.

When the application is run, there should initially be no rows in the report. To populate it, click the Seed Collection button. This will call the page process that loops through the EMP table and inserts a row into the collection for each row in EMP. The value of the SAL column will be encrypted before being stored in the collection. When the page reloads, the report will now contain data from the EMP table and will resemble Figure 14-12.

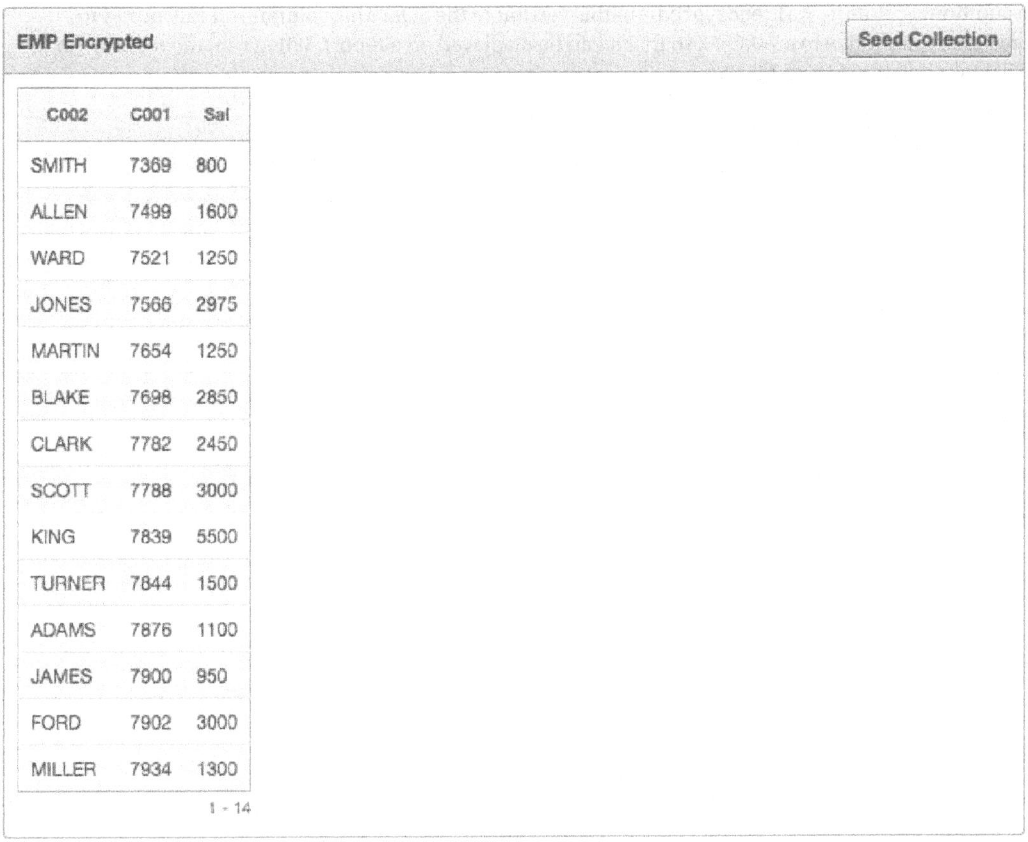
EMP Encrypted

Seed Collection

C002	C001	Sal
SMITH	7369	800
ALLEN	7499	1600
WARD	7521	1250
JONES	7566	2975
MARTIN	7654	1250
BLAKE	7698	2850
CLARK	7782	2450
SCOTT	7788	3000
KING	7839	5500
TURNER	7844	1500
ADAMS	7876	1100
JAMES	7900	950
FORD	7902	3000
MILLER	7934	1300

1 - 14

Figure 14-12. *The report on the EMP_E encrypted collection*

The results of the report after the collection populated are not terribly impressive. In fact, it looks like a simple query directly against the EMP table. However, if the SQL used in the report is altered to include the raw data from the column used to store the encrypted value of the SAL column, things will look different. Edit the report in your application and replace all of the SQL there with that in Listing 14-9.

Listing 14-9. An Updated Version of the SQL Used for the Report on Page 1 of the Application

```
SELECT
  c001,
  c002,
  encrypt_collection_pkg.decrypt_data(blob001) sal,
  utl_i18n.raw_to_char
    (
    data => blob001,
    src_charset => 'AL32UTF8'
    ) sal_encrypted
FROM
  apex_collections
WHERE
  collection_name = 'EMP_E'
```

Notice the additional column—sal_encrypted—in this version of the SQL. This column will call an API to convert the stored encrypted value to a VARCHAR so that it can be displayed on a report. When run, the report with the updated SQL will look similar to Figure 14-13.

Figure 14-13. *The report on the encrypted collection, this time displaying the raw encrypted colum values*

Clearly, the encrypted SAL column has no resemblance to the unencrypted SAL column at all. And without the key—which is stored in encrypted format in APEX session state—there is no way that a malicious user would be able to decrypt those values.

To summarize, implementing collections that incorporate encryption is not a lot of additional work because code is required to manage collections anyway. The problem of storing the key is also solved because it can be randomly generated and then discarded after the duration of the APEX session. Anytime that sensitive data is stored in a collection, the incremental extra effort to ensure that it is encrypted is essential.

Advanced Security Option

The Advanced Security Option is a for-cost feature of the Oracle Database Enterprise Edition only. If you are using either Standard Edition One or Standard Edition, this feature is not available. ASO provides a number of advanced security features that complement the security provided by the database. In regard to APEX applications, there are three main features that are most commonly used: Transparent Data Encryption, column encryption, and network encryption.

Transparent Data Encryption

Transparent Data Encryption (TDE) is a feature of ASO that encrypts either a specific column or an entire tablespace automatically and transparently. The three major shortcomings of using DBMS_CRYPTO are all resolved with TDE. Implementing TDE is completely transparent to all applications; no triggers, views, or additional PL/SQL code is required. Also, storing a key with TDE is more secure because the keys can be stored outside the database and secured via Oracle Wallet Manager. And third, there is little performance impact when using TDE, since the encryption is done at the data file level. When using specific hardware, TDE can even take advantage of hardware acceleration when encrypting and decrypting data, thus making the performance hit negligible.

TDE can be divided into two components: column-level encryption and tablespace encryption. When enabled, column-level encryption will automatically encrypt the values of the columns that it is associated with. Additionally, when the column values are read into the SGA, they will be encrypted there, too. Any undo or redo associated with the column will also be encrypted, ensuring that the data is protected throughout.

Column-level encryption is much preferred over DBMS_CRYPTO for securing data stored in a column, given that the three major drawbacks of DBMS_CRYPTO are not an issue. Also, the fact that column-level encryption can be enabled without changing any code or adding any additional objects is a clear benefit, since the data will be secured when any application—APEX or otherwise—accesses the data.

Tablespace-level encryption is an option that has to be defined before creating a tablespace. Existing tablespaces cannot simply be converted to encrypted ones. Essentially, tablespace encryption will automatically and transparently encrypt all data before writing it to disk and decrypt it as it reads it. While both undo and redo logs are encrypted, the data cached in the SGA from an encrypted tablespace is not.

When using either of these features with APEX, there are no special considerations because they are truly transparent in nature. Simply enable them as you would for any other development tool. You can find more details about the specifics required to configure TDE in the Oracle Database Advanced Security Administrator's Guide.

Network Encryption

Another component of TDE is network encryption, which ensures that all network traffic from a web server or the APEX listener is encrypted as it travels to the database server. Like TDE, no changes to the application are required. Once enabled, network encryption will instantly and automatically begin encrypting packets with a configurable algorithm, such as AES, Triple DES, and RC4.

Think of network encryption as HTTPS for the connection between the web server and the database because that is essentially what it does. Network encryption is an essential component when securing APEX, because without it, there is a noticeable gap. Even though the distance that the packets need to travel from the web server to the database may be short, if a malicious user were to gain access to that part of the network, he would be able to sniff and read the contents of those packets.

Summary

Applications come and go, but data lives forever, as the saying goes. Given that fact, you must take precautions to ensure that sensitive data that does live forever does so with adequate protection. Applying encryption at all points along the path that the data will travel is the only way to ensure that it is not compromised either while in transit or at rest. Unfortunately, there is no single, turnkey solution to do this; rather, a number of different features and techniques need to be applied, as outlined in this chapter.

Index

■ W, X, Y, Z